T0330985

The Complexities
of Sustainability

Science, Technology and Sustainability

Series Editors: David Crowther (*Social Responsibility Research Network, UK*)
Shahla Seifi (*Social Responsibility Research Network, UK*)

Published:

Vol. 1   *The Complexities of Sustainability*
edited by David Crowther and Shahla Seifi

SCIENCE, TECHNOLOGY AND SUSTAINABILITY - VOLUME 1

The Complexities of Sustainability

DAVID CROWTHER

SHAHLA SEIFI

Social Responsibility Research Network, UK

 **World Scientific**

NEW JERSEY · LONDON · SINGAPORE · BEIJING · SHANGHAI · HONG KONG · TAIPEI · CHENNAI · TOKYO

Published by

World Scientific Publishing Co. Pte. Ltd.

5 Toh Tuck Link, Singapore 596224

USA office: 27 Warren Street, Suite 401-402, Hackensack, NJ 07601

UK office: 57 Shelton Street, Covent Garden, London WC2H 9HE

Library of Congress Cataloging-in-Publication Data

Names: Crowther, David, editor. | Seifi, Shahla, editor.
Title: The complexities of sustainability / David Crowther, Shahla Seifi,
     Social Responsibility Research Network, UK.
Description: Hackensack, NJ : World Scientific, [2023] | Series: Science, technology and
     sustainability, 2810-9643 ; 1 | Includes bibliographical references and index.
Identifiers: LCCN 2022021025 | ISBN 9789811258749 (hardcover) |
     ISBN 9789811258756 (ebook) | ISBN 9789811258763 (ebook other)
Subjects: LCSH: Sustainable development--Case studies. | Sustainability--Case studies. |
     Social responsibility of business--Case studies.
Classification: LCC HC79.E5 C61243 2023 | DDC 338.9/27--dc23/eng/20220608
LC record available at https://lccn.loc.gov/2022021025

British Library Cataloguing-in-Publication Data

A catalogue record for this book is available from the British Library.

For any available supplementary material, please visit
https://www.worldscientific.com/worldscibooks/10.1142/12902#t=suppl

Desk Editors: Jayanthi Muthuswamy/Thaheera Althaf/Sandhya Venkatesh

Typeset by Stallion Press
Email: enquiries@stallionpress.com

Printed in Singapore

List of Contributors

Kwame Oduro Amoako, Sunyani Technical University, Ghana
Xinyuan Bao, Shanghai University, China
Dianne Bolton, Western Sydney University, Australia
David Crowther, Social Responsibility Research Network, UK
Victor Ediagbonya, University of Brighton, UK
Miriam Green, Icon College of Technology & Management, UK
Mohshin Habib, Western Sydney University, Australia
Kirsty de Jong, Victoria University of Wellington, New Zealand
Peter Kawalek, Loughborough University, UK
Rim Kheimiri, Polytechnic University of Haut-de-France, France
Terry Landells, Bolton Landells Consulting Pty Ltd, Australia
Katia Lemos, Polytechnic Institute of Cavado & Ave, Portugal
Natallia V. Maltsevich, Belarisian State University, Belarusia
Sonia Monteiro, Polytechnic Institute of Cavado & Ave, Portugal
Frank Nyame-Asiamah, De Montfort University, UK
Tatiana V. Proharava, Belarisian State University, Belarusia
Aliaksandr V. Pyko, Belarisian State University, Belarusia
Rafaela Costa Camoes Rabello, University of Otago, New Zealand
Veronica Ribeiro, Polytechnic Institute of Cavado & Ave, Portugal
Katharina Ruckstuhl, University of Otago, New Zealand
Diane Ruwhiu, University of Otago, New Zealand
Shahla Seifi, Social Responsibility Research Network, UK

Tioluwani Comfort Tioluwani, University of Essex, UK
Nadia Ben Farhat Toumi, University of Paris Saclay, France
Christos Tsatsis, Haute Ecole Francisco Ferrer, Belgium
Hong Wang, Shanghai University, China
Yidan Wang, Shanghai University, China

Contents

Chapter 1

The Many Facets of Sustainability

David Crowther and Shahla Seifi

Abstract

Although the topic of sustainability has become ubiquitous, it is a complex subject, and there is little agreement as to what exactly is meant by the term. This chapter considers a range of issues which need to be addressed in achieving sustainability. It argues strongly that sustainability is a global matter and can only successfully be addressed on a global basis — with the many issues which this raises. In doing so, this chapter acts as an introduction to the volume and sets the scene for many of the issues which are addressed in subsequent chapters.

Keywords: Sustainability; geopolitics; globalisation; regulation; social contract; governance

1. Introduction

There is a certainty in the world that sustainability, as manifest through climate change and its effects as well as increasing pollution, has become the most important issue to be addressed. Many issues are discussed including the climate and associated events, such as fires and floods; air travel and whether it should continue unchanged; electric vehicle transport; renewable energy; pollution and the destruction of habitats; early deaths caused by pollution; and even whether we need to become vegetarian. These are all issues pertinent to achieving sustainability, and all governments are promising some action to address at least some of these issues, despite the fact that ISO 26000[1] became a guide rather than a standard primarily due to the objections of the USA and China to addressing environmental issues. Nevertheless, a consensus seems to have been reached that action is needed. It is noticeably less certain however just what that action should be. And so, governments have grand plans but much less certainty about how to put those plans into action.

It is clear however that sustainability is a complex issue, that many issues need to be addressed at many levels, and that there is a degree of complexity and interaction between these various issues and the steps taken to achieve the desired effects. It is equally clear that Brundtland's three pillars of sustainable development[2] are insufficient to address the issue, even though the WCED (1987) report dwelt on them in detail and stressed that they were three equal pillars. It is also equally inappropriate to describe such development as a "development that meets the needs of the present without compromising the ability of future generations to meet their own needs" (WCED, 1987), as we are plainly affecting future choices through the effects of our actions just as the current generation has been affected by the actions of preceding generations.

Having commenced by issuing these caveats, it must still be accepted that the issue of sustainability needs to be taken seriously and addressed urgently. It is complex and many steps need to be taken. One starting point would be to recognise the complexity and the many issues which need to be addressed and, of course, the interactions between issues and actions in differing arenas. This book attempts to make a start in doing this by addressing various diverse facets which are not normally considered at the same time. In doing, it raises issues for discussion and action rather than offering solutions. This introduction recognises some of these issues, while the subsequent chapters raise many more.

---

[1]Guidance on social responsibility.
[2]Economic, social, and environmental.

2. Manufacturing and the External Environment

Over the last half-century, it has become universally accepted that the external environment is affected to a significant extent by the activities carried out by a company, not just with respect to energy usage and pollution through products but also through social effects and economic dislocations. This necessitates accountability of the company not just to its shareholders but also to the greater audience of society at large. Although this was initially expounded by philosopher-entrepreneurs such as Robert Owen (1816), this necessity was again revived during the 1960s after Rachel Carson's work (1962) and further developed during the 1970s, and some authors have considered the firm's social performance as a member of the whole society. Ackerman (1975) argued that the majority of the businesses have already realised the need to adjust to the recent social environment of accountability towards the community but that the alignment of business to financial outcomes is a constraint for this. In the same way, McDonald and Puxty (1979) argue that shareholders are no longer only owners of the business, but as the firms operate in the society, they are responsible for it. Hence, firms are changing to be more accountable to all stakeholders. It also implies that the external environment, which gets affected by the activities of the firm, is concerned about such activities as the owners of the firm. Moreover, there are a number of stakeholders who have credible concerns regarding the activities of a firm and the business activities' impacts on them. They have both an interest and an influence on the formation of the activities of a firm. Their influence is so substantial that one can say that the power of these stakeholders is a kind of quasi-ownership of the firm. The traditional role of accounting in reporting results was challenged by Gray (1992) and Gray *et al.* (1987) who presented the view that what is required is a stakeholder rather than an ownership approach towards accountability. In effect, this has become known as triple bottom line reporting (Elkington, 1994). This view has become more pronounced recently (e.g. Van der Laan *et al.*, 2008; Mitchell *et al.*, 2015) as shareholders are usually concerned with only profits and dividends, while stakeholders take into account the negative and positive externalities generated by a business as well (see, for example, Hutton, 1997; Sternberg, 1997; Freeman and Reed, 1983). Additionally, writers such as Rubenstein (1992), Kakabadse *et al.* (2005), and Wilburn and Wilburn (2011) went one step ahead and emphasised the need for formulation of social contract between businesses and stakeholders.

The social contract between business and society has been revived in recent decades (Donaldson and Dunfee, 1994). The main concern of this social contract is for the future, and the use of the term "sustainability" is a manifestation of it (Seifi and Crowther, 2012). Such a term appears everywhere either in the discourse of a company's performance or in that of globalisation. Indeed, sustainability is a controversial issue for which there are so many definitions about what one might mean by it (e.g. Toman, 1992; Vos, 2007). The widest definitions of the term are concerned about the impact of present actions on the available options in the future, and this is central to the Brundtland definition of sustainable development (WCED, 1987). By using all the resources now, nothing will remain to be used tomorrow, which is especially important if the amount of such resources is finite. Therefore, the quantity of extractive resources, such as oil, lead, iron, or coal, is finite, and as they are used, they will not be available for later utilisation. This leads to scarcity, and how to deal with this scarcity — either by developing different options or by developing technological solutions which require a lesser quantity of scarce materials — presents itself as the issue. In other words, what is produced needs to be reconsidered not just because of the effects on society but also because of the changing availability of raw materials: In effect, the whole of economic activity needs to be rethought and probably redesigned, which is obviously a major challenge to be addressed.

3. Geopolitical Considerations

As the world grapples with sustainability and its ramifications, it is apparent that the available resources of the world become important, especially as they grow scarcer. It is impossible therefore to consider any approach to sustainability without considering the geographical diversity and location of those resources. This inevitably leads us into the arena of geopolitics (see Seifi and Crowther, 2017). One factor which needs to be considered regarding natural resources, therefore, is the location, and it is an irrefutable fact that a significant proportion of them are located in the BRIC countries (Brazil, Russia, India, and China). These are countries with large populations and which are achieving rapid economic growth and development, and in order to do so, they are inevitably utilising the natural resources which they possess (Wilson, 2015). Naturally, if developing countries continue to grow and to use more of their own resources, then these are no longer available to the rest of the world, especially the developed countries which need these resources in order to continue their own growth and ensure their continuing prosperity.

A review of resources available in these countries (Sidaway, 2012) reveals potentially significant problems. China — the largest country in the world as well as the fastest growing in terms of GDP — has deposits of most of the 150 minerals found so far in the natural world (Clark *et al.*, 1987). It has the largest deposits of 12 minerals and large proportions of 45 more. Brazil has large quantities of mineral resources, such as quartz, diamonds, chromium, iron ore, phosphates, petroleum, mica, graphite, titanium, copper, gold, oil, bauxite, zinc, tin, and mercury. The main natural resources of India are iron ore, bauxite, and copper ore. India is one of the major producers of iron in the world. Gold, silver, and diamonds make up a small part of other natural resources available in India. Russia has the world's largest mineral and energy supply and has 22% of the world's oil, 16% of the world's coal, and 40% of the world's natural gas. It also has the largest quantities of minerals, such as iron ore, nickel, gold, diamonds, zinc, aluminium, tin, lead, platinum, titanium, copper, tungsten phosphates, and mercury (Dubrinski, 2013; Dudin *et al.*, 2016).

It might be argued that the rapid development of these countries has slowed in recent years — indeed it might be further argued that they have slipped into recession with either zero or negative growth (Degaut, 2015). Nevertheless, their economic activity uses significant amounts of their resources, thereby lessening the amount available elsewhere, such as in Europe. This raises one issue regarding sustainability which is concerned with the equalisation, or at least equitable distribution, of both access to resources and the development (with consequent living standards) of the countries and the world. Here also is an area in which inequity is apparent and the possibility of conflicts arises; in fact, it has previously been suggested that conflicts in the Middle East have been concerned with access to resources, primarily oil, and that conflicts have arisen in some parts of the world over the use of water and access to that water.

Many have studied the tragedy of the commons and the problems that ensue. Indeed, recently, Thuestadlsaken *et al.* (2019) have demonstrated experimentally that there is always a tendency to exploit the contributions of others rather than reciprocate. Alfaki (2013) similarly uses game theory (see Seifi, 2021) to show that increased risk in obtaining supplies leads to increased consumption and selfish behaviour resulting in overuse and exploitation of those resources to the detriment of future use. The tragedy of the commons is often used to studied environmental resources and their use. In this manner, Gersani *et al.* (2001) use game theory to show that soybeans compete for space with other species and plants as far as possible. Conversely, Rankin *et al.* (2007) studied competition in biological systems to show adaption strategies, but there still remains the question of whether or not anything supersedes self-interest in determining behaviour. Conversely, Botelho *et al.* (2015) suggest that sometimes cooperation can arise to mitigate the effects of resources shortage in a common-pool resource but only model circumstances in which there are relative similarities in size and power between the actors in the model. Similarly, Janssen (2015) shows that complex behavioural circumstances are necessary to facilitate cooperation in common-pool resources. As access to resources becomes more of an issue, it seems that conflict also becomes likely — possibly inevitable unless alternatives can be found.

4. Managing Global Oversight

Given that sustainability is becoming an increasingly important and urgent issue and there is a clear consensus that the whole world must be involved and must act together, it then seems necessary that a global approach is taken. This requires management, and the COP26[3] conference in 2021 is an example of a global approach but restricted to dealing with climate change. It must be expected that more such coordinations occur as sustainability becomes ever more pressing. Moreover, it is undoubted that these supra-national bodies will require scientific advice about what steps are needed and, of course, about the role technology can play in this. This will require some form of control and regulation.

In order to achieve this, it will require some form of global regulation, and this requires global organisations to exist to both oversee activities and with the power to sanction noncompliance. This in turn requires national governments to surrender some of their sovereignty to these bodies. And this is problematic; even the surrender by the UK of some of its sovereignty to the European Union (EU) has been so difficult that the British people have voted to leave the EU with one of the arguments being about maintaining sovereignty (Gordon, 2016; Ewing, 2017). At a global level, this would require the agreement of all nations. Currently, there are 195 nations, a number which is almost double that of 60 years ago. Some are significantly more powerful — and therefore more influential — than others, but reaching a global agreement is a very difficult process and almost impossible. Even the major countries of the USA, Russia, China, and those in the EU (with possibly the UK added) cannot agree on very much. The 27 countries of the EU, however, have demonstrated in the past that they have difficulty in agreeing about many things (Tallberg, 2004).

It will be observed however that there are some global bodies which manage to exist in a satisfactory way. The principal one is the United Nations which has a number of subsidiary organisations within it. The main ones are the General Assembly, the Security Council, the Economic and Social Council, the Trusteeship Council, and the International Court of Justice. Unfortunately, the regulation of international trading does not fall within its area of responsibility.

---

[3]26th UN Climate Change Conference of the Parties.

For this, the World Trade Organisation exists, starting in 1995 to replace the former GATT.[4] This merely forms a basis for extensive discussion surrounding the reduction of taxes for international trading but has made slow progress because it still needs the agreement of all countries before it is agreed. For example, the Doha Development Round commenced in 2001 and collapsed in 2011. Currently, the Paris Accord (the most recent version of the regulation) became uncertain after the USA's withdrawal despite evidence (Jackson and Grinstead, 2018) supporting its prediction of such global consequences as sea-level rise.

There are however a number of successfully operating global regulation systems that do exist. One significant example is the Basel III Accord which is concerned with the regulation of international banking (King and Tarbert, 2011). Another example is the operation of the international legal system (Krisch and Kingbury, 2006) which is based upon a consent model of regulation although supported by a strong enforcement mechanism for noncompliance. Another system which has been in existence for almost a century is that of the regulation of whaling; although this has been criticised many times (Suhre, 2000), it has remained largely effective, again based primarily upon international consent. There seem to be signs however that this might no longer apply as some countries seem to be revising their whaling policy.

It is undoubted that sustainability must be for the world as a whole and that this cannot be achieved without nations acting in concert or at least in agreement with actions taken. It seems to be reasonable therefore to argue that a global body in a position to establish and monitor a collaborative approach to the functioning of markets in manufacturing goods and resources does not exist. If the need is accepted for a change in the market mechanism, then there would be a need for the establishment of a body to undertake this. This would be necessary but would certainly not be an easy process because global benefits are likely to be in conflict with national

---

[4]General Agreement on Trade and Tariffs.

self-interest as well as corporate self-interest. Indeed, Seifi (2021) argues that corporate interest must be subordinated to the global necessity of managing resources for the world as a whole, with a potential need to revise the whole economic basis for activity — something which is fairly radical.

It is however important to remember the argument of Popper (1957) regarding the poverty of historicism. Here, he contends that an analysis of the past is no guide to the future and that basing any expectations upon what has happened in the past is flawed and unreasonable. Thus, the fact that solutions have always been found previously gives us no cause for either optimism or pessimism in the present and immediate future. This is however a problem which must be addressed and is a part of the complexity of achieving sustainability.

It is a truism that all organisations need some form of governance (Bevir, 2013). At its simplest, governance is merely a set of rules which define the way the individual members of an organisation interact with each other. It is only when the term is used in either a political sense, when it has other connotations, or in a corporate sense, when it refers to relations between the corporation and its investors, that it has a particular meaning. In general, it applies to any organisation of two people or more who need some sort of rules to engage in mutual activity (Jackson *et al.*, 2008). Thus, the markets which exist for raw materials trading need some form of governance (Williamson, 1979) as would these when adapted to a collaborative approach. The whole purpose of governance rules is to share procedures to enable the organisation to function and is based on the principles of transparency, fairness, accountability, and the rule of law.

It seems that the United Nations does not fulfil the role of world governance, although some (e.g. Bull Boas and McNeill, 2004) consider it as a possibility and perhaps desirable. Indeed, the pressure group Forum for a New World Governance[5] exists to promote this concept. Thakur and Van Langenhove (2006) carry this concept

---

[5]http://www.world-governance.org/spip.php?rubrique6&lang=en.

forwards further by proposing regional governance bodies which eventually will become global governance. Such writers however seem to fail to differentiate between governance as a governmental function and governance as simple rules of operation. Thus, governance has become inseparable from the political domain, and it is here where such a proposal will fail, as nations are reluctant to surrender their autonomy and sovereignty. Without these rules however international relations are subject to the uncertain fluctuations of political alliances and to the use of power with the most powerful nations exerting the greatest influence. Those examples of international governance which are operating successfully seem to be always based upon the consent model. Thus, the consent model seems to be confirmed by actual practises, although the argument has also been made that this also needs strong enforcement.

Governance of global trading markets however implies no political content but is merely rules of process and dispute resolution, which is nowhere near as controversial. To an extent, this already exists in the form of international trading — via the WTO rules which act as a default if no alternative between countries has been agreed upon (Isaac and Kerr, 2003) — and especially for international finance (Quinn, 1987). In each case, the regulation is not separated from the political domain, which can cause problems in both monitoring and enforcing sanctions and even in agreeing to change. As the existing forms of regulation are of competitive economic markets, it is indeed difficult to separate their regulation from the use of power and therefore from the political domain, and this is probably one of the major causes of the difficulties which arise in the negotiation of trading regulations. It is helpful therefore to consider both the purpose of regulation and the new environment which will arise.

5. Governance and Regulation

At its simplest, governance is just the set of rules and procedures by which people engage in any form of joint tasks or activities. In general, these need to be written down so that they are available to everyone concerned and it can be seen that everyone is following the same procedures or would take the same actions in the same circumstances (Sama and Shoaf, 2005). If the rules of governance are incomplete or are not fully written down, then this can lead to corrupt activity or the misuse of power. This is true for any form of organisation and is not limited to commercial organisations or to governments. An example of this is FIFA under the Sepp Blatter era, where poor governance[6] was held responsible for the corruption problems experienced. From this, it follows that transparency must exist so that all concerned parties can see how all other concerned parties are behaving and whether they are behaving in the agreed-upon manner. This therefore requires accountability so that people can be held responsible for actions taken or not taken. With accountability comes the need for regulation (Braithwaite *et al.*, 2007), and this therefore requires some form of regulatory oversight.

Regulatory oversight necessitates someone to undertake this function (Boo and Sharma, 2008), and this can be done either internally — by the organisation itself — or externally by either an existing body or one set up expressly for this purpose. The accounting profession provides a prime example of an internally regulated organisation (Johnston and Pelacchi, 2017), while the Enron scandal (Toffler, 2003) provides a prime example of the problems that can ensue from this form of regulation. An example of external regulation by an already existing organisation is given by the WTO and trade regulation which by a body expressly established for the purpose. Another is given in the UK by the Financial Services Authority which has since become two bodies, The Financial Conduct Authority, and the Prudential Regulation Authority, controlled by the Bank of England. As argued above, regulation within a country is not a great problem, as it can be imposed by the government if all else fails. Markets for the trading of raw materials are however a different matter, as this is done in an international manner in global markets. Indeed, the market as such is often virtual as the price mechanism

---

[6]https://www.theguardian.com/football/blog/2015/jun/09/fifa-reform-manifesto-football-sepp-blatter.

works in any competitive environment. Effectively, therefore, this is a global market which would require regulating on a global basis — and the establishment of a regulatory body to provide this oversight and with the power to impose the sanctions agreed upon in the event of noncompliance (Kershaw, 2005).

It is difficult to see how any form of regulation of world activity from a sustainability perspective could be established without the agreement of all nations and certainly the agreement of the most powerful nations, although perhaps there is a role for technology in facilitating this. The evidence suggests that regulation works best with consent. It is of course equally difficult to see how this could be established without any geopolitical considerations. It should also be recognised that at the moment the power probably lies mainly with the consuming countries of those raw materials, as they have the economic resources and extract greater value added from the employment of resources in production. As time progresses however the scarcity of resources, as they become more depleted, will increase, and this will inevitably change the power basis towards those who have the supply of raw materials and away from those that desire them. Conceivably, therefore, Marshall McLuhan's prediction (McLuhan and Fiore, 1968) that future wars will be based on economic criteria has been shown to be both prescient and in need of serious consideration. Dubrinski (2013) has noted that the BRIC countries possess a considerable share of these remaining resources while also developing their industrial capability which will have a significant effect on the current markets for resources and this will become more pronounced as time progresses, as will resource depletion and the development of industrial production capability in these (and other) countries (Nayyar, 2016). This would strengthen the argument for a collaborative approach, at least among the developed but resource-poor countries (such as the UK) but perhaps lessen the desirability among developing but resource-rich countries. This also increases the likelihood of armed conflicts. Such conflicts exist at the present and have been forecast for the future (e.g. Theisen, 2008; Koubi *et al.*, 2014) as well as explained by economic reasons, such as (in part) the invasion of Iraq in 2003 (Bassil, 2012).

The regulation of the market for raw materials in a collaborative environment would require the establishment of a new organisation with a new set of rules (Hallack and Vazquez, 2013). This is possible of course, and the example of the Russian federation after the collapse of the USSR showing us how this can be done is given by de Rosa (2008) who argues that this needs to be done by first establishing a regulatory oversight body to oversee reforms and their quality followed by strengthening the capacity of competition and network authorities. It is therefore possible, but experience shows it to be a lengthy process; moreover, experience shows that at a global level, such things evolve through use and practicality. For the world, it is more complex, as there is not an overarching body which can determine these features and instead consensus must be reached. One of the basic principles of such a market for resources would have to be the allocation of resources. The conventional mechanism for market exchange is that of price, but this would not work in this situation, as price allocates resources to those who can pay the most and therefore probably to the developed countries, whereas the resources would need to be allocated in a way that would enable maximum use to be made of them (De Figueiredo and De Figueiredo, 2002). This raises several problems to be addressed.

Economic theory has of course been developed on the assumption that the best use of any resource can be made by those who will pay the highest price. In other words, the pricing mechanism automatically ensures an optimum allocation of resources. It has been argued (Seifi, 2021) however that this no longer applies when supplies are restricted and cannot be increased, as with natural resources. In this case, pricing might allocate according to economic ability but this differs from utility. Thus, there is a need for some of these resources by all regardless of price or ability to pay. For example, copper is a trace element needed by everyone for living regardless of price. Other minerals are needed for a variety of reasons, and therefore it can be argued that optimum allocation of a scarce resource is best undertaken according to need in order to ensure equity and sustainability. It is apparent of course that technology has a significant role to play in both minimising use of scarce materials and developing alternatives to their use. This is an area which will become of ever greater significance.

Currently, however, use is determined by what is most profitable to that party purchasing which may well not be what is best for the world as a whole. The determining of best use is considered by economists (e.g. Calsamiglia, 1977) to not work satisfactorily without price as the mediator. This also presupposes a short-term view of what is best, whereas a sustainable future might need different decisions when the future is taken into account; in other words, the long-term view might well need to outweigh the short-term view and immediate profitability. A further difficulty is that optimal use is not an absolute concept and competing uses may well be preferred by different people.

Inevitably, it is not possible for nations to separate global needs from their own self-interest and alignment with certain groups of nations. Thus, it is not possible to separate national interests and prejudices from the global allocation process (Francis *et al.*, 2009). Many countries have preferred trading partners, such as the claimed special relationship between the UK and the USA or the reinstated special relationship between commonwealth countries. Equally, many countries are wary of trading with certain others due to such reasons as conflicting ideology or religious differences, or trading preferences from these reasons. It is often claimed that economic utility ignores such preferences and prejudices (Bettis and Prahalad, 1983), but in reality, the trading of increasingly scarce resources can never be separated from either political influences or power relationships.

When resources are fixed in quantity, as are global mineral resources, then it goes without stating that what is used in the present is no longer available for future use. Equally, sustainability requires leaving available choices to future generations. This raises the question of intergenerational resource availability (Padilla, 2002). Optimal resource allocation must therefore take this into account (Howarth, 1991), which is a problem both for present use and for anticipating future requirements. This is certainly one area which needs to be addressed in our drive for sustainability and can of course significantly affect the rate at which resources are utilised or even replenished.

Nations make decisions and take actions according to political processes which consider a wide variety of aims and objectives which are not economic. Indeed, strategic objectives are often more important, and these could outweigh economic benefits in decision-making (Zhuang and Bier, 2010). Thus, the optimal sustainable capability of the world as a whole is almost never considered and does not even rank on most decision-making processes in the political arena. Even if war is engaged in for economic reasons and the outcome might be beneficial for some individual countries, it is never beneficial for the planet as a whole: Some nations become worse off as a result. It is also the case that resources are used for this purpose and therefore diverted from other purposes, so the net productive capacity of the planet is reduced in this manner. As resources become more depleted and therefore made more scarce, this becomes an increasingly important consideration. Wang *et al.* (2017) however show that game theory can deal with this uncertainty in matters of national security. However, they do not consider the effect on the world as a whole.

Regulation is part of governance, and human nature means that procedures may become more lax as they continue in existence. Rules get ignored and corruption inevitably creeps into the system (Shleifer and Vishny, 1993). With most systems of governance, this can be overcome by an oversight of the process — regulating the regulators. At a national level, this is not really a problem, as there is always a higher authority (Builte and Damania, 2008). At a global level, however, such as required by the global market for minerals, there is no higher authority who can check on the world governance of markets.

6. Conclusions

The above analysis illustrates that there are a wide range of issues involved in achieving sustainability. It also illustrates that these issues are complex and diverse and with many overlaps and interactions between the various steps which need to be (or possibly could be) taken in order to achieve sustainability. Technology will most certainly be able to play a significant role in addressing many of these issues, often in unexpected ways. Indeed, technological developments might be regarded as essential as we seek new ways to achieving a sustainable world. Thus, technology can help us down the road towards the goal of sustainable activity and even life (Seifi, 2022). Not all problems can of course be solved through technological development, and some changes in human activity are also required — but again, technological development can help with these changes. Not all the necessary changes can be made in this way, and understanding the limits of technology in providing solutions is equally important.

According to the Gaia theory (Lovelock, 1979, 2006), the Earth will maintain itself in balance and can repair any damage caused which gives ground for optimism. Having said that however, Lovelock (2009) now argues that humans have caused too much change for this to be possible; in other words, the homeostatic system that is on the planet Earth is now broken (Lovelock, 2015). This could imply that there is no hope for the future, or it could imply that it is now down to human ingenuity to repair the damage which we have caused. This of course demonstrates yet again the importance of our need to recreate sustainability. There is much to be done, and the contributions in this book show both that there is much to do and also that there is much hope for the future. It is for each of us to decide how to respond to the challenge.

References

Ackerman, R. W. (1975). *The Social Challenge to Business*, Harvard University Press, Cambridge, MA.

Alfaki, S. (2013). The effects of environmental uncertainty on the tragedy of the commons, *Games and Economic Behaviour*, Vol. 82, November, pp. 240–253.

Bassil, Y. (2012). The 2003 Iraq War: Operations, causes and consequences, *Journal of Humanities and Social Sciences*, Vol. 4, No. 5, pp. 29–34.

Bettis, R. A. and Prahalad, C. K. (1983). The visible and the invisible hand: Resource allocation in the industrial sector, *Strategic Management Journal*, Vol. 4, No. 1, pp. 27–43.

Bevir, M. (2013). *Governance: A Very Short Introduction*, Oxford University Press, Oxford.

Boo, E. and Sharma, D. (2008). Effect of regulatory oversight on the association between internal governance characteristics and audit fees, *Accounting & Finance*, Vol. 48, No. 1, pp. 51–71.

Botelho, A., Dinar, A., Costa, L. M. and Rapoport, A. (2015). Promoting cooperation in resource dilemmas: Theoretical predictions and experimental evidence, *Journal of Behavioral and Experimental Economics*, Vol. 54, February, pp. 40–49.

Braithwaite, J., Coglianese, C. and Levi-Faur, D. (2007). Can regulation make a difference? *Regulation and Governance*, Vol. 1, No. 1, pp. 1–7.

Builte, E. and Damania, R. (2008). Resources for sale: Corruption democracy and the natural resource curse, *The B E Journal of Economic Analysis & Policy*, Vol. 8, No. 1. https://doi.org/10.2202/1935-1682.1890.

Bull, B., Boas, M. and McNeill, D. (2004). Private sector influence in a multilateral system: A changing structure of world governance, *Global Governance*, Vol. 10, pp. 481–498.

Calsamiglia, X. (1977). Decentralising resource allocation and increasing returns, *Journal of Economic Theory*, Vol. 14, No. 2, pp. 263–283.

Carson, R. (1962). *Silent Spring*, Houghton Mifflin, New York.

Clark, A. L., Dorian, J. P. and Fan, P. (1987). All estimate of the mineral resources of China, *Resources Policy*, Vol. 13, No. 1, pp. 68–84.

de Rosa, D. (2008). Regulatory institutions: A blueprint for the Russian Federation, *OECD Working Papers on Public Governance*, No. 10, OECD Publishing. DOI:10.1787/241530366501.

Degaut, M. (2015). *Do The BRICS Still Matter?* Centre for Strategic and International Studies, Washington DC.

Donaldson, T. and Dunfee, T. W. (1994). Toward a unified conception of business ethics: Integrative social contract theory, *Academy of Management Review*, Vol. 19, No. 2. https://doi.org/10.5465/amr.1994.9410210749.

Dubrinski, J. (2013). Sustainable development of mining mineral resources, *Journal of Sustainable Mining*, Vol. 12, No. 1, pp. 1–6.

Dudin, M. N., Frolova, E. E., Artemieva, J. A., Bezbah, V. V. and Kirsanov, A. N. (2016). Problems and perspectives on BRICS countries transfer to green economy and low-carbon energy industry, *International Journal of Energy Economics and Policy*, Vol. 6, No. 4, pp. 714–720.

Elkington, J. (1994). Towards the sustainable corporation: Win-win-win business strategies for sustainable development, *California Management Review*, Vol. 36, pp. 90–100.

Ewing, K. (2017). Brexit and parliamentary sovereignty, *Modern Law Review*, Vol. 80, No. 4, pp. 711–726.

De Figueiredo, J. M. and De Figueiredo, R. J. P. (2002). The allocation of resources by interest groups: Lobbying litigation and administrative regulation, *Business and Politics*, Vol. 4, No. 2, pp. 161–181.

Francis, J. R., Huang, S., Khurana, I. K. and de Pereira, R. (2009). Does corporate transparency contribute to efficient resource allocation, *Journal of Accounting Research*, Vol. 47, No. 4, pp. 943–989.

Freeman, R. E. and Reed, D. L. (1983). Stockholders and stakeholders: A new perspective on corporate governance, *California Management Review*, Vol. 25, No. 3, pp. 88–106.

Gersani, M., Brown, J. S., O'Brien, E. E., Maina, G. M. and Abramsky, Z. (2001). Tragedy of the commons as a result of root competition, *Journal of Ecology*, Vol. 89, No. 4, pp. 660–669.

Gordon, M. (2016). The UK's sovereignty situation: Brexit Bewilderment and beyond, *Kings Law Journal*, Vol. 27, No. 3, pp. 333–343.

Gray, R. (1992). Accounting and environmentalism: An exploration of the challenge of gently accounting for accountability, transparency and sustainability, *Accounting, Organizations & Society*, Vol. 17, No. 5, pp. 399–425.

Gray, R., Owen, D. and Maunders, K. (1987). *Corporate Social Reporting: Accounting and Accountability*, Prentice-Hall, London.

Hallack, M. and Vazquez, M. (2013). European union regulation of gas transmission services: Challenges in the allocation of network resources through entry/exit schemes, *Utilities Policy*, Vol. 25, pp. 23–32.

Howarth, R. B. (1991). Intergenerational competitive equilibria under technological uncertainty and an exhaustible resource constraint, *Journal of Environmental Economics and Management*, Vol. 21, No. 3, pp. 225–243.

Hutton, W. (1997). *Stakeholding and Its Critics*, IEA Health and Welfare Unit, London.

Isaac, G. E. and Kerr, W. A. (2003). Genetically modified organisms and trade rules: Identifying important challenges for the WTO, *The World Economy*, Vol. 26, No. 1, pp. 29–42.

Jackson, C. L., Nicholson, C., Doust, J., Cheung, L. and O'Donnell, J. (2008). Seriously working together: Integrated governance models to achieve sustainable partnerships between health care organisations, *Medical Journal of Australia*, Vol. 188, No. 58, pp. S57–S60.

Jackson, L. P. and Grinstead, A. (2018). 21st century sea-level rise in line with Paris accord, *Earth's Future*, Vol. 6, No. 2, pp. 213–229.

Janssen, M. A. (2015). A behavioural perspective on the governance of common pool resources, *Current Opinion in Environmental Sustainability*, Vol. 12, February, pp. 1–5.

Johnston, R. and Petacchi, R. (2017). Regulatory oversight of financial reporting: Securities and exchange commission comment letters, *Contemporary Accounting Research*, Vol. 34, No. 2, pp. 1128–1155.

Kakabadse, N. K., Rozuel, C. and Lee-Davies, L. (2005). Corporate social responsibility and stakeholder approach: A conceptual review, *International Journal of Business Governance and Ethics*, Vol. 1, No. 4, pp. 277–302.

Kershaw, D. (2005). Evading enron: Taking principles too seriously in accounting regulation, *Modern Law Review*, Vol. 68, No. 4, pp. 594–625.

King, P. and Tarbert, H. (2011). Basel III an overview, *Banking and Financial Services Policy Report*, Vol. 30, No. 5, pp. 1–18.

Krisch, N. and Kingbury, B. (2006). Global governance and global administrative law in the international legal order, *European Journal of International Law*, Vol. 17, No. 1, pp. 1–13.

Koubi, V., Spilker, G., Bohmelt, T. and Bernauer, T. (2014). Do natural resources matter for interstate and intrastate conflict, *Journal of Peace Research*, Vol. 51, No. 2, pp. 227–243.

Van der Laan, G., Ees, H. V. Witteloostuijin, A. V. (2008). Corporate social and financial performance: An extended stakeholder theory and empirical test with accounting measures, *Journal of Business Ethics*, Vol. 79, No. 3, pp. 299–310.

Lovelock, J. (1979). *Gaia*, Oxford University Press, Oxford.

Lovelock, J. (2006). *The Revenge of Gaia*, Penguin, Harmondsworth.

Lovelock, J. (2009). *The Vanishing Face of Gaia*, Penguin, Harmondsworth.

Lovelock, J. (2015). *A Rough Ride to the Future*, Penguin, Harmondsworth.

McDonald, D. and Puxty, A. G. (1979). An inducement — Contribution approach to corporate financial reporting, *Accounting, Organizations & Society*, Vol. 4, No. 1/2, pp. 53–65.

McLuhan, M. and Fiore, Q. (1968). *War and Peace in the Global Village*, Hardwire, San Francisco.

Mitchell, R. K., van Buren, H. J., III Greenwood, M. and Freeman, R. E. (2015). Stakeholder inclusion and accounting for stakeholders, *Journal of Management Studies*, Vol. 52, No. 7, pp. 851–877.

Nayyar, D. (2016). BRICS developing countries and global governance, *Third World Quarterly*, Vol. 37, No. 4, pp. 575–591.

Owen, R. (1816, 1991). *A New View of Society and Other Writings*, Penguin, London.

Padilla, E. (2002). Intergenerational equity and sustainability, *Ecological Economics*, Vol. 41, No. 1, pp. 69–83.

Popper, K. (1957). *The Poverty of Historicism*, Routledge, London.

Quinn, D. (1987). The correlates of change in international finance regulation, *American Political Science Review*, Vol. 91, No. 3, pp. 531–551.

Rankin, D. J., Barum, K. and Kokko, H. (2007). The tragedy of the commons in evolutionary biology, *Trends in Ecology & Evolution*, Vol. 22 No. 12, pp. 643–651.

Rubenstein, D. B. (1992). Bridging the gap between green accounting and black ink, *Accounting Organizations & Society*, Vol. 17, No. 5, pp. 501–508.

Sama, L. M. and Shoaf, V. (2005), Reconciling rules and principles: An ethics-based approach to corporate governance, *Journal of Business Ethics*, Vol. 58, Nos. 1–3, pp. 177–185.

Seifi, S. (2021). *The World's Future Crisis: Extractive Resources Depletion*, Springer, Singapore.

Seifi, S. (2022). Engaging with technological sustainability, *Technological Sustainability*, Vol. 1, No. 1, (forthcoming).

Seifi, S. and Crowther, D. (2012). The ethics game paradox, *Multidisciplinary Journal for Applied Ethics*, Vol. 1, No. 1, pp. 30–37.

Seifi, S. and Crowther, D. (2017). Sustainability and resource depletion, in D. Crowther and S. Seifi (eds.), *Modern Organizational Governance*, pp. 91–105, Bingley, Emerald.

Shleifer, A. and Vishny, R. W. (1993). Corruption, *The Quarterly Journal of Economics*, Vol. 108, No. 3, pp. 599–617.

Sidaway, J. D. (2012). Geographies of development: New maps, new visions? *Professional Geographer*, Vol. 64, No. 1, pp. 49–62.

Sternberg, E. (1997). The defects of stakeholder theory, *Corporate Governance: An International Review*, Vol. 6, No. 3, pp. 151–163.

Suhre, S. (2000). Misguided morality: The repercussions of the international whaling commission's shift from a policy of regulation to one of preservation, *Georgetown International Environmental Law Review*, Vol. 12, pp. 305–330.

Tallberg, J. (2004). The power of the presidency: Brokerage efficiency and distribution in EU negotiations, *Journal of Common Market Studies*, Vol. 42, No. 5, pp. 999–1022.

Thakur, R. and Van Langenhove, L. (2006). Enhancing global governance through regional integration, *Global Governance*, Vol. 12, pp. 233–240.

Theisen, O. M. (2008). Blood and soil? Resource scarcity and internal armed conflict revisited, *Journal of Peace Research*, Vol. 45, No. 6, pp. 801–818.

Thuestadlsaken, E., Brekke, K. A. and Richter, A. (2019). Positive framing does not solve the tragedy of the commons, *Journal of Environmental Economics and Management*, Vol. 95, May, pp. 45–56.

Toffler, B. L. (2003). *Final Accounting: Ambition, Greed and the Fall of Arthur Andersen*, Broadway Books, New York.

Toman, M. A. (1992). The Difficulty in defining sustainability, *Resources*, Winter 1992, pp. 4–6.

Vos, R. O. (2007). Defining sustainability: A conceptual orientation, *Journal of Chemical Technology and Biotechnology*, Vol. 82, No. 4, pp. 334–339.

Wang, Y., Luo, S. and Gao, J. (2017). Uncertain extensive game with application to resource allocation of national security, *Journal of Ambient Intelligence and Humanized Computing*, Vol. 8, No. 5, pp. 797–808.

WCED (World Commission on Environment and Development) (1987). *Our Common Future*, (The Brundtland Report); Oxford University Press, Oxford.

Wilburn, K. M. and Wilburn, R. (2011). Achieving social license to operate using stakeholder theory, *Journal of International Business Ethics*, Vol. 4, No. 2, pp. 3–16.

Williamson, O. E. (1979). Transaction-cost economics: The governance of contractual relations, *Journal of Law and Economics*, Vol. 22, No. 2, pp. 233–245.

Wilson, J. D. (2015). Resource powers? Minerals, energy and the rise of the BRICS, *Third World Quarterly*, Vol. 36, No. 2, pp. 223–239.

Zhuang, J. and Bier, V. M. (2010). Reasons for secrecy and deception in homeland security resource allocation, *Risk Analysis: An International Journal*, Vol. 30, No. 12, pp. 1737–1743.

Part 1

Developments Old and New

https://doi.org/10.1142/9789811258756_0002

Chapter 2

Corporate Responsible Innovation in Science and Technology Organisations: Including Indigenous Worldviews

Rafaela Costa Camoes Rabello, Katharina Ruckstuhl,
Diane Ruwhiu, and Kirsty de Jong

Abstract

Science and technology organisations are increasingly held accountable for addressing global challenges. When such organisations attempt to tackle the "wicked" problems of poverty, hunger, environmental degradation, or climate change, they tend to adopt a classical paradigm or "Western science" approach and run the risk of intensifying or generating new problems. In this chapter, we argue that wicked problems have a better chance of being addressed when such organisations draw on a broader range of worldviews and approaches. The chapter provides a New Zealand exemplar of an inclusive endeavour, whereby an organisation strategically implements an indigenous innovation policy into its core science and technology activities. While the case is singular, there are few empirical models of how inclusive policies operate in science and technology organisations, particularly when such science is upstream or at the ideation phase. This longitudinal study offers pointers that other science organisations may find both useful and inspirational.

Keywords: Responsible innovation; indigenous; organisations; sustainable development; global challenges; wicked problems

1. Introduction

"Rittel's lecture was fascinating but devastating. I went to his office afterwards to ask what can be done if we can't solve 'wicked problems'. 'Oh, we can solve "wicked problems"', he replied with his usual mirth, 'I solve many every day!' The point is, he told me, *that we can't solve them by reference to the logic inherent in the problem*" (emphasis added). (Skaburskis, 2008, p. 277)

Corporations are increasingly expected to help address global challenges, such as poverty, hunger, environmental degradation, and climate change (Buckley *et al.*, 2017; Newenham-Kahindi, 2015; United Nations, 2017; Van Zanten and Van Tulder, 2018). Such large-scale challenges can be viewed as "wicked problems", given that they are complex, ill-defined, and ambiguous, as well as multifaceted and enmeshed in complex social dynamics (Churchman, 1967; Crowley and Head, 2017; Skaburskis, 2008; Termeer *et al.*, 2015).

Often, companies look to science and technology to provide solutions to global challenges (Buckley *et al.*, 2017; Pardey *et al.*, 2016; Sutton and Boag, 2019). In turn, science and technology companies look to science to provide disruptive ideas and technologies (Hautamäki and Oksanen, 2016; Roco *et al.*, 2011). However, the "classical paradigm of science and engineering" can lead to "one-size-fits-all solutions" (Crowley and Head, 2017, p. 541). This classical, or "Western" science, paradigm limits solutions addressing the social complexities of grand challenges. By drawing on the same logic that caused these challenges, other epistemologies that have historically and successfully addressed their particular challenges are overlooked (Watson-Verran and Turnbull, 1995).

In this chapter, we argue that science and innovation on their own are insufficient to respond to such problems. It therefore follows that science and technology organisations should be seeking more diverse approaches to not only science and innovation outputs but also inputs. Such a "politics of diversity" (Crowley and Head, 2017, p. 454) requires inclusive and responsible corporate innovation policies and implementation practises. Inclusivity or "being-in-the-world-with-others" (Roberts, 2003, p. 252) is particularly necessary in respect of the world's 380 million indigenous peoples, who reside in countries that are seen as having many of these challenges, but whose knowledge often is seen as external to the science and technology domain. Such knowledge "has historically been excluded from scientific models that have their origin in Western concepts of rationality, on the assumption that it is inferior" (Puri, 2007, p. 360).

Indigenous knowledge has developed and been tested over centuries, adapting dynamically to local culture, technology, and environment (Sillitoe *et al.*, 2005) and has led to innovative adaptations to address local challenges (Watson-Verran and Turnbull, 1995). We argue that including other knowledge systems as an upstream input into science innovation is a responsible response to addressing complex problems. However, practising a politics of diversity and "being-in-the-world-with-others" is not without its own challenges. This chapter explores the case of a virtual organisation, Science for Technological Innovation (SfTI), which is one of New Zealand's 11 National Science Challenges. In our study, we observe how SfTI meaningfully practises the politics of diversity.

We proceed first by outlining the notions of responsible and inclusive innovation and how through a politics of diversity and "being-in-the-world-with-others" in plural cultural settings (Gudynas, 2011), science and technology corporates can harness other epistemologies to address wicked problems. Next, we contextualise our case study and describe our research methodology. In the third section, we present our research findings, noting the barriers and enablers of inclusive and responsible science and technology policies and practises. We conclude by offering our thoughts on how the case study has wider relevance to corporate responsible practises in the science innovation field.

2. Responsible Innovation as Dialogue with Difference

Wicked problems — complex, ill-defined, and multifaceted problems enmeshed in complex social dynamics — cannot be solved by a "one-size-fits-all solution" (Churchman, 1967; Crowley and Head, 2017; Skaburskis, 2008; Termeer *et al.*, 2015). The term was first coined to refer to grand challenges which derive from a complex class of social-system problems that have no definite formulation, "stopping rule", "true-or-false" status and no immediate solution (Crowley and Head, 2017, p. 541). The United Nations has sought to address wicked problems over many years, most recently articulating these as the 17 Sustainable Development Goals (United Nations, 2017, n.d.). Both governments and businesses, including those in the science and technology realm, have been asked to address these goals (Imaz and Sheinbaum, 2017; Jones *et al.*, 2017).

Globally, there is substantial funding for science and innovation based on the conviction that new technologies will help address wicked problems (Blok, 2014; Blok and Lemmens, 2015; Mitcham, 2003; Stilgoe *et al.*, 2013). Increasingly, this impacts a company's approach to corporate responsibility in relation to innovation (Buckley *et al.*, 2017; Jones *et al.*, 2017; Newenham-Kahindi, 2015; United Nations, 2017; Van Zanten and Van Tulder, 2018).

What then is responsibility in science innovation? Responsible innovation is an approach that builds on concerns about the role of science in society in the context of technological advancements (Genus and Iskandarova, 2018). With substantial investments into national and transnational science to address global challenges as well as drive economies (Blok and Lemmens, 2015; Mitcham, 2003; Schomberg, 2013), responsible innovation requires societal actors and innovators to become mutually responsive to each other through a transparent, interactive process (Von Schomberg, 2012). The responsible science and innovation patchwork should include researchers, businesses, funders, and regulators, as well as members of civil society (Stilgoe *et al.*, 2013). Such social actors should then engage in deliberation — reflecting on their activities and assumptions and responding to stakeholders' and society's values, implying a co-responsibility among actors to address societal concerns (Mitcham, 2003; Stilgoe *et al.*, 2013).

An organisation that wishes to embed responsible scientific and technological innovation will be required to critically unpick the social constituents of the science and technology process through in-depth reflection on the social, political, and ethical implications of a new technology (Callon *et al.*, 2009). However, a scientific way of knowing is not value neutral. It embeds positivistic notions of scientific knowledge, which are entrenched in ideologies of power and domination over others and nature (Aikenhead, 2006; Watson-Verran and Turnbull, 1995). Science, along with its rational and positivist paradigms, has been successful in delivering key technologies (Fallows, 2013); however, a "Western" scientific way of knowing tends to marginalise other knowledge systems (Chilisa, 2017), thereby potentially narrowing science and technology's power to address wicked problems (Crowley and Head, 2017; Flipse *et al.*, 2014; Reinecke and Ansari, 2016; Rittel and Webber, 1973; Skaburskis, 2008). In other words, one "can't solve them [wicked problems] by reference to the logic inherent in the problem" (Hautamäki and Oksanen, 2016, p. 277; Skaburskis, 2008). While scientific knowledge can develop key technologies, there are complex implementation issues and gaps. Hence, broadening innovation policies and practises through a "politics of diversity" may provide one avenue for science and technology corporations to responsibly systematise inclusion (Crowley and Head, 2017, p. 454; Rittel and Webber, 1973).

One way of exercising such a politics of diversity is through the incorporation of indigenous knowledge into science and technology policies and practises. Indigenous knowledge, while tested over centuries, is dynamic and adaptive (Sillitoe *et al.*, 2005). Such knowledge has unique properties, such as the ability to "describe and explain nature in culturally-powerful ways" (Aikenhead, 2006, p. 3) and a place-based prowess at applying innovation to solve local problems (Watson-Verran and Turnbull, 1995).

Historical examples of this dynamism and adaptation abound. For example, between AD 200 and 700, the Anasazi, who lived in the current regions of Colorado, Utah, New Mexico, and Arizona had an urban resident population in the thousands that flourished in the harsh weather of the isolated desert canyons (Lekson *et al.*, 1988; Watson-Verran and Turnbull, 1995). This was only possible through highly complex irrigation, agricultural, and storage systems "with deck dams, reservoirs, canals up to 50 feet wide, irrigation ditches and levelled fields with banks" (Watson-Verran and Turnbull, 1995, p. 6). In a similar way, the Incas, in the extended regions of today's Ecuador, Peru, and Chile in South America, developed highly complex infrastructure and technological systems to support a population of 5 million (d'Altroy, 2014; Davies, 1995; Keatinge, 1988). Through their detailed knowledge of astronomy, the Incas developed a calendar that was intrinsically related to the administration of their empire as well as "irrigation, agriculture, trade, warfare, and all taxes, manpower, and resources" (Watson-Verran and Turnbull, 1995, p. 7). The Micronesian navigators also developed highly efficient technology and wayfinding techniques passed down by oral tradition. In-depth knowledge of sea currents, marine life, weather, winds, and astronomy translated into a complex navigation system. Such systems allowed the Micronesian navigators "to do things that are impossible for a Western navigator, stripped off his instruments" (Hutchins, 1983, p. 192).

The Anasazi, Incas, and Micronesians had dynamic knowledge systems that were adaptive to their local complexities. However, indigenous knowledge has been excluded by a dominant knowledge system based on beliefs of race and civilisation (Smith, 2009) that assumed that indigenous people's knowledge and culture were at a different level of development and therefore uncivilised, leading to assimilationist policies (Stephenson, 2009). Such assimilatory policies, along with a loss of land and resources, resulted in the marginalisation of indigenous people's knowledge, practises, and language (Rewi and Rātima, 2018), reproducing power imbalances and leading to many of today's wicked problems.

By allowing room for other knowledge systems, science and technology organisations can begin the journey to practise responsible and inclusive innovation through "being-in-the-world-with-others" (Roberts, 2003). This involves a "breaking [of] the mirror in which [the] corporation sees only what it chooses to see from behind the high fence and security with which it guards its instrumental interests" (Roberts, 2003, p. 262). Such a notion results in a paradigm shift that moves beyond the logic inherent in the wicked problem that corporates aim to solve. Such a journey requires unpicking individual and institutional value systems that cannot be separated from how we see knowledge and power and how this shapes particular views of human life and relations (Rabello *et al.*, 2018; Stilgoe *et al.*, 2013). Reimagining an ideal of individual and corporate relationships through embracing difference and diversity allows for more humble processes of self-reflexivity and uncertainty that broadens perceptions, "transforming the ways one sees the nature of reality, being and knowledge" (Andreotti and Dowling, 2004, p. 609) and opening up space for the politics of diversity.

However, there are challenges in this for both organisations and individuals. Moving outside one's comfort zone can generate feelings of anger, frustration, denial, disappointment, grief, resistance, or fear (Boler and Zembylas, 2003). Nevertheless, experiencing discomforting feelings "is important in challenging dominant beliefs, social habits and normative practises that sustain social inequities and they create openings for individual and social transformation" (Applebaum, 2017; Boler and Zembylas, 2003; DiAngelo, 2018; Evans-Winters and Hines, 2020; Walsh, 2018; Zembylas, 2015, p. 163).

In the case that we explore here, a mātauranga Māori (Māori knowledge) framework provides the underpinning "other" knowledge system that transforms the praxis of the organisation. Dialoguing with difference (Freire, 1987) is not a rupture with classical or Western science traditions but rather an opportunity for science and technology organisations to create a more responsible approach to addressing grand challenges by recognising that wicked problems can only be solved by moving beyond their inherent logic.

3. Context, Policy Framework, and Research Methodology

In this section, we contextualise how a virtual organisation, New Zealand's SfTI National Science Challenge, has engaged with the politics of diversity through its implementation of Vision Mātauranga, a policy framework to develop science-led innovation for Māori who are the indigenous peoples of New Zealand.

SfTI is one of the 11 National Science Challenges funded by the New Zealand Government. It represents a 10-year, multimillion-dollar programme of research focused on developing novel science to build a more technology-driven and prosperous economy. Demonstrating engagement with Vision Mātauranga is a requirement for much science funding in New Zealand (Davenport *et al.*, 2015; MoRST, 2007). The policy focuses on the untapped potential of Māori knowledge or mātauranga to contribute to New Zealand's economic and social well-being. The policy is underpinned by a value system and its attendant body of theory and practise, known as kaupapa Māori (Awatere *et al.*, 2017; Brewer *et al.*, 2014; Henry and Pene, 2001; Pihama *et al.*, 2002), which refers to "Māori ownership of knowledge, and acknowledging the validity of a Māori way of doing" (Walker *et al.*, 2006, p. 333). Internationally, the policy is unique in that it positions Māori people and Māori knowledge as a key enabler of economic and social prosperity (Ministry of Research Science and Technology, 2009; Ruckstuhl *et al.*, 2019).

Since 2015, a group of social scientists that includes Māori has followed 416 science researchers from 39 different research and innovation organisations to provide insights into the necessary human and relational capacities required by researchers when co-innovating with Māori and industry. The science researchers are organised into eight large projects, called "spearheads", and 69 small researcher-led projects, called "seed" projects.

SfTI projects are multidisciplinary, including engineering, physics, chemistry, earth science, space science, biology, and computer science. The projects support not only the development of advanced technical science but also the researchers' capacity to engage and collaborate across disciplines and industries and with Māori partners. To ensure that Vision Mātauranga permeates SfTI's organisational approach in a meaningful and holistic manner, a series of institutional- and individual-level strategies have been put in place. By combining science, Māori, and industry worldviews, a new research paradigm is being developed, through which transformative outcomes are expected to emerge (Ruckstuhl and Martin, 2019).

At the institutional level, there are six Māori-defined concepts and principles for the implementation of Vision Mātauranga: *kia kōtahi mai* entails a holistic consideration of society beyond the

SfTI organisation; *rapua te pae tāwhiti atu*, an innovation principle meaning to look beyond the immediate horizon; *kia whakapakari mai*, which involves developing and strengthening people's skills, capacities, and understandings, particularly the next generations; *tūhononga*, which involves the integration of people and processes; *mana motuhake*, which acknowledges that Māori will demand a self-determined approach; and *mana whakahaere*, which supports this principle through an empowered leadership (SfTI, n.d.b).

To embed and monitor the six principles, a Kāhui Māori, a group of respected Māori advisors from the science and technology, community, and industry spheres, provides specialist advice to the SfTI board, directors, and team leaders. The Kāhui Māori identify key practises for the institutional, operational, and scientific activities of SfTI. These include identifying opportunities and barriers to research and engagement with and for Māori (SfTI, n.d.a).

At the individual level, SfTI offers researchers a series of capacity-development programmes. These are fully funded training and mentoring activities aimed at building researchers' human and relational capacities. Human capacity refers to a set of competencies that enable an individual to communicate with industry and Māori partners, and relational capacity focuses on the quality of such relationships (Daellenbach and Ruckstuhl, 2018). Vision Mātauranga–related capacity-development programmes encompass activities that initiate or advance researchers' understanding of the Māori world. These activities include workshops, attendance at events in traditional Māori spaces, mentoring, and opportunities for engagement and networking with Māori partners.

How have such policies and activities been perceived? In the next section, we explore individual experiences of and reactions to SfTI's policies and capacity-development programmes to provide empirical evidence of how responsible and inclusive science and innovation is perceived. We interviewed 90 scientists (109 interviews) on their understanding and experiences of engaging with Vision Mātauranga. Group and individual semi-structured and open-ended interviews were conducted, with all participants providing informed consent (Clark *et al.*, 2010). Additional data were collected via surveys and observations and recordings of team meetings, *in situ* and online, as well as project documents, observation notes, and reports provided by SfTI's Building New Zealand's Innovation Capacity (BNZIC) researchers.

Data were organised and coded through NVivo (an electronic database) and analysed through thematic and inductive analyses (Braun and Clarke, 2006; Fereday and Muir-Cochrane, 2006). Individuals' patterns of experiences and ideas were brought together thematically to form a broad picture of the collective experience (Aronson, 1995; Braun and Clarke, 2006). We identified clusters of common experiences relating to both the barriers and enablers of engaging with Vision Mātauranga, from which common themes emerged.

In the following, we outline our findings using emblematic code-named quotations to illustrate key findings.

4. Implementing an Inclusive Innovation Policy: Barriers and Enablers

SfTI researchers talked about two types of challenges they faced when engaging with the Vision Mātauranga policy. The first was their lack of knowledge about the policy and the underlying Māori worldviews, knowledge, and traditions, which justified their lack of involvement with Māori partners and increased their fears of engagement. The second challenge was researchers' view of the policy as a "tick-the-box" initiative rather than one that was truly inclusive and meaningful.

Participants acknowledged their lack of understanding: "I think when it [Vision Mātauranga] first came out, no one knew what it meant. I don't think even the iwi [Māori tribes] knew what it meant" (p. 1) and

> "So I don't really have a feel for that [Vision Mātauranga], because I just don't know. One of the things that I wanted out of this challenge [SfTI] that I haven't quite maybe received or haven't engaged enough, is, I wanted to learn about Māori and the Māori economy. I ticked that on one of the boxes on day one, two years ago, and I'm still not there". (p. 22)

This lack of awareness was also seen in researchers' justification for lack of engagement with the policy and with Māori knowledge, partners, and traditions. A few examples are: "I don't know if I know enough to say much about that [Vision Mātauranga], but no, we've been talking about using it [Vision Mātauranga] for water quality purposes — talking to a lot of the iwi [tribes] about trying to improve the water quality around their resources, but I can't say I've been involved much in any of that" (p. 4) and "I mean, so, if one did want to actually engage with one of the iwi corporations, I'm not actually even sure what the next step would be" (p. 15).

This lack of knowledge around how to engage manifested in frustrations and fear of initiating such engagement.

> "We walked in and a Māori gentleman came out and he basically spoke about his waka [kinship groups descended from a canoe which migrated to New Zealand] and his land and where he comes from, and the whole story, right? Then, they sang a song, and we had to reply with a song. We were all Europeans, so we didn't have a song. So, the person who led the delegation suggested to me to go on YouTube in the morning and try to find a song... The clip played, and we sang along ... They [Māori in the room] were only offended because the song we picked was actually theirs, from their region. So, we stuffed it up in every way we possibly could. Now, that shouldn't have happened, but it was no fault of ours; we just literally — we did not know. We were totally unprepared. We were not briefed. There were no cultural cues to tell us what we were doing was wrong". (p. 53)

The above excerpts highlight a number of issues for organisations. First, an inclusive policy on its own is not enough unless there are regular opportunities to put the policy into practise in a meaningful manner. Second, asking SfTI participants to engage with Vision Mātauranga and incorporate it into their science and technology practises implies asking them to practise "critical inquiry", thereby disrupting the current *status quo* and re-evaluating current paradigms and worldviews. According to Boler and Zembylas (2003), this process of critical inquiry can generate feelings of anger, frustration, denial, disappointment, grief, resistance, or fear. Such discomfort is pedagogically valuable in learning about social justice and as a way to exercise inclusion.

Feelings of denial and a refusal to recognise Vision Mātauranga as legitimate and meaningful for science were also detected across the SfTI community, which at multiple times framed Vision Mātauranga strategies as "tokenist". The following quotes illustrate this: "... This idea that every project should have a Vision Mātauranga box that's ticked, I think is absurd. I mean, I actually just think it's crazy" (p. 14);

> "Personally, I think it [engaging with Vision Mātauranga] is sort of a bit of tokenism going on. I get the impression that the Government is sort of pushing their tokenism down the line and expecting us to do tokenistic things to solve problems that they've identified. I think it's a little bit contrived. They're trying to make it genuine, but it's still the framework, in my opinion, is quite tokenistic". (p. 38)
>
> "I hate saying this, but I've got to be honest here; it feels like when we have a Vision Mātauranga conversation, and there's a Maori researcher like [researcher's name], it's tokenism. To me, it is 100% tokenism. You're a token; I've brought you in the room, so now I can tick the Vision Mātauranga box. That's disgusting. It shouldn't be like that". (p. 40)

We also observed, however, that other researchers who went through such experiences of discomfort had transformed understanding of the importance of Māori knowledge to science and technology: "One thing I've learned in the [SfTI] challenge, and this is something that I kind of... maybe I rolled my eyes at about two years ago, and I'm always honest about that, is around indigenous knowledge. I [now] see indigenous knowledge as fundamental" (p. 22).

4.1. *Vision Mātauranga enablers*

Researchers identified that capacity-development training courses and programmes were key enablers of Vision Mātauranga and hence of responsible and inclusive innovation within SfTI.

For instance, the courses and programmes not only clarified the Vision Mātauranga policy's aims and objectives but also raised awareness of Māori knowledge. "I really enjoyed the discussion that we had — the presentation that we had, and the subsequent discussions on the marae [Māori meeting grounds]; I thought they were very valuable"; (p. 2)

> "I attended the workshops they conducted at the [university name], particularly around Vision Mātauranga and all that; it was really helpful. I attended that workshop. I had a better idea of what it actually means. So it is allowing me to address [science] issues in a better way than what I could have done before the whole thing started. So, it opened up a better insight into the process; what it is and how and what it is, and where it can be connected, and those [science] things". (p. 35)

Another participant mentioned that taking part in Vision Mātauranga workshops had helped her overcome feelings of fear and opened up doors for further engagement with Māori partners, "iwi". One interview excerpt illustrates this:

> "Yeah I've been to the workshops and they've been really useful ... Yeah, so she [names Māori facilitator] delivered one [workshop] through SfTI ..., which was really good, and I went along to as well... So, opening the doors into iwi is definitely something we want to do. It [Vision Mātauranga]'s not something that ... I have a lot of great expertise in, so it's something that's more daunting for me... This is something that she [workshop facilitator] has more experience at doing and having her on the team will make ... easier to open those doors and expand the range of organisations we're working with". (p. 21)

Another benefit of taking part in the workshop and training sessions was an increased awareness of the culture and traditions of Māori and how these intertwined with participants' science and technology activities. One participant, for instance, mentioned how important it was to understand the cultural sensitivities of blood extraction in their project: "It [the workshop] was very interesting and it clearly demonstrates to me that we need to be engaged with the Māori community particularly for the design of the interface and device for extraction of blood because there are issues around the

management of bodily fluids that are particular to their culture"
(p. 11).

Understandings of how indigenous knowledge adds to science and
technology broadened understanding beyond Western science:

> "I now really love sitting down with ... somebody with a Māori
> perspective — around why is this material so special to you — what
> is the significance of this region — why are we concerned about this
> fish waste product, and not concerned about the economy, [and]
> what does it mean to you as a people? ... I can actually reflect
> and go, okay this is important, and it's not important because it's
> a dollar sign; it's important because it means something ... bigger
> than potentially myself ... Yes, there will always be this sense of,
> okay well how can I leverage that, because we're human beings...
> but I think once we understand that Vision Mātauranga is not a
> tag-on, that Vision Mātauranga is a process, I think we'll be better
> off". (p. 22); and
>
> "... you have a tendency to focus on Western-based science,
> at the exclusion of all else, and I think it's quite good to be able
> to actually certainly encourage people to go and think about and
> tap into indigenous knowledge that will be relevant ... and/or
> actually come up with something that is fairly unique and more
> environmentally sustainable". (p. 67)

To help SfTI researchers better understand how Māori might
understand the concepts of technical, human, and relational capacities, a three-dimensional model through time and space was developed (Ruckstuhl and Martin, 2019). The model, "Te tihi o the
maunga", or mountain summit, imagines innovation as a journey
from the sea to the shore and then to the pinnacle of the mountain.
Each part of the journey requires capacities drawn from Māori
knowledge, Māori people, and Māori relationships. Where these
interface with scientific and technical knowledge at the summit, then
there are inclusive innovation gains. For some SfTI researchers, such
models help them embed Vision Mātauranga into their science and
technology practises within and beyond SfTI research, as one quote
illustrates:

> "One of my best article readings were [names a Vision Mātauranga
> BNZIC researcher's] papers around the... from the ocean to the

top of mountain paper. I really like that. Those analogies there were quite useful, and that's something I'm actually using in one of the proposals I have to forward for this year". (p. 68)

5. Concluding Remarks

In this chapter, we have argued that global challenges are wicked problems that cannot be solved by resorting to the same paradigm that underpins them. With corporations expected to do their part in addressing such challenges, particularly through the use of science and technology, a "politics of diversity" is required (Crowley and Head, 2017, p. 454; Rittel and Webber, 1973). In turn, this requires new responsible and inclusive practises to enable such diversity.

We have challenged the view that indigenous knowledge is irrelevant to scientific innovation and shown how SfTI, as a virtual organisation, has developed and implemented inclusive policies and practises. By drawing on Māori knowledge or Mātauranga, practises and, approaches, SfTI has developed a holistic and inclusive approach to embed the Vision Mātauranga policy at both the institutional and individual researcher levels.

The strategies employed, in particular the training programmes, have countered the lack of knowledge about the aims and objectives of the Vision Mātauranga policy and of Māori worldviews. While feelings of discomfort, fear, or frustration have been observed, such experiences have also enabled individual scientists to transform such feelings into a greater awareness of how Māori knowledge and practises can intertwine and strengthen science and technology. SfTI's strategies have supported researchers' ability and willingness to engage with the Vision Mātauranga policy, Māori partners, and Māori practises and have broadened science and technology understandings to include indigenous views and approaches to science. Such an opening up creates a dialogue with difference (Freire, 1987).

There are a number of learnings for other organisations from this case study. First, to promote inclusive science and technology, corporations have to put in place institutional policies that are drawn from and utilise the knowledge system they are striving to dialogue with. Second, companies have to invest in programmes that are more than one-off opportunities in order to not only initiate employees into a "diverse" worldview but also to sustain over time such understandings. Third, shifting the current science and technology paradigm to one that responds to and includes other knowledge systems will be a discomforting and, for some, painful journey at both organisation and individual levels. However, for corporations to address global challenges, which by their very nature are wicked, requires a new logic. Exercising a politics of diversity through a practise of responsible and inclusive science innovation may be one such new logic.

References

Aikenhead, G. S. (2006). Towards decolonizing the Pan-Canadian science framework, *Canadian Journal of Math, Science & Technology Education*, Vol. 6, No. 4, pp. 387–399.

Andreotti, V. and Dowling, E. (2004). WSF, ethics and pedagogy, *International Social Science Journal*, Vol. 56, No. 182, pp. 605–604.

Applebaum, B. (2017). Comforting discomfort as complicity: White fragility and the pursuit of invulnerability, *Hypatia*, Vol. 32, No. 4, pp. 862–875.

Aronson, J. (1995). A pragmatic view of thematic analysis, *The Qualitative Report*, Vol. 2, No. 1, pp. 1–3.

Awatere, S., Robb, M., Taura, Y., Reihana, K., Harmsworth, G., Te Maru, J. and Watene-Rawiri, E. (2017). Wai Ora Wai Māori–a kaupapa Māori assessment tool, *Landcare Research Manaaki Whenua Policy Brief*, Vol. 19, pp. 2357–1713.

Blok, V. (2014). Look who's talking: Responsible innovation, the paradox of dialogue and the voice of the other in communication and negotiation processes, *Journal of Responsible Innovation*, Vol. 1, No. 2, pp. 171–190.

Blok, V. and Lemmens, P. (2015). The emerging concept of responsible innovation. Three reasons why it is questionable and calls for a radical transformation of the concept of innovation, in *Responsible Innovation 2*, pp. 19–35, Springer, Singapore.

Boler, M. and Zembylas, M. (2003). Discomforting truths: The emotional terrain of understanding difference, in *Pedagogies of Difference*, pp. 115–138, Routledge, London.

Braun, V. and Clarke, V. (2006). Using thematic analysis in psychology, *Qualitative Research in Psychology*, Vol. 3, No. 2, pp. 77–101.

Brewer, K. M., Harwood, M. L., McCann, C. M., Crengle, S. M. and Worrall, L. E. (2014). The use of interpretive description within Kaupapa Māori research, Vol. 24, No. 9, pp. 1287–1297.

Buckley, P. J., Doh, J. P. and Benischke, M. H. (2017). Towards a renaissance in international business research? Big questions, grand challenges, and the future of IB scholarship, *Journal of International Business Studies*, Vol. 48, No. 9, pp. 1045–1064.

Callon, M., Lascoumes, P. and Barthe, Y. (2009). *Acting in an Uncertain World: An Essay on Technical Democracy (Inside technology)*, MIT Press, Cambridge, MA.

Chilisa, B. (2017). Decolonising transdisciplinary research approaches: An African perspective for enhancing knowledge integration in sustainability science, *Sustainability Science*, Vol. 12, No. 5, pp. 813–827.

Churchman, C. West. (1967). Wicked Problems. *Management Science*, Vol. 14, No. 4, pp. B141–B142.

Clark, A., Prosser, J. and Wiles, R. (2010). Ethical issues in image-based research, *Arts & Health*, Vol. 2, No. 1, pp. 81–93.

Crowley, K. and Head, B. W. (2017). The enduring challenge of "wicked problems": Revisiting Rittel and Webber, *Policy Sciences*, Vol. 50, No. 4, pp. 539–547.

d'Altroy, T. N. (2014). *The Incas*, Vol. 13. John Wiley & Sons.

Daellenbach, U., Davenport, S. and Ruckstuhl, K. (2017). Developing absorptive capacity for midstream science in open innovation contexts, *International Journal of Technology Transfer Commercialisation*, Vol. 15, No. 4, pp. 447–462.

Daellenbach, U. and Ruckstuhl, K. (2018). *Applying Second Language Communication Theory to Understand Science Collaboration Barriers*, Paper Presented at the ISPIM Innovation Symposium.

Davenport, S., Daellenbach, U., Ruckstuhl, K., Hyland, M. and Leitch, S. (2015). *Rethinking Absorptive Capacity for Open Innovation Contexts*. Paper Presented at the ISPIM Innovation Symposium.

Davies, N. (1995). *The Incas*. University Press of Colorado, Niwot.

DiAngelo, R. (2018). *White Fragility: Why It's so Hard for White People to Talk About Racism*, Beacon Press, Boston.

Evans-Winters, V. E. and Hines, D. E. (2020). Unmasking white fragility: How whiteness and white student resistance impacts anti-racist education, *Whiteness and Education*, Vol. 5, No. 1, pp. 1–16.

Fallows, J. (2013). The 50 greatest breakthroughs since the wheel. Why did it take so long to invent the wheelbarrow? Have we hit peak innovation? What our list reveals about imagination, optimism, and the nature of progress. *The Atlantic*. Available at: https://www.theatlantic.com/magazine/archive/2013/11/innovations-list/309536/.

Fereday, J. and Muir-Cochrane, E. (2006). Demonstrating rigor using thematic analysis: A hybrid approach of inductive and deductive coding and theme development, *International Journal of Qualitative Methods*, Vol. 5, No. 1, pp. 80–92.

Flipse, S. M., De Winde, J. H., Osseweijer, P. and van der Sanden, M. C. (2014). The wicked problem of socially responsible innovation, *EMBO Reports*, Vol. 15, No. 5, p. 464.

Freire, P. (1987). *Pedagogia Do Oprimido*, Vol. 1. Paz e terra, Rio de Janeiro.

Genus, A. and Iskandarova, M. (2018). Responsible innovation: Its institutionalisation and a critique, *Technological Forecasting and Social Change*, Vol. 128, pp. 1–9.

Hautamäki, A. and Oksanen, K. (2016). Sustainable innovation: Solving wicked problems through innovation, in *Open Innovation: A Multifaceted Perspective: Part I*, pp. 87–110, World Scientific, Singapore.

Henry, E. and Pene, H. J. O. (2001). Kaupapa Māori: Locating indigenous ontology, *Organization*, Vol. 8, No. 2, pp. 234–242.

Hutchins, E. (1983). Understanding micronesian navigation, *Mental Models*, pp. 191–225.

Imaz, M. and Sheinbaum, C. (2017). Science and technology in the framework of the sustainable development goals, *World Journal of Science, Technology and Sustainable Development*, Vol. 14, No. 1, pp. 2–17.

Jones, P., Wynn, M., Hillier, D. and Comfort, D. (2017). The sustainable development goals and information and communication technologies, *Indonesian Journal of Sustainability Accounting and Management*, Vol. 1, No. 1, pp. 1–15.

Keatinge, R. W. (1988). *Peruvian Prehistory: An Overview of Pre-Inca and Inca Society*, Cambridge University Press, USA.

Lekson, S. H., Windes, T. C., Stein, J. R. and Judge, W. J. (1988). The Chaco Canyon community, *Scientific American*, Vol. 259, No. 1, pp. 100–109.

Ministry of Research Science and Technology (2009). Evaluation of vision Mātauranga and the Māori knowledge and development output class. Available at: https://thehub.swa.govt.nz/resources/evaluation-of-vision-matauranga-and-the-maori-knowledge-and-development-output-class/.

Mitcham, C. (2003). Co-responsibility for research integrity, *Science and Engineering Ethics*, Vol. 9, No. 2, pp. 273–290.

MoRST (2007). *Vision Mātauranga: Unlocking the Innovation Potential of Māori Knowledge, Resources and People*, New Zealand. Retrieved from: https://www.mbie.govt.nz/assets/9916d28d7b/vision-matauranga-booklet.pdf.

Newenham-Kahindi, A. (2015). Managing sustainable development through people: Implications for multinational enterprises in developing countries, *Personnel Review*, Vol. 44, No. 3, pp. 388–407.

O'Kane, C., Zhang, J. A., Daellenbach, U. and Davenport, S. (2019). Building entrepreneurial behaviours in academic scientists: Past perspective and new initiatives, In *Entrepreneurial Behaviour*, pp. 145–166, Springer, Singapore.

Pardey, P. G., Chan-Kang, C., Dehmer, S. P. and Beddow, J. M. (2016). Agricultural R&D is on the move, *Nature News*, Vol. 537, No. 7620, p. 301.

Pihama, L., Cram, F. and Walker, S. (2002). Creating methodological space: A literature review of Kaupapa Maori research, *Canadian Journal of Native Education*, Vol. 26, No. 1, pp. 30–43.

Puri, S. K. (2007). Integrating scientific with indigenous knowledge: Constructing knowledge alliances for land management in India, *MIS Quarterly*, Vol. 31, No. 2, pp. 355–379.

Rabello, R. C. C., Nairn, K. and Anderson, V. (2018). Rethinking corporate social responsibility in capitalist neoliberal times, in *Redefining Corporate Social Responsibility*, pp. 27–41, Emerald Publishing Limited, Bingley, UK.

Reinecke, J. and S. Ansari, (2016). Taming wicked problems: The role of framing in the construction of corporate social responsibility, *Journal of Management Studies*, Vol. 53, No. 3, pp. 299–329.

Rewi, T. and Rātima, M. (2018). Ngā Hurihanga o te Reo Māori i te Mātauranga: Changes in Māori Language Education, in M. Reilly, S. Duncan, G. Leoni and L. Paterson (eds.), *Te Koparapara: An Introduction to the Maori World*, pp. 304–323, Auckland University Press, Auckland.

Rittel, H. W. and Webber, M. M. (1973). Dilemmas in a general theory of planning, *Policy Sciences*, Vol. 4, No. 2, pp. 155–169.

Roberts, J. (2003). The manufacture of corporate social responsibility: Constructing corporate sensibility, *Organization*, Vol. 10, No. 2, pp. 249–265.

Roco, M. C., Mirkin, C. A. and Hersam, M. C. (2011). Nanotechnology research directions for societal needs in 2020: Summary of international study, Springer, Singapore.

Ruckstuhl, K., Amoamo, M., Hart, N. H., Martin, W. J., Keegan, T. T. and Pollock, R. (2019). Research and development absorptive capacity: A Māori perspective, *Kōtuitui: New Zealand Journal of Social Sciences Online*, Vol. 14, No. 1, pp. 177–197.

Ruckstuhl, K., Haar, J., Hudson, M., Amoamo, M., Waiti, Ruwhiu, D. and Daellenbach, U. (2019). Recognising and valuing Māori innovation in the high-tech sector: A capacity approach, *Journal of the Royal Society of New Zealand*, Vol. 49, No. supl 1, pp. 72–88.

Ruckstuhl, K. and Martin, W. J. (2019). Mätauranga Mäori and the high-tech interface, *New Zealand Science Review*, Vol. 75, No. 4, pp. 87–91.

Schomberg, V. (2013). A vision of responsible innovation, in R. Owen, M. Heintz and J. Bessant (eds.), *Responsible Innovation*, pp. 51–74, John Wiley, London.

SfTI (2018). *Second Tranche Forward Strategy (2019–2024)*. New Zealand.

SfTI (2020). SfTI spearhead 1: Building New Zealand's innovation capacity. Available at: https://www.sftichallenge.govt.nz/assets/Uploads/Our-research/Projects/Spearhead-projects/Building-New-Zealands-innovation-capacity/SfTI-Spearhead-1-Insights-Report-12-Online.pdf.

SfTI (n.d.a). Kāhui Māori — Advisory group. Available at: https://www.sftichallenge.govt.nz/our-people/kahui-maori-advisory-group/.

SfTI (n.d.b). Vision Mātauranga. Available at: https://www.stichallenge.govt.nz/for-researchers/vision-matauranga/.

Sillitoe, P., Dixon, P. and Barr, J. (2005). *Indigenous Knowledge Inquiries: A Methodologies Manual for Development (Indigenous Knowledge and Development Series)*. ITDG Publishing, Bourton Hall, Rugby, UK.

Skaburskis, A. (2008). The origin of "wicked problems", *Planning Theory & Practice*, Vol. 9, No. 2, pp. 277–280.

Smith, G. H. (2009). Mai i te maramatanga, ki te putanga mai o te tahuritanga: From conscientization to transformation, In *Social Justice, Peace, and Environmental Education*, pp. 31–40, Routledge, London.

Stephenson, M. (2009). *Thinking Historically: Maori and Settler Education. Introduction to the History of New Zealand Education*. Auckland, New Zealand: Pearson.

Stilgoe, J., Owen, R. and Macnaghten, P. (2013). Developing a framework for responsible innovation, *Research Policy*, Vol. 42, No. 9, pp. 1568–1580.

Sutton, P. and Boag, J. M. (2019). Status of vaccine research and development for *Helicobacter pylori*, *Vaccine*, Vol. 37, No. 50, pp. 7295–7299.

Termeer, C. J., Dewulf, A., Breeman, G. and Stiller, S. J. (2015). Governance capabilities for dealing wisely with wicked problems, *Administration & Society*, Vol. 47, No. 6, pp. 680–710.

United Nations (2017). UN. Secretary-General, Progress towards the Sustainable Development Goals: Report of the Secretary-General [online]. Available at: https://digitallibrary.un.org/record/3810131 [Google Scholar].

United Nations (n.d.). Sustainable development goals. *Human Rights and the 2030 Agenda for Sustainable Development*. Available at: https://www.ohchr.org/EN/Issues/SDGS/Pages/The2030Agenda.aspx.

Van Zanten, J. A. and Van Tulder, R. (2018). Multinational enterprises and the sustainable development goals: An institutional approach to corporate engagement, *Journal of International Business Policy*, Vol. 1, Nos. 3–4, pp. 208–233.

Von Schomberg, R. (2012). Prospects for technology assessment in a framework of responsible research and innovation, in *Technikfolgen abschätzen lehren*, pp. 39–61, Springer, Singapore.

Walker, S., Eketone, A. and Gibbs, A. (2006). An exploration of Kaupapa maori research, its principles, processes and applications, *International Journal of Social Research Methodology*, Vol. 9, No. 4, pp. 331–344.

Walsh, E. A. (2018). White fragility as an obstacle to anti-racist resilience planning: Opportunities for equity-conscious partnerships, *Journal of Urban Management*, Vol. 7, No. 3, pp. 181–189.

Watson-Verran, H. and Turnbull, D. (1995). Science and other indigenous knowledge systems, in *Handbook of Science and Technology Studies*, pp. 115–139.

Zembylas, M. (2015). Pedagogy of discomfort' and its ethical implications: The tensions of ethical violence in social justice education, *Ethics and Education*, Vol. 10, No. 2, pp. 163–174.

Chapter 3

Features of CSR Ideas Realisation in Belarus During the Pandemic Period of 2020

Tatiana V. Proharava, Natallia V. Maltsevich,
and Aliaksandr V. Pyko

Abstract

This chapter analyses the implementation features of the principles of corporate social responsibility (CSR) at Belarusian enterprises that contribute to reducing social tension and preventing conflicts of interest. The problems of disseminating the ideas of CSR in the business environment and the experience of teaching methods of socially responsible business activities by students of the Belarusian State University are investigated.

Keywords: CSR; stakeholders; training; conflict of interests; COVID-19 pandemic

Abbreviations

1. ISO — International Organisation for Standardisation
2. CSR — Corporate social responsibility
3. CIS — Commonwealth of Independent States
4. WEO — World economic outlook
5. UN — United Nations Organisation
6. BSUIR — Belarusian State University of Informatics and Radio-electronics
7. SB BSU — School of Business of Belarusian State University
8. LLC — Limited liability company

9. JSC — Joint-stock company
10. CJSC — Closed joint-stock company
11. SDG — Sustainable Development Goals
12. NPO — Scientific and Production Association
13. JSSB — Joint-stock savings bank
14. NOC — National Olympic Committee
15. STB — State Standard of the Republic of Belarus

1. Introduction

In 2020, the world community faced serious challenges, which led to a revision of the previously existing principles and methods of interaction between interstate, state, and commercial structures as well as questioned some forecasts of socioeconomic development and forced to look at scientific socioeconomic theories and concepts from a new angle.

In the World Economic Outlook (WEO) reports of June 2020, global growth is projected at 4.9% in 2020. The COVID-19 pandemic has had a more negative impact on activity than anticipated, and the recovery is projected to be more gradual than previously forecast. In 2021, global growth is projected at 5.4% (International Monetary Fund, 2020).

About 90% of the global economic activity has been affected by the pandemic: Transnational trade links and supply chains have been disrupted, consumer demand has fallen, and millions of people have been left out of work. UN experts note that in order to recover from the crisis, it is necessary to focus on creating a more resilient world economic model, strengthening health and social protection systems.

Current world events bring up topics related to the achievement of sustainable development and the use of effective tools of corporate social responsibility (CSR). The importance of assessing the effectiveness of applied social programs and the development of effective strategies for the provision of targeted social assistance is growing. Currently, every country is working hard to overcome the consequences of the crisis caused by the COVID-19 pandemic. Businesses are doing their part to stabilise the situation by helping their employees, customers, and society at large. Sociopolitical problems have arisen in Belarus this year, connected with the disagreement of society with the official results of the presidential elections. In September 2020, this led to a conflict of interest at different levels of government, which must be taken into account when building a CSR policy.

The main objectives of this study are to analyse the peculiarities of the implementation of the principles of CSR at Belarusian enterprises, which contribute to the reduction in social tension, including in the context of a pandemic and protest movements; systematisation and generalisation of the experience of implementing CSR practises at Belarusian enterprises of various industries and fields of activity, preventing conflicts of interest; identification of the most effective methods of teaching socially responsible business activities to students; development of recommendations to improve the effectiveness of CSR training within the framework of the national model of cooperation between business and society, taking into account the experience of foreign countries.

The object of the research is public relations related to the regulation of the implementation of CSR practises in the activities of business structures and business systems in the Republic of Belarus. The subject of the research is innovative approaches that contribute to increasing students' interest in socially responsible attitudes from the standpoint of conflict management within the framework of their future profession.

In the 20th century, the concept of CSR was within the sphere of interest of many economists as well as social scientists and was covered in scientific publications by such authors as A. Caroll, M. Porter, M. Kramer, and Friedman. Research in this area was also carried out by such famous scientists as Wood, L. Burke and J. Logsdon, M. Marrewijk, T. Jones, G. Lantos, P. Heslin and J. Ochoa, L. Trapp, W. Werther and D. Chandler, B. Husted and D. Allen, S. Chuang, S. Huang, and D. Crowther.

The main problems that were considered in the works of these authors concerned the most important aspects of the evolution of CSR, such as the influence of CSR on the decision-making process in an organisation (Jones, 1980), corporate citizenship (Carroll, 2015), the basic principles of CSR (Heslin and Ochoa, 2008), the idea of CSR as a social contract (Lantos, 2001), the influence of CSR on the formation of competitive advantage and the creation of shared values (Porter and Kramer, 2006), and the transformation of CSR from a commitment to strategic necessity (Werther and Chandler, 2005). Particular attention was paid to the fact that CSR creates value and responds to social demands (Werther and Chandler, 2005) as well as the creation of sustainable value as a main CSR objective in business nowadays (Chandler, 2016). The idea of Sustainable Development Goals (SDGs) at the modern stage of CSR was developed by D. Crowther (Crowther *et al.*, 2020).

Belarusian scientists (V. A. Simkhovich, E. A. Danilova, and S. P. Romanova) focused on the pragmatic and social aspects of the applied CSR practises (Simkhovich *et al.*, 2012).

2. Implementation of the Concept of CSR in Belarus

In accordance with the International Standard ISO 26000: 2010, social responsibility is defined as the responsibility of organisations for the impact of their decisions and activities on society and the environment through transparent and ethical behaviour (International Organisation for Standardisation, 2010). CSR is a concept according to which an organisation voluntarily contributes to the development of society, including the social, environmental, and economic spheres, taking on additional obligations beyond those established by law. This concept is considered in many aspects, including as a tool to reduce tension in the relationship of stakeholders, to prevent the emergence of conflict situations, and to prevent the escalation of conflicts. At the present stage, the main goal of CSR is to achieve the SDGs which are understood as meeting the needs of the current generation without creating threats to meet the needs of future generations (Ministry of Economy of the Republic of Belarus, 2017). To date, the SDGs are the internal development goals of Belarus, and a lot of work has been done in the country towards their successful implementation.

In the Republic of Belarus, the concept of CSR began to be widely implemented in 2006 with the support of the United Nations Development Program (UNDP) within the framework of the UN Global Compact initiative. This initiative invites the business community to be guided in its activities by the fundamental principles of human rights, labour relations, environmental protection, and anti-corruption. Due to the common cultural and linguistic traditions and historical past, Belarus in the development of the concept and practise of CSR follows the path of the Russian society. Belarusian researchers, along with their Russian colleagues, focus on the pragmatic aspects of CSR practise, which involves socially responsible restructuring of enterprises in the development of market relations. The greatest attention is paid to charitable and social investments. Leading business associations and consulting agencies, in particular "SATIO", have made a great contribution to promoting CSR ideas in Belarus.

The introduction of socially responsible business practises affects many elements of the internal and external environment of enterprises. The number, composition, and circle of persons interested in sustainable development of enterprises are constantly changing. Accordingly, the problem of timely familiarisation of all stakeholders not only with the global principles and goals of CSR but also with the current tasks and tools used is traditionally relevant.

Corporate sustainability can be viewed as a microeconomic interpretation of the concept of sustainable development. In 2015, Belarus committed itself to the 2030 Agenda for Sustainable Development and committed to ensuring sustainable, inclusive, and sustained economic growth, social inclusion, and environmental protection, as well as promoting peace and security in the world (SATIO, 2019).

Determining the principles of managing an organisation from the standpoint of a socially responsible attitude, enterprises, and institutions are guided by the specifics of their activities, strategic goals, and objectives. CSR should organically fit into the company's management system and permeate all business processes (National Statistical Committee of the Republic of Belarus, 2019).

3. Features of the Belarusian Model of Sustainable Development

The peculiarity of European social policy is that it encourages businesses to actively respond to global and local challenges to sustainable development, ensuring, among other things, the transparency of corporations, respect for human rights, protection of life and health, as well as the environment. Pan-European initiatives, directives, and projects to stimulate CSR are based on the provisions of the International Labour Organisation, the Organisation for Economic Cooperation and Development, World Summits, etc. In turn, the documents adopted at the EU level set the vector of CSR policy in national states.

CSR has national specifics in approaches, methods, and roles of participants. Moreover, a number of researchers point to regional differences in the understanding of the role of the applied CSR strategies.

The Belarusian model of sustainable development is characterised by state and public support for socially unprotected groups of the population. Most of the issues in the social sphere in Belarus are regulated at the state level.

The study of CSR practises in European countries and Belarus, as well as the analysis of legislation and state regulation in this area, shows the difference between Belarus and the rest of Europe in CSR issues. Traditions in the field of CSR have already developed in European countries. CSR practises are developing with the active support of state institutions and businesses and their influence on society is increasing. In most post-socialist states, market transformation did not automatically create a favourable business climate in national economies; it was accompanied by the use of complex, non-transparent institutional technologies of state and corporate management.

The idea of socially responsible business is just beginning to spread in Belarus. According to research by the marketing company Center for Systemic Business Technologies Satio, among successful active enterprises, only 65% are engaged in CSR and only 16%

reflect the results of their activities in reports. CSR projects are mostly implemented by ICT enterprises, banks, and food industry enterprises. At the same time, global experience shows that the effect of CSR increases if it is popularised: In 2017, 75% of the companies are from the top 100 largest companies by revenue in the world report on CSR (SATIO, 2019).

For the majority of Belarusian enterprises, the priority area in social investment is the internal social policy, which is aimed at supporting the employees of their company: ensuring a decent level of wages, providing a social package, and ensuring safe working conditions. In comparison with other countries with economies in transition, the poverty level in Belarus is one of the lowest. Less than 1% of the country's population lives in extreme poverty, which means income of less than USD 2 a day. At the same time, a significant number of Belarusian citizens fall into the low-income category: According to official statistics, in the mid-2000s, the population with incomes below the subsistence level remained relatively high, amounting to over 1.7 million people, or 17.8% of the total population of the country. As in other CIS countries, people living in rural areas, children, and single-parent families are most at risk of poverty.

CSR projects focused on external stakeholders in Belarus are implemented in various forms. Having systematised the data on enterprises, we obtain the following table (Table 1).

For the CSR projects of Belarusian enterprises, it is typical to pay the greatest attention to the issues of charity in the form of support for the most vulnerable categories of the population (assistance to orphans and disabled people).

Having found themselves in a difficult economic situation during the crisis caused by the pandemic, enterprises are looking for new forms of interaction with employees: They are transferred to remote work, given a shorter working day, or granted a part-time work week. Only as a last resort, employers resort to firing employees. The Belarusian people in 2020 have repeatedly demonstrated the ability for self-organisation and self-help. This was especially pronounced in those circumstances when state and administrative structures were

Table 1. Belarusian practise of using CSR forms.

CSR forms	Belarusian practise of application
Charity	Targeted monetary or in-kind assistance (provision of products, transport, prizes, payment of bills, etc.) allocated by the company for conducting social programs. "Interest policy", when each employee decides what % of their income tax to spend on: a kindergarten, a hospital, a foundation, or a public organisation that needs help
Charity marketing	Payment of part of individual financial transactions or part of the cost of products in favour of a chosen good deed (for example, for the installation of internet connection in an orphanage or purchase of necessary things)
Volunteering	Voluntary and free assistance of company employees to the local community. For example, "WAT" plants trees every spring and "ARGO" is engaged in cleaning water bodies
Corporate charity	Providing resources to draw public attention to a specific social issue. For example, COCA-COLA BEVERAGES BELORUSSIA organises Living Water festivals for young ecologists
Social entrepreneurship	Entrepreneurial activity aimed at solving social problems through the organisation of specialised enterprises, primarily for people with disabilities (vision, hearing, etc.). For example, the target activity of the "Tsvetlit" of the "Belarusian Society of the Deaf"
Social investment	A form of financial assistance allocated by the company for the implementation of long-term programs aimed at reducing social tension in the region of its presence and improving the living standards of various segments of society
Social marketing	Holding events or campaigns aimed at changing the behaviour of a specific group of people to improve public health, environmental protection, etc. For example, "SAVUSHKIN PRODUCT" implements the School Milk project to improve the health of schoolchildren in Minsk
Sponsorship	Making a contribution by a legal or natural person (sponsor) (in the form of providing property, rendering services, or performing work) to the activities of another legal or natural person on the terms of a sponsored distribution of advertising by the sponsor. For example, "COCA-COLA BEVERAGES" is a sponsor of the National Olympic Committee of Belarus and "PINSKDREV" is a sponsor of the Association of Wheelchair Disabled People
Philanthropy	Donations in the form of grants, gifts, goods, or services directly to an organisation or individual. "INKO-FOOD" took over the patronage of the children's auxiliary school in Brest and on holidays presents the pupils with gift, and "PRIORBANK" presented a minibus to Belarusian children's hospice in Borovlyany

Source: United Nations in Belarus (2020).

withdrawn from solving problems or did not manage to quickly mobilise budgetary resources. In particular, in the first months of the fight against COVID-19, ordinary residents and business organisations were actively involved in providing assistance to doctors and medical personnel.

Belarusian programmers used mobile applications to create crowdfunding charitable projects on a massive scale. An example of such projects is the KaliLaska project. Through social networks and messengers, they organise material and financial support, in the provision of which everyone is involved; for example, a chat has been created for taxi drivers who are ready to deliver doctors for free. Social assistance from legal entities arises as a result of the activities of proactive individuals.

The need for a broad public discussion and popularisation of successful CSR practises in Belarus is due to the fact that the topic of social responsibility of business in our country is quite new. The local network of the UN Global Compact in Belarus is small and includes only 26 signatories. The Global Compact Network Office is the Good Foundation, founded in 2017. The purpose of the fund is to attract and combine financial, intellectual, and organisational resources and opportunities of Belarusian and foreign individuals and legal entities for the implementation of social, socially useful, and charitable projects, the development of social investments, innovations, and social entrepreneurship in the Republic of Belarus (Samusev, 2018).

In November 2017, the Agreement on the Interaction of Socially Responsible Companies was adopted and signed by 55 organisations. However, 2020 has become a difficult test of the resilience of both health systems and economic systems in all countries of the world. The economic downturn has exacerbated the problems of weak links in the economic complex and in small- and medium-sized businesses.

At the meeting of the Council for Sustainable Development, held in June 2020, it was emphasised that constant monitoring of work on the SDGs and the introduction of innovative projects are important for Belarus. It is important to redirect budgetary resources into initiatives and plans that accelerate the development and modernisation of Belarus. It is necessary to invest in distance learning, telemedicine, digitalisation, and the provision of online administrative services to citizens (Local Social Fund "Dobra", 2019).

4. Problems of Spreading Ideas of CSR in the Business Environment

In connection with the unstable development of the world economy and the aggravation of environmental and demographic problems, issues of CSR are included in the agenda of international organisations. Topics of scientific and scientific-practical international conferences are discussed by government agencies and the business community. Taking into account the global trends in the integration of national economies, when building a strategy for sustainable business development, it is logical to take into account international experience. Among the best-known corporate associations on social responsibility issues are the following: Business for Social Responsibility (BSR), CSR Europe, The Conference Board, Social Responsibility Research Network (SRRNet), and United Nations Global Compact (Cotton, 2009).

The problems of spreading ideas of CSR are common for the post-Soviet space. In Belarus, there is a tendency for the Belarusian state to support CSR practises implemented by companies in certain areas (culture, sports). But the extent of benefits is small, and some incentives for the implementation of CSR practises are temporary and experimental.

At the moment, businesses are not fully building rational relationships with all participants in business processes based on interconnection, interaction, interdependence, and communication. All this complicates the solution of social and environmental problems in society, leading to unreasonable waste of time and money on resolving conflicts.

So, in his dissertation, Petukhov notes such problems as follows:

1. the extremely low level of interest of the Internet audience in the activities of companies in the field of social responsibility;
2. independence of decision-making in the field of CSR by representatives of large businesses without coordination with stakeholders;

3. predominantly advertising and propagandist character of domestic companies towards CSR activities;
4. non-prevalence of the practise of preparing annual non-financial reports (Petukhov, 2012).

As a result of a survey conducted by the International Socio-Economic Fund "Idea", the main reasons for the non-participation of companies in CSR projects were the lack of financial and human resources and low awareness of CSR projects (60.3%). It should be noted that 39.7% of respondents report a lack of knowledge and experience.

Analysing the experience of the EAEU countries, Samusev notes that the system of social responsibility of business is becoming more and more complex; at the same time, it is an integral part of the development strategy of large enterprises in Kazakhstan, Belarus, and Russia.

For Belarusian citizens, social responsibility means, first of all, law-abiding behaviour. At the same time, the role of businesses in carrying out social policy, including through voluntary activities in the field of CSR, is not significant. The current position of the attitude of Belarusian society towards the subjects of social policy can be diagnosed based on the results of sociological research.

The research carried out by the authors through a questionnaire survey of students of the Institute of Business of the Belarusian State University shows that the modern young generation considers state bodies, first of all, to be responsible for solving social issues. Only 16.7% of the respondents understand that this should be a joint effort of all interested parties. While 60.8% believe that social projects should be dealt with by government agencies. This position of enterprise managers can increase the risks of conflict situations. Managers are often unable to conduct a constructive dialogue and find balanced decisions taking into account all the risks of the external environment (National Statistical Committee of the Republic of Belarus, 2020).

The practise of implementation of the CSR concept requires a systematic professional approach, with the availability of special knowledge and skills. A CSR specialist must know the sociology of labour and environmental policy as well as the psychology of management. This specialist should also be familiar with the tools of financial analysis and strategic and investment management, be familiar with reporting, and have the skills of facilitation.

In Belarus, CSR ideas are quite new; therefore, many mechanisms for providing assistance to vulnerable groups of the population are only now starting to work on a systematic basis. At the level of local business, managers of organisations do not always understand how to concretely implement the SDGs, despite the fact that many of their activities are aimed at helping society.

At the initiative of Alexander Skrabovsky, director of the Belarusian social fund Dobra and head of the republican competition of social projects Social Weekend, in 2018, a tool for assessing and self-assessing the activities of companies in the field of sustainable development and CSR was developed and tested in 2019–2020. We are talking about a digital indicator — the index of social responsibility of business or, in short, the "index of goodness" (Morales, 2007). In accordance with the assessment methodology, 134 indicators are determined by experts. They are grouped under four criteria: labour relations and human rights, good business practises, consumers and community participation, and the environment. The index is expressed as a number from 0 to 12 points. Depending on the value of the indicator, there are basic, active, advanced, and outstanding levels of social responsibility.

5. Prevention of Conflicts of Interest by Introducing the Principles of Social Sustainability

A conflict of interest is a real or seemingly real contradiction between the private interests of a person and his official powers, the presence of which may affect the objectivity or impartiality of decision-making as well as the performance or non-performance of actions when exercising the official powers granted to him.

The risks of corporate conflicts and the application of social policy as an element of CSR in the context of internal and external factors are considered by Zaynullin (2016). At the same time, he understands corporate conflicts as disagreements that arise between shareholders, participants, members of management bodies, authorities, stakeholders, other elements of the internal and external environment of the corporation, and the corporation itself. However, little attention is paid to the study of the aspects of drafting a CSR strategy from the point of view of managing stakeholder conflicts of interest.

Basically, the concept of a conflict of interest is applied in cases of contradictions between the interests of various categories of participants in corporate relations (the economic organisation itself, its shareholders/participants, officials of its bodies, consumers of financial services/depositors of banks, and their temporary administrator) and/or between the interests of two or more representatives of the same category (shareholders/participants, officials of bodies of economic organisations of certain types — financial institutions, including banks) concerning the activities of such organisations, including on the issues of decision-making by management bodies, performance of duties of an official of such a body, and temporary administrator of a financial institution/bank). Let's consider what types of conflicts can be resolved using CSR principles (Table 2).

6. Dissemination of CSR Ideas — Social Initiatives of Belarusian Companies

In December 2020, the authors of this chapter conducted a study with the involvement of third-year students in the framework of the scientific laboratory at the Department of Business Administration of the School of Business of BSU.

The main aim of the study was to determine the state of affairs in CSR concept realisation in Belarusian organisations and their activities during the COVID-19 pandemic. As part of the study, the following sectors of the national economy have been selected — the banking sector, the IT sector, the manufacturing sector, and the education sector.

This study examined organisations of various forms of ownership — state and private. Moreover, we have selected leading enterprises and organisations in the above-mentioned industries, which are of particular interest from the point of view of CSR. It

Table 2. Application of CSR principles in resolving conflicts of interest.

Principle	Description	Avoiding conflicts of interest
Accountability	Responsibility to regulatory authorities, compliance with regulations and legislation	Conflict with financial, tax, higher authorities. Conflict with shareholders
Accountability	Presentation of clear and objective information about the social and environmental impact	Conflict with clients on issues of the services or products
Ethical behaviour	Honesty, fairness, and conscientiousness in relation to the environment	A conflict of interest within the organisation through compliance with the standards and norms of ethical behaviour
Respect for the interests of stakeholders	Taking into account and responding to the interests of owners, members, and customers (trustees)	Interpersonal conflicts by increasing the loyalty of employees and customers
Compliance with the rule of law	Equality before the law	Conflict with the law-enforcement authorities
Compliance with the rule of law	Recognition of the importance and universality of human rights, its respect	Emergency conflicts

should be noted that during the pandemic, Belarus followed the Swedish model and did not introduce quarantine and self-isolation measures. This decision was made by the government of the country for the purpose of economic security, and the so-called focal method was chosen as a form of struggle against COVID-19.

Of particular interest is a section that summarises information regarding the response to the COVID-19 crisis in different sectors of the Belarusian economy. A lot of organisations in this period partially (locally) transferred their employees to remote forms of work; in the education sector, they switched locally to distance learning (i.e. there were no centralised decisions at the level of medical organisations — universities themselves decided what to do).

In this study, we set the task to consider organisations in the above-mentioned spheres, and the results are presented in Table 3.

7. Conclusions on the Common Features of the CSR for a Particular Industry

Banking sector: All the banks have similar internal CSR: All of them introduce social benefits to employees and have specific training and education programmes for the staff. Moreover, all of them contribute to charity. Additionally, the response to COVID-19 was more or less the same: All the banks followed the WHO recommendations and created remote workplaces. Most of the banks also had some kind of reporting (except for Belinvest and Technobank). Sadly, it can be seen that, regarding the membership in international organisations, there is either no specific data or no membership at all. It can basically be shown that most Belarusian banks prepare to act locally and not intervene in any international processes and regulations on an official level (except for Belarusbank and Global UN contract). Most of the banks also use ISO standards when it comes to their performance.

IT sector: The Belarusian IT sector is a science-intensive, rapidly developing area, involving mainly young and well-educated personnel. This is an industry with an income level 4.2 times higher than the national average for specialists. The companies offer an extended social package for their employees (includes training and professional development). This sector shows the highest level of activity during the pandemic. The reaction to the COVID-19 crisis in the IT sector was very active and in general was manifested in the following activities:

— transferring funds and equipment to hospitals;
— development of various software applications helping medical staff as well as the other groups of population to operate during the crisis. Access to these apps was free.

Table 3.   CSR activities in Belarusian organisations.

Parameters	Banking sector	IT sector	Industrial sector	Education sector
ISO standards (and other standards regulating CSR)	• ISO 26000 • ISO 14001 • ISO 20121 • ISO 27001 • ISO 9001 • ISO/IEC 20000 • ISO 18295-1: 2017 • ISO 22000 • ISO 13616 The selected standards of GRI G4 are used for the state banks' social responsibility reporting.	The largest IT companies (EPAM, WARGAMING, VIBER) use the following international standards: • ISO 9001 • ISO 27001 • ISO 14001 • ISO 13485 • ISO 26000 • ISO 20121	National standards: • STB ISO 9001-96 • STB ISO 9001-2015 • STB18001-2009 • STB ISO 14001-2017 International standards: • ISO 14001 • OHSAS 18001 • FSSC 22000 • ISO 22716 (GMP) • ISO 9001 • ISO 22000 • ISO/IEC 20000-1 • ISO/IEC 27001 • ISO 50001 • ISO 13485 • ISO 20121 • ISO 22301 • ISO 28000 • ISO/TS 29001 • ISO 55001 • ISO 37001	The largest state university (BSU) uses the following international standards: • ISO 26000 • ISO 21001 Private educational institutions (Streamline, Underground, STEP, Leader, IT-Academy): • ISO 21001 • ISO 27000 • ISO 20000 • ISO 22301 • ISO 29990 National standards (STB) are also used.

Parameters	Banking sector	IT sector	Industrial sector	Education sector
Membership in the international CSR organisations and international social projects	Banks participate in activities of the international organisations and support UN Global Contract and UNICEF to launch a global charity initiative in Belarus. They also operate their own social projects.	IT companies participate in various forms of cooperation with international organisations such as UNICEF (EPAM) and WHO (Viber). "FLO" company through its CSR app is cooperating with international organisations (European Council, UNPF) as well as scientific and educational institutions: • College of Obstetrics and Gynecology • Society for Endometriosis and Uterine Diseases • Texas Christian University • University of Adelaide • Myovant Scientists • UNFPA Bayer Some companies (iTechArt) don't participate in the international CSR organisations. They, however, develop their own social projects in collaboration with universities or companies.	Industrial sector organisations support the international initiative of the UN Global Compact (Savushkin product), EurAsEC (PolotskSteklovolokno), the Skolkovo Foundation as well as cooperation with the international training and consulting companies (Gazprom Transgaz Belarus) and International Alliance for Alcohol Responsible Use (Alivaria). Industrial companies support the membership in the national and international unions (member of the Union of Composites Manufacturers) and the membership in the Entrepreneurs Support Fund.	BSU as a leading state university cooperates with the UNESCO, UNICEF, the European Union, the Council of Europe, and others on social and educational initiatives; participates in the programs ERASMUS+, DAAD, IAESTE, "Horizon 2020"; provides academic exchange programs for students and staff as well as double degree programs. Private educational institutions do the CSR projects with different language school all over the world (EU Business School etc.). Active participation in Olympiads and international championships (Golden Byte, Microsoft Imagine Cup, Cisco Olympiad, NetRiders competition).

(Continued)

Table 3. (*Continued*).

Parameters	Banking sector	IT sector	Industrial sector	Education sector
The reaction to the COVID-19 pandemic crisis	In order to take care of the employees as well as the other stakeholders during the COVID-19 pandemic, Belarusian banks did the following measures: • transfer all possible transactions online; • creation of infrastructure to work on remotely for clients and employees (Internet banking, remote workplaces); • establish masks and social distancing regime; • priority services during the first two hours are given to persons of retirement age;	IT companies did the following measures: • develop new software products and use some innovative solutions in order to help the medical sphere (HealthBuddy application, implemented blockchain technology); • start mask production; • in cooperation with UNICEF in Belarus, ITransition put 171,000 pairs of disposable rubber gloves of different sizes to the emergency response centre of the Ministry of Health;	Industrial enterprises did the following measures: • cancel public festival events; • workers use masks, gloves, and antiseptics at their workplaces; • multiple wet cleaning and mask mode. Medical isolation wards, constant presence of medical workers; • employees move on the distant working (Bielita); • launch a line of antiseptics at a price lower than the offered imported goods (Bielita);	Educational institutions did the following measures: • establish mask regime for students and teachers and regular surface disinfection in classes; • transfer their classes to the distance learning form (conferences in Zoom, online exams and credits); • private companies reduced the cost of training; • reducing the number of students in a group; • allow students to be graded automatically; • provide free Wi-Fi at dormitories (BSU);

Parameters	Banking sector	IT sector	Industrial sector	Education sector
	• organised information campaigns, new insurance programs (online medical insurance with the option "coronavirus infection"); • establish new banking products and services (loans for Belarusian manufacturers of medical equipment and means of protection etc.); • postpone various CSR public events; • introduce a preferential policy of using credit cards for Internet shopping and payments; • organise consultations to clients on mortgage and concessional lending by telephone.	• iTechArt together with Yale University worked on online maps of the spread of COVID-19; • transfer of BYN 10,000 the account of the 4th city clinical hospital; • transfer of BYN 100,000 to fight against the COVID-19 pandemic; • release a chatbot with information about COVID-19; • WHO organisation chatbot.	• provision of personal protective equipment and disinfection of all people and incoming and outgoing vehicles (Gazprom transgaz Belarus); • provide non-alcoholic drinks to Minsk hospital staff (Alivaria); • send shoe covers, medical gloves, hats and masks, respirators, and infrared thermometers to the Minsk infectious diseases hospital (Alivaria); • insurance contract with Belneftestrakh ZASO in Novopolotsk under the STOP-VIRUS COVID-19 program (Naftan); • establish hotlines on COVID-19 issues for senior citizens and the disabled operating around the clock (BelarusKaliy).	

Industrial sector: Having analysed the CSR of some companies, the activity of most companies in the framework of the implementation of CSR projects comes down to two main areas:

- the development of the company's human resources (raising the level of qualifications of employees while providing them with high-quality working conditions); and
- the production of quality goods and services.

Therefore, for this benchmarking analysis, we have selected more advanced businesses that follow the Western lead, create a great environment for their employees, and work hard on their reputation to bring good deeds to life. The number of implemented CSR projects in the industrial sector will potentially continue to grow and will become more attractive in the future. However, it is necessary to understand that in a difficult economic situation, these structures will be less inclined to participate in CSR projects.

Educational sector: The companies have some similarities in internal CSR: All of them use advanced technologies in teaching and take part in professional development seminars and conferences. Moreover, the reaction to COVID-19 was the same: All the educational enterprises created remote workplaces, minimised the number of students per class, and followed the WHO recommendations. All the enterprises achieved some results in interacting with international organisations, which shows that the educational sector in Belarus tries to develop and become prestigious not only in Belarus but also abroad. Unfortunately, not all of them introduced social benefits to their employees and students.

8. Pedagogical Experiment: "CSR Practice in a Pandemic"

The asymmetry of socioeconomic development and the disproportionate development of regions heighten the interest in social responsibility, both among representatives of the real sector of the economy and among representatives of the education system and academia. Universities have traditionally played a key role in the dissemination of innovative ideas and in shaping the thinking and skills of future generations. The importance of education on sustainable development has been addressed by the United Nations since 1972 under the Stockholm Declaration.

Building the trajectory of training future specialists in socially responsible behaviour in business must be carried out systematically, within the framework of the professions they receive.

Higher education institutions are an ideal platform for reflective and critical thinking and play an important role in the process of social reconfiguration (Christie *et al.*, 2013). It is here that suitable conditions are created for interdisciplinary research: in pedagogy, management, and personnel management. Higher educational institutions play a special role in educating influential individuals who value their environment and are able to responsibly interact with it in the future.

However, from the point of view of Cotton (2009), the role of higher education in ensuring sustainable development is limited. This is due to a lack of understanding of the relevance of issues, a gap in the theoretical provisions and practise of social security, a lack of administrative support, pedagogical conflicts, etc. (Gusmão Caiado, 2018). As Slocum *et al.* note in their 2019 study, the orientation of universities to meet market demands impedes pedagogical didactics of teaching for sustainability. In turn, Brazilian researchers note that technical universities refuse to teach students the principles and laws of sustainable development and that the number of university graduates with an understanding of the role of sustainable development for future generations is still small. Abramov (2015), recommends studying independently using special literature, exchanging experience with colleagues and external consultants, and attending special events. The author considers participation in business school courses only as an introduction to CSR issues (Abramov, 2015).

Thus, among the scientific and academic circles of foreign countries, there is no common point of view regarding the role of higher educational institutions in highlighting and promoting the ideas of CSR.

In general, universities are gradually taking responsibility for sustainable development; social and environmental topics are included in the curriculum and a new learning environment is being created to ensure sustainability.

The authors of the chapter believe that at present, higher education institutions can become powerful drivers of corporate sustainability. They are called upon to serve society through education, create advanced knowledge to solve problems on a global scale, and train specialists capable of improving technical and economic indicators without harming the environment and society. Even in a market economy, universities should remain not only centres of knowledge but also a stronghold of universal human values.

The School of Business of the Belarusian State University, along with many companies, enterprises, and other universities, realises the importance of CSR. The administration of the university and the teaching staff conduct a number of activities aimed at the formation of socially responsible business activities among students of 1–4 courses. In particular, theoretical and methodological issues of CSR are studied at lectures and seminars, the best European practises are considered, and business cases devoted to the problems of social interaction are solved.

Roundtables are also held with representatives of business circles and heads of leading Belarusian enterprises. At the meetings, the issues of forming social packages for employees of enterprises, charity, and sponsorship are discussed. The greatest effect is given by outdoor events: excursions to production facilities and visits to orphanages.

Students, at the same time, are accustomed to independently solving issues in providing social assistance. In this direction, at the initiative of student self-government bodies, charity events are held, raising funds to help those in need. A study conducted at the School of Business of BSU shows a high degree of students' readiness to take part in socially significant events: 28% of the respondents took part and 36% (mostly freshmen) were ready to join them.

When organising such events, modern information and communication technologies are actively involved: messengers, social networks, a corporate portal, and a university portal. The use of chatbots and cloud technologies is promising. It is possible to add statistical, analytical, and economic-mathematical methods in terms of quantitative assessment of the development of CSR practises. Information technology makes it possible to form the necessary infrastructure. Unlike other forms of communication with stakeholders, interaction on the Internet allows companies to come into contact with the most active, creative, and motivated audience that can become a source of new competitive advantages for companies. The task of the organisers is to consolidate the positive experience and to demonstrate the possibilities of its application in the workplace (Prokhorova, *et al.*, 2019).

In the context of an urgent transition to a distance learning format, many types of training sessions had to be adapted. At the same time, not only the methods of communication, forms of control, and teaching methods changed but the teachers revised the content of the proposed cases, taking into account the real business situation.

So, the authors of the chapter in May 2020 and students of the School of Business of the Belarusian State University, specialising in Business Administration, were for the first time offered the task of creating video material on the topic of CSR. The essence of the research task consisted in the selection and presentation of video materials of CSR practises, which demonstrate the results of the successful application of CSR of Belarusian businesses in the context of the spread of COVID-19 infection. The end of the school year turned out to be tense for all participants in the educational process. However, the overwhelming majority of students successfully coped with the task offered to them. From the results of the analysis of the presented video material, a number of conclusions can be drawn:

1. More than 60% of the students used the official news YouTube channels of Belarusian television as a source of information search. This indicates the importance of covering socially significant information using this communication tool.
2. More than 85% of the students submitted not just one video for testing (as was required by the assignment) but 3–4 video clips. This may indicate a sufficiently voluminous source material for

selection as well as a deep interest of students in the proposed topic and a desire to present examples of social responsibility as best as possible.

3. Judging by the completed assignment, about 40% of the students understand social responsibility, first of all, as the responsibility of the government and state structures. Thus, part of the video reports was devoted to the topic of state support for small businesses during a pandemic. Accordingly, an additional explanation of the essence of CSR is required on the part of the teacher so that the younger generation of Belarus fully understands the role and tasks of businesses in the sphere of social responsibility.

4. Only 10% of the students filmed videos on their own, the rest used ready-made stories from the Internet. Further research by the authors of the chapter suggests the complication of the task on the topic of "Corporate Social Responsibility" towards collective independent video projects that can be published both on the educational portal of the School of Business and on YouTube.

Higher education institutions can play a leading role in teaching the principles and objectives of and the tools and techniques of socially responsible behaviour and managerial decision-making. A balanced approach to decision-making in complex ambiguous situations will eliminate contradictions and prevent destructive conflicts. The School of Business of the Belarusian State University has the opportunity to implement its own original strategy of social responsibility, which consists in establishing large-scale ties with business circles and in establishing open interaction with all stakeholders in order to provide the Belarusian economy with highly qualified socially responsible leaders (Proharava, *et al.*, 2019).

Thus, the process of forming the qualities of a socially responsible worker begins long before he enters the labour organisation. Studying at the university is one of the most significant stages in the formation of the personal and professional qualities of a future specialist. In addition, stakeholders expect from the university environment the formation of students' personal qualities with an emphasis on the development of self-organisation skills and an active life position based on moral universal characteristics. In turn, the task of the stakeholders is to carry out intra-organisational professional socialisation of future specialists, during which the "rules of the game" and the basic norms of labour behaviour adopted in a particular company are explained. The interaction of universities and companies in the process of training future socially responsible workers can and should be carried out in the field of such competencies as professionalism, the ability to work in a team, and the responsibility for the assigned work.

9. Conclusions

The practical result of the spread of CSR ideas in Belarus is the understanding by Belarusian businesses, on the one hand, of the need to improve the management of the company's sustainable development as a managerial innovation associated with expanding the horizon of business social responsibility and, on the other hand, as a tool for harmonising and realising the interests of stakeholders in order to stimulate the best competitive results of the company and developing the business environment in the long term. In this case, profit is no longer the ultimate goal, which should be guided by management activities. It is one of the economic goals and performs an important function — it acts as a means of achieving the entire set of goals.

Stakeholders turn out to be a key part of business organisations, and stakeholder relationship management becomes the most important characteristic of sustainable business development in the long term.

Each company independently chooses which path of development to follow and which strategy to choose in order to conquer the market, but in modern Belarusian society, where there is close intersectoral interaction, the role of CSR is increasingly growing. Voluntary acceptance of the principles of a socially responsible company testifies to the company's striving for openness, partnership, and respect for human values, providing not only stable conditions for the development of an individual company but also the national economy as a whole, which undoubtedly removes many arguments against the development of CSR aside.

Businesses are is increasingly contributing to sustainable development in Belarus, and the system of social responsibility of businesses is becoming more complex and covers more and more industries. CSR goes from an idea to an integral part of the development strategy of large corporations.

References

Abramov, R. (2015). What and where to learn CSR? Available at: https://soc-otvet.ru/chemu-i-gde-uchitsya-kso/ (accessed 10.12.2020) (in Russian).

Burke, L. and Logsdon, J. M. (1996). How corporate social responsibility pays off, *Long Range Planning*, Vol. 29, No. 4, pp. 495–502. Available at: https://www.sciencedirect.com/science/article/abs/pii/0024630196000416?via%3Dihub.

Carroll, A. B. (2015). Corporate social responsibility: The centerpiece of competing and complementary frameworks, *Organisational Dynamics*, Vol. 44, No. 2, pp. 87–96. Available at: https://www.sciencedirect.com/science/article/abs/pii/S0090261615000170?via%3Dihub.

Chandler, D. (2016). *Strategic Corporate Social Responsibility: Sustainable Value Creation.* SAGE Publications, USA.

Christie, B. A., Miller, K. K., Cooke, R. and White J. G. (2013). Environmental sustainability in higher education: How do academics teach? *Environmental Education Research*, Vol. 19, No. 3, pp. 385–414. https://doi.org/10.1080/13504622.2012.698598.

Chuang, S.-P. and Huang, S.-J. (2016). The effect of environmental corporate social responsibility on environmental performance and business competitiveness: The mediation of green information technology capital, *Journal of Business Ethics*, Vol. 150, No. 4, pp. 991–1009, Springer.

Cotton, D., Bailey, I., Warren, M. and Bissell, S. (2009). Revolutions and second-best solutions: Education for sustainable development in higher education, *Studies in Higher Education*, Vol. 34, No. 7, pp. 719–733. https://doi.org/10.1080/03075070802641552.

Crowther, D. and Seifi, S. (eds.). (2020). Governance and sustainability: International perspectives, 1st edn. 2020 Edition — Part II, Chapter 9. *Features of Functioning of Corporate Entrepreneurial Structures in Agribusiness in Belarus*, pp. 169–189, Springer, Singapore.

Gusmão Caiado, R. G., Quelhas, O. L. G., Leal Filho, W., Luiz de Mattos Nascimento, D. and Ávila, L. V. (2018). A literature-based review on potentials and constraints in the implementation of the sustainable development goals, *Journal of Cleaner Production*, Vol. 198, pp. 1276–1288. https://doi.org/10.1016/j.jclepro.2018.07.102.

Heslin, P. A. and Ochoa, J. D. (2008). Understanding and developing strategic corporate social responsibility, *Organisational Dynamics*, Vol. 37, No. 2, pp. 125–144. Available at: https://www.sciencedirect.com/science/article/abs/pii/S0090261608000132?via%3Dihub.

Husted, B. W. and Allen, D. B. (2007). Strategic corporate social responsibility and value creation among large firms: Lessons from the Spanish experience, *Long Range Planning*, Vol. 40, No. 6, pp. 594–610. Available at: https://www.sciencedirect.com/science/article/abs/pii/S0024630107000738?via%3Dihub.

International Monetary Fund (2020). A crisis like no other, an uncertain. Available at: https://www.imf.org/en/Publications/WEO/Issues/2020/06/24/WEOUpdateJune2020 (accessed 25.07.2022).

International Organisation for Standardisation (2010). ISO 26000:2010. Guidance on social responsibility. Available at: https://www.iso.org/standard/42546.html (accessed 01.09.2020).

Jones, T. M. (1980). Corporate social responsibility revisited, redefined. *California Management Review*, Vol. 22, No. 3, pp. 59–67. https://journals.sagepub.com/doi/10.2307/41164877.

Lantos, G. P. (2001). The boundaries of strategic corporate social responsibility. *Journal of Consumer Marketing*, Vol. 18, No. 7, pp. 595–632.

Local Social Fund "Dobra" (2019). Good index. Available at: https://indexdobra.by/opisanie-indeksa (accessed 25.07.2022) (in Russian).

Ministry of Economy of the Republic of Belarus (2017). National strategy for sustainable socio-economic development of the Republic of Belarus for the period up to 2030. Minsk, BY. Available at: http://www.economy.gov.by/uploads/files/NSUR2030/Natsionalnaja-strategija-ustojchivogo-sotsialno-ekonomicheskogo-razvitija-Respubliki-Belarus-na-period-do-2030-goda.pdf (accessed 10.06.2019) (in Russian).

Morales, A. G. M. (2007). O processo de formaçãoemeducaçãoambiental no ensino superior: Trakectória dos cursos de especialização, *REMEA-RevistaEletrônica Do MestradoEmEducação Ambiental*, Vol. 18, pp. 283–302. https//doi.org/10.14295/remea.v18i0.3554 (in Brazilian).

National Statistical Committee of the Republic of Belarus (2019). National platform for reporting indicators of sustainable development goals (SDGs). Available at: http://sdgplatform.belstat.gov.by/en/sites/belstatfront/home.html (accessed 12.06.2019).

National Statistical Committee of the Republic of Belarus (2020). Nominal gross average monthly earnings in the republic of Belarus by quarters.

Petukhov, K. A. (2012). Corporate social responsibility policy of Russian companies. Abstract of Ph.D. diss. Permian, RU (in Russian).

Porter, M. E. and Kramer, M. R. (2006). *Strategy & society. Harvard Business Review*, December, pp. 1–16. Available at: http://users. metropolia.fi/∼minnak/ipw/Birgit%20Weyer/strategy-society%20 Kopie.pdf.

Proharava, T. V. and Maltsevich, N. V. (2019). The use of artificial intelligence tools in the development of students' communicative competencies, *Innovation Processes and Corporate Governance: Materials of the XI International Extramural Scientific and Practical Conference*, Minsk, 11–25 March, 2019. Minsk, BY, pp. 230–235 (in Russian).

SATIO (2019). CSR in Belarus. Where are we now and where should we go. Available at: https://drive.google.com/file/d/1o3knf5v2ClY4 ChPA-uUPZYKOA-EJibFV/view (accessed 25.07.2022) (in Russian).

Samusev, P. (2018). Socially responsible business: Experience of Belarus, Kazakhstan and Russia. *Eurasia Expert*. Available at: https://eurasia. expert/sotsialno-otvetstvennyy-biznes-opyt-belarusi-kazakhstana-i-ros sii/ (accessed 30.10.2019) (in Russian).

Simkhovich, V. A., Danilova, E. A. and Romanova, S. P. (2012). Social responsibility of modern Belarusian business. Minsk, BY. Available at: https://by.odb-office.eu/files/docs/Socialnaja-otvetstvennost-biznesa-v-RB.pdf (accessed 25.07.2022) (in Russian).

Slocum, S. L., Dimitrov, D. Y. and Webb K. (2019). The impact of neoliberalism on higher education tourism programs: Meeting the 2030 sustainable development goals with the next generation, *Tourism Management Perspectives*, Vol. 30, pp. 33–42. https://doi.org/10.1016/j.tmp.2019.01.004.

Trapp, N. L. (2012). Corporation as climate ambassador: Transcending business sector boundaries in a Swedish CSR campaign, *Public Relations Review*, Vol. 38, No. 3, pp. 458–465.

United Nations in Belarus (2020). Discussion of sustainable development issues in the context of the global economic crisis and pandemic. Available at: https://un.by/novosti-oon/v-belarusi/5031-obsu zhdenie-voprosov-ustojchivogo-razvitiya-v-usloviyakh-globalnogo-ekon omicheskogo-krizisa-i-pandemii (accessed 01.09.2020) (in Russian).

Werther, W. B. and Chandler, D. (2005). Strategic corporate social responsibility as global brand insurance, *Business Horizons*, Vol. 48,

No. 4, pp. 317–324. Available at: https://www.sciencedirect.com/science/article/abs/pii/S000768130400134X?via%3Dihub.

Zaynullin, S. B. (2016). Corporate social responsibility as a method of resolving corporate conflicts, *Internet-zhurnal "NAUKOVEDENIE"* Vol. 8, No. 5. Available at: http://naukovedenie.ru/PDF/12EVN516.pdf (accessed 25.07.2022) (in Russian).

Chapter 4

Collaborating and Competing in Development Agendas: State–Civil Society Tensions in Achieving SDGs

Dianne Bolton, Terry Landells, and Mohshin Habib

Abstract

This chapter's overarching concern is with progression towards the United Nations' (UN) Sustainable Development Goals (SDGs) in a dynamic geopolitical environment increasingly characterised by tensions and competition between a number of signatories. The SDGs constitute an aspirational framework of goals and targets concerning economic, social, and environmental development priorities to which all nations committed in Paris in 2015. In doing so, they affirmed their shared recognition of the complexity of global problems and the need for diverse and autonomous actions to reach voluntary and transparent targets. Goal 17 (UN, 2020a) articulates the need for collaborative action through multistakeholder partnerships (public, public–private, and civil society) "that mobilize and share knowledge, expertise, technology and financial resources" (target 17.16) while "respect[ing] each country's policy space and leadership to establish and implement policies for poverty eradication and sustainable development" (target 17.15). A commitment to global collaborative action has always presented challenges for countries influenced by a variety of political ideologies, power structures, and levels of competitive advantage, as noted by the Brundtland Commission in 1987 (WCED, 1987). However, recently, enhanced tensions have arisen concerning the principles of collaboration embedded in the SDGs and the heightened competition exhibited by the West in relation to the rise of China, given geopolitical tensions in the Indo-Pacific.

Keywords: Collaboration; competition; geopolitics; sustainable development; capitalism; disruptors

1. Purpose

Limited critique exists around the tensions between the ideologies of collaboration, the role of partnerships, and the motivations of key stakeholders in the achievement of the SDGs. This chapter recognises a range of stakeholders in the development agenda, focusing on four groups of stakeholders, namely global institutions, regional blocs framed by dominant ideologies, nation-states, and civil society organisations (CSOs), the latter as representative of civil society in development agendas.

Specifically, we focus on the theme of global "disruptors" that impact the achievement of SDG targets. The opportunities presented by China's Belt and Road Initiative (BRI) to support regional trade interests and partnerships in the South have disrupted existing development paradigms held in the West. These have heightened geopolitical tensions, evidenced in the recent adoption by the G7 of the "Build Back Better World" (B3W) initiative led by the US (Wintour, 2021), and made more transparent the dominance of competitive mindsets influencing development philosophies and agendas in the West. We argue that such dynamics invite a more critical appraisal of the role of partnership in development agendas.

In part one of this chapter, we explore how the political class in both developed and developing nations perceives these disruptions and represents them to their citizens in the form of ideological, political, economic, and social rationales relating to their own development needs. We leverage Gramsci's concept of a capitalist "integral state" to explore the dynamic relationship between the state and civil society, noting how such disruptions might be interpreted and communicated in the state's quest to create hegemonic thinking that supports political stability. While Gramsci's model focused on the role of the integral state in developed capitalism, we see relevance in drawing attention to state and civil society relationships in both developed and developing nations. We also note the extent to which political economy has been influenced by the SDGs and their shared global goals and commitment to collaborative action. Our approach highlights the extent to which the dominant development paradigm, heavily influenced by neoliberal principles, has been disrupted in practise as well as the implications of the B3W in its attempts to regenerate conditional aid, trade, and investment. In part two, we explore the significance of collaboration through exemplifying CSO activity seen as critical to SDG achievement but prone to influence by geopolitical disruptors. Specifically, we identify how disruptors to traditional Western models around trade and aid can have impact on multilateral collaboration in achieving the SDGs. This is pertinent as developing nations pursue more autonomous and localised development agendas. We draw on insights from Bangladesh and the Philippines to explain this perspective.

2. Part one: Geopolitical disruptors and their impact on achieving SDGs

2.1. *Neoliberal agendas around aid and development*

The agendas and influence of aid donors have been debated for many decades. In Theresa Hayter's (1971) classical work, *Aid as Imperialism*, she noted the following:

> "The [international lending] agencies' policies presuppose a liberal form of economic organization and adherence to international rules as defined in the West. They are based on the acceptance and upholding of the international and national framework of the capitalist world ... the international agencies cannot accept changes in developing countries which endanger existing patterns of international trade, foreign private investment, the regular servicing and repayment of debts ... there is a strong emphasis in the agencies' policies and demands on the principles of free enterprise, on reliance on market mechanisms and on respect of private property, domestic and especially foreign. The need for change is, to some extent, acknowledged: but the first priority is stability". (pp. 151–152)

She further acknowledged that, with few exceptions, such stabilisation programmes based on neoliberal premises and supported by international agencies resulted in low or zero rates of growth and in some cases negative rates of per capita growth. Since that time, concern has gradually increased across donors and key institutions around programme effectiveness and the impact of interventions on world poverty. A 2002 World Bank (WB) Policy Research Report focused on the contribution of globalisation to both growth and poverty outcomes from the perspective of a nation's integration into global trade and related opportunities for poverty reduction. Nicholas Stern, the then Senior Vice President and Chief Economist of the WB, noted in that report that during the 1990s, countries with populations adding to 3 billion had successfully broken into the global market for manufacturers, generally supporting poverty reduction, e.g. China, India, Bangladesh, and Vietnam. He estimated that the number of poor declined by 120 million. Poverty reduction was also seen as contingent on a range of domestic reforms to increase stability, including improvements to governance, the investment climate, and social service provision.

The WB's report (2002) was also concerned that 2 billion people were likely to become marginal to the world economy, e.g. in Afghanistan and the DRC, and that within countries which had broken into global manufacturing markets, integration had not necessarily led to greater income equality. Another concern was the requirement for homogenisation of policies to support integration into world markets. The report recognised "... that countries such as China, India, Malaysia and Mexico have taken diverse routes towards integration and remain quite distinctive in terms of culture and institutions" (p. x). A more direct appraisal of the situation was as follows:

> "... some recent developments in the global trading and investment regime are pushing countries towards an undesired standardization. It is important that global trade and investment agreements respect countries freedoms in a range of areas from intellectual property rights, cultural goods, and environmental protection to social policies and labour standards. Globalization does not need homogenization. There is also the real danger that the imposition of global standards could be used as the excuse for a resurgence of rich country protectionism". (pp. x–xi)

Long (2003) echoed these concerns especially in relation to the role of multilateral organisations including the WB, International

Monetary Fund (IMF), and the World Trade Organisation (WTO), suggesting that "... despite differences in their responsibilities, operational domains and administrative make-up, they frequently convey a degree of consensus when it comes to more general goals and means of development ... espous[ing] a broadly common economic and political rationality" (p. 24). He added that this "... neoliberal club of market-led development thinkers ... assigns the state a much-reduced role in initiating and steering development, as compared to the space allotted to private enterprise and civic associations, both local and global" (p. 24).

The limited outcomes of such neoliberal strategies and value sets were obscured by claims around the need for improved governance i.e. poor development outcomes were not due to the structure and conditions underpinning acceptance of WB and IMF assistance but to ineffective institutions and implementation. Key strategies for improved governance and political stabilisation included institutional development and more participation and empowerment of CSOs (WB, 2002). Stiglitz (1999) further noted that for half a century, the WB's core mission had remained the promotion of economic growth and the eradication of poverty in less developed nations but that overall lending policies were increasingly based less on individual projects and more on "... indicators of macroeconomic and sectoral policies and institutions, as well as governance, because these variables are strong predictors of performance on poverty reduction", thus consolidating a neoliberal package of measures. Cognisant of the limited outcomes of poverty reduction strategies, a broader focus on more sustainable and equitable development and commitments to universal goals around the elimination of poverty became a key development concern and potential disruptor of the neoliberal agenda.

The Brundtland Commission was inaugurated in December 1983 and responded to an urgent call by the United Nations General Assembly (UNGA) to frame a global agenda for change towards achieving more sustainable development by the year 2000 and beyond. Their report, *Our Common Future* (WCED, 1987), expressed growing concern around the characteristics of development and its impact, recognising that global agendas to alleviate poverty required global recognition and collaboration across a broad range of interconnected diverse issues which were multilateral, multifaceted, multilayered, complex and tension-ridden, and would require changes in conceptualising development in both developed and developing nations.

Reporting on 15 years of Millennium Development Goals (MDG), the UN (2015) noted that the eight MDGs had "... helped to lift more than a billion people out of extreme poverty, to make inroads against hunger, to enable more girls to attend school than ever before and to protect our planet. They generated new and innovative partnerships, galvanized public opinion and showed the immense value of setting ambitious goals". However, the uneven progress of development was also highlighted, suggesting commitment to the 17 SDGs replacing the MDGs would require collective long-term effort to tackle the root causes of poverty and integrate the economic, social, political, and environmental drivers of development. However, as Bolton and Landells (2020, p. 152) noted, "[t]aking action around multifaceted and contentious [sustainable development] issues often requires non-traditional, expansive, and synergised thinking across inter-connected institutions and actors in diverse economic, social, environmental and political arenas often characterized by ill-defined interlinkages".

This mindset might appear to require a break with hegemonic thinking around development agendas described earlier. Rigorous debate has ensued as to the extent to which the SDGs accommodated neoliberal assumptions and practises. Commentators such as Weber (2017) suggest that whereas the MDGs were largely non-specific in relation to implementation methods, the more detailed SDGs allow "... the implementation of highly contested neoliberal policies [as] part of the explicit goals of the SDG framework" (p. 400). Thus, conflicting claims around the breadth of SDG agendas and the accompanying rhetoric that promulgates the autonomy of signatories to implement the SDGs according to their national priorities are reflected in Long's (2003) questions concerning the extent to which hegemonic strategies characterise global institutional frameworks for development planning. He asks whether they might have a deeply seated impact on development strategies or whether they might prevail as disruptors of the apparent neoliberal consensus around "global" agendas for development. We argue that the pursuit of hegemonic neoliberal discourse concerning global trade, aid programmes, investment conditions, and institutional practise is being increasingly disrupted by paradigmatic shifts in the ecology of development; the influence of alternative development rationales and means of progression is being deemed more relevant to the aspirations of many autonomous nation-states.

We conclude that the politics of disruption (increasingly heightened by geopolitical and economic power shifts) is helping key stakeholders better appreciate emergent opportunities for development in a more autonomous South seeking regional strategies for development, including new and alternative forms of aid, trade, and investment. Such innovation was anticipated when the SDGs were adopted in 2015. However, the contemporary return to Cold War mindsets of key geopolitical players challenges the conceptualisation of new forms of collaborative activity in an increasingly polarised world.

2.2. *Disruptors to the neoliberal development paradigm*

Goal 17 of the SDGs is to "Strengthen the means of implementation and revitalize the global partnership for sustainable development" (UN, 2020a), in recognition that the SDGs can only be realised with strong inclusive partnerships at the global, national, regional, and local levels. Its emphasis on international cooperation around finance, technology, capability building, trade, and systemic issues identifies the importance of multistakeholder partnerships, including public, public–private, and civil society partnerships at a global, regional, and local levels. Achieving such highly aspirational aims, particularly in crisis conditions such as those currently experienced by the impact of COVID-19 on growth, debt, and development, further tests shared understanding among stakeholders around the nature of interconnectedness and commitments to the SDGs. We posit that any significantly disruptive circumstances, such as pandemics, impacts of climate change, global financial crises, and increased geopolitical tensions, will require reflection on and reconceptualisation of stakeholder roles and engagement with the SDGs. Currently, these pressures largely coincide, thus increasing the dynamism, unpredictability, and diversity of national and international responses.

Mulakala (2021) discusses forms of disruption to the pattern of global consensus which are heavily influenced by the neoliberal paradigm noted earlier. She acknowledges that the achievement of the SDGs and Agenda 2030 require "... beyond-aid resources, strategies and partnerships" (p. 522). She argues that South–South cooperation (SSC) has fostered new combinations of development partnership and finance, with significant geopolitical implications, and that "[t]oday development finance is less about aid and more about trade, foreign direct investment, export credits and other resource flows, including remittances ..." (p. 520). The disruption emanates from the fact that "... today SSC is big, bold, and SSC investments have predominantly a Chinese face" (p. 521). This reality has confronted the West, regenerating politics of global competition and challenging the potential of multilateralism, cooperation, and partnership anticipated in the SDGs and Agenda 2030.

2.3. *The integral state*

So, how might we better understand the responses of nation-states towards new forms of collaborative action to achieve globally agreed goals, both nationally and internationally? To help conceptualise this phenomenon, we critique Gramsci's concept of the "integral state" that theorises the dynamic interaction between the state and civil society under state leadership in the development of stable forms of government. Importantly, Gramsci identifies "... an interconnection and dialectical unity between the state and civil society" (Humphrys, 2018, p. 147), recognising that the integral state will to some extent always be unstable as it grapples with tensions and antagonisms and sense-makes the approach of the political class. An important feature of the ongoing instability is that it embeds, among other things, emergent narratives of equality and inequality (including national and international power relations and other

antagonisms) into its existing hegemonic discourse and then "...
normalises ideas as 'common sense' in the service of social stability"
(Hawksley and Georgeou, 2019, p. 29). State-managed discourse
around its response to global challenges becomes "common sense",
with hegemonic "domination" occurring by the normalisation and
integration of tensions through discourse that adapts, shapes, and
ultimately validates state responses to pressures and constituencies,
ostensibly through diverse forms of democratic process.

Our focus here is how the "integral state" creates political
stability through a manufactured "common sense" by absorbing
tensions around contested development strategies. Figure 1 illustrates tensions between the civil and political societies that are
managed by the integral state. The areas of tension identified
reflect issues and practises associated with the state's alignment
or diffusion of tension associated with the political economy of
development strategy, including the achievement of the SDGs.
The diagram also aims to reflect abstract tensions between civil
society and political society that might be experienced by both
developed and developing nations. It can be assumed that these
tensions can be aggravated or diminished by the re-emergence of
competitive geopolitical tensions that appear to fly in the face of new
forms of collaborative practise identified in the Brundtland Report
(WCED, 1987) as underpinning global action to address global
inequities.

The diagram exemplifies how the state in developed and developing economies is faced with the challenge of sense-making development paths and outcomes for its citizens by aligning tensions
between the civil and political society. Tensions might manifest
around multiple and complex approaches to development strategies; support for localisation agendas versus tied or conditional
approaches to development principles (all of which impact decisions
on the mixes of public and private, national and international
resourcing); and the benefits of global and regional partnerships.
This conceptualisation of the dynamics of the integral state helps
exemplify how diverse *national* "common senses" might facilitate
new forms of collaboration in complex and competitive *regional*

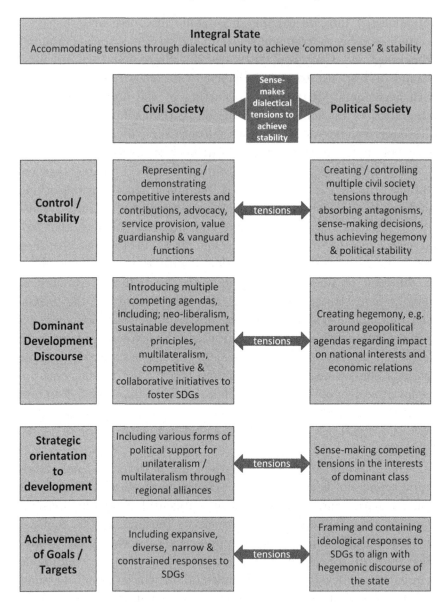

Figure 1.   Role of integral state: Issues in tension in development discourse and action.

and *global* environments; supports an understanding of how nation-state interests are being realigned through new forms of multilateralism in regional development blocs that potentially challenge the common sense of the old neoliberal order; and how contemporary emergent Cold War mindsets might impact evolving development rationales and strategies. Additional influences on state–civil society tension include commitments to the SDGs manifest in a nation-state's development planning and their implications for collaborative partnerships underpinning national development goals. A key issue is the extent to which initiatives such as B3W can influence such agendas by constraining certain development opportunities through new forms of conditionality around aid, trade, and investment.

For example, as a counterpoint to Northern domination of the South through development support, commitment to multilateralism is now firmly embedded in global discourse around North–South, South–South and triangular cooperation, and such discourse now infiltrates global strategic, diplomatic, and economic relations. The sustainability discourse around holistic and integrated international agendas increasingly respects national autonomy in determining development pathways and characterises many "integral states" in the South. Public awareness around commitments to the SDGs often frame or inform national plans and political administrative structures in many developing nations. These frameworks are shaping expectations around emergent responses to global challenges, such as pandemics and climate change, also potentially influencing attitudes to global partnerships in achieving the SDGs. Thus, in many developing nations, achievement of the SDGs underpins a range of political and ideological stances around development goals and planning. The attempts by the US and its strategic partners to introduce new forms of multilateralism driven openly once more by strategic considerations (following US withdrawal from many forms of multilateral activity under the Trump presidency) again appears to regenerate neoliberal competitiveness as a driver of aid and collaboration. This contrasts with China's hands-off philosophy, particularly in South–South engagement and facilitation of development initiatives through voluntaristic trade and infrastructure development.

Of relevance to this new form of geopolitics underpinning development discourse in 2021, it might be useful to reflect upon Long's (2003) argument that it is not the direct influence of opposing rational discourses that shapes development ideologies and logics. Rather, in line with Gramscian thinking, fragmented attempts are made to embed counterposing philosophies and ideologies into a dominant discourse, e.g. "letting the market do its job" being accompanied by alternative discourses on equity and the problems of marginalisation. The presentation of US' positions by Presidents Trump and Biden highlight and leverage the political pressures of the day, e.g. Trump resorted to increased protectionism to counteract China's economic ascendancy and Biden through B3W appears to have leveraged the ambiguity and chaos of the COVID-19 impact on global economic performance to regenerate a US-led political economy that reflects neoliberal orthodoxy as a precondition of strategic and economic cooperation. This is not to deny Long's argument that individuals, as representatives of organisations or informal groups, have potential to help recast discourse and presumably "common sense" around development initiatives.

Hawksley and Georgeou (2019) suggest that the SDG framework already represents "... the common sense neoliberal view of the challenge of sustainable development being met by the tripartite system of state, market and civil society" (p. 44), including deregulation, marketisation, commoditisation, and hyperextension of workers. By contrast, others acknowledge the affective dimensions of the SDG framework "... as not only generating particular subjectivities but also offering a sense of a world that is moving on a particular pathway and towards something that can produce a sustainable, goal oriented and 'better' world" (Gabay and Ilcan, 2017, p. 338). We embrace both perspectives while acknowledging the tensions. The SDG framework attempts to reconcile the otherwise competing interests of the private, public, and non-government sectors by a common focus on goals to address global development challenges affecting or affected by all nations and sectors. Yet, frameworks for achieving, SDGs and associated policies, projects, and practises also appear to allow large and smaller global players to compete, collaborate, and synergise alternative development approaches. It is suggested later that developing nations are becoming well versed in tolerating, critiquing, and synergising multiple and diverse ideologically driven initiatives within their own national development plans and strategies for meeting critical SDGs in local contexts in the wake of new configurations of global power. It is also suggested that aspirational SDG goals have assisted some developing nations' legitimate alternative development ideologies that consider simultaneous growth and equity agendas, in contrast to neoliberal orthodoxy and practise. Escobar (1992) identified the "autopoietic" character of social movements, i.e. the extent to which "through their own action they establish a distinct presence in their social and cultural environment" (pp. 44–45), thus highlighting the likely impact of domestic CSOs (as representatives of civil society) to defend a hard-fought localisation agenda. Initiatives from the North to revise aid, trade, and investment programmes that reinforce conditionality of adherence to neoliberal principles of development, working against autonomous development choices, might expect tension between INGOs and local NGOs. In this light, the B3W programme is considered in the following.

There is evidence that achieving the SDGs has occurred increasingly through a range of development avenues and resourcing options as developing nations exert increasing autonomous control over development planning. However, it appears that post-COVID-19 these options are becoming more constrained, as the incentives to "rebuild better" are framing aid agendas in more openly political rather than collaborative terms. At the G7 meeting, President Biden "convinced both European and Asian allies to weave together an anti-China front and reinserted the United States into a global leadership position to 'build back a better world'" (Liang, 2021) based on their shared values around democracy and rules-based liberalism. As one US senior administration official was quoted, "We believe we will beat the BRI by offering higher-quality choice and we'll offer that choice with self-confidence about our model that reflects our shared values" (Widakuswara, 2021). This seems in tension with the more open WB's position that BRI transport projects offer benefits that can assist the decrease in poverty by lifting around 7.6 million out of extreme poverty and up to 32 million from moderate poverty (World Bank, 2019).

Strategic details around the B3W agenda such as "affordability" of loans (given heavy reliance on private finance in a post-COVID-19 recovery); claims around "no strings attached"; lack of collaboration and cooperation with Chinese initiated projects; and constraints on the initiatives of partners, e.g. Japan and Italy, to continue involvement in BRI projects, have raised concerns about broader implications for multilateral systems and interests. This contrast, with the premise that multilateralism, as a keystone of the SDGs, "require[s] countries to recognise differences, manage conflicts and work cooperatively towards common goals …lead[ing] the world towards a more sustainable future in a more inclusive way" (Liang, 2021).

B3W appears to reflect the US integral state's creation of new discourse around conditions for multilateral development cooperation in the face of increasing strategic and global challenges, seeking to absorb antagonisms and tensions created by the increasing influence of China. Earl (2021) notes that new tensions between state and civil society in the US could arise from its pursuit of this role concerning the funding required for global leadership initiatives. Global tensions might also arise from diverse but nonetheless global commitments to the SDGs, the urgent challenges of climate change, and the widely accepted need for more inclusive forms of leadership that collaborate to fill the massive gap of resources and activity required. Such sentiments were echoed by António Guterres' address to the 15th session of the UN Conference on Trade and Development (UNCTAD 15) in October 2021, calling for the levelling of the playing field by a debt action plan to address COVID-19-related economic decline through more open and fair trade rules (UN, 2021). Another point of tension is the politicisation of China's efforts to operate within the WTO and more recently in the Comprehensive and Progressive Agreement for Trans-Pacific Partnership (CPTPP), which according to Earl (2021) "… is a natural recruiting ground for scaling up the old Trans-Pacific Partnership (TPP) towards a free trade area of the Asia-Pacific". He suggests that the gap between it and China's existing international obligations might be much narrower than people think.

Thus, the differences between cooperation concerning adherence to principles and shared goals is being challenged by players wanting to keep China out of trade agreements. As Earl (2021) noted, in relation to China's attempts to join the CPTPP, if the US continues to reject the TPP it once advocated and countries, including New Zealand, Singapore, and Malaysia, are prepared to consider the application, opposition to China's agenda will present other Asia-Pacific countries, such as Australia, with difficult choices. He notes that New Zealand's approach seems to be more consistent with that of developing nations in trying to balance the interests and expectations of the larger geopolitical players and yet pursue more open, collaborative, and independent options. Civil societies will respond to tensions in these agendas, shaping and challenging characteristics of a new "common sense" and the level of political stability that it generates.

The next section traces the history of global thinking and tensions around commonly shared goals in the form of a sustainable development agenda. The integral states of both developed and developing nations will need to absorb these tensions in determining the new common sense for appraisal by civil societies. A key feature has been the global agreement about the importance of autonomy in developing states to determine local agendas. We are interested in the extent to which this agenda is threatened by increasingly transparent geopolitical rivalries.

2.4. *SDG as a development framework*

By the 1980s, the focus on sustainable development had shifted from a singular concern with increased growth and economic output to that around alleviating poverty and inequality as a feature of economic growth patterns, requiring action by both developed and developing countries. The Brundtland Report of 1987 framed a global agenda for achieving sustainable development by the year 2000 and beyond, "... recognis[ing] the broad range of interconnected issues underpinning the diverse [and] multilateral, multifaceted, multilayered, complex and tension-ridden agendas of member states and other stakeholders" (Bolton and Landells, 2020, p. 151). At the

2015 UN Sustainable Development Summit, the SDGs were adopted, suggesting a new form of multilateralism to be achieved through an evolving "... dynamic and interactive trajectory between commitment and capability to undertake multiple forms of action by member states within a framework of shared goals of achieving [sustainable development]" (p. 151). Such an approach relied on emergent shared values and collaborative practise, also recognising the importance of local agendas and the selection, resourcing and partnerships that met local political, social, economic, and environmental goals.

2.4.1. *Busan and BRICS: influence on SDGs*

So, how do these aspirations impact the dominance of neoliberal approaches to aid, trade, and investment? Weber (2017, p. 400) expressed concern that the "... SDG framework presents a highly contested approach to development as *'the'* agenda for *global* development ... the implementation of highly contested neoliberal policies [being] itself part of the explicit goals of the SDG framework", tracing the continuity of this approach back to the structural adjustment policies and poverty reduction strategies of the WB and the IMF. We argue that the SDG framework and its focus on global goals has also encouraged some developing countries to engage discriminately and critique aid and trade development partnerships from the perspective of their outcomes over time rather than passively accept constraints of trade partners in practise. Weber also concedes that the 2011 Busan Partnership Agreement (BPA), preceding the SDGs, paradigmatically shifted the discourse of international development assistance to one of global development. Principles stated in the BPA included ownership of development priorities by developing countries, shared principles for cooperative development, development partnerships led by developing countries to implement approaches tailored to country-specific situations and needs, and transparent practises as a key element of accountability by all stakeholders (OECD, 2011).

Principle 2 of the BPA stresses that "... the nature, modalities and responsibilities that apply to South–South cooperation differ from those that apply to North–South cooperation" (OECD, 2011), advocating increased efforts to support effective cooperation based on specific country situations and goals. The goals and activities of BRICS countries reflect such differences and an emergent paradigm of development partnerships and cooperative engagement across diverse politico-economic philosophies and cultures. The 12th BRICS summit (BRICS, 2020) reaffirmed commitment to "... strengthening and reforming international governance so that it is more inclusive, representative, democratic with meaningful and greater participation of developing countries in international decision-making and better attuned to contemporary realities" (para. 6). A more reformed multilateral system would encompass the UN, the WTO, the WHO, the IMF, and other international organisations.

This BRICS statement recognises tensions in the North's domination of the development agenda, given historical legacies and unpredictable and subsequent multilateral interactions, but also that alternative development perspectives and partnerships were gaining ground. So, was a new "common sense" arising around increasing local determination of development agendas?

2.4.2. *Disruption of Washington Consensus: Belt and Road Initiative (BRI) and Aid-for-Trade (AfT)*

John Williamson, who coined the term Washington Consensus, concluded that its overall results on growth, employment, and poverty reduction were disappointing in many countries, a sentiment echoed by US President Obama in 2018 (Norton, 2018) and previously identified by UNCTAD (2010). Kazi (2020) highlighted how

"China has disrupted this euro-centric model by investing in infrastructure abroad to improve connectivity and develop the countries in the global south through trade. China has developed its own parallel development institutions to lead South–South cooperation and emancipate people from poverty, hunger and disease". (p. 144)

China's BRI introduced in 2013 constitutes a plan through partnerships to enhance six overland economic corridors across Eurasia and a maritime Silk Road connecting regions and sea across Asia, Africa, and Europe. Titumir and Rahman (2019a) concur that the "BRI offers an alternative to hitherto dominant forms of global market order created by the so-called Washington Consensus ... popularly known as neoliberalism, deregulation and privatization". However, they also conclude that a participating country's potential gains would depend on

> "...changes in the level of production, export and import conditions that would benefit local capital and business enterprise, participating country's location in the Chinese production network, the type of goods — primary, intermediate or finished — a country can supply to Chinese markets as well as to the wider export market in the region within the new aura of enhanced connectivity and cooperation". (p. 14)

For Bangladesh, they added that the BRI presented opportunities to expand labour-intensive activities. However, they saw little difference between Chinese multilateral investment banks, SOEs, and private commercial bank lending, these being similar forms of funding incurring similar risks. They further noted a lack of evidence of innovation in technology transfer arrangements on which Bangladesh is highly dependent. They noted that the involvement of local populations and benefit identification and sharing was critical to Bangladesh, perhaps implying an enhanced role for civil society organisations.

Of prime geopolitical significance is China's clarification of its approach as non-interventionist outside the trade partnership, respectful of the SDGs, and collaboration-based rather than a competition-based approach to trade. Conditionality on loans is also less than the WB and the Asian Development Bank (ADB), while China's official development assistance does not impact the effectiveness of grants and loans from Western multilateral aid and lending agencies (Dreher *et al.* 2021). But risk-increasing debt burden can arise if project selection does not include local input into decision-making and delivery.

Titumir and Rahman (2019a) include the term "normative legitimacy" as a criterion for effective development, a term that might be considered in the context of consensus building by an integral state. For instance, in the case of Chinese aid, they note the need for support of the political and economic class and the community as well as consensus of interests between China's and Bangladesh's political processes, deemed as essential to realising gains from BRI or presumably other initiatives such as B3W. Otherwise, it would appear "... regime centric, with limited potential gains" (p. 27). To that end, the extent to which the SDGs provide a forum for developing such normative and political legitimacy seems important. They see China's lack of interest in intervening in domestic politics as a key element of normative legitimacy, its main driver being transformation of its domestic economy.

However, as noted earlier, China's agenda is seen by the West through a competitive geopolitical lens centred on China's strategic and economic ascendancy, whereas other players in the South have identified a key benefit of the BRI as its accommodation of their development aspirations that supersede the limitations of free-trade rhetoric. "[T]he approach taken is 'equiangular development diplomacy' that calls for a balanced pathway to progress, basing countries' relations on mutual development needs and priorities rather than on divergent geopolitical interests or disputes" (Titumir and Rahman, 2019b; p. 45).

The WTO has also emphasised its own centrality to achieving the SDGs through trade in areas such as poverty reduction, health, and the environment by delivering pro-growth and pro-development trade reforms "... continuing to foster stable, predictable and equitable trading relations across the world" (WTO, 2020). The OECD and the United Nations Development Programme (UNDP) also claim "... that aid alone is not enough to achieve our shared development goals, [requiring] recognition of an evolving and increasingly complex development "architecture" characterised by a greater variety of actors, country contexts and new forms of partnerships" (OECD/UNDP, 2014, p. 20). They promote the aid for trade (AfT) philosophy and programme and multilateral cooperation to advance both development and business outcomes as mutually reinforcing.

Langan and Scott (2014) note that AfT initiatives are presented as instruments that constitute "... an innovative form of donor support in the post-Washington Consensus ... enhancing the well-being of the poor within developing societies — since increased trade will bring about livelihood creation and 'trickle down' prosperity for vulnerable citizens" (p. 144). They question this form of support when poor countries are excluded from core negotiating forums and that "assisting developing countries to understand and implement the obligations of such agreements through trade-related assistance ... does nothing to address the inequities of the rules themselves" (p. 153).

The OECD has acknowledged the complexity of developing countries opening economies to international trade:

"The benefits of a liberalised trade regime will only be realised in an economy with efficient infrastructure linking local producers to domestic, regional and global markets and a regulatory environment that encourages a vibrant private sector. Developing countries ... require help in building their trade-related capacity — in terms of information, policies, procedure, institutions and infrastructure — to integrate and compete effectively in global markets". (OECD, n.d)

Perhaps these assumptions and concerns warrant further investigation of the operationalising of B3W with its rules-based, neoliberal agenda. For example, a significant aspect of rules-based approaches by the WTO and the OECD is the measurement of progress towards the trade and development targets of partner countries. This focus now claims: to ensure that outcomes are context specific; that "sea changes" in the global landscape of development assistance have occurred, including new actors supporting South–South cooperation; and a tightened fiscal environment exists, impacting ODA levels, as well as increased pressure for transparency and accountability. The WTO's review of AfT (WTO, 2019) notes that a growing number of South–South partners have actively engaged in AfT and stresses the programme's contribution to SDG 8: "Promote sustained, inclusive and sustainable economic growth, full and productive employment and decent work for all".

However, concerns about the use of effectiveness indicators have been raised. In Bangladesh, Mozumder (2012) has acknowledged some improvements, such as simplification of customs procedures, but questions the attribution of such initiatives with trade and development outcomes, suggesting that AfT effectiveness indicators need to acknowledge the broad-based and multiple factors involved. Ancharaz (2013) assessed the success of integrating developing countries in the AfT schemes and noted difficulties in understanding AfT schemes, differentiating them from other ODA, lack of information about projects, AfT resources overall not being additional, lack of project capacity to recognise and address local capacity constraints, lack of local ownership and involvement of local stakeholders, misalignment of donor objectives with host country priorities, and lack of donor coordination. A broader appreciation of trade reform (particularly the recognition of the more proactive role played by China within the WTO framework) might be warranted, with the BRI initiative being perceived by developing nations as an integral part of the multilateral trade environment, a reality now perceptibly denied by B3W.

According to Li and Qi (2021), the history of global multilateral partnerships for development is marked by cynicism among certain developing countries concerning its purpose and drivers because the institutionalisation of the OECD's Development Assistance Committee (OECD-DAC) established a system led by "Western" countries. They describe this initiative as ostensibly to ensure programme quality "... but more importantly as a strategic effort to reinforce the political interests of the United States and its allies in the Cold War context". Li (2017) notes the subtle creation of Western political hegemony around aid achieved by depoliticising technological drivers and development values to equate with concepts such as basic needs strategy, gender and development, participatory development, sustainable development, and poverty reduction to establish shared values and consent to aid conditions. Mosse (2011) describes this as bureaucratisation of development aid which covers up its political face and intentions.

Debates about the legitimacy of OECD forums versus UN forums emphasise the need for developing economies to claim a stake and demonstrate relevant forms of leadership in the international development process. However, disagreements about the role of OECD-DAC and other development effectiveness forums, such as the Global Partnership for Effective Development Co-operation (GPEDC) (supported by the OECD and UNDP), emphasise the narrowness of such agendas. "The emerging powers, in particular China, believe that promoting development for developing countries requires different discussions that should relate to how development cooperation can promote trade, investment, agriculture and industrialisation so that economic growth can be accelerated" (Li and Qi 2021, p. 403). The refusal of the US and Japan to join the Asian Infrastructure Investment Bank (AIIB) foreshadowed obstacles to active cooperative engagement to achieve the SDGs despite the GPEDC's claims concerning commitment to them. B3W openly continues the politicisation of development collaboration.

The GPEDC claims to promote development effectiveness through building better partnerships and a whole-of-society approach (including South–South and triangular cooperation), despite it not being fully supported by China, India, Brazil, and South Africa (Li *et al.*, 2018). It also claims to monitor GPEDC's strategic priorities towards "strengthen[ing] multi-sector engagement and generat[ing] political momentum and *behaviour change*" (GPEDC, 2020, p. 4, emphasis added) as well as promoting partnership with an effective private sector. The potential tensions with the B3W concerning the characteristics of collaborative practise deserve further consideration in part two.

3. Part two: Collaborative practises, CSOs, and achieving SDGs

3.1. *A shrinking civil society space?*

We have discussed earlier the extent to which neoliberalism still characterises Western thinking and practise in influencing agendas to address the SDGs, particularly the extent to which stakeholder agendas deserve critique in this context. We exemplify the perceived lack of criticality around the role of stakeholders in achieving collaborative goals and suggest that the conceptualisation of key stakeholder functions, as envisaged in development objectives and achievement of the SDGs, might benefit from reflection on geopolitical shifts.

For example, commentors (Anheier *et al.*, 2019; Brechenmacher and Carothers, 2019) suggest that CSOs face shrinking civil society space and that their contributions in fulfilling traditional development roles are diminishing, as the relations between governments and organised civil society becomes increasingly complex, diverse, and often tension ridden. We introduce limited critique of this debate, specifically noting that effective and adaptive forms of CSO activity have long needed reform, including new regulatory frameworks to re-establish how "... the goals, ways and means of governments, and civil society be better coordinated and reconciled" (Anheier *et al.*, 2019) whether these be "... full democracies ... flawed democracies ... hybrid regimes [or]... authoritarian regimes" (p. 4).

Although authoritarian politics in the North and the South is being highlighted as a driver of shrinking civil society space, little attention is being given to the likely impact of geopolitical shifts and tensions. Factors for consideration include the following: the rise of China's capability to offer development opportunities to development partners in the North and South, recognised by the WB as potentially helping decrease poverty levels significantly through trade opportunities; China's engagement with the SDGs in delivering on a development and infrastructure agenda through working with multiple partnerships across public and private sectors; the declining but still significant role of aid as a percentage of development funding in the South; the changing face of autonomous national agendas in the South and the potential impact on engagement with development partners including CSOs; and the importance of understanding individual state perspectives and needs in reconstituting civil society space and CSO roles in meeting urgent development needs. Anheier *et al.* (2019, p. 13) ask "How can profoundly adversarial relations be transformed into complementary or supplementary ones without endangering the fundamental independence of civil society". This suggests perhaps the need for reconsideration of CSO roles, seen through less ethnocentric lenses to maximise the well-being of local communities. The involvement of CSOs could provide increasing opportunities for practising a broader and reconstituted role more relevant to the needs of developing countries. This is a core question in an era in which the need for urgent collaborative action around the global agendas of the SDGs has become increasingly obvious in the limited global commitments to support the South concerning the COVID-19 impact which may herald the worst economic downturn since the Great Depression (UN, 2020b).

As noted earlier, state–civil society dynamics associated with the Gramscian integral state might help explain the shrinking space of civil society in complex, diverse, and tension-ridden North–South, South–South, and triangular divisions, particularly concerning cooperation around the SDGs. For example, the increasing tension between competitive geopolitical mindsets and commitments to new forms of global cooperation to resolve emergent and increasing threats, such as COVID-19 and climate change, will elicit contextual responses from developed and developing integral states, consistent with the accommodation of pressures arising from their respective civil societies. Such complex tensions demand critique of ongoing Northern domination of development agendas rather than collaborating around aid, trade, and investment. A history of such critique is described in the following.

3.2. *CSOs and partnerships: The Busan legacy*

After the 2008 Accra High-Level Forum on aid effectiveness, the establishment of the 2010 Istanbul Principles on development effectiveness, and the 2011 Busan Partnership Agreement, there was a significant shift towards inclusion of multiple stakeholders from civil society, requiring appropriately diplomatic engagement. The Istanbul Principles included pursuing equitable partnerships and solidarity that create and share knowledge and commit to mutual understanding, including the realisation of positive and sustainable change.

Tensions around principles of collaborative practise and individual values and goals were recognised by respondents to a BetterAid CSO survey (Tomlinson, 2012). The survey highlighted the challenges of managing political and ideological tensions through cooperative practises. The first tension identified by interviewees was the global engagement of CSOs versus their status as independent development actors. It was noted that complex agendas challenge actors to uphold human rights in concrete situations and work towards a changed vision of development and development cooperation. These were systemic issues that went beyond a development effectiveness agenda. It was seen as critical that CSOs continued to undertake advocacy roles, as the effectiveness of the Busan Partnership was seen as politically driven not just purporting technical solutions, the political agendas of Western-driven aid being understated. This approach appears to ignore the potential for flexibility to accommodate principles of cultural relativism in interpreting the concept of rights in the development process.

Similarly, the second challenge was sustaining a focus on country-level implementation through initiating conversations with governments and broad-based stakeholders. CSOs that were mainly service-oriented wanted to develop further capacity and commitment to support the Istanbul Principles. An enhanced focus on relationships with governments was seen to challenge CSOs' capacity to provide critique and feedback to government concerning domestic and international agendas around effective development and resource limitations restraining this capability.

The third issue set concerned how CSOs might simultaneously live up to national and international commitments. The challenge of being heard in multilateral forums was seen as fundamental for shaping the critical contributions of CSOs in regional forums. One participant suggested the following:

"[The goal of effectiveness] is achieved by encouraging new organizational cultures and new directions for interacting with other actors, leaving behind the perception that it is merely an issue of procedures, which tends towards bureaucratization. In this sense, CSOs must demonstrate their capacity for innovation and adaptation to changing contexts, searching for the best manner to insert themselves in collective action". (Tomlinson, 2012, p. 132)

Some CSOs felt constrained in advocating change in perceptibly dysfunctional aid systems with few incentives for donors to alter their attitudes towards providing more relevant and positive impacts for people living in poverty and provide appropriate accountability.

A fourth and related concern was how CSO inclusion in multilateral processes could be strengthened. It was noted by one participant that the UN needs to acknowledge that "... in reality [it] is also controlled by the powers...The UN is also in a flux of conflict between the global powers and the BRICS and the G77, who have achieved some momentum and strength" (Tomlinson, 2012, p. 136).

The report concluded that thousands of CSOs were ready to work with the principles of reform embedded in the Busan Global Partnership but questioned the willingness of political leadership to support that outcome. It is argued here that these comments reflect a shifting mindset towards goal achievement through multilateral partnership, requiring greater transparency to shared commitments and outcomes by all stakeholders, including CSOs.

It is worth noting that the OECD's (2020) overview on enabling civil societies through effective development cooperation identifies the OECD-DAC channelling nearly USD 21 billion, or 15% of all bilateral official development assistance to CSOs, and that an enabling environment should enhance their legitimacy through more flexible process in steering of funds and programmes. It notes also that the role of CSOs is based on appreciation of their "... ability to identify new and often systemic obstacles to social, economic *and democratic development* and for their capacity to innovate, elaborate and implement solutions" (emphasis added), aligning with the goal of strengthened development partnerships in a whole-of-society approach towards the achievement of the SDGs.

It might therefore be asked: What are the implications of geopolitical shifts in the shaping of CSOs' perspectives around multilateral collaboration, as envisaged by the SDGs? Both the BRI and AfT claim to be catalytic in facilitating new approaches to connectivity as a basis for development. However, connectivity appears to have increasingly strengthened ideological drivers, as embedded in the B3W and other recent strategic alliances aimed at containing China's rise as a global power.

We now exemplify how collaborative approaches to the achievement of the SDGs are engaging CSOs in the political agendas of the state in Bangladesh and the Philippines, as a point of reflection on opportunities for synergies underpinning innovation.

3.3. *Reporting on collaborative practise to achieve SDGs*

Goal 17, towards strengthening implementation of the SDGs through global partnership for sustainable development, describes CSOs and collaborative partnerships as vital elements of collective society-wide efforts to achieve sustainable development outcomes through North–South, South–South, and triangular regional and international cooperation. Assistance to developing countries includes support for multistakeholder partnerships involving public, private, and civil society sectors. CSOs' roles are seen as crucial by state governments and donors in implementing SDG strategies, particularly in supporting localisation of strategic approaches by the private and public sectors individually and in collaboration.

In a review of Voluntary National Reviews (VNRs) of SDG progress presented to the UN between 2016 and 2019, the UN's Department of Economic and Social Affairs asserted the following:

> "... multistakeholder engagement and durable partnerships with diverse stakeholders will be key to realizing progress on the ... SDGs ... and ensuring that no one is left behind. Governments at all levels, citizens, parliaments, academia, civil society, the private sector, trade unions, youth and others can accelerate transformative actions through individual and collaborative efforts on sustainable development". (UNDESA, 2020, p. 5)

Reporting guidelines for VNRs post 2019 detail stakeholder engagement as representing a "whole-of-society" approach. CSO stakeholders engage in preparation for the VNR, review progress towards the SDGs, help adapt institutional frameworks to ensure stakeholder perspectives are being considered, and engage stakeholders in implementation. We draw on examples from Bangladesh and the Philippines to illustrate specific features of actual collaborative practise.

Bangladesh submitted VNRs in 2017 and 2020, providing evidence of NGO and CSO engagement. The VNR claimed that CSOs played a significant role in ensuring that SDG activity (in economic, social, and environmental domains) maintained relevance to local context at the country, district, and sub-district levels. CSOs were also represented on the Sustainable Development Goals Implementation and Review Committee, a multistakeholder steering committee for review and implementation of the 2030 Agenda. Partnerships between the government and NGOs provided services in remote areas where services could not be provided affordably, government–CSO partnerships "facilitating the process of social change" (Government of the People's Republic of Bangladesh, 2020, p. 13). CSOs were also involved in the review of the SDGs for the VNR; consulted on implementation of the whole-of-society approach adopted; represented on the SDGs Working Team (providing recommendations to the steering committee) and on three committees implementing and coordinating SDG localisation at the divisional, district and sub-district levels; and in discussions regarding improved data collection.

The NGO Affairs Bureau in Bangladesh sees its role as communicating with line ministries to ensure projects align with national priorities and SDG targets directed towards the most marginalised and vulnerable. An ex-senior executive officer who had been responsible for country-level coordination of the SDGs in Bangladesh confirmed the significant role allocated to CSOs in meeting them and particularly their importance in delivering Bangladesh's localisation agenda in which each sub-district provides one additional local target to add to the 39 targets that Bangladesh has prioritised from the 169 targets of Agenda 2030.

Bangladesh's 2020 VNR briefly addressed the urgency of the COVID-19 response and the Rohingya crisis, sense-making key areas of tension to be addressed by the state. Subsequently, Western governments and CSOs have supported the Bangladesh government's five-year plan and its COVID-19 Preparedness and Response Plan 2020 as well as the UN Joint Response Plans for the Rohingya Humanitarian Crisis and related COVID-19 appeals. China has also supported responses to these crises while also facilitating bilateral negotiations between Bangladesh and Myanmar for safe repatriation of Rohingyan refugees. This approach appears to illustrate agreement across the three players concerning the benefits of a regional resolution to political tensions associated with the Rohingyan situation and the value of regional practical cooperation in addressing political challenges in alignment with the SDGs, such as improving livelihood and eliminating poverty in border areas between Myanmar and Bangladesh (Reliefweb, 2021).

The Philippines submitted VNRs in 2017 and 2019, the latter being focused on Goals 4, 8, 10, 13, 16, and 17 (Republic of the Philippines, 2019) and providing insight into the role of CSOs in progressing its development agenda in line with the SDGs. The 2019 report indicated that international CSOs were involved in planning for the 2019 VNR through feedback on the High-Level Political Forum process and that CSOs were involved in regional consultations in the three major island groups of the Philippines to gather data and inputs into the VNR. Some of these consultations revealed the need for CSO engagement platforms to better direct and coordinate their functions and resources to support the SDGs and for improved consultation between the government and CSOs. In a discussion on the progress against the goals, CSO involvement was detailed, e.g. that concerning service delivery in education. The VNRs suggest that government bodies, comprising representatives from CSOs and government agencies, were also established to ensure women, children, indigenous peoples, and people with disabilities are considered in the development discourse.

The Philippines, localisation agenda is claimed to be facilitated through partnerships between local governments, CSOs, and "people's organisations" in the selection and monitoring of infrastructure projects and addressing policy gaps in local service delivery. Country assistance strategies (CASs) are considered aligned with the pursuit of the SDGs and the Philippine Development Plan (2017–2022) through which Agenda 2030 is managed. The VNR indicates that inclusive partnerships are being pursued to that end. Of the development partners, 90% engage CSOs, 80% consult the private sector, and 55% engage other stakeholders in the formulation of their respective CASs. Thus, the perspectives of civil society in shaping local agendas as responses to CSOs appear to be significant, as do donor agendas.

Discussions with a CEO of a large microfinance institution in the Philippines provided a richer perspective on civil society engagement. He suggested that recently, large CSOs can experience increased autonomy from the government. For the first time in 50 years, the ADB had made a direct loan to his NGO rather than through the government. Negotiations were lengthy in dealing with each layer of the funding organisation and associated sub-cultures. To gain this loan, the ADB evaluated the proposal against eight SDGs. He believed the assessment of their credibility included the strength of their networks (with partners also expected to achieve the SDGs) demonstrating relevant insight and collaborative skills.

Similarly, an administrative officer in a regional office at the National Economic Development Authority (NEDA) described the local culture in which the achievement of the SDGs is seen as embedded in the Philippines' development plan, investment programme, and the country's vision described in AmBisyon Natin 2040. CSOs are seen as essential in crafting such plans and in bringing specific and sectoral insights and skills to the four regional committees (economic, social, infrastructure, and governance). In the regions, there is often opportunity for CSO representation to chair committees, as their competence in shaping stakeholder mindsets is appreciated, many having had prior experience within government. He saw this CSOs' role as particularly important given the imminent implementation of the Mandanas Ruling which is anticipated to increase local government budgets by 30–40% in 2022 (World Bank, 2021). Meniano (2021) lists the functions assigned to local governments including agriculture programmes, local infrastructure, environmental services, revenue mobilisation, health services, maintenance of peace and order, employment facilitation, transportation, tourism, and housing. This ruling will constitute a significant increase in local government influence on the choice of development projects and possibly provide a very different perspective about how the local economy might be envisaged, an environment in which the role of CSOs might need to be radically reimagined.

In Bangladesh and the Philippines, the impact of the SDGs has included a focus on the machinery of government to ensure increased localisation of agendas and civil society involvement to that end. In line with the SDG philosophy, this has involved a breadth of partnership that meets local needs. Ideological constraints on CSOs based on reservations about their alignment with the state seem at odds with the views of state players described here which appear to seek partnership that provides productive feedback to meet local agendas. Our reading of VNRs suggests the need for considering CSO roles as providing support for local initiatives in a manner that reflects local democratic principles cognisant of cultural relativity and shared understanding between salient stakeholders.

3.4. *Global institutions fostering collaborative, localised development*

The World Bank (2019, p. 5) estimated that the BRI could increase GDP by 3.4% in BRI countries and by 2.9% in the rest of the world. We have noted how some developing countries perceive the value of alternative opportunities provided by China. Rabena (2018, p. 688) suggested that for the Philippines "... BRI membership translates into greater access to the 'red market' and positions Manila on the radar of Chinese investors and creditors". He also notes that BRI is attractive because of the Philippines' history of chronic infrastructure problems. The bilateral agreements attempt to align their respective development goals and interests along five dimensions of cooperation, i.e. policy coordination, infrastructure development and connectivity, trade and investment facilitation, financial coordination and integration, and people-to-people ties and connectivity. However, it appears the way forward will rely on new forms of feedback, collaboration, and negotiation between development partners to optimise localisation strategies. The CEO we interviewed in the Philippines described a potential lack of opportunity for CSOs to shape projects in BRI initiatives as detrimental to the maintenance of established and emergent CSO roles in development initiatives, including the capacity to accommodate local agendas and holistic project performance improvement.

In considering China's capacity for collaboration around local agendas, Straube (2020) notes that in China's centrally planned economy, CSOs have been closely integrated with state activities and thus have limited experience in prosecuting debates within China and between China and partner countries. He suggests that the BRI has the potential to reshape China's approach to the mechanics of collaboration, such as working more closely with CSO partners on BRI projects.

In critiquing collaborative approaches to localised development, the OECD has also recognised the dangers of oversteering funding by the West. Universal acceptance of the SDGs includes adherence to a philosophy that nations will reach goals through their own interpretations of viable approaches, consistent with regional and local opportunities and needs. Consequently, a return to Cold War mindsets, which fragments the shared understanding of global goals and operational approaches to achieving them, has the capacity to diminish the outcomes envisaged by the SDGs. Against this background, we shall now reflect on possible implications for collaboration in the context of disruptors described earlier.

3.5. *Collaboration and conditionality: Tensions highlighted by SDGs*

This chapter has elaborated on the shifts, tensions, and paradoxes experienced by key stakeholders in pursuit of collaborative practises to achieve the SDGs in environments that are increasingly disrupted by competitive Cold War agendas spilling over into development agendas. We have considered these against the SDGs' broad and somewhat aspirational agenda. We have noted that the SDGs have provided a framework for developing nations to plan, report, and measure progress, leveraging trade, aid, and investment across a variety of geopolitical players. As the economic and strategic power of China has increased, Western agendas around trade, aid, and investment are made increasingly transparent, as demonstrated by the B3W infrastructure plan to rival China's BRI. Geopolitical strategies in the West continue to emphasise binary and competitive development options at the expense of diverse, multilateral, and collaborative inputs to achieving the SDGs. The term "multilateral" seems increasingly constrained to blocs of ideologically aligned actors.

However, attempts to strengthen conditional approaches to aid, trade, and investment activity seem challenged by shifts in global institutional philosophy and practise spawned by both the failure of prior conditional Northern development approaches and the success of Southern nations in adopting diverse forms of political economy that have delivered growth and equity outcomes to meet local agendas. We have argued that the lens of the SDGs, with its focus on collaborative partnerships to address urgent global problems, highlights tensions between the state and civil society in both the North and the South, aggravated by the recent geopolitical reversion to politics of competition and Cold War as drivers of Northern-backed development agendas.

We extended Gramsci's conceptualisation of pressures on the "integral capitalist state" to absorb such tensions and antagonisms manifest between civil and political societies, focusing on those embodied in local and global approaches to development. The SDGs allow for a wide range of interpretation and action at a nation-state level, being goal focused yet acknowledging differentiated responsibilities and capabilities. The adoption of the SDGs by developing nations has in some instances strengthened the alignment between the state and civil society. On the other hand, when a developed capitalist nation adopts the SDGs, it can challenge economic, political, and social values around principles of sustainable development, highlighting inherent tensions between competitive and collaborative approaches to global development agendas, and perhaps even the essence of neoliberal premises.

China's BRI has operated as a key disruptor of the West's development agenda from a number of perspectives. First, its philosophy of non-conditional and cooperative support for the South increasingly contrasts with the approach of the US' B3W that intends to "... beat the BRI by offering a higher-quality choice ... *that reflects our shared values*" (Widakuswara, 2021, emphasis added). Liang (2021) has noted the following:

> "... while Biden espouses "no strings attached". It is hard to imagine the United States won't demand changes if recipient countries are deemed to be violating western standards, given the emphasis on democratic values that coalesce the G7 and underpin the "better world". The US track record also suggests that structural adjustments may be imposed as a conditionality of finance. Strong beliefs in the private sector and the dismissal of the efficacy of governments could also present tremendous challenges for the G7 to trust and work with public agencies in the developing world".

Second, China's main message in its 2021 VNR (People's Republic of China, 2021) champions the SDG values and aims to increasingly promote synergy between the BRI and the 2030 SDG agenda as a form of deepening South–South cooperation, showing willingness to fill the void in multilateral action left by the US' withdrawal from many forms of multilateral cooperation. The B3W attempts to redefine and reclaim leadership in the development space. Third, China's flexibility in its terms of financial and other assistance to developing nations creates fewer domestic tensions between its civil and political societies and its focus on tangible infrastructure and trade benefits for partners are clearly identifiable by their partners as directly related to growth and poverty reduction. By contrast, the B3W is more heavily dependent on private sector investment and governance reform.

Liang (2021) suggests that a weakness in the logic of the B3W is that G7 countries are also engaged in a range of complex projects and trade arrangements with China that are unlikely to be compromised by the B3W focus on improved governance and democratic process. The Chinese approach appears to be that for developing nations, the democratic process evolves from achieving development outcomes in practise rather than as a precondition to undertaking development initiatives. Furthermore, at the various stages of evolution from less developed to developing nations, many of the latter now operate with the realisation that the aid, trade, and investment environment offers multiple opportunities to structure development in line with post-Busan principles of their increased autonomy. Chakma (2019, p. 17) notes how geopolitical tensions are managed skilfully by the Bangladesh government in owning and optimising its own development opportunities. "[W]hilst Dhaka accepted BRI funding selectively, it remained respectful to India's concerns. Importantly it persistently maintained policy autonomy notwithstanding pressure from both powers". Discussions with key development agencies suggest that both Dhaka and Manilla play their socioeconomic cards carefully in tense geopolitical situations.

In Bangladesh and the Philippines, adherence to the SDGs appears to have influenced political and administrative frameworks and required engagement of civil societies to this end, including shaping and leveraging skills of CSOs in advocacy, service provision and project implementation to achieve localisation objectives embedded in the SDGs and to strengthen safeguards and reduce risks around implementation. Syal *et al.* (2021) identify the need "... for a more differentiated approach to the study of state-civil society collaboration under conditions of restricted civic space ...". We suggest that the notion of state–civil society collaboration through complex multistakeholder engagement in project and service environments will be appropriately critical of the B3W agenda if the latter attempts to limit diverse economic and social development opportunities in achieving the SDGs, as embedded in country plans.

Buffardi (2011) concluded that the US's foreign assistance policy often "... demonstrates the perils of policies without publics, identifying conditions under which narrow interest involvement can impede rather than facilitate policy reforms" (p. 33). Attempts to address such shortcomings at an institutional level (e.g. Paris Declaration, Accra Agenda for Action, Busan Principles, GPEDC) have been consistent, and some accrual of change to strengthen localisation agendas is evident in ensuing frameworks and practises, although the GPEDC has struggled to maintain the engagement of key global stakeholders. Lundsgaarde and Engberg-Pedersen (2019), in reflecting on the invisibility of the Paris Declaration (2005) principles in current development practise, suggest that many donor countries have engaged selectively with the declaration's principles around autonomous local approaches to development, requiring that "... the multitude of actors involved needed to work better together, and the effects of interventions should be documented and analysed". Of significance here is the continuing relevance of these points, particularly that "[w]hile governments supported the aid effectiveness agenda in international meetings, neither donors nor partner countries seemed very much inclined to make the necessary political adjustments" (Lundsgaarde and Engberg-Pedersen, 2019). The impact of the promises of the B3W or the BRI alternative remains to be seen, especially concerning their capacity to impede or stimulate multilateral action to meet the SDGs. The extent to which developing nations have achieved sufficient autonomy to critique and select these offerings that are now more ideologically and practically separated also deserves further exploration. A key focus for future consideration might be whether increased regional trade fostered through investment in infrastructure can also engender a sharing of goals and aspirations around autonomous realisation of targets framed by the SDGs, utilising embedded principles of collaboration.

4. Conclusion

Finally, we have noted that although the SDGs are aspirational, they have provided a set of order-generating principles and targets around which responses to key global problems can be monitored. In so doing, they make transparent individual national development strategies and outcomes, identifying priorities, synergies, and tensions between economic, social, and environmental goals. Stacey and Griffin (2005) suggest that in highly complex environments, tensions and paradoxes are unresolvable and need to be held and that it is more important to witness the gestures and understand the intent of actors in dynamic and iterative interplay. We have briefly described the complex gestures of developed and developing nations in response to perceived opportunities and disruptions intimated by the rise of Chinese economic power, with its implications for South–South cooperation to achieve the SDGs. Certain frameworks appear important in influencing attitudes and gestures. For example, the SDG framework, *inter alia*, has sought accountability for global commitment to the increasing autonomy of developing nations in shaping their responses to emergent environmental shifts, threats, and opportunities. Specifically, we have noted that since the Brundtland Report, the processes of collaborative action and shifts in collaborative mindsets have been seen as critical in moving towards the goals of more sustainable development. Accordingly, the response of the West to China's increased capacity to contribute to sustainable development in the South appears to contradict previous global acknowledgement concerning the importance of collaborative practise and China's potential contribution to decreasing global poverty levels through increased infrastructure and trade.

The Brandt Report (Independent Commission on International Development Issues, 1980) was quite clear that global development should move forward on the basis of Western political and economic philosophies, orthodoxies, and economic science. The Brundtland Report (WCED, 1987) and its philosophies of collaboration and cooperation (embodied in the SDGs) envisaged developing countries taking a more autonomous role in defining political pathways towards development, guiding principles to that end being increasingly refined in fora, such as Paris 2005, Accra 2008, and Busan 2011, and also reflected in actions, such as the boycotting of the GPEDC by some BRICS members.

Thus, a revival of what have been described as Cold War approaches, limiting collaborative groupings to meet the SDGs to ideologically aligned players, seems to have the intent of constraining options and choices of developing nations around collaborative partnerships. These geopolitical tensions will be ongoing and will not be resolved directly as a precondition for the achievement of sustainable development. They will however add to tensions between the state and civil society in developed and developing nations around achieving alignment of and synergies between economic, social, and environmental objectives, priorities, and planning. These developments in turn increase the challenge for the "integral state" in absorbing such antagonisms and sense-making its politico-economic stance on what constitutes sustainable development. This is a necessary function of the state in order to report on the contribution to SDG attainment which will have greater or lesser importance for different nation-states in diverse political scenarios.

Accordingly, each developing nation will prioritise its most urgent challenges to meet political priorities. We have noted, as an example, that Bangladesh emphasises its interpretation of the SDGs as promoting growth with equity, with implications for its alignment of economic, social, and environmental targets and practises. We suggest that a major contribution of the SDGs has been to surface political priorities underpinning development strategies at a state level, thus making more transparent alignments and tensions between economic, social, and environmental objectives. This outcome itself can be seen as a democratic act, as the "integral state" sense-makes its decisions in the broader context of public good, exercising its mandate to manage geopolitical tensions while focusing on locally prioritised development goals within the SDG framework.

Increasing experience and emergent skills have been demonstrated by some developing countries in managing international and geopolitical tensions, for instance, in acquiring resources to manage the COVID-19 pandemic. Thus, the tactics of the North to limit cooperation through geopolitical competition might be less effective this time around, given the new "common sense" shared by the South concerning the need for diverse inputs and partnerships to meet global challenges affecting their citizens' well-being in the short and long terms. We have argued that not only is there a clear mandate to empower diverse collaborative partnerships but also that the South is now experiencing the benefits of multiple options for development in addressing and aligning its economic, social, and environmental priorities. Thus, it appears that a key challenge in developing partnerships to achieving the SDGs will be to maintain the autonomy of developing nations by respecting political choice and acknowledging cultural relativism through diverse and innovative forms of collaboration that optimise development opportunities in working to meet agreed global targets (as an order-generating agenda). This approach appears to constitute a new "common sense" around sustainable development that can either align or disrupt the relationship between the state and civil society concerning their engagement at a global level in responding to the urgency of global agendas as identified through the SDGs.

References

Ancharaz, V. (2013). Assessing the effectiveness of aid for trade: Lessons from the ground. Available at: https://www.cepal.org/sites/default/files/events/files/presentacion_vinaye_dey_ancharaz_ictsd.pdf.

Anheier, H. K., Lang, M. and Toepler, S. (2019). Civil society in times of change: Shrinking, changing and expansion spaces and the need for new regulatory approaches, *Economics: The Open-Access, Open-Assessment e-Journal*, Vol. 13, (2019-8), pp. 1–27. http://dx.doi.org/10.5018/economics-ejournal.ja.2019-8.

Bolton, D. and Landells, T. (2020). Brundtland and after: Through commitment to capability, in D. Crowther and S. Seifi (eds.), *The Palgrave Handbook of Corporate Social Responsibility*, pp. 149–175, Palgrave MacMillan, Switzerland. DOI:10.1007/978-3-030-22438-7_9-1.

Brechenmacher, S. and Carothers, T. (2019). Defending civic space: Is the international community stuck? Available at: https://carnegieendowment.org/2019/10/22/defending-civic-space-is-international-community-stuck-pub-80110.

BRICS. (2020). XII BRICS summit moscow declaration. Available at: https://www.gov.br/mre/en/contact-us/press-area/press-releases/xii-brics-summit-moscow-declaration.

Buffardi, A. L. (2011). Institutional influence: The role of international donors in shaping development goals, implementation and effectiveness. PhD dissertation. University of Washington. Available at: https://digital.lib.washington.edu/researchworks/bitstream/handle/1773/19502/buffardi%20dissertation%20final.pdf?isAllowed=y&sequence=1.

Chakma, B. (2019). The BRI and Sino-Indian geo-economic competition in Bangladesh: Coping strategy of a small state, *Strategic Analysis*, Vol. 43, No. 3, pp. 227–239. DOI:10.1080/09700161.2019.1599567.

Dreher, A., Fuchs, A., Parks, B., Strange, A. and Tierney, M. J. (2021). Aid, China, and growth: Evidence from a new global development finance dataset, *American Economic Journal: Economic Policy*, Vol. 13, No. 2, pp. 135–174. DOI:10.1257/pol.20180631.

Earl, G. (2021). Economic diplomacy: After AUKUS in trade, aid and technology, *The interpreter*, Lowy Institute. Available at: https://www.lowyinstitute.org/the-interpreter/economic-diplomacy-after-auk us-trade-aid-and-technology.

Escobar, A. (1992). Imagining a post-development era? Critical thought, development and social movements, *Social Text*, Vol. 3, No. 32, pp. 20–56. DOI:10.2307/466217.

Gabay, C. and Ilcan, S. (2017). Leaving no-one behind? The politics of destination in the 2030 sustainable development goals, *Globalizations*, Vol. 14, No. 3, pp. 337–342. DOI:10.1080/14747731.2017.1281623.

Global Partnership for Effective Development Cooperation (GPEDC) (2020). How we partner together for sustainable development: 2020–2022 work programme. Available at: https://www.effectivecooper ation.org/content/2020-2022-global-partnership-work-programme.

Government of the People's Republic of Bangladesh (2020). Voluntary National Reviews (VNRs) 2020. Available at: https://sustainable development.un.org/content/documents/26303VNR_2020_Bangladesh_ Report.pdf.

Hawksley, C. and Georgeou, N. (2019). Gramsci "makes a difference": Volunteering, neo-liberal "common sense", and the sustainable development goals, *Third Sector Review*, Vol. 25, No. 2, pp. 27–56. DOI:10.3316/INFORMIT.929306512882392.

Hayter, T. (1971). *Aid as Imperialism*, Pelican Books, Middlesex, England.

Humphrys, E. (2018). Anti-politics, the early Marx and Gramsci's "Integral State", *Thesis Eleven*, Vol. 147, No. 1, pp. 29–44. DOI: 10.1177/0725513618787638.

Independent Commission on International Development Issues (1980). *North–South — A Programme for Survival.* Pan Books, London.

Kazi, K. J. (2020). South–south cooperation: Development impact of China's belt and road initiative (BRI), *Pakistan Social Sciences Review*, Vol. 4, No. (IV), pp. 144–159. DOI:10.35484/pssr.2020(4-IV)10.

Langan, M. and Scott, J. (2014). The aid for trade charade, *Cooperation and Conflict*, Vol. 49, No. 2, pp. 143–161. DOI:10.1177/0010 836713482880.

Li, X. (2017). Evolution and prospects of the global partnership for effective development cooperation, *Journal of Learning and Exploring*, Vol. 6, pp. 107–113.

Li, X., Gu, J., Leistner, S. and Cabral, L. (2018). Perspectives on the global partnership for effective development cooperation, *IDS Bulletin*,

Vol. 49, No. 3. Available at: https://bulletin.ids.ac.uk/index.php/idsbo/article/view/2986/Online%20article.

Li, X. and Qi, G. (2021). Should China join the GPEDC? Prospects for China and the global partnership for effective development cooperation, in S. Chaturvedi, H. Janus, S. Klingebiel, L. Xiaoyun, A. de Mello e Souza, E. Disdiropoulos and D. Wehrmann (eds.), *The Palgrave Handbook of Development Cooperation for Achieving the 2030 Agenda*, Palgrave Macmillan, Switzerland. Available at: https://doi.org/10.1007/978-3-030-57938-8_31.

Liang, Y. (2021). Can the G7 really build back a better world? *East Asia Forum*, 24 July, 2021. Available at: https://www.eastasiaforum.org/2021/07/24/can-the-g7-really-build-back-a-better-world/.

Long, N. (2003). Contesting policy ideas from below, in M. Bøås and D. McNeill (eds.), *Global Institutions and Development: Framing the World?* pp. 24–40, Routledge, London and New York.

Lundsgaarde, E. and Engberg-Pedersen, L. (2019). Revisiting the aid effectiveness agenda: Has the paris declaration disappeared? *Danish Institute for International Studies*. Available at: https://pure.diis.dk/ws/files/2914827/Erik_og_Lars_Paris_Agenda_disappearedWEBFINAL1207.pdf.

Meniano, S. (2021). Region 8 agencies brace for transfer of functions to LGUs. Philippines News Agency, 27 April, 2021. Available at: https://www.pna.gov.ph/articles/1138120.

Mosse, D. (ed.). (2011). *Adventures in Aidland: The Anthropology of Professionals in International Development*. Berghahn Press, Oxford and New York, NY.

Mozumder, K. (2012). Managing aid for trade and development results: Bangladesh case study: Draft report. OECD. Available at: https://www.oecd.org/dac/aft/Bangladesh_Case_Study.pdf.

Mulakala, A. (2021). The Asian century: The transformational potential of Asian-led development cooperation, in S. Chaturvedi, H. Janus, S. Klingebiel, L. Xiaoyun, A. de Mello e Souza, E. Disdiropoulos and D. Wehrmann (eds.), *The Palgrave Handbook of Development Cooperation for Achieving the 2030 Agenda*, Palgrave Macmillan, Switzerland. Available at: https://doi.org/10.1007/978-3-030-57938-8_24.

Norton, B. (2018). Obama admits bipartisan capitalist "Washington consensus" fueled far-right & multiplied inequality. Available at: https://therealnews.com/obama-admits-bipartisan-capitalist-washing ton-consensus-fueled-far-right-multiplied-inequality.

OECD (n.d.). Promoting effective aid for trade. Available at: https://www.oecd.org/development/promotingeffectiveaidfortrade.htm.

OECD (2011). Busan partnership for effective development co-operation. Available at: https://www.oecd-ilibrary.org/docserver/54de7baa-en. pdf?expires=1633941988&id=id&accname=guest&checksum=B90E39 F7ED136E72F8160BECFDBF6EC9.

OECD (2020). Overview: Enabling civil society through effective development cooperation. Available at: https://www.oecd-ilibrary.org/sites/ f2aef4ad-en/index.html?itemId=/content/component/f2aef4ad-en.

OECD/UNDP (2014). *Making development co-operation more effective: 2014 progress report*, Paris: OECD Publishing. DOI:10.1787/97892642 09305-en.

People's Republic of China (2021). Main message. Available at: https:// sustainabledevelopment.un.org/index.php?page=view&type=30022& nr=81&menu=3170.

Rabena, A. J. (2018). The complex interdependence of China's belt and road initiative in the Philippines, *Asia and the Pacific Policy Studies*, Vol. 5, No. 3, pp. 683–697. DOI:10.1002/app5.257.

Reliefweb (2021). China, Myanmar and Bangladesh reach positive consensus on accelerating the repatriation of rohingya refugees, (21 Jan 2021). Available at: https://reliefweb.int/report/bangladesh/china-myanmar-and-bangladesh-reach-positive-consensus-accelerating-repat riation.

Republic of the Philippines. (2019). The 2019 voluntary national review of the Philippines. Available at: https://sustainabledevelopment.un.org/ content/documents/23366Voluntary_National_Review_2019_Philippines. pdf.

Stacey, R. and Griffin, D. (2005). Introduction: Leading in a complex world, in Griffin, D. and Stacey, R. (eds.), *Complexity and the Experience of Leading Organizations*, pp. 1–16, Routledge, Oxon, UK.

Straube, C. (2020). The belt and road initiative and civil-society participation, *Rosa Luxemburg Stiftung*. Available at: https://www.rosa lux.de/en/news/id/43409/the-belt-and-road-initiative-and-civil-society -participation?cHash=9476fa170bafcca504de90f5dd06370b.

Stiglitz, J. E. (1999). The World Bank at the millennium, *The Economic Journal*, Vol. 109, November, pp. F577–F597.

Syal, R., van Wessel, M. and Sahoo, S. (2021). Collaboration, co-optation or navigation? The role of civil society in disaster governance in India, *Voluntas*. DOI:10.1007/s11266-021-00344-8.

The World Bank (2002). *Globalization, Growth, and Poverty: Building an Inclusive World Economy. A World Bank Policy Research Report.* World Bank and Oxford University Press, Washington, DC. Available at: https://openknowledge.worldbank.org/handle/10986/14051.

The World Bank (2019). Belt and road economics: Opportunities and risks of transport corridors. Available at: https://www.world bank.org/en/topic/regional-integration/publication/belt-and-road-eco nomics-opportunities-and-risks-of-transport-corridors.

The World Bank (2021). Philippines: Mandanas ruling provides opportunities for improving service delivery through enhanced decentralization. Available at: https://www.worldbank.org/en/news/press-re lease/2021/06/10/philippines-mandanas-ruling-provides-opportunities-for-improving-service-delivery-through-enhanced-decentralization.

Titumir, R. A. M. and Rahman, M. Z. (2019a). Economic implications of China's belt and road initiative (BRI): The case of Bangladesh, *China and the World: Ancient and Modern Silk Road*, Vol. 2, No. 4, pp. 1–38. DOI:10.1142/S2591729319500214.

Titumir, R. A. M. and Rahman, M. Z. (2019b). Strategic implications of China's belt and road initiative (BRI): The case of Bangladesh, *China and the World: Ancient and Modern Silk Road*, Vol. 2, No. 3, pp. 1–59. DOI:10.1142/S2591729319500202.

Tomlinson, B. (2012). CSOs on the Road from Accra to Busan: CSO Initiatives to Strengthen Development Effectiveness. IBON Books, Philippines. Available at: https://concordeurope.org/wp-content/ uploads/2012/09/csos_on_the_road_from_accra_to_busan_final.pdf.

United Nations (UN) (2015). Millennium development goals report 2015. Available at: https://www.un.org/millenniumgoals/2015_MDG_ Report/pdf/MDG%202015%20rev%20(July%201).pdf.

United Nations (UN) (2020a). Sustainable development goals: Goal 17: Revitalize the global partnership for sustainable development. Available at: https://www.un.org/sustainabledevelopment/globalpartner ships/.

United Nations (UN) (2020b). COVID-19: Growth forecast at −3 per cent, as IMF offers debt relief to most vulnerable nations in Africa, Asia, Middle East and Caribbean. *UN News*, 14 April, 2020. Available at: https://news.un.org/en/story/2020/04/1061712.

United Nations (UN) (2021). Secretary-General, at United Nations Conference on Trade and Development Session, Urges Strategies to Address Debt, Climate Crises, Expand Fair Trade, Investment. Available at: https://www.un.org/press/en/2021/sgsm20950.doc.htm.

United Nations Conference on Trade and Development (UNCTAD) (2010). Trade and development report, 2010. Available at: https://unctad.org/ system/files/official-document/tdr2010_en.pdf.

United Nations Department of Economic and Social Affairs (UNDESA) (2020). Jointly building belt and road towards SDGs: Bangladesh. Available at: https://www.brisdgs.org/project-countries/bangladesh.

Weber, H. (2017). Politics of leaving no one behind: Contesting the 2020 sustainable development goals agenda, *Globalizations*, Vol. 14, No. 3, pp. 399–414. DOI:10.1080/14747731.2016.1275404.

Widakuswara, P. (2021). US to offer alternative to China's belt and road initiative. Available at: https://www.voanews.com/a/usa_us-offer-alternative-chinas-belt-and-road-initiative/6206928.html.

Wintour, P. (2021). G7 backs biden infrastructure plan to rival China's belt and road initiative. Available at: https://www.theguardian.com/world/2021/jun/12/g7-global-infrastructure-plan-to-rival-chinas-belt-and-road-initiative.

World Commission on Environment and Development (WCED) (1987). Our common future. Available at: https://sustainabledevelopment.un.org/milestones/wced.

World Trade Organization (WTO) (2019). *Aid for trade global review 2019.* Available at: https://www.wto.org/english/tratop_e/devel_e/a4t_e/gr19_e/glossy_summary_report_e.pdf.

World Trade Organization (WTO) (2020). The WTO and the sustainable development goals. Available at: from https://www.wto.org/english/thewto_e/coher_e/sdgs_e/sdgs_e.htm.

Chapter 5

Lessons from the Evolution of the Accounting Tool: From the Genesis up to the Roman Period

Christos Tsatsis[*]

Abstract

Littleton (1993) points out that "***Accounting is relative and progressive***. (...) *Older methods become less effective under altered conditions;* (...) *surrounding conditions generate fresh ideas* (...) *as such ideas and methods prove successful they in turn begin to modify the surrounding conditions*" (Littleton, 1933, p. 361).[1] We argue that "accounting crises", such as the use of the system in a way that was not designed or the voluntary disclosure of wrong data is, according to Littleton's terminology "new problems" that "older methods" are not designed for. The succession of accounting debt crises of the first 21st century is a perfect example of the history which continually repeats. To demonstrate this, the chapter aims to identify from the early history of accounting elements linked with economic crises and in response, how the accounting system does evolve. To fulfil this objective, we used a harmonised methodology in the four major periods for analysing accounting crises.

Keywords: Accounting; economy; history; financial disclosure; civilisation; evolution

---

[*]The author wants to thank Profs Faska Khrouz and Walter Hecq (+) for their support and Mrs. Meltem Caliscan and Nicole Blondeel for their material support. Finally, I would like to thank Prof Seifi for her sincere and friendly review and her outstanding patience which on the one hand made this chapter clearer and on the other hand allowed me to become a better writer.
[1]The full statement is reproduced in Section 5.

1. Introduction

Economists and finance specialists pay little attention to the techniques of accounting. Most of the time, they take financial statements for granted and they do not look further. Boyns and Edwards (1991) underlined the fact that ignorance of how and why data are compiled in such a way *can lead to erroneous conclusions* (Boyns and Edwards, 1991).

In this chapter, we would like to explain a few interrelationships between accounting statements and the finance world. To be more precise, how past financial crises and accounting scandals may modify the financial statement disclosures.

To answer this question, we take a historical approach to accounting. Practitioners, historians, and the public link accounting to the double-entry accounting technique (DEB), the father of which is Luca Pacioli with his work in 1494. This parallelism seems straightforward since almost all accounting techniques are based on the foundation of a double accounting system. We should, somehow, add two remarks to this general belief.

First, Pacioli in his book *simply described a method used by merchants in Venice during the Italian Renaissance period.* (Smith, 2013, Abstract). Yamey (1994) told us the story of Simone Boccanegra, who was elected Doge of the city of Genoa in 1339, where *the earliest surviving ledger is that of* 1340, *for long thought to have been the earliest example of double-entry bookkeeping (DEB).* (Yamey 1994, p. 376). Pacioli is not the founder but the first who describes this DEB system.

Second, all the accounting ledgers are not made in the double-entry technique. The recent survey of 2018 launched by the International Federation of Accountants reported that 37 *governments (25% of jurisdictions covered by the Index) reported on accrual in their last set of published financial statements* (IFAC, 2019, p. 2), while the others report on a cash basis. The link between accrual and DEB is that accrual drives DEB. Let's explain: Accruals are the moment a transaction is recognised when it occurs (IFAC, 1993, p. 4), while cash basis recognises a transaction when cash is paid or received. This simple change of moment of recognition shapes the ledgers that accounting is providing. For instance, in a cash basis, *the elements of the financial statement will be cash receipts, cash disbursements and cash balances* while in accruals *The elements of the financial statements will be assets, Liabilities, net assets/equity, revenues and expenses* (IFAC, 1993, p. 4), which can be generated only if a DEB is set up.[2]

But Pacioli's reputation as the father of modern private sector accounting is still valid. Even if he is not the inventor, his work was the first to describe the "Venetian account systems", which later became our "classic" double-entry accounting as our accounting teachers taught us.

This chapter will go back to the roots of accounting systems. We focus on the period prior to Pacioli's work and prior to double-entry accounting technique to just accounting which is *the process of identifying, measuring and communicating economic information.*[3]

Because accounting has more than 5,000 years of history,[4] and according to Walton (1995), *regulations are developed in incremental basis* knowing "why", "where", "when", and "how" should permit a better understanding of accountancy, its rules, and the impact of the accounting reporting on the "economy".

We focus on the evolution of accounting techniques over time in four ancient civilisations, namely Sumerian, Egyptian, Greek, and Roman, and their legacy on today's practises.

But since accounting is the reporting process of a whole economic/social and legal environment, we must make a broader analysis

---

[2]For instance, Germany uses only cash accounting to report their federal accounts. https://www.bundesfinanzministerium.de/Web/DE/Themen/Oeffentliche_Finanzen/Bundeshaushalt/Haushalts_und_Vermoegensrechnungen_des_Bundes/haushalts_vermoegensrechnungen_des_bundes.html.

[3]The American Accounting Association (1966) defined accounting as "*the process of identifying, measuring and communicating economic information to permit informed judgments and decisions by users of the information*" (American Accounting Association, 1966).

[4]Jean-Guy Degos, *Histoire de la comptabilité*, Que sais-je? (Presses Universitaires de France — PUF, 1998); John R. Alexander, "History of Accounting" (Association of Chartered Accountants in the United States, n.d.); Douglas Garbutt, "The origins of Accounting and Writing", *The Accounting Historians Notebook* 4, No. 2 (1981): 10–11.

to understand how accounting system operates. To do it, we analyse each civilisation in sections, and each section is divided into smaller subsections:

- The first subsection describes the general context of the period. Accounting is a way to describe exchange, trade, facts, and the general context is likely to influence this technique.
- The second subsection describes the technical evolution of the period. Since accounting has to be materialised in a support, the technical evolution of civilisation plays an important role in the accounting technique.
- The third subsection describes the accounting characteristics themselves. Those characteristics are both influenced by the general context and the techniques available at this time.
- The fourth subsection explains the accounting innovations, which helps us to understand how and why the accounting techniques evolve in that way. This section is influenced by all three previous subsections.
- The fifth subsection tells us how the accounting education is done and how the accounting profession is organised. The education is meant to transmit actual knowledge and practises to new generations.
- The sixth subsection describes how control — what we call today as audit — in accounting was done.[5]
- The seventh subsection describes accounting pitfalls/frauds discovered and how we deal with them.
- The last subsection is a wrap-up of all previous subsections.

In that context, two assumptions should be made. First, this chapter is not an exhaustive review; for decades, scientists have added their own contribution to history. In our analysis, we tried to consider the most recent contributions with some intrusions into older works. Second, this is not a historian's chapter; this means that the facts we analyse are "the general accepted historical facts", disregarding controversies that historians have raised. In this work, we explore

---

[5]The only exception is in the Greek Civilisation. Subsection 4 deals with *public accounting*, while Subsection 6 deals with *banking accounting*.

how accounting crises can shape the accounting practises using past accounting crisis example and their accounting evolution.

2. Sumerian Civilisation

2.1. *General context*

History Begins at Sumer (Kramer, 1973). Sumerian civilisation has prospered in Mesopotamia since the 4th millenary BC. The spatial situation between the Tigris and the Euphrates rivers allowed agriculture to flourish but only to a certain extent. Their poor soil put pressure on the Mesopotamians to import almost every raw material. This very particular situation allows the commercial exchanges[6] to grow fast as well as to develop in parallel an efficient system of exchange and organise trade (Oppenheim, 1954).

2.2. *Technical evolution*

The development of writing and laws allowed trade to grow. A very interesting example is the code of Hammurabi (2000 BC) in which, according to Vlaemminck (1956), we can already find passages which proves the existence of bookkeeping.[7] Keister (1963) stipulates that the development of the civilisation seemed constant: *There were almost no significant changes in these (accounting) records* (Robson, 2004).

2.3. *Accounting characteristics*

Ancient Mesopotamians were obsessive bookkeepers (Garbutt, 1981, p. 11). The use of receipt tablets, debt records, purchase tablets,

---

[6]As stated by Carmona and Ezzamel (2007), *In both civilizations (Mesopotamia and Egypt), some of the key elements suggested by Polanyi were present; well-defined market locales, buyers and sellers exchanging commodities at agreed prices but without coinage mediating the exchange, and markets that satisfied local needs.* (Carmona and Ezzamel, 2007, p. 181).

[7]Original text in French is *Déjà dans le monument juridique d'Hammourabi, on trouve des textes qui attestent la tenue des comptes, tel celui qui est relatif au contrat de commission et qui semble bien constituer l'obligation légale, sinon de la tenue d'une véritable comptabilité, tout au moins, de l'enregistrement en forme de comptes de certaines transactions* (Vlaemminck, 1956, p. 15).

allowance tablets, pay list tables, and inventory records were very common (Keister, 1963). Mesopotamians also used to make summary disclosures (Degos, 1998). All those tablets seemed to be used as proof and the need for control was permanent. Vlaemminck (1956) wrote that some tablets were authentic and in some others, marks such as checks were often found. The technique used by the scribes was very accurate.[8] The accounts had all the elements of today's actual accounts (Vlaemminck, 1956). Cossu (1996) learned that accounts were made on a daily basis and annual disclosures permit establishing the physical balance sheet (Cossu, 1996).

2.4. *Accounting innovations*

Tablets appeared only in the 4th millennium BC (Schmandt-Besserat, 1982, p. 875). Before that, as the technology was not available, Sumerians used tokens in order to record commercial transactions (Garbutt, 1981). According to Carmona and Ezzamel (2007), Mattessich's work shows that *each token shape is a type of account, and the number of tokens contained in a clay envelope or on a string indicates the quantity of specific items* (Carmona and Ezzamel, 2007, p. 185). Later, those tokens were sealed inside a clay envelope which, according to Mattessich, was the correspondence of contents[9] which permits a tautological and physical control.

2.5. *Accounting education*

The training of scribes was accurate in order to achieve their future duties. As Carmona and Ezzamel wrote, *Scribes who were*

---

[8] *According to Rivero Menendez (2000, p. 283), it was customary to call the scribe to the temple, palace, or private domain to record commercial transactions, irrespective of their volume. Written accounts of transactions were signed by the transaction parties, witnesses and the scribe* (Carmona and Ezzamel, 2007, p. 185).

[9] *The symmetry between the tokens on the inside and the impressions on the surface of the envelope confirms the correspondence to modern double-entry where most physical manifestations are recorded on the debit side while social relations appear on the credit side* (Mattessich, 1998, pp. 3–4).

carefully trained to acquire the necessary literary and arithmetic skills and were held responsible for documenting commercial transactions (Carmona and Ezzamel, 2007, p. 183).

2.6. *Control*

Last but not least, we should point out that Sumerians used an early system of cost accounting and budgeting procedures applying the notion of "standard costs" (Mattessich, 1998; Carmona and Ezzamel, 2007). We should also underline the belated role of temples which, with time, became both a marketplace and an early bank relay (Vlaemminck, 1956; Cossu, 1996).

2.7. *Accounting pitfall/frauds*

Furthermore, writing on clay was an *irreversible process* (Vlaemminck, 1956), and *the fragility of the writing support material was a warranty of its own authenticity since attempting to falsify it would probably destroy (the tablet).*[10]

2.8. *Wrap-up*

Sumerian civilisation gave to modern historians the very first evidence of an organised system based on trade. Advanced systems of exchanges recorded in tokens and clay tablets are some great pieces of evidence.

3. Egyptian Civilisation

3.1. *General context*

As Ezzamel said, **Egyptians** also have an *obsession with bureaucratic details* (Ezzamel, 1997, p. 564). Unlike the Sumerians, commerce is not the issue but a centralised power system highly influenced by the temples and the royal palace (Carmona and Ezzamel, 2007, p. 189). A very strong centralised system, which controls many activities, needs

---

[10]Translated from French is *La fragilité même du matériau était une garantie de sa sécurité puisqu'une tentative de falsification avait des grandes chances d'entrainer sa destruction* (Degos, 1998, p. 11).

a very strong internal control and auditing system (Wilkinson, 1999; Ezzamel, 1997, 2005; Stone, 1969). *Although the state and temples dominated the economic landscape of ancient Egypt, a significant private sphere also exited* (Carmona and Ezzamel, 2007, p. 184).[11]

3.2. *Technical evolution*

Techniques also evolved since Sumer. The abundance of papyrus permits a large control system to be installed[12]; a more complex form of writing called hieratic (a simplified version of hieroglyphs) and a decimal counting system giving the ability to master the four basic operations allow them to master the record-keeping activities.[13] As shown by Ezzamel's work, accounting in Egypt did evolve during the 4,000 years of Egyptian era.[14] However, we can say that during this period, the major change was the Greek influence on Egypt.[15] We thus first discuss the Egypt accounting system and then analyse later the Greek influence on this country.

3.3. *Accounting characteristics*

Accounting in Egypt was broadly used in public and private spheres.[16] Accounting documents include *journals, ledgers, lists and*

---

[11]More discussion about this topic could be found in the works of Ezzamel (1994, 1997).

[12]*Record keeping was facilitated by the abundance of cheap writing material.* (Hain, 1966, p. 701).

[13]Hayes (1961) wrote that *Numerous sample problems in arithmetic, worked out and explained in this papyrus, show that the Egyptian of the Middle Kingdom was well acquainted with the four arithmetical operations-addition, subtraction, multiplication, and division — could handle fractions, and possessed a well-defined system of decimal notations* (Ezzamel, 1994, p. 234).

[14]We should point out that, according to Ezzamel, during the Egyptian era, the power of a centralised system was very strong in the Old Kingdom during 2700–2200 BC, declined during the Middle Kingdom (2080–1780 BC) *reaching its most extreme form during parts of that period when tax commission became the only real link between central government and the provinces* (Ezzamel, 1997, p. 570), and regained its centralised power with the New Kingdom (1552 BC).

[15]Even if, according to historians, the Greek period of Egypt officially starts at 332 BC with the invasion by Alexander the Great.

[16]Ezzamel note that *As numerous sources (...) make clear, detailed accounting records were kept not only for taxation purposes but also to document daily*

tables with multiple columns (Ezzamel, 1994, p. 237). Like for the Sumerians, those documents served to record transactions as proof[17] (Ezzamel, 1997). As explained by Carmona and Ezzamel, *accounts were kept on a daily basis, with separate columns for each type of commodity, and they matched daily supplies and provisions* (Carmona and Ezzamel, 2007, p. 190).

3.4. *Accounting innovations*

Accounting innovations, such as specific terminology (Ezzamel, 2005, p. 29) or the use of alternative ink (red and black), allowed to improve visibility (Ezzamel, 2005, p. 39; Carmona and Ezzamel, 2007, p. 190). The use of columns helps to note on the same line and follow and clear debts and duties. Like Sumer, Egypt was a "non-monetary economy"; but this seems not to be a problem since the Egyptians introduced a standardised unit of measurement, "the shat" (Degos, 1998, p. 24; Vlaemminck, 1956, p. 22), later on replaced by the Deben which is a multiplier of the Shat[18] (Daumas, 1977, pp. 427–428).

3.5. *Accounting education*

The scribe had a central role in this system. According to Stone (1969), his duty was to record, audit, and forecast activities.[19] A very long training period of 15 years permitted him to master fields such as writing, counting, and measuring. Ezzamel suggests that organised scribe schools were common since the Middle Kingdom

---

income for temples, lists of inventory for equipment and personal wealth, wages of workers on the necropolis sites, barter transactions in village markets, and detailed activities in other state institutions such as dockyards, workshops and breweries (Ezzamel, 1997, p. 564).

[17] *Accounting was [also] called upon to facilitate the quantification, documentation and reporting of the performance of subordinates* (Ezzamel, 1997, p. 573).

[18] The shat equals 7.5 g of gold, while the deben equals 12 shats which is 90 grams of gold (Daumas, 1977, pp. 427–428).

[19] *A developed bureaucratic system reveals and actively promotes a specific human trait: a deep satisfaction in devising routines tor measuring, inspecting, checking, and thus as far as possible controlling other people's activities. (...) It draws upon a particular aptitude, as distinctive and important for a society as the genius of its artisans and architects, or the bravura of military men. We call a member of this class a "scribe"* (Kemp, 1989, p. 111).

(Ezzamel, 1994). Ancient teachers probably used standardised manuals, such as the "Rhind Mathematical Papyrus" (Degos, 1998, pp. 22–23; Vlaemminck, 1956, p. 21).

3.6. *Control*

Greek influence in Egypt is visible since 500 BC. Greeks imported into Egypt tools and techniques they used in Greece. Those included a new language (the demotic), probably a new numerical system, a monetary system (coins), and a modern banking system with the use of bank transfers.[20] It is also during this period, in Egypt, that we find the first clear evidence of accounting manipulation. The Zenon Papyri[21] demonstrate a perfect task division. Accounts were made on a daily basis, and a new balance appeared after every operation. Audit evidence is found in accounting ledgers. Those are small dots in front of accounting operations to mark that a verification is made. Audits could also lead to corrections or margin notes in ledgers. Audits were also used to track assets[22] or expenses.

3.7. *Accounting pitfall/frauds*

Audits were also made for track fraud.[23] Scribes had to implement a very strong "internal control system".[24] Fraud was very severely

---

[20] *At debit of Appolonios, 700 drachms he owes to Ariston, son of Antipatros At the credit of Ariston, son of Antiparotros, 700 drachms* (Vlaemminck, 1956, p. 23; Cossu, 1996, p. 26).

[21] *A collection of more than one thousand documents, are mainly concerned with the private estate of Apollonios, who was the chief financial minister of Ptolemy Philadelphos* (Hain, 1966, p. 699).

[22] Ezzamel (1997) shows us an example of an audit: *Deliveries of grain from the granaries to the bakery were reconciled with deliveries of bread from the bakery to the storehouse by matching numbers of loaves expected (using appropriate conversion ratios) against those delivered, and corroborating this by reference to the total weight of bread in deben* (Ezzamel, 1997, p. 582).

[23] An example is reported by Hain (1966) which *the supervisor who detected the fraud promptly reports it to Zenon and asks him to make sure that a similar situation does not arise again* (Hain, 1966, p. 701).

[24] *Lines were drawn by the inspectors to indicate that inspection took place* (Carmona and Ezzamel, 2007, p. 190).

punished.[25] Fraud examples could be found in the Heronimos archives. Bingen work (1951) reported by Vlaemminck revealed how Egyptians were able to record fictitious operations (Bingen, 1951). For instance, Vlaemminck reports that damaged goods continued to be kept in stocks until the day that an inspector discovered the "disaster" (Vlaemminck, 1956, pp. 26–27). Other examples demonstrate that some sales were fictitious operations. Indeed, workers were paid with wine; Heronimos wrote in his books, on the one hand, that wages were paid in coins and, on the other hand, that wine was sold.

3.8. *Wrap-up*

Egyptian scribes were able to produce full-length accounting books. Accounts were used not only to record information but also, in order to track performance, to make forecasting and improve productivity. In this centralised economy, audits were frequent, and negligence was severely reprimanded. Greek influence brought about major changes in Egyptian civilisation.

4. Greek Civilisation

Ancient Greece covers a period from the first civilisation of Mycenae in the 17th century BC until the Roman period of the 1st century BC. We focus on the accounts of Athens during the 5th century BC. Athens at this time was the first democracy in the world; the activities of the citizens consisted of "public affairs", arts and crafts industry, and farming. The central position of Athens in Greece (and the development of Piraeus Harbor[26]) helped commerce to flourish.

---

[25]Wilson (1951) wrote that *This was not a code of law, but rather a series of police regulations directed against specific malpractices and also a reorganization of the administrative machinery in the land, in order to control future abuses... The punishments meted out are very harsh for minor cases of plundering or corruption. The alarming spread of official dishonesty must have called forth an extreme severity of penalties* (Wilson, 1951).

[26]*42. Again, since the different populations did not in any case possess a country that was self-sufficing, each lacking in some things and producing others in excess*

This was facilitated by the probably very first "full coined economy" and a very strong coin, the silver drachma (Vlaemminck, 1956, p. 33). In Athens, democracy influenced public accounting and the coined money played a major role in the development of banking in Greece.

Greeks used not only papyrus but also ostraca (which are fragments of pottery), stones, and marble (Harris, 1994). We should not forget the millions of pages written by Greek philosophers, thinkers, poets, and public personalities. The development of mathematics also played an important role in the Greek economy since mathematics allows banks to make basic financial computations (Cossu, 1996, p. 27). Since that time until 330 BC and Alexander the Great, every city was a different state; differences existed not only across time but also space.[27] For our analysis, we only focus on the most elaborate ancient Greek accounting technique in the 5th century BC in Athens.

Accounting in ancient Greece was dual; there was a public accounting relating to the city accounts and a private accounting related to the bank accounts. Public accounting documents included paradosis,[28] accounts of public works, money-lending records, records

---

of their needs, and since they were greatly at a loss where they should dispose of their surplus and whence they should import what they lacked, in these difficulties also our city came to the rescue; for she established the Piraeus as a market in the center of Hellas — a market of such abundance that the articles which it is difficult to get, one here, one there, from the rest of the world, all these it is easy to procure from Athens trans. (Isocrates, 1928) translated from (George Norlin). Original text can be found in Appendix 1.1 http://www.perseus.tufts.edu/hopper/text?d oc=Perseus%3Atext%3A1999.01.0143%3Aspeech%3D4%3Asection%3D42.

[27]We argue that radical changes made in the 6th and 5th centuries BC would influence accounting techniques, and for this particular reason, we state that accounting in Mycenae in the 16th century BC (writing in Linear B) was not the same type of accounting as that in Athens in 5th century BC; accounting in space seems to be quite homogeneous; for instance, inscriptions found in marble in many temples such as Delphi does not vary much from those in Parthenon.

[28]Paradosis ("delivery, receipt" in Greek) was a particularity of Athens. Public accounts were kept by Athenian citizens. Those citizens were chosen randomly for one year. At the end of this year, they hand over the accounts to the next ones. The accounting books of their duty were called "paradosis" which means "rendition" (Harris, 1994).

of income, and records of expenditure (Davies, 1994, p. 207). Private banking accounting documents include the ephimerides and trapezitika gramateia.[29] Although commerce and recording were very developed in ancient Athens, we have very little information concerning their "books". As Athens was dug during the last two centuries in search of evidence, the lack of information could mean that even if there was an organised form of private accounting or accounting practises, they did not survive so far.

Public accounting was based on democratic principles.[30] Harris pointed out that during the tyrannical period in Athens, public accounting was cancelled. Public account recordings on papyrus and tablets were numerous,[31] while information disclosed on marble concerned exclusively sacred accounts. The city was administered by 10 public treasurers who were chosen by lot; they had the duty to preserve and to increase the national treasure, and they could also levy taxes and pay the city expenditures. Most of the time, accounting documents are inventories which facilitate the audit. Audit was also a privilege of democracy, as citizens randomly chosen were put on duty to control accounts. Moreover, the final word belongs to citizens who can raise any question to the treasurers in front of the assembly.[32] This random control seems to be the first historical evidence of a regular control by a revenue court "the Logistai Court" complemented, in second place by an audit organisation, "the Euptymes College". We should also add that Athens society was one of the first civilisations to set up control of

---

[29] According to Vlaemminck (1956, p. 31) and Cossu (1996, p. 28), the literally, first word means *journals* and the second terms *words book of banks*.

[30] *Publication was a prerequisite for democracy* (Hansen, 1991).

[31] *Master lists of the registry of citizens, tax incomes and expense accounts, city religious calendars and priest lists and more documents for housekeeping purposes of administration must have been written records* (Harris, 1994, p. 216).

[32] *The ten treasurers sent their records to a board of ten accountants (logistai) and ten advocates (synēgoroi), both groups selected by lot, for review. A finding of maladministration would result in a trial before a jury for theft. If the financial records proved accurate, the ten Treasurers then appeared before the Boule. Any citizen could voice a complaint at this public hearing* (Harris, 1994, p. 214).

the marketplace in order to protect customers, which maybe another heritage of democracy.[33]

Harris raised here a major controversy in Athens economy court decisions and other administrative acts were published: *There is no indication that the Athenian democracy valued or promoted mass literacy: above all, there was no state subsidized education* (Hedrick Jr., 1994, p. 164). But why could a system which chooses their public managers randomly afford not to educate them? A selection existed since candidates were chosen according to their background.[34]

Unlike Sumer and Egypt where bankers were priests, in Greece, they were metics.[35] Banking in ancient Greece was first created to fulfil the need of exchange. From that time, until the late 5th century BC, every city state pressed its own silver coins (Flament, 2007). The little information we have about accounting in ancient Greek banks suggests that bookkeeping was meticulous, accurate, and honest, which was very often quoted as proof of tribunals (Cossu, 1996; Migeotte, 2007; Vlaemminck, 1956). Greek bankers recorded in their register all amounts they handled with entry and exit dates; every

---

[33][1] *Also Market-controllers are elected by lot, five for Peiraeus and five for the city. To these the laws assign the superintendence of all merchandise, to prevent the sale of adulterated and spurious articles.* [2] *Also ten Controllers of Measures are appointed by lot, five for the city and five for Peiraeus, who superintend all measures and weights, in order that sellers may use just ones.* [3] *Also there used to be ten Corn-wardens elected by lot, five for Peiraeus and five for the city, but now there are twenty for the city and fifteen for Peiraeus. Their duties are first to see that unground corn in the market is on sale at a fair price, and next that millers sell barley-meal at a price corresponding with that of barley, and baker-women loaves at a price corresponding with that of wheat, and weighing the amount fixed by the officials — for the law orders that these shall fix the weights.* [4] *They elect by lot ten Port-superintendents, whose duty is to superintend the harbor-markets and to compel the traders to bring to the city two-thirds of the sea-borne corn that reaches the corn-market.* (Aristotle, 1920) Translation of (H. Rackham) translated by H. Rackham. Cambridge, MA, Harvard University Press 1954. Original text can be found in Appendix 1.2 http://www.perseus.tufts.edu/hopper/text?doc= Perseus%3Atext%3A1999.01.0045%3Achapter%3D51.

[34]Harris (1994) specifies that *Were drawn from the wealthiest class of citizens which ensured that they had some experience in dealing with money and finance* (Harris, 1994, p. 218).

[35]Free men who were non-citizens of Athens.

customer also had an account opened to his name with one page for assets and one page for liabilities[36]; Demosthenes, in one of his defence speeches, shows us how banks operate.[37] Greek banks used bank transfers and checks, while deposits and borrowing activities were promoted by the absence of regulation in interest rates.

Evidence of accounting manipulations appeared in the classic writer's work. Manipulations occur both in the private and public lives. In public life, an example of Timotheus shows us how he introduced copper coins, pretending that they have the same value as silver.[38] In private accounting, we have an example of Agyrrhius trying to avoid taxation.[39]

---

[36] Even if the Sumerians and Babylonians, also recorded operations for "third party", it was the first time in history that we have evidences of a personal account (in comparison to general accounts) (Vlaemminck, 1956, p. 32).

[37] *He instructed Archebiades and Phrasias to point him out and introduce him to my father, when he should return from his journey. It is the custom of all bankers, when a private person deposits money and directs that it be paid to a given person, to write down first the name of the person making the deposit and the amount deposited, and then to write on the margin "to be paid to so-and-so"; and if they know the face of the person to whom payment is to be made, they do merely this, write down whom they are to pay; but, if they do not know it, it is their custom to write on the margin the name also of him who is to introduce and point out the person who is to receive the money.* (Demosthenes, 1939) Translation of Demosthenes from Norman W. DeWitt, Ph.D., and Norman J. DeWitt, Ph.D. Cambridge, MA, Harvard University Press 1949 original text can be found in Appendix 1.3 (Demosthenes 1949) http://www.perseus.tufts.edu/hopper/text?d oc=Perseus%3Atext%3A1999.01.0080%3Aspeech%3D52%3Asection%3D4.

[38] *Timotheus of Athens during his campaign against Olynthus was short of silver, and issued to his men a copper coinage instead. On their complaining, he told them that all the merchants and retailers would accept it in lieu of silver. But the merchants he instructed to buy in turn with the copper they received such produce of the land as was for sale, as well as any booty brought to them; such copper as remained on their hands he would exchange for silver.* (Aristotle, 1935) Translated by G. C. Armstrong. Cambridge, MA, Harvard University Press original text could be found in Appendix 1.4 http://www.perseus.tufts.edu/hopper/text?doc =Perseus%3Atext%3A1999.01.0048%3Abook%3D2%3Asection%3D1350a.

[39] [133] *I will tell you the reason for this change of front. Last year and the year before our honest Agyrrhius here was chief contractor for the two per cent customs duties. He farmed them for thirty talents, and the friends he meets under the poplar all took shares with him. You know what they are like; it is my belief that they meet there for a double purpose: to be paid for not raising the bidding,*

Athens was the only city to date where almost any information was freely available in the public space. From this city full of paradoxes, we retain that democracy brings public disclosure and public control. Athens was also the first full monetary economy. This permits Athenian banks to bloom by creating some basic practises. This development was also the result of politics which helped commerce grow without any barriers while state institutions were created to protect citizens and keep an eye on abuses and frauds.

5. Roman Civilisation

The Roman era was from 753 BC (the birth of Rome) to AD 476 (the fall of the Roman Empire of Occident). The Roman legacy includes numerous archives, such as law texts, accounting documents, and defence/accusation speeches (mostly from Cicero). Roman documents describe themselves as a nation where details and meticulousness were the basic characteristics of their accounting.

Technical evolution includes abacus which facilitates the computation tasks (Minaud, 2005, p. 188), but also, the Roman numbers themselves were a major revolution since *on hard surfaces they render falsification work more difficult.*[40] Evidence pointed out by

---

and to take shares in taxes which have been knocked down cheap. [134] *After making a profit of six talents, they saw what a gold-mine the business was; so they combined, gave rival bidders a percentage, and again offered thirty talents. There was no competition; so I went before the Council and outbid them, until I purchased the rights for thirty-six talents. I had ousted them. I then furnished you with sureties, collected the tax, and settled with the state. I did not lose by it, as my partners and I actually made a small profit. At the same time I stopped Agyrrhius and his friends from sharing six talents which belonged to you.* (Antiphon and Andocides, 1941) Translated from Antiphon Andocides, English translation by K. J. Maidment, M.A. Cambridge, MA, Harvard University Press; London, William Heinemann Ltd. 1968. Original text could be found in Appendix 1.5 http://www.perseus.tufts.edu/hopper/text?doc=Perseus%3Atext%3A1999.0 1.0018%3Aspeech%3D1%3Asection%3D134.

[40] Free translation by the author, original text is *le système des chiffres romains* (...) *rend les falsifications plus difficiles sur les matériaux durs* (Cossu, 1996, p. 30).

Minaud's work reveals that there are almost no changes in accounting principles during the Roman period.

Accounting books of Rome were the "aduersaria" and the "codex accepti et expensi". Cicero describes how Roman accounting worked.[41] Purser sums up accounting in Rome: *Each Roman citizen had at least two accounts books. Aduersaria: a kind of waste book, or a day-book, the Italian Memoriale, in which he entered day by day, according as they occurred, the several transactions in which he took part (...) The codex accepti et expensi, also called tabulae, codices, domestic ratio, into which, the entries of aduersaria were carefully posted each month* (Purser, 1887, p. 209).

Romans had set the details in accounting very thoroughly; they already used classifications by nature, third-party accounts, and double-entry accounts (but not double-entry bookkeeping). Six hundred years later, all those factors will contribute to the rise of double-entry bookkeeping in Italy while some other features such as qualitative budgeting were "rediscovered" in the 20th century (Minaud, 2005).

There is no evidence of specialised education in accounting (Minaud, 2005, p. 25). However, Roman elementary school education was teaching basic mathematics which, according to Cicero, was enough for computing.[42]

---

[41] *II. (...) Why is it that we write down memoranda carelessly, that we make up account-books carefully? For what reason? Because the one is to last a month, the other for ever; these are immediately expunged, those are religiously preserved; these embrace the recollection of a short time, those pledge the good faith and honesty of a man for ever; these are thrown away, those are arranged in order. Therefore, no one ever produced memoranda at a trial; men do produce accounts, and read entries in books.* Translation from (Cicero, 1903). Original text could be found in Appendix 1.6 http://perseus.uchicago.edu/perseus-cgi/citequery3.pl?d bname=LatinAugust2012&getid=1&query=Cic.%20Q.%20Rosc.%204.

[42] [5] *in summo apud illos honore geometria fuit, itaque nihil mathematicis inlustrius; at1 nos metiendi ratiocinandique utilitate huius artis terminavimus modum.* (Charles Duke Yonge, 1877) Translation of Cicero *Geometry was in high esteem with them, therefore none were more honorable than mathematicians. But we have confined this art to bare measuring and calculating,* Cicero's *Tusculan Disputations: Also Treatises On The Nature Of The Gods And On The Commonwealth* (New York: Harper and Brothers, Publishers, 1877).

The Roman paterfamilias (head of the family) was the only one who had, by law, the obligation to hold a codex[43]; this document was so important that in the case of a trial, codex was used as a proof.[44]

Accounting manipulations were also present in Roman economy; Cicero's orations give us several examples; we take up two of them. The first is about Fonteius. He was a quaestor who abused a law permitting Roman citizens to pay only one-fourth of the old tax debts. Fonteius managed to "record" new debts he received as old ones and keep three-fourths for himself (Minaud, 2005, p. 45; Vlaemminck, 1956, p. 36). The other example quoted by Minaud relates to the case of Longinus, who was on duty in Spain. He taxed the citizens heavily, but he allowed the amounts to be transferred to his own account as a loan instead of a tax levy (Minaud, 2005, pp. 140–141).

Roman civilisation was probably the only one which imposed citizens to keep a very specific set of accounts.[45] The meticulousness and the detail that the Romans applied to their books probably made the Roman Empire the precursor of medieval Italian accounting (which gave birth to the double-entry bookkeeping). But, between those periods, in the dark ages, we have no evidence of any elaborate accounting systems in Western Europe.

---

[43] *Tabulas qui in patris potestate est nullas conficit.* Traduction of (Cicero, 1903) *In the first place, he, who is still under the power of his father, keeps no accounts.*
[44] [175] *And that these things were done in this manner, you may know, O judges, both from the public documents of the cities, and from their public testimonies; in all which you will find nothing false, nothing invented as suited to the times. Everything which we speak of is entered in the returns and made up in a regular manner, without any interpolations or irregularities being foisted into the people's accounts, but while they are all made up with deliberation and accuracy* (Cicero, 1903). Original text could be found in Appendix 1.7. http://perseus.uchicago.edu/perseus-cgi/citequery3.pl?dbname=PerseusLatinTexts&getid=1&query=Cic.%20Ver.%202.3.175.
[45] Later, those obligations will be only for private companies.

6. Discussion

Based on the Littleton statement, which is our guideline, we can argue that accounting techniques are influenced (1) by the political and economic environment and (2) by the technology available. Those evidences are also present in the periods we study in this contribution.

The <u>environment</u> shapes accounting. We saw that factors such as laws, economy, and central power tend to shift the emphasis of accounting. The brightest example is the Greek democracy which required that public information was publicly disclosed. This "simple requirement" had a dramatic effect on the way that accountancy was recorded, as it led to basic requirements such as what type of information to disclose, how to disclose it, in which periodicity, who will be in charge, and how to control the accuracy of given information.

<u>Technology</u> also plays a major role in accountancy. The term technology should be understood here in a broad sense. This includes the writing and numerical system, the writing support, any helping device, science development, commerce development, and the layout of books. Technology determines accounting characteristics. Let's take again our Athenian example: Even if there were institutions in Sumer and Egypt that lent and borrowed resources,[46] banks actually developed in Greece due to environmental and technological facts, such as (1) full coined economy, (2) advances in mathematics, and (3) regulations. Coins (and monetary economy) enhance commerce since there is no need to find a deal to exchange two goods but also because coins can be carried easily; advances in mathematics with free regulations allow bankers to assess their risk and offer the appropriate interest rates. This allowed banks to raise funds from deposits (that) they can borrow. This situation forced bankers to "set up" a new way to keep their accounts by which they can check the status of every customer (personal accounts).

---

[46]Since Egyptian and Sumerian civilisations were not always a "coined civilisation", we prefer to use *resources* instead of *money*.

Table 1 summarises the descriptors we selected in the introduction by periods. The table is organised by using the seven subsections described in Introduction, with Subsections 1 and 4 divided for better visibility.

6.1. *Drivers for changes*

But accounting systems, just like the society they reflect, are not perfect. They may no longer reflect the actual environment or else be challenged by people who try (legally or not) to overcome the system.

Napier (2001) stated that *accounting methods become obsolescent partly because of changes in the available technologies for accounting — methods developed in the manual or punch card era can be refined greatly in the computer era — but also because of changes in the nature of the problem for which accounting is the proposed solution* (Napier, 2001, p. 18). During this early period, we have the example of Sumer which changed from a token accounting to a writing accounting after the invention of writing (and probably the invention of clay tablets). Those changes are traditionally slow to operate but usually create "major improvements" in accounting techniques.

The second type of change is driven by the fact that the accounting system has pitfalls[47] that people will use (legally or not) in order to make an unexpected profit. This was the case with the introduction of copper money in Greece. In such situations, the accounting system will both integrate the practise as legal and create the appropriate checks and balances. In Greece, copper money was introduced little after Timotheus, but it represents a smaller quantity than silver coins (Flament, 2007) — or it will reinforce law and controls in order to avoid the practise. This was one of the consequences of 2007–2009 IAS/IFRS crises with fair-value notions. Those changes are usually fast but do not change (only improve) the current accounting system.

---

[47]In the abstract, we called them "accounting crises".

Table 1.   Accounting evolution over the past period.

	1. General environment	1b. Writing, counting system	2. Technical evolutions	3. Accounting characteristics
Mesopotamia, 4000–538 BC	Commerce, market for exchange physical goods	Tokens, clay tablets, cuneiform writing, base-60 counting system	From tokens to writing (on clay)	Tablets used as proof, accounts, balances, recapitulations, etc.
Egypt, 3100–332 BC; Greek period, 332 BC–AD 642	Mostly religious (importance of temples); mainly exchange of goods but coins were introduced by Greeks	Mostly papyrus hieratic (demotic in the Greek period) writing a base-10 counting system. Four basic operations were used	From clay to papyrus	Accounting was broadly used, mostly lists counting several columns
Greece, 1700–100 BC	Democracy, commerce, rise of monetary economics	Greek alphabet and counting system, use of stones, ostraca, and papyru	Development of mathematics permitting exact computation in borrowing system	Public accounting: mostly budgeting accountant with public disclose and public control. Banks: use of personal accounts
Rome, 753 BC–AD 476	Civilisation ruled by laws, with a powerful centralised system which shapes citizen behaviour, No monetary unicity	Roman alphabet and writing system, no decimal system, same writing support as Greece	Abacus, Roman numbers permitted to avoid falsification	Citizens were obliged to keep books. Two books were held, one as a memorandum and one as a general book

(*Continued*)

Table 1. (Continued).

	4. Accounting evolutions	4b. Commercial evolutions	5. Accounting education	6. Control/audit	7. Fraud
Mesopotamia, 4000–538 BC	Unifying norms of performance. First cost accounting and budgeting techniques	Credit letter, borrowing system	Careful training of scribes for literary and arithmetic skills	The first auditors: physical control, checks, copies of counts for control	The fragility of material avoids falsification. Writing was an irreversible process
Egypt, 3100–332 BC. Greek period, 332 BC–AD 642	Standardised unit of measurement (shekel), visual improvements through the use of different inks	In Greek period, bank transfer and checks	Organised education of scribes (high studies)	Very developed since it was a way for central administration to control economic activities	Writing tricks was already known (Heroninos accounts), but a severe system of control and sanctions existed
Greece, 1700–100 BC	First revenue court and audit organisation in history. Use of personal accounts	Introduction of the first coins. First real banks; free market with regulations for the most "weaker"	No evidence of specific accounting training	Fulfilled by the people (demos) in the public affairs. No evidence of a bank audit	Heavily tracked by the boulae, the board of logistion and astymonian (police)
Rome, 753 BC–AD 476	Nature classification, third-party accounts, double entry accounts, auxiliary books	Accounting books were (almost) an irrefutable proof of justice	No training in accounting but a basic mathematics for computation tasks	No evidence of a centralised system of auditing	From Cicero, we can argue that law and courts were on the watch for frauds

The third type of change is initiated by frauds. It concerns people who will deliberately disclose false information to "fool" third parties. Heronimos archives and Longinus' manner of levying tax are some examples we exposed in this chapter. Usually, this kind of situation will require a very quick response but will not change at all the accounting system since it is neither obsolete nor challenged. Only improvement will be a reinforcement of internal and external controls, besides both examples were discovered during an external control.

7. Accounting Pitfalls and their Response

In this work, we explore how accounting crises can shape the accounting practises using past accounting crisis examples and their accounting evolution.

The following Table 2 summarises the different pitfalls that could occur in the accounting system.

We should point out that the whole chapter is based on historical facts. Those facts highlight the habits of ancient societies. This means that our knowledge is based on facts that (1) we found and (2) we could decode. History should have been seen as an actual interpretation of testimonies found by archaeologists and interpreted by specialists. Our interpretation is, therefore, a reconstructed reality of ancient times based on previous works.

8. Conclusion

Based on the Littleton statement, which is our guideline for this study, we have seen that accounting, political and economic environment, and technology influence each other. Like this, accounting is really relative and progressive.

We have seen that altered conditions in the accounting practise, such as pitfalls, frauds or a new technique, have all different levels of threads in accounting practise. This leads either to the embracement of this new tool, or to the improvement of the actual technique, or to the avoidance of such practise by an enforcement of the rule or the law.

Table 2. Accounting pitfalls and their response.

Diagnostic	Practises don't reflect the actual environment	Pitfalls occurring in the common practises but they are legal	Pitfalls occurring in the common practises and they are illegal	Frauds are discovered
Solution	New techniques needed to be implemented in order to consider the new parameters	Regulators decide to incorporate the pitfall as legal by making minor adaptations to the common legal system	Regulators decide that pitfall is not legal and then decide to reinforce regulation to (1) avoid those pitfalls and (2) increase control	The accounting system is not challenged; the only solution is to increase control
Adoption time/speed	Slow or very slow	Since the pitfall is discovered, it can take time to decide if it is legal or not. Then, legislation could be done very quickly		Usually very fast
Accounting change	Major improvement leading to radical changes	Improvement of common practises	Improvement of common practises leading to a greater legal control	Small improvement observed except a major reinforcement of legal control

Accounting crises are not all the same. They should be analysed in order to discover their main roots. Are they a brutal evolution of technical, political, or economic environment? Or are they a loophole discovered in the accounting practise or related to misleading information given by mistake or on purpose by others?

All those roots prove that accounting is not a frozen technique for all the seasons. Accounting did change in the past and will continue to evolve. Accounting crises are just the big eruption in the continuous flow of evolution. Results provided by accounting techniques are given through the prism of this particular science which is bounded by the economic, political, technical, and social boundaries which by themselves change.

To extend the debate, further discussion of the social role of accounting could be done, especially in light of the huge accounting literature review done by Walker (2016), but it would exceed the scope of this contribution.

Finally, the final conclusion of this chapter was written almost 90 years ago:

> "Accounting is relative and progressive. The phenomena which form its subject matter are constantly changing. Older methods become less effective under altered conditions; earlier ideas become irrelevant in the face of new problems. Thus surrounding conditions generate fresh ideas and stimulate the ingenious to devise new methods. And as such ideas and methods prove successful, they in turn begin to modify the surrounding conditions". (Littleton, 1933, p. 361)

References

American Accounting Association (1966). *A Statement of Basic Accounting Theory*. American Accounting Association, Evanston, IL.

Antiphon and Andocides (1941). *Minor Attic Orators, Volume I: Antiphon, Andocides*, Translated by K. J. Maidment. Loeb Classical Library. https://www.amazon.com/gp/product/0674993403?ie=UTF8 &tag=theperseusprojec&linkCode=as2&camp=1789&creative=9325& creativeASIN=0674993403.

Aristotle (1920). *Atheniensium Respublica*, Edited by Sir F. G. Kenyon. 1st edn. Clarendon Press, New York.

Aristotle (1935). *Aristotle: Metaphysics, Books 10–14. Oeconomica. Magna Moralia*, Translated by Hugh Tredennick and G. Cyril Armstrong, Harvard University Press, Cambridge, MA.

Bingen, J. (1951). Les comptes dans les archives d'Héroninos, *Chronique d'Egypte*, Vol. 26, No. 52, pp. 378–385. https://www.brepolsonline.net/toc/cde/1951/26/52.

Boyns, T. and Edwards, J. R. (1991). Do accountants matter? The role of accounting in economic development, *Accounting, Business & Financial History*, Vol. 1, No. 2, pp. 177–195.

Carmona, S. and Ezzamel, M. (2007). Accounting and accountability in ancient civilisations: Mesopotamia and ancient Egypt, *Accounting, Auditing & Accountability Journal*, Vol. 20, No. 2, pp. 177–209.

Caumeil, R. B. (2006). Londres, 29 Juin 1973: Naissance de l'IASC, *Revue Française de Comptabilité*, Vol. 384, p. 24.

Cicero, M. T. (1903). *The Orations of Marcus Tullius Cicero Volume 1*, Translated by C. D. Yonge. George Bell.

Cossu, C. (1996). *Les Pratiques Comptables en Mésopotamie, Après l'invention de l'écriture*, AFC, Tours.

Daumas, François. (1977). Le Problème de La Monnaie Dans l'Egypte Antique Avant Alexandre, *Mèlanges de l'Ecole Francaise de Rome. Antiquité*, Vol. 89, No. 2, pp. 425–442.

Davies, J. (1994). Accounts and accountability in classical Athens, in *Ritual, Finance, Politics: Athenian Democratic Accounts Presented to David Lewis*, by Robin Osborne and Simon Hornblower, pp. 201–212. Oxford University Press, USA.

Degos, J.-G. (1998). *Histoire de La Comptabilité*, Que Sais-Je? Presses Universitaires de France — PUF.

Demosthenes (1939). *Demosthenes: Orations*, Translated by A. T. Murray, Harvard University Press, Cambridge, MA.

Demosthenes (1949). *Demosthenes. Demosthenes with an English Translation*, Translated by Norman W. DeWitt and Norman J. DeWitt, Harvard University Press, London.

Ezzamel, M. (1994). The emergence of the "accountant" in the institutions of ancient Egypt, *Management Accounting Research*, Vol. 5, Nos. 3–4, pp. 221–246. https://doi.org/10.1006/mare.1994.1014.

Ezzamel, M. (1997). Accounting, control and accountability: Preliminary evidence from ancient Egypt, *Critical Perspectives on Accounting*, Vol. 8, No. 6, pp. 563–601.

Ezzamel, M. (2005). Accounting for the activities of funerary temples: The intertwining of the sacred and profane, *Accounting and Business Research*, Vol. 35, No. 1, pp. 29–51.

Flament, C. (2007). *Une Economie Monetarisee: Athenes a l'epoque Classique (440–338): Contribution a l'etude Du Phenomene Monetaire En Grece Ancienne (Collection d'Etudes Classiques)*. Peeters Publishers. https://www.amazon.fr/Une-%C3%A9conomie-mon%C3%A9tari s%C3%A9e-classique-Contribution/dp/9042919582.

Garbutt, D. (1981). The origins of accounting and writing, *The Accounting Historians Notebook*, Vol. 4, No. 2, pp. 10–11.

Hain, H. P. (1966). Accounting control in the Zenon Papyri, *Accounting Review*, Vol. 41, No. 4, pp. 699–703.

Hansen, M. H. (1991). *The Athenian Democracy in the Age of Demosthenes: Structure, Principles, and Ideology*. OUP, Oxford. https://www.amaz on.com/dp/0806131438.

Harris, D. (1994). Freedom of information and accountability: The inventory lists of the Parthenon, in *Ritual, Finance, Politics: Athenian Democratic Accounts Presented to David Lewis*, pp. 213–226, C D L Press, New York.

Hedrick Jr., C. W. (1994). Writing, reading and democracy, in S. Hornblower and R. Osborne (eds.), *Ritual, Finance, Politics: Athenian Democratic Accounts Presented to David Lewis*, pp. 157–174. Oxford University Press, USA.

IFAC (1993). Study 2 — Elements of the financial statements of national governments. New York. Available at: https://www.ifac.org/publi cations-resources/study-2-elements-financial-statements-national-gove rnments.

IFAC (2019). International public sector financial accountability index 2018. Available at: https://www.ifac.org/knowledge-gateway/suppor ting-international-standards/discussion/international-public-sector-fin ancial-accountability-index.

Isocrates (1928). *Isocrates, Volume I: To Demonicus. To Nicocles. Nicocles or the Cyprians. Panegyricus. To Philip. Archidamus*, Translated by George Norlin, Harvard University Press, Cambridge, MA.

Keister, R. O. (1963). Commercial record-keeping in ancient mesopotamia, *The Accounting Review*, Vol. 38, No. 2, pp. 371–376.

Kemp, J. B. (1989). *Ancient Egypt: Anatomy of a Civilisation*, Routledge. ISBN: 978-0415063463. https://www.amazon.com/dp/0415063469.

Kramer, S. N. (1973). *History Begins at Sumer*. Doubleday. ISBN: 978-0385094054. https://www.amazon.com/dp/0385094051.

Littleton, A. C. (1933). *Accounting Evolution to 1900*. American Institute Publishing Co., Inc. ASIN: B0014KT76I. https://www.amazon.com/ dp/B0014KT76I#detailBullets_feature_div.

Mattessich, R. (1998). Recent insights into Mesopotamian accounting of the 3rd millennium B.C. — Successor to token accounting, *Accounting Historians Journal*, Vol. 25, No. 1, pp. 1–27.

Migeotte, L. (2007). *L'économie Des Cités Grecques: De l'archaïsme Au Haut-Empire Romain*, 2e édn revue et augmentée. Ellipses Marketing. ISBN 272983608X. https://www.amazon.fr/dp/272983608X.

Minaud, G. (2005). *La Comptabilité à Rome: Essai d'histoire Économique Sur La Pensée Comptable Commerciale et Privée Dans Le Monde Antique Romain*. Presses Polytechniques et Universitaires Romandes.

Napier, C. J. (2001). Accounting history and accounting progress, *Accounting History*, Vol. 6, No. 2, pp. 7–31. https://doi.org/10.1177/10323732 0100600202.

Oppenheim, A. L. (1954). The seafaring merchants of Ur, *Journal of the American Oriental Society*, Vol. 74, No. 1, pp. 6–17.

Pacioli, L. (1494). *Summa de Arithmetica, Geometria, Proportioni & Proportionalita*. https://books.google.gr/books?id=iqgPe49fhrsC&pri ntsec=frontcover&hl=fr&source=gbs_ge_summary_r&cad=0#v=onep age&q&f=false.

Purser, L.-C. (1887). The roman account-book, Vol. VI, No. 13, pp. 209–218.

Robson, E. (2004). Accounting for change: The development of tabular book-keeping in early Mesopotamia, in *Creating Economic Order: Record-Keeping, Standardization, and the Development of Accounting in the Ancient Near East*, pp. 107–144.

Schmalenbach, E. (1955). *Dynamische Bilanz*, (version 12. A.). 12. A. Wissenschaftl.Buchgesell.

Schmandt-Besserat, D. (1982). The emergence of recording, *American Anthropologist*, Vol. 84, No. 4, pp. 871–878.

Smith, M. (2013). Luca Pacioli: The father of accounting, *SSRN Electronic Journal*, January. https://doi.org/10.2139/ssrn.2320658.

Stone, W. E. (1969). Antecedents of the accounting profession, *Accounting Review*, Vol. 44, No. 2, pp. 284–291.

Vlaemminck, H. J. (1956). *Histoire et Doctrines de La Comptabilité*. Éditions du Treurenberg, Bruxelles.

Walker, P. S. (2016). Revisiting the roles of accounting in society, *Accounting, Organizations and Society*, Reflecting on 40 years of Accounting, Organizations and Society — Part II, Vol. 49, No. Supplement C, pp. 41–50. DOI: https://doi.org/10.1016/j.aos.2015.11. 007. https://www.sciencedirect.com/science/article/abs/pii/S0361368 215300064?via%3Dihub.

Walton, P. (1995). *European Financial Reporting: A History*. Walton, Academic Press, London.

Wilkinson, A. H. T. (1999). *Early Dynastic Egypt*, Routledge, London, New York. ISBN 9780415186339.

Wilson, A. J. (1951). *The Culture of Ancient Egypt*. University of Chicago Press.

Yamey, B. (1994). Accounting in history, *European Accounting Review*, Vol. 3, No. 2, pp. 375–380.

Yonge, C. D. (1877). *Cicero's Tusculan Disputations: Also Treatises on the Nature of the Gods and on the Commonwealth*. Harper & Brothers, Publishers, New York.

Appendix

Appendix 1.1

"ἔτι δὲ τὴν χώραν οὐκ αὐτάρκη κεκτημένων ἑκάστων, ἀλλὰ τὰ μὲν ἐλλείπουσαν τὰ δὲ πλείω τῶν ἱκανῶν φέρουσαν, καὶ πολλῆς ἀπορίας οὔσης τὰ μὲν ὅπου χρὴ διαθέσθαι τὰ δ᾽ ὁπόθεν εἰσαγαγέσθαι, καὶ ταύταις ταῖς συμφοραῖς ἐπήμυνεν· ἐμπόριον γὰρ ἐν μέσῳ τῆς Ἑλλάδος τὸν Πειραιᾶ κατεσκευάσατο, τοσαύτην ἔχονθ᾽ ὑπερβολήν, ὥσθ᾽ ἃ παρὰ τῶν ἄλλων ἓν παρ᾽ ἑκάστων χαλεπόν ἐστι λαβεῖν, ταῦθ᾽ ἅπαντα παρ᾽ αὐτῆς ῥᾴδιον εἶναι πορίσασθαι.

Appendix 1.2

κληροῦνται δὲ καὶ ἀγορανόμοι ι#, πέντε μὲν εἰς Πειραιέα, ε# δ᾽ εἰς ἄστυ. τούτοις δὲ ὑπὸ τῶν νόμων προστέτακται τῶν ὠνίων ἐπιμελεῖσθαι πάντων, ὅπως καθαρὰ καὶ ἀκίβδηλα πωλήσεται. [2]

κληροῦνται δὲ καὶ μετρονόμοι ι#, πέντε μὲν εἰς ἄστυ, ε# δὲ εἰς Πειραιέα. καὶ οὗτοι τῶν μέτρων καὶ τῶν σταθμῶν ἐπιμελοῦνται πάντων, ὅπως οἱ πωλοῦντες χρήσονται δικαίοις. [3]

ἦσαν δὲ καὶ σιτοφύλακες κληρωτοὶ ι#, πέντε μὲν εἰς Πειραιέα, πέντε δ᾽ εἰς ἄστυ, νῦν δ᾽ εἴκοσι μὲν εἰς ἄστυ, πεντεκαίδεκα δ᾽ εἰς Πειραιέα. οὗτοι δ᾽ ἐπιμελοῦνται, πρῶτον μὲν ὅπως ὁ ἐν ἀγορᾷ σῖτος ἀργὸς ὤνιος ἔσται δικαίως, ἔπειθ᾽ ὅπως οἵ τε μυλωθροὶ πρὸς τὰς τιμὰς τῶν κριθῶν τὰ ἄλφιτα πωλήσουσιν, καὶ οἱ ἀρτοπῶλαι πρὸς τὰς τιμὰς τῶν πυρῶν τοὺς ἄρτους, καὶ τὸν σταθμὸν ἄγοντας ὅσον ἂν οὗτοι τάξωσιν. ὁ γὰρ νόμος τούτους κελεύει τάττειν. [4]

ἐμπορίου δ᾽ ἐπιμελητὰς δέκα κληροῦσιν· τούτοις δὲ προστέτακται τῶν τ᾽ ἐμπορίων ἐπιμελεῖσθαι, καὶ τοῦ σίτου τοῦ καταπλέοντος εἰς τὸ σιτικὸν ἐμπόριον τὰ δύο μέρη τοὺς ἐμπόρους ἀναγκάζειν εἰς τὸ ἄστυ κομίζειν.."

Appendix 1.3

δεῖξαι δ᾽ αὐτὸν τῷ πατρὶ τῷ ἐμῷ καὶ συστῆσαι τῷ Ἀρχεβιάδῃ καὶ τῷ Φρασίᾳ προσέταξεν, ἐπειδὴ ἥκοι ἐκ τῆς ἀποδημίας. εἰώθασι δὲ πάντες οἱ τραπεζῖται, ὅταν τις ἀργύριον τιθεὶς ἰδιώτης ἀποδοῦναί τῳ προστάττῃ, πρῶτον τοῦ θέντος τοὔνομα γράφειν καὶ τὸ κεφάλαιον τοῦ ἀργυρίου, ἔπειτα παραγράφειν "τῷ δεῖνι ἀποδοῦναι δεῖ", καὶ ἐὰν μὲν γιγνώσκωσι τὴν ὄψιν τοῦ ἀνθρώπου ᾧ ἂν δέῃ ἀποδοῦναι, τοσοῦτο μόνον ποιεῖν, γράψαι ᾧ δεῖ ἀποδοῦναι, ἐὰν δὲ μὴ γιγνώσκωσι, καὶ τούτου τοὔνομα προσπαραγράφειν ὃς ἂν μέλλῃ συστήσειν καὶ δείξειν τὸν ἄνθρωπον, ὃν ἂν δέῃ κομίσασθαι τὸ ἀργύριον.

Appendix 1.4

Τιμόθεος Ἀθηναῖος πολεμῶν πρὸς Ὀλυνθίους καὶ ἀπορούμενος ἀργυρίου, κόψας χαλκὸν διεδίδου τοῖς στρατιώταις. ἀγανακτούντων δὲ τῶν στρατιωτῶν ἔφη αὐτοῖς τοὺς ἐμπόρους τε καὶ ἀγοραίους ἅπαντα ὡσαύτως πωλήσειν. τοῖς δ᾽ ἐμπόροις προεῖπεν, ὃν ἄν τις λάβῃ χαλκόν, τούτου πάλιν ἀγοράζειν τά τ᾽ ἐκ τῆς χώρας ὤνια καὶ τὰ ἐκ τῶν λειῶν ἀγόμενα: ὃς δ᾽ ἂν περιλειφθῇ αὐτοῖς χαλκός, πρὸς αὐτὸν ἀναφέροντας ἀργύριον λαμβάνειν.

Appendix 1.5

"[133] ἐγὼ ὑμῖν ἐρῶ διότι οὗτοι ταῦτα νῦν γιγνώσκουσιν. Ἀγύρριος γὰρ οὑτοσί, ὁ καλὸς κἀγαθός, ἀρχώνης1 ἐγένετο τῆς πεντηκοστῆς τρίτον ἔτος, καὶ ἐπρίατο τριάκοντα ταλάντων, μετέσχον δ᾽ αὐτῷ2 οὗτοι πάντες οἱ παρασυλλεγέντες ὑπὸ τὴν λεύκην, οὓς3 ὑμεῖς ἴστε οἷοί εἰσιν: οἳ διὰ τοῦτο ἔμοιγε δοκοῦσι συλλεγῆναι ἐκεῖσε, ἵν᾽ αὐτοῖς ἀμφότερα ᾖ, καὶ μὴ ὑπερβάλλουσι4 λαβεῖν ἀργύριον καὶ ὀλίγου πραθείσης μετασχεῖν. [134] κερδήναντες δὲ ἓξ1 τάλαντα, γνόντες τὸ πρᾶγμα οἷον εἴη, [ὡς πολλοῦ ἄξιον,]2 συνέστησαν πάντες, καὶ μεταδόντες τοῖς ἄλλοις ἐωνοῦντο πάλιν τριάκοντα ταλάντων. ἐπεὶ δ᾽ οὐκ ἀντεωνεῖτο οὐδείς, παρελθὼν ἐγὼ εἰς τὴν βουλὴν ὑπερέβαλλον, ἕως ἐπριάμην ἓξ καὶ τριάκοντα ταλάντων. ἀπελάσας δὲ τούτους καὶ καταστήσας ὑμῖν ἐγγυητὰς ἐξέλεξα τὰ χρήματα καὶ κατέβαλον τῇ πόλει καὶ αὐτὸς οὐκ ἐζημιώθην, ἀλλὰ καὶ βραχέα ἀπεκερδαίνομεν οἱ μετασχόντες: τούτους δ᾽ ἐποίησα τῶν ὑμετέρων μὴ διανείμασθαι ἓξ τάλαντα ἀργυρίου".

Appendix 1.6

II. (...) Quid est quod neglegenter scribamus aduersaria? quid est quod diligenter conficiamus tabulas? qua de causa? Quia haec sunt menstrua, illae sunt aeternae; haec delentur statim, illae seruantur sancte; haec parui temporis memoriam, illae perpetuae existimationis fidem et religionem amplectuntur; haec sunt disiecta, illae sunt in ordinem confectae. Itaque aduersaria in iudicium protulit nemo; codicem protulit, tabulas recitauit.

Appendix 1.7

"[175] Atque haec ita gesta esse, iudices, cognoscite et ex litteris publicis civitatum et ex testimoniis publicis, in quibus nihil fictum, nihil ad tempus accommodatum intellegetis; omnia quae dicimus rationibus populorum non interpositis neque perturbatis neque repentinis, sed certis, institutis, ordine relata atque confecta sunt".

Appendix 2: How to Explain the Development of Double-Entry Accounting

Littleton (1933) describes seven "key ingredients" which led to the creation of a double-entry accounting:

1. Private property: bookkeeping is concerned with recording property transactions.
2. Capital: without capital, little commerce and no credit.
3. Commerce: in a brooded sense in order to create the need to organise systems to replace existing record-keeping.[48]
4. Credit: in order to record transactions of future goods.
5. Writing: permits to bypass human limit of memory.
6. Money: "common dominator" of exchange.
7. Arithmetic: to compute monetary details.

As we saw before, many of these factors date back from antiquity, but they are never found together until the Middle Ages. But even though those elements were found together, the genius mind of Pacioli was needed in order to allow other scholars to understand, copy, and expand the double-entry technique.

Appendix 3: Genesis and Major Milestones of Accounting

Many accounting professionals do not care about accounting history because they are too busy running their own business. Others — mostly scholars — believe that accounting starts with Luca Pacioli with his best-seller *Summa de arithmetica, geometria, de proportioni et de proportionalita* (Pacioli, 1494). Very few know that accounting started with Mesopotamians: in 3500 BC, as Garbutt stipulates, *The evidence certainly suggests that accounting preceded writing* (Garbutt, 1981, p. 11).

Even if Pacioli is not the starting point, his work marks a milestone in accounting history. As argued by Degos, *Before him (Pacioli) since Sumer, accounting vestiges are found in tokens, tablets, registers, books essentially material supports. After, we look for history in the accounting books, in abstract thought: the*

---

[48] Also cited by J. F. Peck, "Accounting in the industrialization of Western Europe", in *European Financial Reporting: A History*, by Peter Walton (Academic Press, 1995), pp. 11–28.

accounting science will replace the art of accounting.[49] According to Degos, Pacioli admits that he is not the creator of the double-entry book, his work is a summary of the "Venetian method", but he *has been obsessed by bookkeeping procedures designed to minimize the opportunities for fraud and to enhance accounting books' acceptability in legal proceedings* (Yamey, 1994, p. 376).

Another milestone is the first regulations about accounting. According to Schmalenbach (1955) *In 1673 the commercial ordinance appeared as the first commercial code setting out the accounting obligations of business. The Napoleonic Code followed that and from that source the accounting obligations of business flowed into the legal machinery of all Europe* (Walton, 1995, p. 5). Schmalenbach (1955) underlines that this reform was made necessary *by the vast number of fraudulent bankruptcies which were a feature of French economic and financial life at the time.*

The last milestone could be the attempt of the International Standard Account Committee founded in 1973 and replaced since 2001 by the International Accounting Standards Board. As described on their website, "Our mission is to develop, in the public interest, a single set of high quality, understandable and international financial reporting standards (IFRSs) for general-purpose financial statements". (International Accounting Standards Board, 2009). This attempt of international standardisation is driven by "the need of a common language and common rules"[50] as it was exposed at the 10th international congress of accounting which took place in Australia in 1970 (Caumeil, 2006).

Major developments in accounting techniques were made in order to make accounting more reliable. It is not very surprising that the three milestones were initiated by scholars (Pacioli), legal

---

[49] Free French translation from author. Original text is *avant lui, depuis Summer, les vestiges comptables étaient des jetons, des tablettes, des registres, des livres, essentiellement sur des supports matériels. Après lui, on recherchera l'histoire dans les traités de comptabilité, dans la pensée abstraite, la science des comptes se substituera à l'art des comptes.* Degos. Que sais-je? *Histoire de la comptabilitÃ©,* pp. 66–67.

[50] Which will permit a bigger transparency and comparability.

authorities (Colbert), and professionals (ISAC) because of the scope of accounting stakeholders. But those changes are not "a spontaneous generation", they are the results of a long evolution which includes the seven points of Littleton (1933).

https://doi.org/10.1142/9789811258756_0006

Chapter 6

Following the Science: The UK Government's Response to "Herd Immunity" During Early COVID-19

Miriam Green

Abstract

The aim of this chapter is to discuss the importance and impact of scientific advice on the government's response to the COVID-19 pandemic. This is a subject worthy of more than one book, so the topic is confined to the question of "herd immunity" or "mitigation": a strategy considered in the United Kingdom (UK) during the early appearance of the virus in the first months of 2020. This chapter also considers definitions of science and problems within science itself and how these have impacted considerations of herd immunity during the first months of the pandemic. The relationships between the scientists who have advised the government, the politicians involved, and the impact this has had on the scientific advice given and implemented are discussed, as are the problems regarding the concept of "following the science". The practise of herd immunity is outlined, as are attitudes to these in the UK in the first quarter of 2020. Finally, the position of science and scientists in relation to the responses to COVID-19 is considered in the broader political and ideological context of 21st century Britain.

Keywords: Following the science; herd immunity; COVID-19; government response; scientific advisers; modelling; austerity; neoliberalism

1. Introduction

There are difficulties with the scientific information relating to the COVID-19 pandemic and with the government's response to the advice given by its scientific advisors. This is partly because of the fast spread of the virus and the need for rapid development of the scientific research and knowledge about the virus, which could lead to rapid changes in the advice given by scientists to the government.[1] This was further complicated by differences among the scientists themselves.

At the same time, the government, not unnaturally, had an agenda of its own with concerns other than those solely to do with the virus. In the best-case scenario, the government ran the risk of interpreting the advice in ways not strictly in accord with what scientists intended; in the worst case, it used the information "politically" — for example, by being selective about the information received or distorting it to realise its own agenda, regardless of the risks to public health.

Because this is all so recent, the sources relied upon are mostly from the media. Although many of the articles used have been published in *The Guardian*, many of those are not by in-house journalists or editorial writers but by independent medical scientists who have been writing and speaking across different media. The other main source of information used is from the chief government advisory body, the Scientific Advisory Group for Emergencies (SAGE).

One of the problems with SAGE is that the documents made available to the public are short, and although most of the names of the people belonging to that body were later published, it is not documented as to who was responsible for the findings and the advice given and who might have disagreed with either the findings or their interpretation. We also are not told what other documents there

---

[1]The main government advisory body, the Scientific Advisory Group for Emergencies (SAGE), emphasised the transitoriness of its advice. The SAGE documents had introductory paragraphs highlighting the uncertainty of the information and advice given. https://www,gov.uk/government/publications/sages-priorities-26-f.

might have been presented to the government that are not publicly available.

At the very least, the SAGE documents show some of the information available to the government and when it was in its possession. They specify particular findings, conclusions, and recommendations, at particular times. What one can see from the other sources is how various medical and other scientists not in SAGE evaluated those findings in so far as they had access to them.

2. Science and Scientists

2.1. *The science*

Discussing the role of science and scientists as advisers to governments in times of crisis raises many issues and potential difficulties. However, before they are considered, there are more fundamental problems with science — as fundamental as questions as to what science is. This issue came into prominence with the development of positivism in the early 20th century with its rigorous and constrained definitions as to what constituted science, and more than that, what was true knowledge, many types of intellectual inquiry being discarded as invalid and nonsensical (Turner, 2001). This is a controversy that has continued not only regarding the natural sciences but also regarding the application of scientific methods to social science research (Green, 2019).

Logical positivism, developed by an eminent group of philosophers, mathematicians, and scientists, the "Vienna School", took an extreme positivist view: science and therefore true knowledge were derived only from empirical investigation of observable, natural elements in the universe, attained through rigorous methods based on statistical analyses of quantitative data. This knowledge was value-free, eliminating the subjectivities inevitable through the study of people and their potential biases and ignorance. It was based on "scientific" rather than qualitative methods of analysis, thereby avoiding the subjectivities of the researcher and of the subject being studied (Turner, 2001). It was considered to be an objective approach that should also be applied also to the social sciences if they were to be regarded as being scientific. Social forces, metaphysics, and mental thought processes were all to be avoided as they did not match up to these criteria (Halfpenny, 2001).

There was a reaction to this view of science from philosophers and historians of science, notably Thomas Kuhn (1970), and a critique of these methods as applied in the social sciences by many, including Bourdieu (1990). Kuhn, along with others, such as Hanson (1972) and Feyerabend (1993), offered serious challenges to positivism. Science was much broader than encompassing only the type of knowledge stipulated by the logical positivists. Kuhn defined science as "any field in which progress is marked" (Kuhn, 1970, p. 162). Methods of inquiry were necessarily and legitimately far more varied than those described above. In order for science to progress, there had to be new scientific paradigms, which by definition involved new conceptualisations of the problems, new questions, new research methods and ways of handling data, with new solutions (Kuhn, 1970).

The claim that positivist methods of inquiry and the knowledge resulting from these were value-free has also been challenged. Hanson (1972) used the example of the two astronomers Tycho Brahe and Keppler, who would interpret the dawn in different ways, not because the data were different, but because of their different existing preconceptions. Kuhn (1970) highlighted the importance of community in influencing what scientists did. In fact, one of his definitions of a scientific paradigm was "model problems and solutions to a community of practitioners" (Kuhn, 1970, p. viii). The importance both of preconceptions and of social context in influencing scientists in their thinking should become apparent later on in relation to scientists' advice to government ministers.

All in all, science was claimed by these later theorists to be much more haphazard in its choice of subject matter and methods than were assumed by positivists and are also assumed by some currently. Scientific "revolutions" according to Kuhn meant just that — an upending of what had previously been orthodox approaches. Feyerabend put this firmly and clearly as follows:

"Philosophers ... suspected for some time that there is not one entity 'science', with clearly defined principles but that science contains a great variety of ... approaches and that even a particular science such as physics is but a scattered collection of subjects ... each one containing contrary tendencies". (Feyerabend, 1993, p. x)

This broadening of the conception of science is relevant in the context of COVID-19, particularly in view of the uncharted territory and the rapidity with which scientists' research findings were needed for decisions regarding public health. The waters were muddied by the close relationship some scientists had, and had to have, with government ministers, particularly with the prime minister and the minister for health and social care (DHSC). There were further complications because there were many interested scientists who did not have this close relationship, some highly critical of what they perceived as the scientific advice to the government to be.

3. The Scientists

3.1. *Differences among scientists*

Professor Devi Sridhar, chair of global public health at Edinburgh University, has pointed out that there are different, diverse views of science depending on the scientist's particular field of knowledge — as was evident in the early days of the pandemic when the number of infections was rising, and various choices were available to the government based on different scientific advice (Devlin, 2020).

On the one hand, there were proposals to take radical measures to scotch the virus, for example, by banning mass gatherings, enforcing measures such as social distancing and more radically, imposing a lockdown on the population as a whole; on the other, to allow the infection to take hold with a view to arriving at herd immunity, "mitigation" or "delaying the spread" of the virus within the general population. SAGE's advice on 4 February, 2020, for example, was to delay the arrival and spread of the virus outside of winter, as this would allow the NHS time to get ready for an outbreak of the virus and allow it to concentrate for the moment on regular winter respiratory illnesses (SAGE, 4 February, 2020).

3.2. *Public expectations*

The scientists who have acted as advisors during this pandemic have been subject to new stresses and pressures. One is the new pedestal upon which scientists have frequently been placed. Al-Khalili (2020b) points to the change from people for long having dismissed scientists, with "experts" being a derogatory term, to them now largely deciding to "trust the science" and follow its recommendations. This, writes Al-Khalili, has put strains on scientists. As well as trying to win the continuous race to save lives against the spread and infectivity of the virus, scientists are now more in the public eye than ever before and have to provide a running commentary on and justification for their work — for failures as well as successes; for the different views held by them and for the changes in their own advice. They also risk the public losing trust in their work through unrealistic expectations (Devlin, 2020).

3.2.1. *Time span*

The newness of the virus and its rapid spread have made scientists have to deal with uncertainty and to start from what science historian Daston has called "empirical ground zero" (Sodha, 2020). The time in which scientists are expected to deliver has proved difficult. Buranyi (2020) makes the point that scientific research normally is based upon years of review and further testing for replication. In this case, scientists have had to work in a much shorter time span, where not all the information about the virus is known. Nor has there been time for a resolution regarding scientists' different opinions and recommendations, potentially affecting the type of strategies used and their timing. There has also been no time for lengthy consideration and further research in such dangerous and potentially calamitous circumstances.

4. Scientists Working with the Government

Scientists working with the government have, not unnaturally, resulted in further complications.

4.1. *Differences between scientists and politicians*

Al-Khalili (2020a) has highlighted some important differences in the ways science and politics work. Scientists making mistakes is a natural part of scientific progress. Like Kuhn (1970), Al-Khalili sees science developing through scientists making errors and through current knowledge being replaced with more accurate results, allowing for a deeper understanding. Politicians, on the contrary, often do not want to admit to any mistakes, as this could be regarded as a form of weakness.

A related difference, linked to attitudes to making mistakes, is the acceptance by scientists of uncertainty. Scientists allow doubt to govern their work and have to be ready to abandon existing ideas if a new observation or finding emerges. In science, uncertainty is seen as a way of progressing knowledge. Al-Khalili points to the importance in this pandemic of being able to admit doubt and change course, thereby avoiding the possibility of catastrophe. He emphasises that being ready to change strategy is a strength, not a weakness (Al-Khalili, 2020a).

There is the additional difficulty regarding the interconnection of science with politics at a time of heightened crisis. The UK government, as indeed any government, has other responsibilities arguably equally pressing. These include protection of the economy on which everyone is dependent and protection of the public — not only from the pandemic but from its effects in other areas, such as employment, education, and mental health if, for example, a lockdown is instituted. Then, there is the NHS — ensuring its capacity not only to deal with people infected by the virus — a daunting task in itself — but also looking after people with other illnesses, particularly life-threatening ones. This can put further strain on scientists, particularly when they may have different mindsets and objectives from those of the politicians they are advising.

4.2. Lack of transparency

One of the problems in understanding the role of the scientists in their relationship with the government has been the lack of information and transparency regarding their communications and interactions, particularly as there were often claims by government ministers that the government had followed the "best science", in the face of some serious, negative consequences from the virus.

This lack of transparency has been true of the government's advisory group, SAGE. Its composition and deliberations were for some months kept secret. Anthony Costello, Professor of International Child Health and Director of the UCL Institute for Global Health, pointed out that an advisory group of scientists needed to be open, independent, and diverse in order to be successful. But it was only in May 2020 that the government released the names of 50 scientific advisers that sat on SAGE. Not all were named, some having asked specifically for their names not to be disclosed (Costello, 2020a).

It was not only the public which was not informed. Other medical scientists were also not a party to information about SAGE. Professor Sheila Bird, formerly of the biostatics unit of the Medical Research Council, University of Cambridge, was concerned that it was not known who sat on SAGE and that the scientific bases for the government's decisions were not clear (Devlin, 2020). Sir David King, a former chief scientific adviser to the government, argued that publishing the names of some of the people in SAGE did not constitute sufficient transparency. One needed to have the discussions made public, including the advice given by scientists as distinct from what the strategy advisers advocated (Sample and Mason, 2020).

The composition of the scientific bodies advising the government was taken up by Costello (2020a, 2020b). He pointed out that SAGE would have been better served and a herd immunity strategy quashed had independent public health experts been included in that body. He was keen for the policy failures not to be attributed to public health colleagues (Costello, 2020b). The composition of the SAGE members, he claimed, was biased in favour of a medical view of science, ignoring public health epidemiologists with experience of the virus in, for example, China, such as Professor Gabriel Leung, an infectious diseases expert at the World Health Organization (WHO); Dr Mike Ryan, an epidemiologist and Executive Director of the WHO Health Emergencies Programme; and with no social scientists for community engagement and no logicians who could help with resources and supplies (Costello, 2020a).

In fact, there was a group of behavioural scientists advising SAGE — the Independent Scientific Pandemic Insights Group on Behaviours (SPI-B). Its report, published in early April 2020, with advice as to how the public might respond to lockdown measures, was heavily redacted, with large portions of text containing criticisms of the government's policy entirely blanked out — one insight into the relationship between the government and some of its scientific advisers. The SPI-B members' conclusions were that the government didn't want any criticism; their own independence was put at risk; the government's secrecy undermined public trust, the position of scientific experts, and their advice (Lewis and Conn, 2020).

4.3. *Following the science*

Politicians, against the advice of many scientists, have been reluctant to take decisions they regard as likely to be unpopular until the last minute, at times using uncertainty as the reason, and often with disastrous results (Hanage, 2021a). As mentioned above, there were other exigencies the government had to face, with additional pressure at times from fellow ministers, from vociferous backbenchers, and from the public. Scientists might then have to explain the variance between their publicly available advice and government policies. Government assertions that they were following the science claimed both by Prime Minister Johnson and President Trump might have made this task even more difficult (Buranyi, 2020).

Scientists and their work face politicisation in relation to government policies and demands. This might lead to the government's ignoring their advice, perhaps justifiably, as it might see a dialectic between the nation's health and the nation's economic or psychological well-being. However, it has been argued by many, including Hanage, a professor of the evolution and epidemiology of infectious disease at Harvard, that mistakes made early on in the pandemic, against scientific advice, resulted in the UK suffering not only among the worst number of deaths but also among the worst economic disruption in the developed countries (Hanage, 2021b).

Scientific advice was varied. The SAGE's documents from February 2020 indicate that some of the scientific advice supported what became the government's strategy. This was for a cautious mitigating approach delaying the spread of the virus rather than encouraging a more active strategy to destroy the virus completely (see e.g. SAGE, 4 February, 2020). But of course, this may have been the brief they were working to rather than their independent framing of the issues.

4.4. *Pressures on scientists to support government policies*

Scientists have been seen to support government policies, sometimes against their own judgement. Paton (2020), an emeritus professor of health policy at Keele University, accused government advisers of speaking in code and inverted logic to protect the government and in particular the prime minister. One example he gives is of Professor Chris Whitty, who is the UK Government's chief medical officer and chief medical adviser to the DHSC. In March 2020, at the beginning of the first wave of the pandemic, Whitty put forward an argument that testing had had to be abandoned because of the cases being too numerous but, at the same time, arguing that the figures were not high enough for a lockdown (Paton, 2020).

Whitty's arguments, as set out by Paton and backed by the government, resulted in two serious errors that led to England and Wales having one of the largest numbers of deaths per capita among industrialised nations (Sample, 2020b). There were other examples of inconsistencies which are perceived as support for the government. Sir Mark Walport is a scientist who was purported to have changed his mind over the importance or otherwise of a test-and-trace policy in reducing the infection rate of the virus in those crucial early months (Costello, 2020b). It has been suggested that scientific and medical advisers made some proposals based not on their scientific knowledge but on the exigencies of the moment — in this instance, against testing because there was no provision for it because of hugely inadequate manpower and equipment in the NHS (Alderson, 2020).

Dr Richard Horton, editor of the *Lancet*, one of the oldest and best-known general medical journals, made a similar point. In May 2020, in an excoriating article against what he saw as the increasingly collusive relationship between scientists and ministers who "appear to have agreed to act together in order to protect a failing government", he gave as one of his examples the justification that testing was so poorly carried out because of its inappropriateness for the UK, instead of the admission that the WHO's recommendations had been ignored (Horton, 2020a). The government's scientific advisers had become "the public relations wing of a government that had betrayed its people". He concluded with the warning that what was at stake was not one adviser but "the independence and credibility of science and medicine" (Horton, 2020b).

This criticism was supported by Professor Greg Philo of Glasgow University. He compared what was happening in China on 19 March, 2020 (the announcement that there were no new cases of the virus) with the UK government's chief medical adviser's assertion that social distancing, if implemented too early, would have "almost an unmeasurable impact on the epidemic". Philo claims the contrary: China could have reduced its infection rate by 66% had it acted just one week earlier. He does not give any evidence for this but supports his argument for early action with a plea that now was "not the time to continue defending a bankrupt theory that the World Health Organization called wrong and dangerous" (Philo, 2020). The WHO had declared a public health emergency on 30 January, 2020 and by 24 February had warned that the virus was highly contagious, capable of enormous health and societal consequences (Conn *et al.*, 2020).

The fact that Cummings, the prime minister's former chief political adviser, took part in the SAGE meetings could also have seriously compromised the discussions and the final advice given to the government. King warned about the quality of the advice because of Cummings' presence. He questioned from whom the prime minister was getting the advice — from Cummings or from the government's chief medical adviser. King's conclusion was that "Suddenly you get a confusion" (Sample *et al.*, 2020).

4.5. *Manipulation of scientific views*

Differences in views among scientists can be manipulated. Hanage (2021a) points out that because science is not monolithic, and because scientists' conclusions do not follow the same single path, this can be used unscrupulously by government ministers, delaying action because there are differences of opinion or choosing the advice which suits. " 'Taking scientific advice' is not the same as asking a bunch of experts the same question until one of them says something you want to hear" (Hanage, 2021a).

Even more problematic for scientists is when politicians declare they are "being led by the science" and are accompanied by scientists at public press conferences but in fact are ignoring scientists and, worse still, are using public acceptance of policies in the belief that they are supported by science to push through policies which are in fact not supported by those scientists. Sridhar complained that

> "As a scientist, I hope I never again hear the phrase "based on the best science and evidence" spoken by a politician . . .. This phrase has become basically meaningless". (Devlin, 2020)

Siddique claims that the government has consistently avoided criticisms of its policies with regard to the pandemic by declaring that it was "following the science". Sir Venkatraman Ramakrishnan, president of the Royal Society and Nobel prize-winning biochemist, acknowledged that the science was complicated as were the government's decisions as to how to implement it. While scientists did not always get everything right, "the beauty of science" was that scientists could change their minds as new evidence came to light. A more truthful phrase, according to him, would be that the government was "heeding the science advice [and] considering it when we make our decisions" (Siddique, 2020).

One step further down is when government failures are attributed to scientists. There is at least one instance when government failures were blamed directly on science. Thérèse Coffey, Secretary of State at the Department for Work and Pensions, attributed the government's inability to protect care homes to "wrong" scientific advice. However, to be fair to the government, this was repudiated by the prime minister's office. It was also condemned by Ramakrishnan, who pointed out that this compromised the freedom with which scientists could give advice freely and frankly (Siddique, 2020).

It has been suggested that some scientists are beholden to the government for funding, which may be an added source of pressure on them. Sodha (2020) has pointed out that Vallance was in line for being appointed chief executive of UK Research and Innovation, a funding body with an annual budget of GBP 7 billion. Sodha argues that this would put any scientist in a difficult and unprotected position regardless of their integrity, particularly in view of the lack of transparency regarding the advice given to government by its scientific advisory bodies and by the prime minister's former chief political advisor (Sodha, 2020).

The Guardian supported this in its conjecture that Cummings'[2] influence might have been strengthened in SAGE's discussions for the very reason of his potential influence over government funding (Editorial, *The Guardian*, 27 April, 2020). This was modified by Professor Peter Ayton, City University of London. The problem, according to Ayton, was not that scientists might compromise their positions because of the connection between government funding and Cummings' presence. Rather, it was that their scientific advice might not be reliably relayed by Cummings to the government. In his letter to *The Guardian*, he continued the following:

> "The government's notion that reports from dilettante observers at SAGE can improve on the chief scientific officer's briefing to enhance government understanding and decision-making is not reassuring". (Ayton, 2020)

---

[2]Cummings, as mentioned previously, was the prime minister's former chief political adviser who recently fell out with him and was dismissed by the prime minister's office.

5. Herd Immunity

A recent definition of herd immunity is that it is "the indirect protection from a contagious infectious disease that happens when a population is immune either through vaccination or immunity developed through previous infection" (Gavi, 2020).[3] Therefore, when enough people have become immune either through vaccination or infection, they act as a buffer and protect the population as a whole, including those who have not been vaccinated or who have not had the disease. One of the great successes of herd immunity in the past was the elimination of smallpox (Gavi, 2020).

There are challenges to the achievement of herd immunity, particularly if one takes the direction of encouraging infection in the population. One of the reasons for the high death rate in the UK was the potential for high mortality and serious illness among those most vulnerable — principally the elderly. Another serious consequence is the strain this puts upon medical services. This is why governments have generally sought to achieve herd immunity by vaccination (Gavi, 2020).

However, this is not to say that herd immunity through vaccination is risk-free. There is the danger of virus mutation which may not be as susceptible to the current vaccines; immunity may last only for a period as with the flu vaccine; and there is human capriciousness — opposing or abstaining from having the vaccine for various reasons, not all based on the most reliable knowledge available. If enough people did not have the vaccine, this would weaken herd immunity and put people in danger of infection (Gavi, 2020).

6. Scientific Support for Herd Immunity by Infection

The government was supported in this approach by Professor Sunetra Gupta, Oxford University professor of theoretical epidemiology. She argued that one could not know the number of deaths, given the absence of testing. If half the population might have had a mild

---

[3] Although this chapter comes from the Gavi, the Vaccine Alliance, the author (not named) states that these views are personal.

infection, as the figures suggested, this would show a much lower death rate than originally assumed. And if this was the case, preferable to closing down the economy might be warning people against crowds and putting resources into the NHS. (In her defence, Gupta had been concerned about lockdowns causing breakdowns in food supply chains, leading to starvation among the poorest in many countries (Wikipedia/Great Barrington Declaration).)

At the time, some other scientists were in agreement with Gupta. The death rate from COVID-19 was played down by John Ioannidis, pandemic forecaster at Stanford University; by Professor Spiegelhalter of Cambridge University, who thought the virus would last only a few weeks; and by John Lee, a former NHS pathologist, who suggested deaths of the elderly were being recorded differently in different countries and that their deaths from COVID-19 were exaggerated (Jenkins, 2020).

7. Official Scientific Advice in Favour of Delaying the Spread

When looking at the advice given by SAGE and its related subcommittees, one has to take into account the brief or parameters for the committee, which may have been set by the government rather than arrived at independently by the scientists themselves. Interestingly, in the documents published by the SAGE and the bodies reporting to it in February 2020, the phrase "herd immunity" did not appear. Instead, the terms used were "to delay the spread", "mitigation", and "containment".

A report from the Scientific Pandemic Influenza Group on Modelling, an operational sub-group (SPI-M-O) for SAGE, was submitted on 3 February, 2020. Given the uncertainties in the situation, their difficulties, as with the other SAGE groups, were as follows:

> "This evidence was compiled very rapidly during a fast-moving response .... The paper presented here is the best assessment of the evidence at the time of writing, and the conclusions were formed on this basis. As new evidence or data emerges, SAGE updates its advice accordingly". (SPI-M-O, 3 February, 2020)

In this case, the brief was to investigate "the impact of possible interventions to delay the spread of a UK outbreak of 2019-nCov" (SPI-M-O, 3 February, 2020). This report recommended restricting travel from countries with outbreaks, quarantining people returning from China, mass closure of schools early in the case of an epidemic in the UK, and voluntary home isolation of those with respiratory symptoms and their household contacts in the case of significant levels of asymptomatic transmission. These were far more stringent than the suggestions made one day later by SAGE, but nevertheless, the aim in both reports was to delay a UK epidemic but not to stop it (SPI-M-O, 3 February, 2020).

The minutes from the SAGE meeting held on 4 February, 2020, also supported the idea of mitigation, and, as mentioned, its advice was less restrictive:

> 3. A delay now in the arrival and spread of WN-CoV in the UK would be beneficial for improving NHS readiness and ability to manage a UK outbreak and importantly may push any outbreak beyond the winter respiratory season.

The reason given for this suggestion was that

> The NHS is currently facing winter pressures, and outside of the winter respiratory season there will be fewer people presenting at hospital with similar symptoms to WN-CoV.

A further suggestion which was against taking more restrictive action was that

> 5. SAGE agreed that, based on current evidence, domestic measures such as shutting down public transport or restricting public gatherings would probably be ineffective in creating any meaningful delay in spread of WN-CoV. (SAGE, 4 minutes, 4 February, 2020)

Public Health England (PHE), which described itself as an executive agency to protect and improve the nation's health and well-being, was asked by SAGE to prepare a paper to make proposals both to contain the virus and also to slow the spread of an outbreak. "Containment" was limited to single cases or small clusters; "slowing the spread" was interpreted as minimising the number of new cases each day. Containment fell short of a strategy to eradicate the virus, but the PHE recommendations for containment went much further than the measures other SAGE groups were recommending and that the government took. The PHE recommended contact tracing, isolation of high-risk contacts, daily active health monitoring, community decontamination, rapid access to assessment and testing including asymptomatic contacts, the isolation of PCR-positive cases, and closures of schools or residential settings (PHE, 24 February, 2020). These were measures the government was later severely criticised for not taking. Some of the reasons as to why the government decided to aim for mitigation rather than eradication of the virus might have been, as has been suggested, the lack of resources in the NHS and a lack of national preparedness.

The option of taking more active, direct measures against infection had certainly been offered, even if it was not the strongest that could be chosen, i.e. lockdown and closing the country's borders. But certainly, until 16 March, 2020, SAGE was recommending less restrictive containment policies:

1. There are currently no scientific grounds to move away from containment efforts in the UK ....

14. SAGE agreed there is no evidence to suggest that banning very large gatherings would reduce transmission. Preventing all social interaction in public spaces, including restaurants and bars, would have an effect, but would be very difficult to implement ....

18. Cocooning of older and vulnerable patients can start later, and would have to continue longer, than other measures. (SAGE, 13 minutes, 5 March, 2020)

It was only on 16 March that SAGE's advice changed, to advocate measures including additional social distancing and a significant increase in testing, with a warning that additional measures might be necessary (SAGE, 16 minutes, 16 March, 2020).

Thus, the government had had a range of restrictions offered by different groups reporting to SAGE. There was also other scientific advice publicised, often recommending far more severe measures, with the aim of eradicating rather than containing the virus. (As seen in the following, the government chose, until late in March 2020, to adopt the least stringent recommendations — more akin to a herd immunity policy, perforce by infection, as there were no vaccines yet.)

8. Scientific Opposition to Herd Immunity by Infection

Many scientists were strongly opposed to a strategy of herd immunity by infection and to the fact that preoccupations with herd immunity prevented scientists from paying enough attention to other, more active measures to deal with the virus.

8.1. *Unproven assumptions regarding herd immunity by infection*

Despite the advice given by SAGE and by other bodies, such as the modelling sub-committee, there was strong opposition to herd immunity strategies from many scientists. One trenchant criticism of the modelling used to justify a strategy of herd immunity was that it relied upon a set of unproven assumptions. Taleb, professor of risk engineering at New York University, and Bar-Yam, president of the New England Complex Systems Institute, in the third week of March 2020 wrote a critique of the modelling used. They first clarified that modelling was based on showing what would happen following a preselected set of actions. The modelling was based on a set of assumptions fed into models, and the conclusions used to make policy recommendations. But, Taleb and Bar-Yam asked, what if the assumptions were flawed? Their answer was that "people die". They claimed the following:

> The idea behind herd immunity was that the outbreak would stop if enough people got sick and gained immunity. Once a critical mass of young people gained immunity, so the epidemiological modellers told us, vulnerable populations ... would be protected ....

Their conclusion was

> this idea was nothing more than a dressed up version of the "just do nothing" approach. (Taleb and Bar-Yam, 2020)

They then continued to list the problems because of the assumptions made — flaws which individuals and scientists the world over had publicised: One could not ensure that only young people would become infected; young people neither in the UK nor anywhere else constituted the 60–70% population needed to become infected and recover; and there was no evidence that immunity rather than a recurrence of the virus would result (Taleb and Bar-Yam, 2020).

8.2. *Necessity to test, trace, quarantine, and practise social distancing*

Costello points out that a herd immunity strategy also contradicted WHO advice to test intensively, trace contacts, quarantine, and practise social distancing. In fact, population testing and contact tracing had been practised originally but were stopped early on. According to Costello (2020a), the UK had been among the first to develop a COVID-19 test as early as mid-January 2020, which had been approved by the WHO. Its national research infrastructure gave it the capability to respond to the virus, yet the WHO instructions were ignored. Costello concluded that the discussions in SAGE in February must have led to a different strategy of delaying the spread of the virus and instead

> "allowing it to move through the population so that we eventually acquired "herd immunity" at a delayed speed". (Costello, 2020a)

In Costello's opinion, this decision had been illogical and reckless:

> "So, at the moment when the UK had fewer than 10 deaths from COVID-19 and less than 500 confirmed cases of coronavirus, the government, informed by SAGE, decided to stop all community testing and tracing". (Costello, 2020c)

Costello points to perplexity in the public health community. He had argued in an earlier chapter that such a policy would cause a serious spread of the virus with more infections and mortalities. He had claimed, which many would regard as a matter of common sense, that it would have been better to take precautionary measures, contain the pandemic, and consider herd immunity later when more evidence might be available. He estimated that had the government policy been followed to the end — which was to allow 40 million people to become infected — it could have meant six million hospital admissions, of whom two million might have required intensive care with over 400,000 deaths (Costello, 2020c).

One explanation for halting the test-and-trace policy was a lack of capacity. It was not to do with scientific advice. Sir Mark Walport, chief executive of UK Research and Innovation and, according to Costello, a key member of SAGE, on 14 March, 2020, affirmed that "Advice from the scientific community was always to test as much as possible". The problem was that people in the laboratories and Public Health England were unable to put this into effect (cited in Costello, 2020b). Costello points out that the next day, 15 March, in an interview with Sky News, Walport went back on his view about the importance of testing, instead praising the government's "world class" modelling and its allowance of mass gatherings. On 29 March, he again defended the government's social distancing policy as being preferable to testing when it came to lowering infection rates for the general population (Costello, 2020b).

8.3. *Possibility of high death rates*

However, the government had also been given different advice. It was informed of potentially catastrophic consequences of COVID-19 by one of the three expert groups advising SAGE. SPI-M, the group modelling the spread of the virus, informed the government on 2 March, 2020, that the virus was highly contagious; each person could infect up to three more; and 80% of the population (53 million people) could become infected, with a death rate estimated at between 0.5% and 1% of the population — between 250,000 and 500,000 people. On 14 March, 500 British scientists signed a letter opposing herd immunity as a viable strategy (Conn *et al.*, 2020).

Al-Khalili's characterisations of scientists are evident with regard to scientists' understandings of and recommendations with respect to COVID-19. Although mistakes had been made regarding what kind of virus it was and how different it was from flu epidemics, the acceptance of uncertainty by many scientists enabled them to admit doubt and change course. While this may be seen as a strength among scientists (Al-Khalili, 2020a), it was not so easy for politicians. This may have led to their obstinacy in pursuing a particular policy designed to mitigate the effects of the virus for longer than was credible, rather than taking more stringent and active measures as had been advised by many scientists. So, on the one hand, many scientists did change their position with regard to the problems a herd immunity strategy would create, seeing the necessity for test and trace and lockdown policies. On the other, the government persisted in what might be described as a *laissez-faire* policy for too long.

9. The UK Government's Response to the Concept of Herd Immunity Early 2020

The government had obviously been faced with conflicting advice from scientists both within the SAGE groups and from those outside as to how serious the pandemic was likely to be and what measures should be taken. The measures that were taken by the government were in the first months of 2020 always on the side of doing the minimum — measures akin to a herd immunity policy by infection. As mentioned previously, this may have been due to the other and potentially conflicting demands perceived by the government regarding the economy, employment, education, and NHS readiness.

Ministers, notably the previous Health and Social Care Secretary, Hancock, have persistently denied backing a herd immunity approach (Conn *et al.*, 2020). However, there are many indications that a herd immunity approach had been supported by the government. A senior source from the DHSC affirmed that discussions about herd immunity were still being considered after 16 March, 2020. This is after SAGE changed its advice to recommend additional, more direct interventions. Costello, also a former WHO director, was under the impression that the government had supported herd immunity:

> "the government appears to have concluded that it is inevitable most people will get the disease, so we should let the epidemic

proceed to allow 60% of the population to become infected and build herd immunity through the wild virus". (Costello, 2020c)

According to Horton (2020c), Graham Medley, one of the government's scientific advisers, affirmed on Newsnight in mid-March 2020 that the government's policy, on the recommendation of scientists, was as follows:

> "to allow a controlled epidemic of large numbers of people, which would generate "herd immunity" ... a situation where the majority of the population are immune to the infection. And the only way of developing this in the absence of a vaccine, is for the majority of the population to become infected". (cited in Horton, 2020c)

The aim would be to have "a nice big epidemic" among the less vulnerable while reducing to a minimum the exposure to the virus of the vulnerable (Horton, 2020c).

Cummings has recently stated that a herd immunity strategy had indeed been the government's plan "A" pursued by the Health and Social Care Secretary until 16 March, 2021 (Elgot *et al.*, 2021).[4]

The government in fact did claim something like herd immunity as a strategy at the prime minister's daily press conferences, flanked by the government's chief scientific adviser and chief medical officer, Vallance and Whitty. These had been set up from 16 March, 2020:

> "The policy was containment and mitigation. The sick would be treated. Crowds should be avoided. "Herd immunity" should rise to 60% or 70%, and time would do the rest". (Jenkins, 2020)

Sixty percent of the population, it has been pointed out, would amount to 40 million people becoming infected (Conn *et al.*, 2020).

Despite warnings both from within SAGE and from scientists outside, the government chose not only to ignore these but also to cancel some of the measures that were already in place against the pandemic. The first phase of a test-and-trace strategy was ended on

---

[4]The fact that Cummings had recently been dismissed by the prime minister's office should perhaps be taken into account when criticisms of the government are made.

2 March, and a "mitigation" plan was instituted, aimed at isolating infected people and then their households for a fortnight. At some point in the future, efforts would be made to shield vulnerable people (Conn *et al.*, 2020). However, the virus was still not taken with the seriousness beginning to be urged by the government's scientific advisers. At the first televised press conference on 3 March, 2020, the prime minister, flanked by his chief medical and scientific advisers, stated the following:

> "I was at a hospital the other night where I think there were actually a few coronavirus patients and I shook hands with everybody".

He advised the following:

> "We should all basically just go about our normal daily lives ... The best thing you can do is to wash your hands with soap and hot water while singing Happy Birthday twice". (Conn *et al.*, 2020)

There was no further advice, for example, given to elderly and vulnerable people to shield.

This advice was given at a time when other governments in Europe, cognisant of the effects of the pandemic in Italy, were beginning to take measures including lockdowns and border closures. No such safeguards were introduced into the UK. In fact, the number of people coming into the country between January and the end of March is thought to have been 18 million, of whom a tiny fraction — 273 — were quarantined (Monbiot, 2020). The fact that Italy and Spain had three weeks earlier faced these problems and been shown to have made inadequate preparation and provision did not help concentrate the minds in the UK. Even after the lockdown was announced, 95,000 people are estimated to have entered the country without being subject to any restrictions (Monbiot, 2020).

Equally, if no less inexplicably, information about the measures taken by some governments in South East Asia, which were successfully combatting infections from the virus, also appears to have been ignored. From a WHO situation report on 18 March, 2020, it has been estimated that the number of deaths in South Korea, China, Japan, and Taiwan with a population together totalling about 24 times that of the UK, with less warning, between them had recorded fewer than 3,500 deaths. By March 2020, life was moving back to normal in China — attributed to extensive testing and tracing (Rowland, 2020). Jeremy Hunt, a former health secretary and since 2020 chair of the Health and Social Care parliamentary select committee, described the government's focus on influenza and its failure to learn from the experiences of Asian countries as "one of the biggest failures of scientific advice to ministers in our lifetime" (Pegg, 2020).

In the UK, occurrences, which perhaps can also best be explained by a strategy of herd immunity by infection, were the continuance of large crowd sporting events. Those most remembered are the Cheltenham horse racing festival 10–13 March with over 60,000 spectators each afternoon, the Liverpool vs. Atletico football match, 11 March, which hosted 52,000 people including 3,000 from Madrid, a city already under partial lockdown, and the Stereophonics concert in Cardiff on 14 March which played to a packed house (Conn *et al.*, 2020). On March 7, the prime minister himself attended a crowded rugby match at Twickenham (Toynbee, 2020). It is thought that these events constituted a major cause for the spread of the pandemic at that time — they were "superspreader" events, language catching up with the effects of the virus.

By 22 April, 2020, the Gloucestershire Hospitals NHS trust which covers Cheltenham had recorded 125 deaths, a figure roughly double that of two neighbouring trusts (Sabbagh *et al.*, 2020). However, according to Dr Andrew Preston, reader in microbial pathogenesis at Bath University, the lack of testing and tracing meant that one could not know for certain what the Cheltenham festival's role was with regard to the spread of the virus, although the higher death rates in that trust two weeks after the festival made it likely (Sabbagh *et al.*, 2020).

Yet, some of the government's advisers were still supporting a herd immunity policy. For example, Sir Patrick Vallance on the Radio 4 Today programme asserted on 13 March the following:

"because the vast majority of people get a mild illness, to build up some kind of herd immunity, so more people are immune to this disease, and we reduce the transmission. At the same time we protect those who are most vulnerable to it". (cited in Conn *et al.*, 2020)

This was despite the WHO's further declaration on March 11 that COVID-19 constituted a pandemic and despite its strong criticism of some countries' "alarming levels of inaction" (Conn *et al.*, 2020).[5] Costello drove the point home about the government and its advisers' secrecy. He suggested that the decision about herd immunity might have been avoided if people with public health and primary care expertise had been included in the SAGE group. And had the discussions and intended courses of action been made public, the wider scientific community could have contributed to the final decisions and possibly saved thousands of lives (Costello, 2020a).

Weeks later, the government changed course and decided to pursue a test, trace, and isolate policy but still, according to Costello, with the aim of "flattening the curve" rather than eradicating the virus by finding every case (Costello, 2020a). Professor Neil Ferguson of Imperial College London is thought to have influenced a change in direction in the government's policy. Ferguson estimated on 16 March, 2020, that under a mitigation policy, in which herd immunity was one option, 250,000 people would die (Conn *et al.*, 2020). Costello writing in late April 2020, estimated that by late May 2020, there could be 60,000 or more deaths. It was estimated that by 19 May, without testing, tracing, and isolating, there would be between the official estimate of 35,000 and the Financial Times estimate of 62,000 deaths (Costello, 2020b).

10. Consequences

The results, as is widely known, were disastrous. Between mid-February and the end of May 2020, England's and Wales' deaths from all causes — the virus and cancelled medical treatment for

---

[5]Much earlier warning signs of the potential seriousness of the virus include the *Lancet's* warning on 24 January, 2020, and the warnings already mentioned that the WHO had given in January and February 2020 (Conn *et al.*, 2020).

other ailments — had excess deaths that were 37% higher than expected and were among the worst per capita of 21 industrialised countries, exceeded only by Spain, with 38%. The virus spread widely during the first three weeks of March 2020 and by the end of April had claimed more than 21,000 lives in hospitals alone, possibly the highest death toll in Europe (Conn *et al.*, 2020). According to the journal *Nature Medicine*, the reasons for this were delays in going into lockdown and the absence of effective community-based test-and-trace procedures. The UK, as mentioned, had put a stop to its test-and-trace programme, according to some because of lack of capacity (Sample, 2020b).

11. Explanations

With the benefit of hindsight and with a burgeoning blame game, the likely culprits can only be the government, its scientific advisers, or more broadly "the science" as it was known and publicised at the time. And with a public inquiry, however much delayed, in the offing, it is a question that must be answered with the possibility of the reputation of the government, the scientists and science, or all of them, being on the line.

12. Scientists' Assumptions

12.1. *Resemblance of the virus to influenza*

The assumption that the pandemic would resemble influenza was initially made by many scientists, according to Horton. He points out that what he calls the "key government committee", the New and Emerging Respiratory Virus Threats Advisory Committee on 21 February, 2020, advised that they supported Public Health England's assessment of the risk as "moderate". This was after the WHO had declared that the virus constituted an international public health emergency. Horton called this decision "a genuinely fatal error of judgment" (Horton, 2020a). Costello confirms this. In his view, SAGE paid too much attention to the influenza pandemic, which had a much lower death rate, a lower R value[6] (1.3 approximately) and a short incubation period, making testing redundant (Costello, 2020a).

12.2. *Scientific modelling*

One of the problems the scientists faced is that they could not immerse themselves in the "long effort" which, Bourdieu had argued, scientific work required (Bourdieu, 1990, p. 16). One of the ways scientists arrived at decisions as to what was going to happen and therefore what actions might be taken was through scientific modelling. The problem with modelling, as mentioned earlier, is that it is based on assumptions made by the modeller, necessary in the absence of hard data. But as Sample (2020a) points out, because they are based on assumptions that may turn out to be incorrect, modelling results cannot be accepted uncritically.

In one case, scientists at Oxford University estimated that a high proportion of the population in the UK (68%, or over 34 million) had been exposed to the virus in early 2020 and that only a fraction were at risk of serious illness. The 68% figure was described by Klenerman, one of the Oxford University researchers, as "the most extreme" result. Klenerman said that a result at the other extreme would be that only a tiny proportion of the population had been exposed to the virus, and that the actual result was likely to be somewhere in between (Sample, 2020a).

Another set of modelling done by Imperial College also under-played the likely risks from the virus, this time regarding the need for intensive care facilities. The model was based on the assumption that the demand for intensive care for COVID-19 would be the same as the findings of a previous model regarding a possible influenza pandemic. Because the demand was estimated to be much lower than what eventually transpired, the government again was supported in its inclination to allow the country to ride the epidemic out, letting

---

[6]R is the number of people that one infected person will pass on a virus to, on average. So if, for example, a person with the virus infected three other people, the R value would be 3.

infection sweep through the population with the expectation that this would create herd immunity (Sample, 2020a).

Sample points out that the Imperial College model was flawed also in what it did not consider — the potential benefits that widespread rapid testing, contact tracing, and isolation strategies might bring in the early stages of a pandemic, nor did it consider the effects of a lockdown (Sample, 2020a). Sample's conclusion was that models should not therefore be rejected; rather, their limitations should be acknowledged and they should be used only in conjunction with other sources of information.

13. Government Ministers' Assumptions

Many reasons have been suggested for the government's attraction to a herd immunity strategy rather than to testing and tracing or to the other measures suggested such as lockdown and border controls — measures successfully adopted in some other countries.

13.1. *The influence of the influenza virus*

One explanation is that the government's mindset and preparations were based on influenza pandemics, as had been the case with many scientists. That was what attracted its attention, perhaps because that was where the funding had been directed (Professor Graham Medley, cited by Conn *et al.*, 2020). The difference between COVID-19 and flu was not sufficiently appreciated. With regard to flu, its spread was rapid, but it became milder as it mutated; people could develop immunity and the population become resistant. COVID-19, on the other hand, was far more dangerous, its properties more uncertain, and herd immunity strategies by infection far riskier (Conn *et al.*, 2020).[7]

---

[7]Herd immunity was not discarded as a policy, according to Cummings. He published plans showing government documents from three meeting held by COBRA (COBR is the acronym for Cabinet Office Briefing Rooms and is the Civil Contingencies Committee that is convened to handle matters of national emergency or major disruption. Its purpose is to coordinate different departments and agencies in response to such emergencies. These plans were published in

Pegg (2020) gives this as an explanation for the government's failure to act appropriately in dealing with COVID-19. However, Pegg himself points out that UK governments had had experience with previous emergencies, including periodic outbreaks of infectious diseases, fuel protests, floods, foot and mouth disease, bird flu scares, and the aftermaths and implications of the 9/11 and 7/7 terrorist attacks in the US and London, respectively. There had also been several government and public health bodies set up to predict UK's future responses to such emergencies and to recommend how governments should handle them (Pegg, 2020).

13.2. *The government's preparedness*

Where there might have been a vision previously, this was not followed with action in the early months of the pandemic. Rhodes, head of the Centre for the Study of Existential Risk at Cambridge University, scheduled to give evidence to a House of Commons joint committee on the national security strategy on preparations with regard to infectious diseases, told *The Guardian* that while the UK had planned reasonably well for a pandemic, there did seem to be "a significant gap between recognition of the risk and planning, and action on preparedness" (Carrington, 2020).

Horton was scathing in his criticism of the government's planning to deal with the virus. He compared the UK's response with China's:

> "When its government realised that a new virus was circulating, officials didn't advise handwashing, a better cough etiquette and disposing of tissues. They quarantined entire cities and shut down the economy". (Horton, 2020a)

13.3. *Economic considerations*

The government's concern for the economy, understandable though this was, has been given as a reason many times during this pandemic

---

early March 2020, which demonstrated the government's intention to follow a herd immunity strategy later on in September (Elgot *et al.*, 2021). This despite the fact that governments in many other countries were taking more immediate, direct, and stringent measures.

for not taking action. According to a "well-placed source" at a Cabinet Office Briefing Rooms (COBRA) meeting, the government feared that a lockdown would be economically disastrous and, in any case, itself could result in many deaths (Conn *et al.*, 2020). However, there were arguably other more fundamental and far-reaching economic factors at play — those to do with government expenditure and ideology. Cost was another economic consideration, certainly in the early stages of the pandemic, as also mentioned in the following. The alternatives to a herd immunity policy were regarded as being too costly. One of these alternatives, along with other simultaneous measures was testing, tracing, and isolation, a strategy recommended by the WHO (Summers, 2020a). However, this was expensive (Summers, 2020a) and was delayed until May 2020 (Booth, 2020).

13.4. *Ideological considerations*

Cost can be linked with the government's ideology and consequent funding policies for over a decade and could well be the most important factor regarding the degree of preparedness and willingness to act, including its openness to the idea of herd immunity from infection, mitigation or delaying the spread of the virus. Cost cuts in public funding have been an important part of the government's strategy since the conservative/liberal democrat government took office in 2010, with its severe and wide-ranging austerity programme. This has been in line with its increasingly strong neoliberal ideology of decreasing state involvement in supporting public services and of encouraging privatisation (Green 2016). Some of the consequences of the austerity policy introduced by this government were reduced resources in the NHS, in other public services, and in local organisations, including local authorities, which could have been used to roll out programmes such as test and trace. However, these were not used initially.

Horton, along with others, supports this line of argument. He puts the failure of the government to act down to its austerity programme, which had the aim of reducing the role of the state.

This left the country poorly prepared and fatally weakened (Horton, 2020a). According to Toynbee, the 10 years of austerity had

"crippled every service ... the Andrew Lansley reforms blew the NHS into fragments; social care was stripped bare; and local government, responsible for public health, was shredded". (Toynbee, 2020)

Monbiot (2020) takes this argument further, attributing to the government what can be described as ideological, partisan, and possibly nefarious intent. He gives as an example the government allowing untested patients to be moved from hospitals to care homes. The Cygnus exercise in 2016 had emphasised the dangers that an epidemic would pose for residents in care homes. The government's disregard for this warning and breach of its own procedures was neither because of lack of knowledge nor of capacity.

Monbiot identifies this as a cost-averse strategy and links it with the granting of lucrative monopolies to "friends in the private sector". He paints a stark picture of this ideology and the policies arising from it. He equates the present UK government's policies with those of Bolsonaro in Brazil and with those of the former Trump administration in the US. In his opinion, they represent a particular kind of economic interest, which is in conflict with the people who are front-line workers and others performing useful services that enable us to carry on with our lives:

"This political conflict is always fought on behalf of the same group: those who extract wealth. The war against utility is necessary if you want to privatise public services, granting lucrative monopolies or fire sales of public assets to friends in the public sector. It's necessary if you want to hold down public sector pay and the minimum wage, cutting taxes and bills for the same funders and lobbyists. It is necessary if corporations are to be allowed to outsource and offshore their workforces, and wealthy people can offshore their income and assets". (Monbiot, 2020)

Monbiot's explanation is one that is evidenced by the government's austerity programme, underpinned by a neoliberal ideology that has sought to reduce the role of the state and the resources provided by it, in favour of the privatisation of public services and the policy of making individuals responsible for their circumstances, with diminishing support from the state (Green, 2016).[8] This policy has been continued relentlessly over the past 11 years, resulting in the huge public service cuts described above by Toynbee. This is not to mention the costs borne by the poorest and most disadvantaged in British society, from reductions in benefits, through reduced housing provision to people dying from being deprived of basic help (Green, 2016).

Given successive governments' willingness to continue with such policies in the face of these consequences, intended or not, Monbiot's explanation for the government's lack of action and its consequences is one that should be taken seriously. He argues that because the government had the knowledge and capacity, not acting was a conscious decision, the underlying strategy being not to frontload any costs.

14. Conclusion

Freedland's expectation that the government would, when reckoning comes, use as a get-out the excuse that it was "following the science" and nicely positioning the scientists as the "fall guys" is possible. There have been indications of this already. However, it might be argued that the government was not entirely to blame. From what

---

[8]This ideology is again being played out at the time of writing this. On 5 July, 2021, the government declared that all COVID-19 restrictions were to be lifted on 19 July, 2021. All current restrictions, such as the wearing of masks and social distancing, would be voluntary, even in closed spaces and public transport. Professor Stephen Reicher of the University of St. Andrews and a member of one of the sub-committees advising the government commented particularly on the government's passing responsibility for decisions as to how to behave to individuals: He is reported as saying how frightening it was "to have a 'health' secretary who still thinks COVID is flu. Who is unconcerned at levels of infection. Who doesn't realise that those who do best for health, also do best for the economy. Who want to ditch all protections while only half of us are vaccinated". His most severe criticism was as follows: "Above all, it is frightening to have a 'health' secretary who wants to make all protections a matter of personal choice when the key message of the pandemic is "this isn't an 'I' thing, it's a 'we' thing" (Allegretti and Geddes, 2021).

has been described above about the problems facing scientists and between scientists and government ministers, one can well arrive at Freedland's conclusion that

> "there is no such thing as "the science" — that there are always going to be competing views over how to act on data once you've got it". (Freedland, 2020)

One can go further in unpacking the concept of "the science" and showing the concept in its extreme to be chameleon-like or phantasmagorical — one can query what did the science consist of and what of it held in the rapidly changing situation. What was "the science" when there were different views among scientists and when the information to hand in relation to the virus was interpreted so differently by different experts and when it was changing so rapidly? Also, were the scientific recommendations unaffected by scientists' knowledge about whether there were the resources, capabilities, and political will to implement them?

But the government must also bear responsibility. What did its "following the science" amount to? Was it to follow what was politically convenient, choosing between different scientists' views on political rather than scientific grounds, sometimes waiting till the "right" answer came up and a convenient recommendation made? Or was it simply to ignore the scientific recommendations when they did not suit? And had the science been followed, would the government strategies have led to the disastrous consequences they did? Ultimately the government's (and scientific advisers') "way out" may be their consensus that the scientists' role was to advise and that it was for the government to take the final decisions, bound as it always was by other considerations as well.

These questions might have become clearer had the analysis been extended over a longer time period and more of the issues investigated, particularly the timing and stipulations regarding the lockdowns, the success of the test and trace rollouts, and the vaccination programme.

Freedland's conclusion and Sridhar's comments still stand, that there is no such thing as "the science", let alone "following" it.

The science and the scientists were part of a process that involved different scientific views and findings based on different assumptions and comparisons, which philosophers such as Feyerabend would have regarded as normal. In this case, the rapidity with which the scientists had to come up with results in a far from neutral context greatly complicated the situation.

The government's policy of minimal public responsibility and minimal resourcing particularly in early 2020 at the beginning of the pandemic overrode much of the scientific advice it was being given at least from early and mid-March 2020. Ultimately, the government's legacy of austerity and its neoliberal ideology may have then been the most important factors determining its policies and their consequences.

References

Alderson, F. (2020). Letter to *The Guardian*, 15 April, 2020.

Al-Khalili, J. (2020a). Our politicians must learn the value of doubt. *The Guardian*, 22 April, 2020.

Al-Khalili, J. (2020b). Scientists fought covid, now they're battling misinformation. *The Guardian*, 29 December, 2020.

Allegretti, A. and Geddes, L. (2021). Backlash from scientists as Johnson prepares to lift all covid restrictions. *The Guardian*, 5 July, 2021.

Ayton, P. (2020). Letter to *The Guardian*, 29 April, 2020.

Booth, R. (2020). Test and trace: What has gone wrong, from slow results to centralisation. *The Guardian*, 14 October, 2020.

Boseley, S. (2020). Herd immunity: No evidence to support tactic, Medics Warn. *The Guardian*, 15 October, 2020.

Bourdieu, P. (1990). *The Logic of Practice*, Translated by R. Nice, Stanford University Press, Stanford.

Bourdieu, P., Chamboredon, J.-C. and Passeron, J.-C. (1991). *The Craft of Sociology: Epistemological Preliminaries*, in B. Krais (ed.), Translated by R. Nice, Walter de Gruyter, Berlin.

Buranyi, S. (2020). The scientists' advice on covid is clear, Despite the dissenters. *The Guardian*, 29 September, 2020.

Carrington, D. (2020). UK strategy to tackle pandemic was not implemented, says ex-chief scientist. *The Guardian*, 30 March, 2020.

Conn, D., Lawrence, F., Lewis, P., Carrell, S., Pegg, D., Davies, H. and Evans, R. (2020). Revealed: The inside story of the covid-19 crisis in the UK. *The Guardian*, 30 April, 2020.

Costello, A. (2020a). No 10's secret science group has a shocking lack of expertise. *The Guardian*, 28 April, 2020.

Costello, A. (2020b). How did sage get it so wrong? *The Guardian*, 19 May, 2020.

Costello, A. (2020c). First, suppress this pandemic. Then plan for the next stage. *The Guardian*, 17 March, 2020.

Devlin, H. (2020). Growing exasperation among experts over politicians who claim they "follow the science". *The Guardian*, 24 April, 2020.

Elgot, J., Allegretti, A. and Stewart, H. (2021). "We're killing the vulnerable", key claims in cummings' latest attack on government. *The Guardian*, 17 June, 2021.

Elgot, J. and Davis, N. (2021). Johnson being urged to impose blanket covid border controls. *The Guardian*, 24 January, 2021. https://www.the guardian.com/world/2021/jan/24/boris-johnson-urged-blanket-covid-border-controls-uk.

Feyerabend, P. (1993). *Against Method*, 3rd edn. Verso, London.

Freedland, J. (2020). This government should be on the rack. The evidence that it botched crucial decisions at crucial moments is piling up. *The Guardian*, 2 May, 2020.

Gavi. The vaccine alliance. 26 March, 2020. Available at: https://www.gavi.org/vaccineswork/what-herd-immunity?gclid=EAIaIQobChMI6 9LD76WP8QIVQwCiAx039wmDEAAYAiAAEgIIevD_BwE.

Green, M. (2016). Neoliberalism and management scholarship: Educational implications. *Philosophy of Management*, Vol. 15, No. 3, pp. 183–201. DOI:10.1007/s40926-016-0042-x.

Green, M. (2019). *Management Scholarship and Organisational Change: Representing Burns and Stalker*. Routledge, London.

Habermas, J. (1972). *Knowledge and Human Interests*, Translated by J. J. Shapiro. Heinemann, London.

Halfpenny, P. (2001). Positivism in the twentieth century, in G. Ritzer and B. Smart (eds.), *Handbook of Social Theory*, pp. 371–385, SAGE, London.

Hanage, W. (2021a). A year on, we cannot afford to forget the covid failures. *The Guardian*, 23 March, 2021.

Hanage, W. (2021b). There are no excuses for Hancock's care homes strategy. *The Guardian*, 17 June, 2021.

Hanson, N. R. (1972). *Patterns of Discovery: An Inquiry into the Conceptual Foundations of Science*. University Press, Cambridge.

Harvey, I. (2020). [Emeritus Professor of Public Health, UEA] Letter. *The Guardian*, 10 October, 2020.

Horkheimer, M. (1937). *Critical Theory*, Herder and Herder, New York.

Horton, R. (2020a). Covid-19 is the greatest science policy failure in a generation. *The Guardian*, 10 April, 2020.

Horton, R. (2020b). How can any scientist now stand by this government? *The Guardian*, 28 May, 2020.

Horton, R. (2020c). Why did the UK fail to act on coronavirus months ago? *The Guardian*, 19 March, 2020.

Jenkins, S. (2020). Was I wrong? Even scientists still don't agree on covid-19. *The Guardian*, 3 April, 2020.

Jones, O. (2014). *The Establishment: And How They Get Away with it*. Penguin Books, UK.

Kucharski, A. (2020). How covid-19 models work, and why we need them. *The Guardian*, 12 November, 2020.

Kuhn, T. (1970). *The Structure of Scientific Revolutions*. 2nd edn. Chicago University Press, Chicago.

LBC Reiter News. 22 January, 2021. Available at: https://www.lbc.co.uk/news/heathrow-airport-huge-crowds-queues-incredibly-worrying-shadow-health-secretary/.

Lewis, P. and Conn, D. (2020). Scientists' Fury as advice on lockdown is censored before being published. *The Guardian*, 9 May, 2020.

Mannheim, K. (1952). *Essays on the Sociology of Knowledge*. Routledge and Kegan Paul Ltd., London.

Monbiot, G. (2020). The UK was ready for this virus. Then we un-prepared. *The Guardian*, 20 May, 2020.

Nicolson, D. (2021), Participant in Ridge, S. (2021) Cove crisis: Learning the lessons, sky news, 9 February, 2021. Available at: https://news.sky.com/video/covid-19-assessing-the-uks-responsae-12212791.

Paton, C. (2020). Letter to *The Guardian*, 19 October, 2020.

Pegg, D. (2020). A disaster plan: How Britain was blindsided by the virus. *The Guardian*, 22 May, 2020.

PHE (2020). If there is evidence of a cluster of covid 19 cases in the UK what will the PHE proposal be, 24 February, 2020. Available at: https://www.gov.uk/government/publications/phe.

Philo, G. (2020). Letter to *The Guardian*. 20 March, 2020.

Reiter, S. A. and Williams, P. F. (2002). The structure and progressivity of accounting research: The crisis in the academy revisited, *Accounting, Organizations and Society*, Vol. 27, No. 6, August, pp. 575–607.

Ridge, S. (2021). Cove crisis: Learning the lessons, sky news, 9 February, 2021. Available at: https://news.sky.com/video/covid-19-assessing-the-uks-response-12212791.

Rowland, A. (2020). Letter to *The Guardian*, 20 March, 2020.

Sabbagh, D., Morris, S. and Cook, C. (2020). Virus death toll leads to new call for inquiry into Cheltenham festival. *The Guardian*, 22 April, 2020.

SAGE 4 Minutes: Coronavirus (COVID-19) Response, 4 February, 2020. Available at: https://www.gov.uk/government/publications/sage-min utes-coronavirus-covid-19-response-4-february-2020/sage-4-minutes-coronavirus-covid-19-response-4-february-2020.

SAGE 12 Minutes: Wuhan Coronaviurs, 3 March, 2020. Available at: https://www.gov.uk/government/publications/sage-minutes-corona virus-covid-19-response-3-march-2020.

SAGE 13 Minutes: Coronavirus (COVID-19) Response, 5 March, 2020. Available at: https://www.gov.uk/government/publications/sage-minutes-coronavirus-covid-19-5-march-2020.

SAGE 16 Minutes: Coronavirus (COVID-19) Response, 16 March, 2020. Available at: https://www.gov.uk/government/publications/sage-min utes-coronavirus-covid-19-response-16-march-2020.

Sample, I. (2020a). Scientific modelling is valuable — But remember the limitations. *The Guardian*, 26 March, 2020.

Sample, I. (2020b). Excess deaths: England and Wales among the worst hit. *The Guardian*, 15 October, 2020.

Sample, I., Carrell, S. and Pegg, D. (2020). Sage: Names of scientific advisers to be published. *The Guardian*, 28 April, 2020.

Sample, I. and Mason R. (2020). More calls for clarity as no 10 partially reveals sage list. *The Guardian*, 5 May, 2020.

Scally, G. (2021). Government decisions have paved the way to this crisis. *The Guardian*, 12 January, 2021.

Scott, G. (2021). Boris Johnson refuses call for coronavirus public inquiry while country is still "working flat out" to tackle crisis. *Yorkshire Post*, 27 January, 2021. Available at: https://www.yorkshirepost.co.uk/hea lth/coronavirus/boris-johnson-refuses-call-coronavirus-public-inquiry-while-country-still-working-flat-out-tackle-crisis-3114819.

Siddique, H. (2020). Protest after minister hints "wrong" science led to government mistakes. *The Guardian*, 21 May, 2020.

Sodha, S. (2020). The covid crisis means that we need to cut the bias in science. *The Guardian*, 24 July, 2020.

SPI-M-O (2020). Consensus view on the impact of possible interventions to delay the spread of a UK outbreak of 2019-nCov, 3 February, 2020. Available at: https://assets.publishing.service.gov.uk/government/up loads/system/uploads/attachment_data/file/888388/s0007-spi-m-o-co nsensus-view-impact-interventions-030220-sage4.pdf.

Sridhar, D. (2021). Participant in Ridge, S (2021) Cove crisis: Learning the lessons, sky news, 9 February, 2021. Available at: https://news.sky .com/video/covid-19-assessing-the-uks-response-12212791.

Summers, C. (2020a). The WHO's new test is a gamechanger. *The Guardian*, 30 September, 2020.

Taleb, N. and Bar-Yam, Y. (2020). No 10's "science" is almost evidence-free. *The Guardian*, 26 March, 2020.

The Guardian (2020). Editorial. 27 April, 2020.

Tolhurst, A. and Langford, E. (2020). Boris Johnson has claimed the UK will have a "world-beating" system to test, track and trace for coronavirus up and running by 1 June. *Politics Home*, 20 May 2020. Available at: https://www.politicshome.com/news/article/pm-claims-uk-will-have-worldbeating-test-track-and-trace-system-up-and-running-by-1-june.

Toynbee, P. (2020). Johnson is the wrong man in the wrong job at the wrong time. *The Guardian*, 21 April, 2020.

Turner, J. H. (2001). The origins of positivism: The contributions of Auguste Comte and Herbert Spencer, in G. Ritzer and B. Smart (eds.), *Handbook of Social Theory*, pp. 30–42, SAGE, London.

Vince, G. (2020). Under the microscope. Available at: *The Guardian Review*, 5 December, 2020, pp. 6–9.

Wikipedia. Available at: https://en.wikipedia.org/wiki/Great_Barrington_Declaration (accessed 17 June, 2021).

Part 2

Implementation and Governance

Chapter 7

Cohered Emergent Theory for Designing and Implementing Multinational Mining Sustainability Practise in Ghana

Frank Nyame-Asiamah, Kwame Oduro Amoako, and Peter Kawalek

Abstract

This chapter applies cohered emergent theory to explain how multinational mining corporations operating in Africa can design and implement their sustainability practises to equalise the economic, environmental, and social dimensions of sustainability. We used thematic analysis to analyse interview data from 16 diverse stakeholders of a multinational mining company in Ghana. The findings suggest that the company's economic, environmental, and social sustainability practises were designed and implemented as a social inclusivity process that revolved around rational planning and power, critique from "less powerful" stakeholders and emergent events, and regular adjustments to senior managers' planned actions. These design and implementation processes will help senior managers to manage business activities ethically and mitigate potential sustainability implementation risks that can damage organisational reputation, harm community welfare, and destroy the environment. The study also has implications for governments and policy think tanks of developing countries to rectify corporate sustainability policies that can foster fair allocation of royalties and taxes from multinational mining companies to the mining communities and to reduce rural poverty. The outcome of the study manifests the theoretical value of the cohered emergent discipline in practise.

Keywords: Cohered emergent theory; economic sustainability; environmental sustainability; social sustainability; multinational mining; Ghana

1. Introduction

Extractive companies create jobs and wealth for economic development, yet their activities degrade the environment, deprive the livelihoods of many people living in the mining communities, and raise concern for social justice (Gerlak and Zuniga-Teran, 2020). The leftover mining materials cause severe damage to arable land, water bodies, vegetation, and the environment (Sun *et al.*, 2018). Policy discourse has intimated that the present wealth creation objectives should not be pursued carelessly to compromise the future use of scarce resources (Hansmann *et al.*, 2012) or disadvantage people whose livelihoods and well-being depend on equitable use of resources (Essah and Andrews, 2016; Gerlak and Zuniga-Teran, 2020). The United Nations requires companies to operate responsibly and balance their financial benefits with ecological and social expectations of their diverse stakeholders in order to achieve the Sustainable Development Goals and make our world fairer (Tsalis *et al.*, 2020).

The former Norwegian Prime Minister, Gro Harlem Brundtland, had earlier summarised such a sustainable development initiative as one that "seeks to meet the needs and aspirations of the present without compromising the ability to meet those of the future" (World Commission on Environment and Development, 1987, p. 7). Brundtland ratifies that sustainable development must be designed, implemented, and practised equally around economic, environmental, and social sustainability dimensions (Senior, 2003). Her sustainability advocacy was advanced through the triple bottom line framework which uses economic, environmental, and social dimensions of sustainability to explain how companies should organise their production and communication activities to provide reasonable opportunities for their primary stakeholders, preserve healthy environment, and promote social justice for communities (Elkington, 1997, 2013; Norman and MacDonald, 2004).

The contention is that managing and balancing economic, environmental, and social dimensions of sustainability is a complex and challenging task for both private and public sector organisations (Fischer *et al.*, 2020). First, the foci of these three sustainability dimensions are different and often conflicting. Economic sustainability focuses more on wealth creation and financial stability for businesses, their primary investors, and internal stakeholders (Elliott, 2005). Environmental sustainability emphasises the conservation of ecological systems and reduction of risks of pollution and harm to natural resources (Scott, 2003), while social sustainability addresses concerns about injustices, social inequalities, and exploitation of vulnerable groups (Adonteng-Kissi, 2017). Companies' efforts to achieve financial objectives connotate clear, measurable, and short-term indicators, whereas social and environmental measurements are mostly ambiguous and uncertain (Epstein *et al.*, 2015). While a company may pursue moderate social and environmental goals for public benefits, their financial goals are usually aggressive to boost competition or risky to yield higher returns (Epstein and Buhovac, 2014; Godelnik, 2021).

Some researchers see the relationship between economic, environmental, and social goals is one that is characterised by short-term competition and firm-centric interests which are inconsistent with long-term public benefits (Mackey *et al.*, 2007; Meyer and Gauthier, 2013). There is therefore an increasing need for effective sustainability implementation that can address the challenges of equalising the three dimensions (Chofreh and Goni, 2017; Shakeel *et al.*, 2020; Ghadge *et al.*, 2020). Research studies have continued to explore a holistic and result-oriented approach to implementing corporate sustainability practises that align with corporate vision and can promote globalisation and continuous improvement (Lloret, 2016).

Although the Global Reporting Initiative (GRI, 2021) has offered principles and reporting frameworks to guide environmental, and social sustainability practises of mining corporations, the initiative has been criticised for supplying unreliable information and its deficiency of site-level performance indicators (Fonseca *et al.*, 2013). The question is how can multinational mining companies design and implement their sustainability practises to achieve equality between the economic, environmental, and social dimensions of sustainability? Existing studies continue to encourage researchers to find ways of developing sustainability initiatives that can integrate the three dimensions equally and meet the expectations of stakeholders of mining companies, including the companies themselves (Asr *et al.*, 2019; Azapagic, 2004; Niesenbaum, 2020).

This chapter applies cohered emergent theory to explain how multinational mining corporations operating in Africa can design and implement their sustainability practises to equalise the economic, environmental, and social dimensions of sustainability. Cohered emergent theory is a social inclusivity theory that prescribes how stakeholders with diverse interests can negotiate, collaborate, and contribute to sustainable design and implementation initiatives (Nyame-Asiamah, 2020; Nyame-Asiamah and Kawalek, 2021). We utilise the case of Precious Gold Mining Limited (pseudonym) subsidiary in Ghana and explore the narratives of the company's internal and external stakeholders based on cohered emergent theory to explain how the company implemented its economic, environmental, and social sustainability initiatives.

The outcomes of the study will encourage multinational mining companies to empower local communities and other stakeholders in designing and implementing their sustainability initiatives to meet the needs of those whose interests are impacted by the companies' operations. It will also motivate environmental agencies and policymakers in developing countries to enact mining policies that can encourage ethical mining business and improve lives in mining neighbourhoods.

The rest of the chapter is organised as follows: First, we discuss existing literature and frameworks for implementing sustainability practises to highlight their merits and challenges. Second, we introduce cohered emergent theory and explain how it can help companies to integrate their economic primacies with environmental and social values of their communities and adhere to ethics of responsible business. Third, we introduce the context of Precious Gold Mining Limited in Ghana and discuss our research methods. Fourth, we interpret the data and proceed to discuss our findings. Finally, we conclude the chapter with a summary of our contribution and implications for practise and research.

2. Sustainability Implementation Frameworks

Research studies have highlighted several sustainability models that explain how companies can report their environmental and socio-economic performances to their stakeholders, but there are challenges with existing models for designing and implementing sustainability initiatives (Azapagic, 2004; Morioka *et al.*, 2017; Niesenbaum, 2020).

First, the GRI framework outlines a wide range of sustainability performance indicators that help organisations to measure and disclose the impact of their activities on economy, environment, and society in a way to improve the value and credibility of their reports (Diouf and Boiral, 2017; Thomas, 2019). The framework seeks to promote accountability and openness in reporting activities of 10 industries, which include mining & metals, electric utilities, and oil & gas (Global Reporting Initiative, 2021; Gallego-Alvarez *et al.*, 2019; Pisani *et al.*, 2017). The difficulty is that GRI standards are generic; they lack site-specific data and allow opportunities for companies to manipulate their reports to manifest their consciously planned sustainability outlook (Fonseca *et al.*, 2013). The implication of this is that good sustainability reporting does not necessarily mean good sustainability performance. For instance, Belkhir *et al.* (2017) examined carbon emissions data of 40 companies reporting on GRI and those which did not report on it and found that there was no relationship between GRI reporting and better sustainability performance. It is even far more difficult to use GRI standards to compare the economic sustainability of private companies with local benefits for communities (Amoako *et al.*, 2017; Thomas, 2019) and to access non-financial reports and compare them evenly between different companies (Brown and Farrelly, 2009).

Second, the International Organization for Standardization (ISO), an independent, non-governmental international organisation with a membership of 165 national standards bodies, has set out a series of environmental management standards (ISO 14000 series) to help organisations to reduce energy use, cut material waste, and protect the environment (Gleckman and Krut, 2017; Bravi *et al.*, 2020). The key objectives of ISO 14000 include minimising business impact on air, water, and land and ensuring that companies comply with environmental policies, laws, and regulations (Testa *et al.*, 2014; Mazzi *et al.*, 2020). A survey of 1,508 Italian ISO 14001-certified companies which implemented ISO standards confirm that the companies considered the standards useful for reducing energy and waste as well as preventing and monitoring environmental risk (Bravi *et al.*, 2020). Notwithstanding the benefits, another study involving a survey of 361 ISO 14001-certified corporations in Spain found that the cost of implementing the standards and maintaining the certification was expensive (Heras-Saizarbitoria *et al.*, 2016). Another criticism is that the ISO 14000 series is exclusive to environmental protection and does not focus on the social dimension of sustainability, such as operational health and safety issues (Curkovic and Sroufe, 2011). Others contend that companies may even need time to adjust to revised versions of ISO 14000 before they can achieve the expected outcomes of the standards (Boiral and Henri, 2012; Vílchez, 2017). This justifies the need for flexible budgeting and standards in corporate project management (Bartley *et al.*, 2017; Patel, 2007; Roth, 2008).

Third, the Carbon Disclosure Project which was initiated in early 2000 as an international non-profit organisation encourages cities and the 500 largest global companies to disclose their greenhouse gas emission data, supply chain activities, and other climate-change-related information and to take proactive actions to make their activities carbon neutral (Siddique *et al.*, 2021). The limitation is that environmental disclosures do not necessarily lead to improved market value (Matsumura *et al.*, 2014; Hassan and Kouhy, 2014), and some companies even fail to divulge their carbon emissions (Stanny, 2013). Matsumura *et al.* (2014) collected emissions data on Standard and Poor's firms through a Carbon Disclosure Project questionnaire and found that the companies' carbon emissions were significantly negatively related to their market value. Hassan and Kouhy (2014) also examined the relationship between environmental disclosure and performance of oil and gas industry in Nigeria by analysing annual reports, press releases, and fact sheets of the studied firms' activities. They found that the firms' disclosure content related negatively with their carbon emission performance. Some studies argue that the Carbon Disclosure Project is a market and risk predicting tool that encourages firms to use disclosed information to create more real financial incentives for investors through stock price appreciation than to highlight sustainability benefits for employees and local communities (Alsaifi *et al.*, 2020; Nizam *et al.*, 2019).

Fourth is the triple bottom line theory which explains how an integration among economic, environmental, and social dimensions of sustainability can be used to measure the total impact of a companies' actions around profit, planet, and people (Senyo and Osabutey, 2021; Shim *et al.*, 2021; Zaharia and Zaharia, 2021). By employing the triple bottom line framework, Shim *et al.* (2021) examined the relationship between corporate social responsibility dimensions and the market value of restaurants by using data from 32 publicly traded restaurants in the US between 1999 and 2012. They reported that the economic responsibility activities increased the value of the restaurants through their community services and improved consumer products, whereas the environmental responsibility activities reduced the market value of the restaurants. In another study, Tjahjadi *et al.* (2021) adopted the triple bottom line framework to examine the impact of corporate sustainability programmes on good corporate governance, which included education of the board of commissioners of non-financial firms listed on the Indonesian Stock Market between 2013 and 2017. They found that education of the board of commissioners had negative effects on the companies' economic and environmental sustainability and no effect on social sustainability, although the size of the board correlated positively with economic sustainability performance. The outcome did not match the theoretical hopes of a triple bottom line, and it is supported by the critique that in spite of the benefits of a triple bottom line, it does not fully capture the social and emotional expectations of many stakeholders which are often unpredictable (Boje, 2016). As researchers continue to explore holistic sustainability frameworks to integrate and equalise the economic, environmental, and social sustainability of company behaviour (Elkington, 1997; 2013; Roberts and Cohen, 2002) and encourage complexity-based models for addressing sustainability challenges (Brown, 2008; Cohen, 2001; Korten, 2005; Kuhmonen, 2017), we apply cohered emergent theory to explore fresh insights into corporate sustainability design and implementation.

3. Cohered Emergent Theory

Designing sustainability practises to equalise the economic, environmental, and social domains of sustainability and to meet diverse expectations of multiple stakeholders of mining companies is not a straightforward activity for corporate managers. It is a complex process that involves power plays, compromises, moral judgements, and regular interactions between stakeholders who are affected by the sustainability agenda. This goes beyond the consideration for balancing the three domains of sustainability to include emergent actuality, a system design process which uses power negotiation, knowledge sharing, and understanding of unexpected occurrences to address sustainability expectations of stakeholders (Nyame-Asiamah and Kawalek, 2021).

It is based on the idea that the processes of designing and implementing corporate responsibility practises must draw on emergent and adaptive system approaches to allow managers to utilise their decision-making powers sensitively to address the concerns of people whose lives are affected by business activities (Brown, 2008; Cohen, 2001; Bastola and Nyame-Asiamah, 2016; Schianetz and Kavanagh, 2008). These propositions are firmly nested in cohered emergent theory (cohered emergent transformation model), a social inclusivity model that prescribes how stakeholders with diverse interests can negotiate, collaborate, and contribute to sustainable design and implementation initiatives (Nyame-Asiamah, 2020; Nyame-Asiamah and Kawalek, 2021). The theory uses learning and self-organising behaviours to explain how complex and continuous interactions between multiple stakeholders can facilitate a collaborative shift of power between corporate managers and other stakeholders to address conflicts of interest and centralised controls within sustainable design initiatives.

Cohered emergent theory draws on the complexity view that a system has several independent agents who interrelate spontaneously and continuously within their environment to create unified patterns and coherent outcomes (Nyame-Asiamah, 2013). The agents adapt to actions and reactions that emerge from their continuous interactions, which is not controlled centrally by a single individual or a group of agents (Kuhmonen, 2017; Schianetz and Kavanagh, 2008). The multiple and adaptive interactions by agents are complex and non-linear, yet they follow simple rules to generate greater outcomes than the sum of individual agent's contributions to the system. Cohered emergent theory therefore follows the principles of complexity, sets out four interrelated modules to govern its operationalisation, and explains how managers can design sustainability practises to address emergent actuality of diverse stakeholders' concerns. One is the complex adaptive system (CAS) domain that describes the self-organising space for diverse stakeholders to interact and co-create sustainable innovations, and there are learning and decision outcomes that emerge from stakeholders' multiple and complex interactions (Nyame-Asiamah and Patel, 2010; Nyame-Asiamah 2020; Nyame-Asiamah and Kawalek, 2021). These are illustrated in Figure 1 to highlight the conceptual application of the theory to corporate sustainability and consumer behaviour fields as a cohered corporate sustainability model.

The CAS module represents an evolutionary system that can allow corporate managers, employees, investors, community members, and other stakeholders, such as regulators, environmental activists, non-governmental organisations, political actors, and the United Nations to interact, design, and implement sustainability practises to benefit the interests of multistakeholders and their environment (Nyame-Asiamah and Kawalek, 2021). The CAS module removes managerial power exertions from collective discussions that aim to achieve healthy ecology, effective production, and inclusive society. As demonstrated in Figure 1, the outcomes of the stakeholders' interactions emerge through the planned learning module (A), the emergent learning module (B), or the deferred learning module (C) to typify the usual sustainable development actions of corporate managers/executives, the communities and employees (consuming public), and other groups, such as regulators and policy-makers/environmentalists.

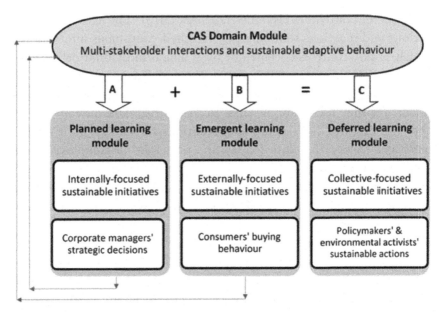

Figure 1. Cohered corporate sustainability model derived from cohered emergent theory.

Source: Adapted from Nyame-Asiamah and Kawalek (2021).

The planned learning module explains the rational planning decisions of corporate managers which prioritise internally focused sustainability practises to make their companies more competitive in the market and maximise the rewards of their investors. Planned learning uses strategic-driven measures to design and implement sustainable development activities. It emphasises more on economic sustainability than ecological preservation, social inclusion, and emotional needs of communities and non-managerial staff of companies which often emerge unpredictably.

The emergent learning module encourages moral, communal, and emotional expectations that are essential for environmental and social sustainability practises. It is an externally focused process which stimulates collaboration and negotiations between corporate managers and "less powerful" stakeholders, such as ordinary community members and non-managerial staff, who have minimal influence on corporate responsibility decisions. Emergent learning is an innovative process of learning because it empowers "less powerful" stakeholders to engage effectively in sustainable development initiatives. It creates a democratic space to critique weaknesses with existing sustainability initiatives and provide feedback for improving environmental and social sustainability practises. By responding to the emergent knowledge of the "less powerful" stakeholders, corporate managers will modify, postpone, or defer their rational plans for sustainability in an attempt to equalise the three dimensions of sustainable initiatives.

The deferred learning module describes a learning and decision-making process that motivates corporate managers to use suggestions by the "less powerful" stakeholders, regulators, policymakers, environmentalists, and other interest groups to modify and improve their sustainability practises. It draws insights from the deferred model of reality, a theoretical construct that explains how software designers can design information systems flexibly to encourage users to shape the design processes in emergent conditions (Nyame-Asiamah, 2013; Patel, 2006; Ramrattan and Patel, 2010). The deferred learning module also creates the opportunity for policymakers and environmental activists to negotiate sustainability initiatives directly with big corporations and encourage them to implement sustainability practises that can promote a healthy environment (Nyame-Asiamah and Kawalek, 2021).

Cohered emergent theory is a nascent theory that has been tested, utilised, and welcomed in many situations to address power issues, conflicting stakeholder interests, and system design tensions in different contexts. The theory was employed as a thematic analysis model to analyse comprehensive data from eight higher education institutions in Nepal that aimed to improve their curriculum provisions and student experience (Bastola, 2019). Its practical merits were acknowledged through extensive qualitative research in Komfo Anokye Teaching Hospital in Ghana, where 20 recommendations were made to narrow the manager–clinician tension in (re)designing healthcare knowledge base (Nyame-Asiamah, 2013, pp. 334–335). Cohered emergent theory was applied to study how healthcare managers and clinicians adopted video consultations in the Alliance

(University Hospitals of Leicester) in the UK, with informed change recommendations to increase the utilisation of video consultations in the hospital (Gilbey, 2021).

The capability of the theory has also been recognised in the Information Technology for Development editorial report as research that can underpin effective healthcare ICTs implementation and improve health outcomes in areas with socioeconomic inequality during pandemic emergencies (Qureshi, 2020). There are also ongoing research projects applying the theory at De Montfort University and Cardiff Metropolitan University, respectively, to explain how to: (i) implement enterprise policy and programmes effectively for small and medium enterprises in Nigeria and (ii) evaluate and design employee reward and motivational packages in Nigerian commercial banks. We further examine the theoretical merits of cohered emergent theory by utilising our multinational mining case study to explore empirical data on the theory and explain how multinational mining corporations operating in Africa can design and implement their sustainability practises effectively. This will unveil the theoretical advancement of cohered emergent theory to understand how companies can equalise the economic, environmental, and social dimensions of sustainability in practise.

4. Methodology

4.1. *Research context of Ghana and Precious Gold Mining Limited*

This study was conducted on Precious Gold Mining Limited, a subsidiary company of a South African multinational mining corporation operating in Ghana. Ghana itself is the biggest gold-producing country in Africa (Forbes, 2020). The recent number of companies exploring gold, bauxite, diamonds, and manganese undertakings in Ghana is about 90, with over 300 registered small-scale miners and 90 mine support service companies (Essah and Andrew, 2016). Gold mining industry has contributed to improving Ghana's export income since the 1980s (Tuokuu *et al.*, 2018). The Minerals Commission estimates that 3% of gross sales of gold is paid to the government as royalties. Of this, 80% goes to the consolidated fund of the Ghanaian government, 10% is distributed to mining administrative departments, and the remaining 10% is allocated to local communities (Aryee, 2001; Tuokuu *et al.*, 2018). The sector is one of the highest paying industry jobs in Ghana, although there are inequalities in employees' remuneration (Ankrah *et al.*, 2017).

Despite the socioeconomic contribution of mining, the sector has been heavily criticised for polluting the environment, contaminating water bodies, disfiguring the landscape, and disturbing the social structures (Idemudia *et al.*, 2020). Mining activities have displaced many communities and taken over farmlands from local residents who cultivate the lands as a source of livelihood (Essah and Andrews, 2016). To address these challenges, the Minerals and Mining Law of 1986 was implemented to reconcile the possible conflicts between economic development and natural resource management (Akabzaa and Darimani, 2001; Tuokuu *et al.*, 2018). Unfortunately, this law failed to balance the economic benefits of minerals with effective management of natural resources, as it allowed the multinational mining companies to repatriate more profits from mining activities to their countries of origin. Subsequently, the national environmental policy was adopted to mandate the Environmental Protection Agency of Ghana in protecting the environment and promoting sustainable use of economic resources (Environmental Protection Agency, 1995). The power of the Environmental Protection Agency (Act 490) enables them to conduct environmental impact assessments, punish those who contravene environmental regulations, and grant environmental permits to mining companies (Tuokuu *et al.*, 2018). The Ministry of Lands and Natural Resources also established the Ghana Minerals Commission under Article 269 of the Constitution of 1992 and the Minerals Commission Act to contribute to the formulation, implementation, and monitoring of the national mining policies and regulations (The Minerals Commission of Ghana, 2021). The Minerals and Mining Act 2006 also empowers the Commission to investigate, assess, and approve prospective mining exploration. The act has facilitated an increased foreign presence in Ghana's large-scale mining sector and a subsequent increase in mineral production. Unfortunately, research suggests that policy efforts to address environmental problems in Ghana's mining sector have not been effective, and there are several cases of illegal mining activities in the country (Hilson, 2004; Tuokuu *et al.*, 2018; Kpienbaareh *et al.*, 2021).

Precious Gold Mining Limited has three mining subsidiaries. These are "A" Gold Mine, "B" Gold Mine, and "C" Gold Mine. The company is located in the southern part of the Western Region of Ghana. It is about 300 km by road from the west of Accra, Ghana's capital. The study was conducted at "C" Gold Mine of Precious Gold Mining Limited, one of Ghana's largest gold mines. We chose "C" Gold Mine because of its long-standing record of sustainability in Ghana (Teschner, 2013), its global leading position in corporate best practises throughout its history, and its repeated commitment to sustainable mining practises (*Precious Gold Mining Limited*, 2021). "C" Gold Mine is dedicated to environmental protection and community development programmes, such as entrepreneurship training, educational scholarships, and infrastructure building (Sadik, 2013).

Precious Gold Mining Limited employs about 6,500 people. The mining company has contributed USD 13 million towards community development and procured USD 394 worth of its logistics locally. Furthermore, the company pays taxes and royalties of USD 109 million to the Ghana government (*Precious Gold Mining Limited*, 2021). In 2005, the company's foundation launched the Sustainable Community Empowerment and Economic Development (SEED) programme, a five-year community development programme worth USD 5 million to improve the livelihoods and quality of life of 30,000 underprivileged men, women, and children in its 16 primary stakeholder communities. Recent research indicates that the company has constructed schools, clinics, public libraries, and roads for communities in the catchment areas of its operations (Ansu-Mensah *et al.*, 2021; Amoako, *et al.*, 2018). In 2020, the news media reported that the company's foundation has spent GHS 8.79 million (approximately USD 1.47 million) to develop the agricultural sector within its mining host communities (Ghana News Agency, 2020). To understand the nuances of the reported contribution, we sought the stakeholders' views to explore how the company's economic sustainability and benefits compare with the environmental and social aspects of sustainability which are externally focused.

4.2. *Data collection*

We utilised the pragmatist tradition and case study strategy to explain how cohered emergent theory informs multinational mining corporations operating in Africa to design and implement their sustainability practises to equalise the economic, environmental, and social dimensions of sustainability. Pragmatism is a "problem-centred", "pluralistic", and "practise-oriented" methodology that tests theoretical constructs on empirics through a rigorous research design which captures the economic, social, political, and historical context of the problem being studied (Creswell, 2014; Kaushik and Walsh, 2019). A case study is an outward-looking research strategy which is used to examine a research problem in a real-life context where the boundaries between the research phenomenon and context are not quite clear (Yin, 2013). It allows researchers to use rich data to understand nuances of a single environment and advance theories in qualitative research (Crane and Glozer, 2016; Eisenhardt, 1989).

We used purposive and snowballing sampling techniques to invite participants to take part in the study after obtaining their consent. Seven internal and nine external stakeholders of the company's provided responses to our semi-structure interview questions which covered: the nature of the company's sustainability practises, the design and implementation processes of the sustainability practises, the challenges with sustainability design and implementation processes, and how to improve sustainability practises to meet diverse stakeholders' expectations. The internal stakeholders constituted the managers and employees of the company, while the external stakeholders were selected community residents, the Ghana Environmental Protection Agency, and the Ghana Police Service. These external stakeholders emanated from the catchment communities of the company's mining sites, which include Subri, Damang, Huni-Valley, and Koduakrom, and had experienced the company's sustainability practises as well as the impact of mining on local people

Table 1. Research participants' affiliations, positions, and interview duration.

Participants affiliation	No. of participants	Position and codes	Average interview duration
Precious Gold Mining Limited	4	Senior Managers (Senior Manager A, B, C, D)	54 minutes
Precious Gold Mining Limited	3	Junior Managers (Junior Manager A, B, C)	45 minutes
Mining communities	5	Community residents (Community resident A, B, C, D, E)	60 minutes
Environmental Protection Agency (EPA), Ghana	2	Regulators (Regulator A, B)	75 minutes
Ghana Police Service	2	Police officers (Police officer A, B)	43 minutes

and the environment. The profile of the participants and the duration of the tape-recoded interviews are summarised in Table 1.

4.3. *Method of analysis*

We transcribed the recorded interviews and applied thematic analysis (Braun and Clarke, 2006; Eisenhardt, 1989) to identify common themes and patterns from the participants' responses that related to the individual participant groups' views and experiences of designing and implementing sustainability practises to reflect their varied interests. We carried out several iterative processes to find variations between the managers' rationale for initiating and approving sustainability activities and other stakeholders' expectations for ecological quality and social value, and how these affected the balance between economic, environmental, and social sustainability (Yin, 2013). During these iterative processes, we inductively selected statements/phrases that pointed to our research question and offered new insight into our understanding of how the company attempted to equalise the three sustainability dimensions. We then grouped statements/phrases of similar characteristics into the following four categories which manifest the core modules of cohered emergent theory: implementing sustainability as a collective agenda; budget, power, and economic sustainability; unexpected issues affecting sustainability design; and changing cause to equalise the three dimensions of sustainability. We interpreted the findings around these core categories of thematic analysis and further discussed how fresh data are explored using cohered emergent theory to understand the meaningful way multinational mining companies can design and implement their sustainability practises to equalise the economic, environmental, and social dimensions of sustainability.

5. Findings and Interpretation

5.1. *Implementing sustainability as collective agenda*

The data suggest that the mining company operated within a complex system which involved many stakeholders with different and sometimes conflicting sustainability goals which include financial costs and benefits of implementing sustainability initiatives, protection of environment, development of community infrastructure, and promotion of social well-being. Balancing and achieving these conflicting goals were challenges for the diverse stakeholders whose expectations, interactions, and decision-making were often marred by power, control, and self-centredness.

Some managers accused the accounting and financial management team of the company for disapproving and delaying their requests for environmental and social sustainability initiatives. Senior Manager C stated his frustration as follows:

> Accounting guys are troublesome as they dictate our expenditure. Once they say there is no money, it's very difficult to convince them. They control our spending which is good but their work is at the same time a challenge to us. They should understand that it's not only production related expenditure that must be approved.

This argument for allocating and approving funds for sustainability projects was contrasted by a counter-claim that the company's investments in sustainability had not brought direct economic returns. Junior Manager C opined the following:

> We don't see gold coming from environmental management; what your money is doing is not bringing gold. Just imagine, I want to extract water and the processing fee alone is $3000. But you don't have a choice; you have to do it because you cannot use water illegally.

A critical analysis of the quote tells us that the company's sustainability might have been driven by regulatory requirements rather than a moral judgement. One junior-level manager working at the Environmental Unit held the view that sustainability is not only about allocating funds and claiming money or cost minimisation but it has more to do with reducing consumption. He clarified as follows:

> Sustainable development is not solely about the money. If I reduce my quantity, the cost will go down, so that's the whole idea… if in capturing data for GRI, I don't capture the usage, that's the cost without the quantity, the data is incomplete. (Junior Manager B)

The manager's view suggests that economic sustainability can be compensated for environmental and social sustainability through effective management, sustainable production, and green consumption.

Senior Manager D extended the discussion around sustainability understanding to developing better relationship between the company and the mining communities and to ensuring that the ethics of sustainability is practised by the company, the community, and all other stakeholders. He believed that the community itself did not practise sustainable life:

> The communities don't understand yet the importance of sustainability. They think the mine, once it's here, we must take care of them and everything. When you tell them that they will suffer when the mine is shut down, they say how do you know what will happen when you leave? How we will survive is none of your business. So,

it's giving us a lot of headaches trying to explain to them. (Senior Manager D)

While the company staff considered community engagement and collective decisions as better ways to implement and practise sustainability, some community members felt they were not adequately involved in decisions about sustainable projects for the community apart from holding the quarterly stakeholder meetings with the community leaders. One resident announced his disappointment as follows:

As for good community relations with the mine, it is somehow bad. They hardly interact with the community members directly, unless something pops up, then through their community affairs office they may convey such information. Rather, most often it is some NGOs around that organise some forums. (Community resident B)

This quotation explains the need to engage the community actively to understand their sustainability expectations in order to implement projects that address their social, environmental, and economic needs. The data suggest that better interactions between the company and the community were critical for effective designing social and corporate sustainability initiatives for the mining residents and their communities. Regulator A from the Environmental Protection Agency feared that the community members were not fully aware of the consequences of the mine wastes and they needed to understand the reasons for providing environmental and social sustainability projects. His concern was corroborated by Regulator B as follows:

Many community members are not well informed about the dangers of staying close to the mine waste. We advise them to stay away from the waste but they don't care the safety and health issues.

A further discussion around community safety and social sustainability initiatives revealed that sustainable projects could be implemented effectively if the community leaders would use their social positions to support sustainable mining policies that can improve socioeconomic and environmental development of the community. Police Officer B said that both traditional and political leaders interfered with law enforcement activities that aimed to control illegal mining and community protection, while Police Officer A confirmed this as follows:

> This is a small town and almost everyone knows each other. The leaders in this area are fond of pleading on behalf of these illegal miners whenever they have issues with the police. This makes it very difficult to prosecute offenders because our system is such that we need the support of these leaders to make our work easier. (Police Officer A)

Our analysis of data suggests that the company's sustainability practises were complex and required the understanding of power positions, conflicts of interest, and how to plan rationally to address uncertainties and emergencies.

5.2. *Budget, power, and economic sustainability*

The planning and implementation of the company's sustainability initiatives were heavily shaped by budget which tilted towards the economic dimension. Senior Manager B who was responsible for finance and budget argued that the concept of sustainability as centred on "money" and it is a manager's job to find alternative ways of minimising costs. He said the following:

> Everything boils down to money irrespective of how fancy the idea of sustainability looks like. If you look at the environment and the community guys, they will think this is the only approach but when it comes to the finance we do cost benefit analysis of other alternatives to achieve the same purpose.

While money is a predictable factor for sustainable development plans and favours economic sustainability, the interpretation from the above quotation is that managers have alternative paths towards budgetary allocations and their plans should not be always static. In addition, Junior Manager A explained that they followed strict and expensive ISO guidelines to provide safe mining activities:

> The ISO 14001 is the engine of our environment department system and it is very expensive to keep the system. If the system tells to

you employ five officers you have to, else your certificate will not be renewed on expiry. (Junior Manager A)

It also noted that the power positions of the local chiefs and assemblymen (local government representatives) were often used to gain some contracts from the mining company and these were expected to bring some social benefits to the community, but this was not the case. Community resident E reported his concerns as follows:

> What I know is sometimes they allocate some kind of royalties to chiefs in the town and they also award some kind of contract to the assemblyman. With these kinds of offers to these leaders, it is expected that they can also contribute something to the community. (Community resident E)

Some residents considered the behaviour of chiefs and community leaders in the sustainability implementation processes as self-centred. Community resident D added his desperation to this rationalist view of managing resources to suit people with authority:

> Chiefs and leaders bring people from different places and take money from them in exchange for community members' employment opportunities with the company.

Community resident C also criticised the chiefs' influence on the company's sustainability agenda of the company which did not benefit the ordinary members of the community and looked up to God.

> We, the residents here, need help but some of the chiefs behave selfishly. They rather side with the mining officials, with some of them getting contracts from the mining firm. Over here it's only God who can help us.

The expression "only God can help us" signifies the helpless situation of the community members who felt that they did not benefit from the company's lucrative remuneration which was far better than many white-collar jobs regardless of the staff's academic qualifications. This gave reasons for the chiefs and community leaders to act as middlemen and connected job seekers who did not necessarily live in the community with mining jobs which, according to Senior Manager A, offered the lowest-paid worker a basic monthly salary of USD 500 excluding allowances, 30% overtime of the basic salary, and six-month generous bonus. Community resident B corroborated the manager's claim as follows:

> Compared to other cities like Kumasi and Accra [two largest cities in Ghana] you can't get access to a good paying job unless you have a high certificate. But here with some little training at junior high school, one earns a good salary. The money a junior high school graduate is earning by working with the mine, even if you have your MBA or lecture at a university, you can't get that money.

A deeper interpretation of this quotation is that the company attached more importance to the financial welfare of their staff which echoes the assertion that economic welfare subjugates the need for environmental and social sustainability (Böhling *et al.*, 2019; Garvin *et al.*, 2009).

5.3. *Unexpected issues affecting sustainability design*

Aside from the (estimated) cost involved in developing and implementing sustainability projects for the community, we identified some emergent factors such as acid rock drainage, encroaching behaviour, and other uncertainties that influenced or changed the rational sustainability design. Senior Manager B explained that acid rock drainage can often leak into the stored mined rocks to increase the estimated costs for chemical treatment. He elaborated as follows:

> On the side of environment, we are dealing with material in higher ARD [acid rock drainage]. Sometimes you mine the material and you store them in the storage pits and, before you could say Jack Robinson [say someone's name], acid is coming out of it into the environment and that needs to be treated which costs very high. (Senior Manager B)

Junior Manager A gave an account of how the company abandoned a biogas project because of their inability to obtain expert advice on biogas, a problem which was not anticipated at the planning stage. Instead, the company used financial limitation as a cover story to explain why this environmental project did not go ahead. He said the following:

> Some time ago we wanted to do bio-gas, instead of land fill waste but it was so difficult to get somebody who is not versed in environmental issues to understand. Rather, emphasis was placed on the financial situation of the company and the project was not approved. When your hands are tied like that, you only do what is critical. You don't get room to do what might not be critical but necessary. (Junior Manager A)

Our interactions with the company staff revealed that some intruders and local hunters entered the rehabilitated areas and used fire to drive rodents out from their holes which often ignited dry plants and cause bushfires. Junior Manager C cautiously narrated one incident where some acres of reclaimed land caught fire through such intruding behaviour and it unexpectedly increased the company's environmental sustainability costs:

> Here is the case where the community encroaches on rehabilitated land...whether those people were hunting or...the place is burnt and about ten to fifteen acres is gone. These are areas we have spent money to rehabilitate the land so when EPA confirms it has matured, it reduces the bond we have to pay to the Ghana Government. All of a sudden it becomes an extra cost for us.

The implication of these unexpected occurrences is that the company would find it difficult to secure funds for projects that fell outside their budget. Junior Manager A summarised such challenges as follows:

> Sometimes unexpected issues may come up that need attention. For example, you planned to work only at site A this year and then in the course of the year something comes up and it becomes necessary to go to site B. There is no budget allocation for the environmental impact assessment that needs to be done there and that is a problem.

Probing the activities of the intruders further, the research participants from the company indicated that some of the trespassers surprisingly stole vegetables and food crops which had to be tested for human consumption from the company's simulation farms.

They were frustrated by such unexpected actions of the intruders that could reduce the quality of environmental data needed to verify the safety of the produce harvested from the reclaimed lands. Although the community members agreed that people trespassed the mining site, they believed that some intruders were not community residents. One of them argued as follows:

> Yes, I agree that there are times that some people do trespass on the property of the mining company. However, this place is a mining area and it attracts a whole lot of people from Ghana and even outside Ghana. I don't think it's always that encroachers do come from our communities. (Community resident A)

The critical interpretation of the data is that the company's planned actions can be distorted by encroachers and their activities regardless of where they come from.

Our conversation with the participants also revealed that the cost of maintaining some facilities provided by the company was a tussle between the company and the community. Senior Manager D argued that the company needed to implement more water projects for communities which did not have potable water than focusing on repairs for communities which were already benefiting from facilities. He articulated as follows:

> There are communities that have not received any water project and are also expecting us to provide them with water. So, if those communities enjoying the water want us to come and repair it when it is broken down then it's a quite difficult situation. (Senior Manager D)

While the manager's argument seems logical, some residents criticised the company's expectation that the community should pay for water maintenance which residents could not afford. Community resident E said the following:

> We were enjoying free water from nature and if mining activities have polluted such sources of water, it is their obligation to provide another alternative for free. Hence the company has no option than to repair them when broken down.

The sense-making of the resident's critique is that it is the company's social responsibility to restore any damaged natural resources in the community that emerge as a consequence of their mining operations.

5.4. *Changing cause to equalise the three dimensions of sustainability*

As the interview progressed, we noted that the managers understood the insatiable needs of the community, used flexible budget to address some unexpected costs of sustainability, met quarterly to discuss sustainability matters, and responded to the community youth protest and critical comments by changing their recruitment practises.

While the funding formula for social and environmental sustainability projects was based on USD 1 worth of ounce of gold produced plus 1% of profit for the community, the participants explained that the falling production levels and gold prices were an obstacle to the company's sustainable development projects. Such uncertainties put pressure on the company and required the application of a flexible budget. Senior Manager D described his experiences and challenges as follows:

> The need of communities around the mine is insatiable and that is where I face challenges in resource allocation. The pressure from the communities are just too much.

To meet the community's sustainability expectations, the company applied a flexible budget which allowed us to make adjustments to the planned spending and switched money between alternative projects. Junior Manager A explained how he might manage contingencies as follows:

> If I have the budget for A and B, when it comes to using that budget and I need more for A, I should have that flexibility to go and take funds from B and add it to A, as long as what will be left for B will be enough.

Managers with costing and budgeting responsibilities shared opinion on how other managers could handle unplanned social responsibility expenditure:

> We understand that there could be unexpected cost, so we tell them
> to inform us on such issues so that we discuss the way forward.
> (Senior Manager B)

Our conversation with the residents showed that the company
met the community members every quarter to discuss the needs and
concerns of the residents and what they (the company) were doing to
support the community. However, the residents wanted their requests
to be addressed more than the company reporting their plans and
performance to the community:

> We meet quarterly and they set the agenda for the meeting and
> most often they give a report on the performance of the company.
> We will be happy if we can make an input into projects that they
> should do for us before executing such projects, instead of them
> just determining projects that they should do for us whilst our
> immediate need lies unattended. (Community resident A)

The interpretation of the data is that the residents wanted the
company to shift from the rationalist view of designing social
and environmental sustainability activities towards a more inclusive
approach that could address the community needs. Although they
were displeased about the previous recruitment process of the
company which denied many community job seekers the opportunity
to secure operational management roles, they felt that their critical
feedback had changed some practises of the company's social responsibility design. Community resident C narrated a situation where the
youth protested against the company's recruitment process to bring
change:

> They will bring their own people and that made the youth rise
> against them, leading to the change in trend. We think that, if noth-
> ing at all, the menial jobs should be given to the nearby villagers
> and this has changed the trend a bit. (Community resident C)

The meaning of the "changed trend" denotes how the company
had used the critique and negative feedback to improve their social
sustainability practise although they felt that more could still be
done. Community resident A summarised this as follows:

The employment situation was worse until about seven years ago when the youth here demonstrated violently against the management of the mining company. After that the mining firm started recruiting but even still I think it's not enough.

One manager confirmed that the recruitment process has improved to offer more opportunities for the community members:

The percentage of our employees and contractors from the catchment areas is 56% as at the last quarter. What we do is to make sure that most of the recruitment that we do comes from the communities. It is only scarce skills that we don't get from the communities. (Senior Manager A)

The manager's narrative substantiates that postulate of cohered emergent theory that critical knowledge of "less powerful" stakeholders can cohere with managers' rationality to bring sustainable change but this should not be done through violent protests (Nyame-Asiamah and Kawalek, 2021).

6. Discussion

This chapter applied cohered emergent theory to explain how multinational mining corporations operating in Africa can design and implement their sustainability practises to equalise the economic, environmental, and social dimensions of sustainability. Our findings suggest that the company perceived sustainability design and implementation as a collective process which involves decisions and participation of many stakeholders with conflicting interests. The design process was planned and initiated by managers and people in positions of power whose actions were often influenced by resource availability and economic priorities. The managers' conscious actions were affected by the changing socioeconomic needs of the community residents, their critical feedback, and unexpected occurrences. Managers responded to the residents' feedback and unpredicted events by modifying their (managers') sustainability plans, pausing the planned implementation process, or redirecting their scarce resources as they attempted to equalise economic, environmental, and social aspects of sustainability. The participants' narratives exemplify the features of complex adaptive behaviour, planned learning, emergent learning, and deferred learning when explored using cohered emergent theory to explain corporate sustainability implementation (Nyame-Asiamah, 2013; Nyame-Asiamah and Kawalek, 2021).

First, the findings suggest that extractive companies prioritise economic sustainability for many reasons. They aim to secure greater returns on investment, pay their staff adequately, and use economic models like cost-benefit analysis to minimise their operational costs or maximise revenue. These revealing objectives fortify senior managers' and cost accountants' roles in setting financial targets and persuading others to follow within the organisations. Operating within many regulatory frameworks, managers of multinational mining rationalise their spending to reflect the demands of environmental standards. Improvising from the junior manager's narrative, Precious Mining Gold Limited had to comply with the expensive ISO 14001 standards including the obligation to employ a minimum number of technical staff before satisfying environmental (re)certification requirements.

In this unique case, the managers' aim to prioritise economic sustainability overlaps some environmental sustainability targets. They use their decision-making powers to orchestrate sustainability activities. Their decision-making behaviours lean towards sustainability practises that can make their company more competitive. The managers' actions manifest the planned learning path of cohered emergent theory (Nyame-Asiamah, 2020; Nyame-Asiamah and Kawalek, 2021). Quite surprisingly, the community leaders and chiefs who collaborated with the managers to implement sustainability activities were repeatedly alleged to have utilised their positions of power to induce the social responsibility initiatives, such as the community recruitment quota, for their own interest. Despite its strategic benefits, planned learning is exclusively not sufficient to discharge sustainability initiatives to meet the expectations of diverse stakeholders. This echoes the view that planned actions must respond to emergence to achieve sustainable development initiatives (Nyame-Asiamah, 2020; Nyame-Asiamah and Patel, 2010; Patel, 2006; Ramrattan and Patel, 2010).

The findings from this study reveal many characteristics of emergence that were different from rational sustainability design. For instance, the community residents reminded the company to take the responsibility for repairing water projects and bringing back the *natural* state of water that had been tampered with by the mining activities in the community. This knowledge of business ethics was more incidental to the company's plans to develop new water projects than maintaining the existing ones but essentially needed to improve social sustainability expectations of the community.

There were similar emotionally charged actions by the residents that encouraged the company to recruit more mining workers from the community and helped them to improve their social responsibility activities for the locals. The risk of acid rock drainage which increased operational costs and encroachers' actions which distorted the simulation farm data or caused bush fires to the prohibited land were also unpredictable events that emerged through the company's interactions with its physical or social environment. The warning signs of these negative events prompted the company to think about flexible budgeting and management approaches which were not based on strict standardised activities or inputs (Patel, 2007; Singh *et al.*, 2009). Flexible budgets create buffers for companies to manage financial uncertainties and apply alternative modes of executing sustainability initiatives effectively (Bartley *et al.*, 2017; Roth, 2008). These are unknown elements of rational sustainability planning which emerge through human interactions with their environment, learning, and adaptation. It signals features of emergent learning that empowers "less powerful" stakeholders to negotiate with senior managers and address lapses in rational sustainability design.

The interaction effect of negotiating sustainability decisions between "less powerful" stakeholders and senior managers is revealed through our case study where the company increased their recruitment quota for the community residents as a response to the residents' protest and critique. This was a better social sustainability outcome achieved through a collaborative shift of power from corporate executives to the "less powerful" stakeholders of the community.

By changing their recruitment plans to accommodate the social responsibility expectations of the residents, the managers' actions reflect deferred learning (Nyame-Asiamah and Kawalek, 2021; Patel, 2006). The company discussed the sustainability issues with the community on a quarterly basis to understand the local stakeholders' expectations and environmental concerns and attempted to address these matters collectively. Although the company emphasised more the economic dimension of sustainability due to the apparent financial constraints, they committed a lot of resources to delivering environmental and social sustainability activities to meet most expectations of their community residents. They adopted a pragmatic approach to designing and implementing sustainability practises to equalise the economic, environmental, and social dimensions of sustainability. Their sustainability implementation efforts were characterised by continuous interactions between the company and its stakeholders that fostered negotiations, power shift, and adaption to exemplify the discipline of cohered emergent theory.

7. Conclusion

7.1. *Contribution to theory and practise*

We applied cohered emergent theory (Nyame-Asiamah, 2020; Nyame-Asiamah and Kawalek, 2021) to explain how multinational mining corporations operating in Africa can design and implement their sustainability practises to equalise the economic, environmental, and social dimensions of sustainability. The application of the cohered emergent discipline is our contribution to theory and practise. By utilising the case of Precious Gold Mining Limited and empirical data from the company's stakeholders, we have contributed fresh insights into the literature on corporate sustainability implementation that encourages participation, inclusion, and empowerment of "less powerful" stakeholders in corporate sustainability decisions. It adds to the body of knowledge that explains corporate responsibility and sustainability practises from emergent and adaptive perspectives (Brown, 2008; Cohen, 2001; Korten 2005) and emphasise the value of cohered emergent theory in a different sector and within a pragmatist philosophy. The theory enhances our understanding of how to address power issues, conflicts of interest, and emergent actuality in sustainable design agenda (Nyame-Asiamah, 2020).

The application of cohered emergent theory will motivate sustainable development advocates to design and implement sustainability projects as a collective initiative that aligns with the CAS module and its interrelated planning and the emergent and deferred learning processes now and in the future. This contribution will make the implementation of existing rational sustainability standards and reporting frameworks more meaningful to local contexts where emergence and changing community expectations can be adequately accommodated expectations can be adequately accommodated into corporate responsibility and sustainability practises (Patel, 2007; Polacek *et al.*, 2012; Schianetz and Kavanagh, 2008). By validating the merits of cohered emergent theory through a pragmatist philosophy and a case study strategy, we also contribute a rich empirical case to support teaching in academia now and in the future.

The immediate implications of this study for corporate managers and executives are to utilise the findings to identify and mitigate potential sustainability implementation risks that can lead to crises and damage organisational image, harm community welfare, and destroy the environment. For instance, we can draw a conclusion from Community resident A's narrative that companies can empower their local communities to participate in corporate sustainability implementation processes, address their local needs, and eventually prevent any potential violent protests that the "less powerful" stakeholders might use to damage corporate reputation. As a matter of fair business practise, designing sustainability practises proportionately and ethically will benefit corporations and society in the long run. The findings of this study also offer prospects for policymakers and governments in developing countries to rectify corporate sustainability policies that can foster fair allocation of royalties and taxes from multinational mining companies to the mining communities and to reduce rural poverty.

7.2. *Implications for the sustainability readership*

Through the nascent lens of cohered emergent theory, our study has introduced a new perspective to sustainability design and implementation in the mining sector which has implications for sustainability scholars and practitioners to implement sustainable development projects effectively. It is our hope that the reader will apply the merits of this study to different contexts and sectors where companies and institutions are encouraged or required to implement sustainability activities collectively to address power relations, conflicts of interest, and emergent actuality. The theoretical value of the study has greater scope and implications for the reader who studies, implements, and evaluates sustainable development goals to design and execute such initiatives through the modules of cohered emergent theory and to achieve positive outcomes. Embracing this knowledge will bring the scientific community of sustainability closer to equalising the economic, environmental, and social dimensions of sustainability in practise.

References

Adonteng-Kissi, O. (2017). Poverty and mine's compensation package: Experiences of local farmers in prestea mining community, *Resources Policy*, Vol. 52, pp. 226–234.

Akabzaa, T. and Darimani, A. (2001). Impact of mining sector investment in Ghana: A study of the Tarkwa mining region, *Third World Network*, Vol. 11, No. 2, pp. 47–61.

Alsaifi, K., Elnahass, M. and Salama, A. (2020). Carbon disclosure and financial performance: UK environmental policy, *Business Strategy and the Environment*, Vol. 29, No. 2, pp. 711–726.

Amoako, K. O., Lord, B. R. and Dixon, K. (2017). Sustainability reporting: Insights from the websites of five plants operated by newmont mining corporation, *Meditari Accountancy Research*, Vol. 25, pp. 186–215.

Amoako, K. O., Amoako, I. O. and Marfo, E. O. (2018). Comparing sustainability disclosures on corporate websites: A case study of newmont mining corporation's plant sites in Ghana, *International Journal of Multinational Corporation Strategy*, Vol. 2, Nos. 3–4, pp. 241–275.

Ankrah, P. W., Gbana, A. M., Emmanuel, A. D., Arthur, A. and Agyapong, S. (2017). Evidence of the income inequality situation in the mining industry of Ghana, *Journal of Economics*, Vol. 5, No. 1, pp. 79–90.

Ansu-Mensah, P., Marfo, E. O., Awuah, L. S. and Amoako, K. O. (2021). Corporate social responsibility and stakeholder engagement in Ghana's mining sector: A case study of newmont Ahafo mines, *International Journal of Corporate Social Responsibility*, Vol. 6, No. 1, pp. 1–22.

Asr, E. T., Kakaie, R., Ataei, M. and Mohammadi, M. R. T. (2019). A review of studies on sustainable development in mining life cycle, *Journal of Cleaner Production*, Vol. 229, pp. 213–231.

Azapagic, A. (2004). Developing a framework for Sustainable development indicators for the mining and minerals industry, *Journal of Cleaner Production*, Vol. 12, No. 6, pp. 639–662.

Bartley, J., Chen, A., Harvey, S., Showalter, S., Zuckerman, G. and Stewart, L. (2017). Lies, damn lies, and statistics: Why a widely used sustainability metric fails and how to improve It, *Journal of Applied Corporate Finance*, Vol. 29, No. 2, pp. 109–114.

Bastola, M. (2019), A deferred-based framework for evaluating the quality of privatised curriculum provision to improve student experience in Nepal. Unpublished PhD thesis, Cardiff Metropolitan University.

Bastola, M. and Nyame-Asiamah, F. (2016). Reframing service sector privatisation quality conception with the theory of deferred action, *International Journal of Economics and Management Engineering*, Vol. 10, No. 10, pp. 3312–3317.

Belkhir, L., Bernard, S. and Abdelgadir, S. (2017). Does GRI reporting impact environmental sustainability? A cross-industry analysis of CO2 emissions performance between GRI-reporting and non-reporting companies, *Management of Environmental Quality: An International Journal*, Vol. 28, No. 2, pp. 138–155.

Böhling, K., Murguía, D. I. and Godfrid, J. (2019). Sustainability reporting in the mining sector: Exploring its symbolic nature, *Business & Society*, Vol. 58, No. 1, pp. 191–225.

Boiral, O. and Henri, J. F. (2012). Modelling the impact of ISO 14001 on environmental performance: A comparative approach, *Journal of Environmental Management*, Vol. 99, pp. 84–97.

Boje, D. M. (2016). Critique of the triple bottom line, in G. A. Rosile (ed.), *Tribal Wisdom for Business Ethics*, pp. 181–198, Emerald Group Publishing Limited.

Braun, V. and Clarke, V. (2006). Using thematic analysis in psychology, *Qualitative Research in Psychology*, Vol. 3, No. 2, pp. 77–101.

Bravi, L., Santos, G., Pagano, A. and Murmura, F. (2020). Environmental management system according to ISO 14001: 2015 as a driver to sustainable development, *Corporate Social Responsibility and Environmental Management*, Vol. 27, No. 6, pp. 2599–2614.

Brown, C. (2008). Emergent sustainability: The concept of sustainable development in a complex world, in H. G. Brauch *et al.* (eds.), *Globalization and Environmental Challenges: Reconceptualizing Security in the 21st Century*, pp. 141–149, Springer, Berlin.

Brown, R. R. and Farrelly, M. A. (2009). Challenges ahead: Social and institutional factors influencing sustainable urban stormwater management in Australia, *Water Science and Technology*, Vol. 59, No. 4, pp. 653–660.

Chofreh, A. G. and Goni, F. A. (2017). Review of frameworks for sustainability implementation, *Sustainable Development*, Vol. 25, No. 3, pp. 180–188.

Cohen, M. J. (2001). The emergent environmental policy discourse on sustainable consumption, in *Exploring Sustainable Consumption*, pp. 21–37, Pergamon, London.

Crane, A. and Glozer, S. (2016). Researching corporate social responsibility communication: Themes, opportunities and challenges, *Journal of Management Studies*, Vol. 53, No. 7, pp. 1223–1252.

Creswell, J. W. (2014). *A Concise Introduction to Mixed Methods Research*. SAGE Publications.

Curkovic, S. and Sroufe, R. (2011). Using ISO 14001 to promote a sustainable supply chain strategy, *Business Strategy and the Environment*, Vol. 20, No. 2, pp. 71–93.

Diouf, D. and Boiral, O. (2017). The quality of sustainability reports and impression management: A stakeholder perspective, *Auditing and Accountability Journal*, Vol. 30, No. 3, pp. 643–667.

Eisenhardt, K. M. (1989). Building theories from case study research, *Academy of Management Review*, Vol. 14, No. 4, pp. 532–550.

Elkington, J. (2013). Enter the triple bottom line, in *The Triple Bottom Line*, (pp. 23–38), Routledge.

Elkington, J. B. (1997). *Cannibals with Forks: The Triple Bottom Line of 21st Century Business*. Capstone Publishing, Oxford.

Elliott, S. R. (2005). Sustainability: An economic perspective, *Resources, Conservation and Recycling*, Vol. 44, No. 3, pp. 263–277.

Environmental Protection Agency (1995). *Environmental Impact Assessment: Procedures*. Ghana.

Epstein, M. J. and Buhovac, A. R. (2014). A new day for sustainability, *Strategic Finance*, Vol. 96, No. 1, p. 25.

Epstein, M. J., Buhovac, A. R. and Yuthas, K. (2015). Managing social, environmental and financial performance simultaneously, *Long Range Planning*, Vol. 48, No. 1, pp. 35–45.

Essah, M. and Andrews, N. (2016). Linking or de-linking sustainable mining practises and corporate social responsibility? Insights from Ghana, *Resources Policy*, Vol. 50, pp. 75–85.

Fischer, D., Brettel, M. and Mauer, R. (2020). The three dimensions of sustainability: A delicate balancing act for entrepreneurs made more complex by stakeholder expectations, *Journal of Business Ethics*, Vol. 163, No. 1, pp. 87–106.

Fonseca, A., McAllister, M. L. and Fitzpatrick, P. (2013). Measuring what? A comparative anatomy of five mining sustainability frameworks, *Minerals Engineering*, Vol. 46, pp. 180–186.

Forbes (2020). Top 10 gold producing countries. Available at https://www.forbes.com/sites/greatspeculations/2021/06/23/updated-top-10-gold-producing-countries/?sh=7c3eafc92ce2.

Gallego-Alvarez, I., Lozano, M. B. and Rodriguez-Rosa, M. (2019). Analysis of social sustainability information in a global context according to the new global reporting initiative 400 social standards, *Sustainability*, Vol. 11, No. 24, p. 7073.

Garvin, T., McGee, T. K., Smoyer-Tomic, K. E. and Aubynn, E. A. (2009). Community–company relations in gold mining in Ghana, *Journal of Environmental Management*, Vol. 90, No. 1, pp. 571–586.

Gerlak, A. K. and Zuniga-Teran, A. (2020). Addressing injustice in green infrastructure through socio-ecological practise: What is the role of university–community partnerships? *Socio-Ecological Practice Research*, Vol. 2, No. 2, pp. 149–159.

Ghadge, A., Er Kara, M., Mogale, D. G., Choudhary, S. and Dani, S. (2020). Sustainability implementation challenges in food supply chains: A case of UK artisan cheese producers, *Production Planning & Control*, pp. 1–16.

Ghana News Agency (2020). Goldfields spends GH¢ 8.79 million to develop agricultural sector. *News Ghana*. Available at: https://www.goldfields.com/news-article.php?articleID=9003.

Gilbey, J. (2021). How managers and clinicians have adopted video consultations to improve clinic utilisation and patient experience in the alliance (UHL) secondary care outpatient setting. Unpublished Masters Dissertation, De Montfort University.

Gleckman, H. and Krut, R. (1997). Neither international nor standard: The limits of ISO 14001 as an instrument of global corporate environmental management, in C. Sheldon (ed.), *ISO 14001 and Beyond*

Environmental Management Systems in the Real World, pp. 45–50, Greenleaf Publishing, Sheffield.

Global Reporting Initiative (2021). The Global standards for sustainability reporting. Available at: https://www.globalreporting.org/standards/.

Godelnik, R. (2021). The evolution of sustainability-as-usual, in *Rethinking Corporate Sustainability in the Era of Climate Crisis*, pp. 15–39, Palgrave Macmillan, Cham.

Precious Gold Mining Limited (Anonymised) (2021). About gold fields Ghana Foundation. Available at: https://www.goldfields-ghana.com/about-gold-fields-ghana-foundation.php (accessed 16 July, 2021).

Hansmann, R., Mieg, H. A. and Frischknecht, P. (2012). Principal sustainability components: empirical analysis of synergies between the three pillars of sustainability, *International Journal of Sustainable Development & World Ecology*, Vol. 19, No. 5, pp. 451–459.

Hassan, A. and Kouhy, R. (2014). Evaluating gas-flaring-related carbon emission performance in the Nigerian upstream sector: A comparison of Duo methods, *African Journal of Economic and Sustainable Development*, Vol. 3, No. 3, pp. 254–271.

Heras-Saizarbitoria, I., Boiral, O. and Arana, G. (2016). Renewing environmental certification in times of crisis, *Journal of Cleaner Production*, Vol. 115, pp. 214–223.

Hilson, G. M. (2004). Structural adjustment in Ghana: Assessing the impacts of mining-sector reform, *Africa Today*, pp. 53–77.

Idemudia, U., Kwakyewah, C. and Muthuri, J. (2020). Mining, the environment, and human rights in Ghana: An area of limited statehood perspective, *Business Strategy and the Environment*, Vol. 29, No. 7, pp. 2919–2926.

Kaushik, V. and Walsh, C. A. (2019). Pragmatism as a research paradigm and its implications for social work research, *Social Sciences*, Vol. 8, No. 9, 1–17.

Korten, D. C. (2005). Sustainable development: Conventional versus emergent alternative wisdom, *Development*, Vol. 48, No. 1, pp. 65–69.

Kpienbaareh, D., Kansanga, M. M., Konkor, I. and Luginaah, I. (2021). The rise of the fourth estate: The media, environmental policy, and the fight against illegal mining in Ghana, *Environmental Communication*, Vol. 15, No. 1, pp. 69–84.

Kuhmonen, T. (2017). Exposing the attractors of evolving complex adaptive systems by utilising futures images: Milestones of the food sustainability journey, *Technological Forecasting and Social Change*, Vol. 114, pp. 214–225.

Lloret, A. (2016). Modeling corporate sustainability strategy, *Journal of Business Research*, Vol. 69, No. 2, pp. 418–425.

Mackey, A., Mackey, T. B. and Barney, J. B. (2007). Corporate social responsibility and firm performance: Investor preferences and corporate strategies, *Academy of Management Review*, Vol. 32, No. 3, pp. 817–835.

Matsumura, T., Akiba, Y., Borrill, J., Chinone, Y., Dobbs, M., Fuke, H., . . . and Yotsumoto, K. (2014). Mission design of LiteBIRD, *Journal of Low Temperature Physics*, Vol. 176, No. 5, pp. 733–740.

Mazzi, A., Spagnolo, M. and Toniolo, S. (2020). External communication on legal compliance by Italian waste treatment companies, *Journal of Cleaner Production*, Vol. 255, p. 120325.

Meyer, C. R. and Gauthier, J. (2013). Navigating challenging fitness landscapes: Social entrepreneurship and the competing dimensions of sustainability, *Journal of Social Entrepreneurship*, Vol. 4, No. 1, pp. 23–39.

Morioka, S. N., Bolis, I., Evans, S. and Carvalho, M. M. (2017). Transforming sustainability challenges into competitive Advantage: Multiple case studies kaleidoscope converging into sustainable business models, *Journal of Cleaner Production*, Vol. 167, pp. 723–738.

Niesenbaum, R. A. (2020). Artisanal gold mining in Las juntas de Abangares, Costa Rica: Approaches and barriers to achieving sustainability objectives, *Environmental Science & Policy*, Vol. 114, pp. 470–477.

Nizam, E., Ng, A., Dewandaru, G., Nagayev, R. and Nkoba, M. A. (2019). The impact of social and Environmental sustainability on financial performance: A global analysis of the banking sector, *Journal of Multinational Financial Management*, Vol. 49, pp. 35–53.

Norman, W. and MacDonald, C. (2004). Getting to the bottom of "triple bottom line, *Business Ethics Quarterly*, Vol. 14, No. 2, pp. 243–262.

Nyame-Asiamah, F. (2013). The deferred model of reality for designing and evaluating organisational learning processes: A critical ethnographic case study of Komfo Anokye teaching hospital. Brunel University Brunel Business School PhD Theses, Ghana.

Nyame-Asiamah, F. (2020). Improving the 'manager-clinician' collaboration for effective healthcare ICT and telemedicine adoption processes — A cohered emergent perspective, *Information Technology for Development*, Vol. 26, No. 3, pp. 525–550.

Nyame-Asiamah, F. and Kawalek, P. (2021). Sustainability and consumer behaviour: Towards a cohered emergent theory, in D. Crowther and S. Seifi (eds.), *The Palgrave Handbook of Corporate Social Responsibility*. Palgrave Macmillan, Cham. https://doi.org/10.1007/978-3-030-42465-7_23.

Nyame-Asiamah, F. and Patel, N. V. (2010). Informing knowledge management systems design and evaluation with the theory of deferred action,

The International Journal of Technology, Knowledge and Society, Vol. 6, No. 2, pp. 191–210.

Patel, N. V. (2006). *Organization and Systems Design: Theory of Deferred Action.* Palgrave Macmillan, London.

Patel, N. V. (2007). Deferred action: Theoretical model of process architecture design for emergent business processes, *International Journal of Business Science & Applied Management,* Vol. 2, No. 3, pp. 4–21.

Pisani, N., Kourula, A., Kolk, A. and Meijer, R. (2017). How global is international CSR research? Insights and recommendations from a systematic review, *Journal of World Business,* Vol. 52, No. 5, pp. 591–614.

Polacek, G. A., Gianetto, D. A., Khashanah, K. and Verma, D. (2012). On principles and rules in complex adaptive systems: A financial system case study, *Systems Engineering,* Vol. 15, No. 4, pp. 433–447.

Qureshi, S. (2020). Outrage and anger in a global pandemic: Flipping the script on healthcare, *Information Technology for Development,* Vol. 26, No. 3, pp. 445–457.

Ramrattan, M. and Patel, N. V. (2010). Web-based information systems development and dynamic organisational change: The need for development tools to cope with emergent information requirements, *Journal of Enterprise Information Management,* Vol. 23, No. 3, pp. 23–377.

Roberts, B. and Cohen, M. (2002). Enhancing sustainable development by triple value adding to the core business of government, *Economic Development Quarterly,* Vol. 16, No. 2, pp. 127–137.

Roth, H. P. (2008). Using cost management for sustainability efforts, *Journal of Corporate Accounting & Finance,* Vol. 19, No. 3, pp. 11–18.

Sadik, A. (2013). *Corporate Social Responsibility and the Gold Mining Industry: The Ghana Experience,* Montclair State University.

Schianetz, K. and Kavanagh, L. (2008). Sustainability indicators for tourism destinations: A complex adaptive systems approach using systemic indicator systems, *Journal of Sustainable Tourism,* Vol. 16, No. 6, pp. 601–628.

Scott, M. I. T. (2003). *Dimensions of Sustainability.* Taylor & Francis.

Senior, K. (2003). Brundtland's legacy, *The Lancet Oncology,* Vol. 4, No. 1, p. 3.

Senyo, P. K. and Osabutey, E. L. (2021). Transdisciplinary perspective on sustainable multi-tier supply chains: A triple bottom line inspired framework and future research directions, *International Journal of Production Research,* pp. 1–16.

Shakeel, J., Mardani, A., Chofreh, A. G., Goni, F. A. and Klemeš, J. J. (2020). Anatomy of sustainable business model innovation, *Journal of Cleaner Production*, Vol. 261, p. 121201.

Shim, J., Moon, J., Lee, W. S. and Chung, N. (2021). The impact of CSR on corporate value of restaurant businesses using triple bottom line theory, *Sustainability*, Vol. 13, p. 2131.

Siddique, M. A., Akhtaruzzaman, M., Rashid, A. and Hammami, H. (2021). Carbon disclosure, carbon performance and financial performance: International evidence, *International Review of Financial Analysis*, Vol. 75, p. 101734.

Singh, R. K., Murty, H. R., Gupta, S. K. and Dikshit, A. K. (2009). An overview of sustainability assessment methodologies, *"Ecological Indicators*, Vol. 9, No. 2, pp. 189–212.

Stanny, E. (2013). Voluntary disclosures of emissions by US firms, *Business Strategy and the Environment*, Vol. 22, No. 3, pp. 145–158.

Sun, W., Ji, B., Khoso, S. A., Tang, H., Liu, R., Wang, L. and Hu, Y. (2018). An extensive review on restoration technologies for mining tailings, *Environmental Science and Pollution Research*, Vol. 25, No. 34, pp. 33911–33925.

Teschner, B. (2013). How you start matters: A comparison of gold fields' Tarkwa and Damang mines and their divergent relationships with local small-scale miners in Ghana, *Resources Policy*, Vol. 38, No. 3, pp. 332–340.

Testa, F., Rizzi, F., Daddi, T., Gusmerotti, N. M., Frey, M. and Iraldo, F. (2014). EMAS and ISO 14001: The differences in effectively improving environmental performance, *Journal of Cleaner Production*, Vol. 68, pp. 165–173.

Tuokuu, F. X. D., Gruber, J. S., Idemudia, U. and Kayira, J. (2018). Challenges and opportunities of environmental policy implementation: Empirical evidence from Ghana's gold mining sector, *Resources Policy*, Vol. 59, pp. 435–445.

The Minerals Commission of Ghana (2021). Organisational profile. Available at: https://www.mincom.gov.gh/organisation-profile/.

Thomas, E. A. (2019). How useful is the global reporting initiative (GRI) reporting framework to identify the non-financial value of corporate social performance (CSP)? in *Responsible Business in Uncertain Times and for a Sustainable Future*, pp. 37–87, Springer, Cham.

Tjahjadi, B., Soewarno, N. and Mustikaningtiyas, F. (2021). Good corporate governance and corporate sustainability performance in Indonesia: A triple bottom line approach, *Heliyon*, Vol. 7, No. 3, p. e06453.

Tsalis, T. A., Malamateniou, K. E., Koulouriotis, D. and Nikolaou, I. E. (2020). New challenges for corporate sustainability reporting: United nations' 2030 agenda for sustainable development and the sustainable development goals, *Corporate Social Responsibility and Environmental Management*, Vol. 27, No. 4, pp. 1617–1629.

Vílchez, V. F. (2017). The dark side of ISO 14001: The symbolic environmental behavior, *European Research on Management and Business Economics*, Vol. 23, No. 1, pp. 33–39.

World Commission on Environment and Development (1987). *Our Common Future*, Oxford University Press, Oxford.

Yin, R. K. (2013). Validity and generalization in future case study evaluations, *Evaluation*, Vol. 19, No. 3, pp. 321–332.

Zaharia, R. M. and Zaharia, R. (2021). Triple bottom line, in D. Crowther and S. Seifi (eds.), *The Palgrave Handbook of Corporate Social Responsibility*. Palgrave Macmillan, Cham. https://doi.org/10.1007/978-3-030-42465-7_2.

Chapter 8

Sustainability Reporting and the Sustainable Development Goals in Higher Education: A Portuguese University Case

Sonia Monteiro, Veronica Ribeiro, and Katia Lemos

Abstract

The year 2015 represented a historic mark for sustainable development, with the approval of the 2030 Agenda at the United Nations (UN) summit, which defined 17 Sustainable Development Goals (SDGs). The UN 2030 Agenda provides a universal framework to which each country, region, and community can prioritise its needs and address them locally. Higher education institutions (HEIs) can and must provide a holistic approach to the 2030 Agenda and advance it since the SDGs are a key aspect of their social responsibility (Vilalta *et al.*, 2018). The UN Agenda 2030 represents an opportunity for the improvement of university management, the relationship with stakeholders and the community, and the articulation and consolidation of education policies with the SDGs. Sustainability education can provide students with the in-depth competence to incorporate sustainability into the consciousness of the future, as citizens and professionals. Thus, HEIs will need to be able to plan, evaluate and monitor their contributions to the SDGs, and review their strategies accordingly. Therefore, reports can play a key role, informing HEIs' progress towards sustainability in four main areas (learning and teaching, research, organisational governance, and external leadership) and shaping future commitments and actions. This chapter aims to develop a longitudinal study regarding the evolution of the sustainability report in a Portuguese Public University — the University of Minho — seeking to analyse how this University includes its contributions towards the SDGs of the 2030 Agenda in its disclosures. The study methodology is based on content analysis of the information disclosed in the sustainability reports published until 2016, referring to the period 2010–2015. The results indicate that the university adopted the Global Reporting Initiative guidelines. The alignment with the UN goals was made for the first time in the last sustainability report.

Keywords: Sustainability reporting; sustainable development goals; higher education; global reporting initiative; accountability; social responsibility

1. Introduction

The United Nations (UN) 2030 Agenda represents an opportunity for the improvement of higher education institutions' (HEIs) management, the relationship with stakeholders and the community, and the articulation and consolidation of education policies with the Sustainable Development Goals (SDGs). HEIs cannot remain apart in the reflection of sustainable development (SD) since they play an important role in the students' formation and transfer of knowledge of future professionals/future citizens, who will have to democratically promote human rights and the common good. HEIs should consider sustainability as a mechanism that, in addition to seeking academic success, should give significant contributions to the community within its area of influence, region, and country in general. This implies promoting sustainability as a strategic model in the mission, vision, and objective of the HEIs, carrying out activities of social commitment.

After committing to become sustainable, HEIs need to be held accountable. Stakeholders are attentive to the acts practised by HEIs; analysing if they have sustainable behaviours. In order to do this, the dissemination of information about SD allows us to understand the concerns and strategies that guide decision-making, contributing to the image they intend to pass on to the community in which they are placed. Therefore, reporting should be considered an important way to provide an overview of current progress towards the SDGs. Reporting is both an important measure for accountability and evaluation and a huge opportunity for HEIs that engage with the SDGs.

Over the last few decades, reporting frameworks/guidelines have been developed to help assess and manage the current state of an organisation's sustainability and communicate it to stakeholders. The guidelines/standards developed by the Global Reporting Initiative (GRI) are singled out as the world's foremost internationally recognised and globally accepted sustainability reporting framework (KPMG, 2015).

Sustainability reporting acquired great importance in the last decades; however, the information disclosed is not always presented in a context of a business model or an organisational strategy, making it difficult for stakeholders to understand how sustainability (social, economic, or environmental) can affect the value creation process of an organisation (Eccles and Serafeim, 2015). In this context, the integrated report emerges as a viable alternative because it has the potential to make the strategies and business models of the organisations more transparent to stakeholders.

The aim of this chapter is to develop a longitudinal study about sustainability reporting on a Portuguese public university — Minho University — analysing its content and also analysing if the University's disclosure includes its contributions towards the SDGs.

This work is structured in six sections. The first and second sections address the social responsibility and accountability in HEIs in an SD context. The third and fourth sections emphasise the role of education to promote sustainability awareness and the importance of integrating the SDGs into sustainability reporting. The research design is presented in section five, which consists of the case study of a Portuguese HEI, through a longitudinal analysis of its sustainability reports in the period 2010–2015. In the last section, the results of the study are analysed, and finally, the main conclusions are presented.

2. Social Responsibility of Higher Education Institutions in Favour of Sustainable Development

Social responsibility assumes the organisations' voluntary character towards the impacts of their decisions and activities in society and the environment through a transparent and ethical behaviour that contributes to SD, taking into account the expectations of stakeholders (Chen *et al.*, 2015).

In the context of the public sector, Social Responsibility (SR) is a function of the state itself since its main objective is to promote better living conditions for citizens, through the implementation of public policies, with effective and efficient use of available resources. Higher education is an important factor of social transformation and can influence the models and orientations of the economic, social, and cultural development of the surrounding community.

In the context of HEIs, public universities are typically larger and more complex than private universities. As a result of their size, circulation of people and vehicles, high consumption of materials, and development of complex activities, they can even be considered "small cities" (Alshuwaikhat and Abubakar, 2008). Taylor *et al.* (1994) even consider universities as "silent destroyers" due to their environmental impacts.

Therefore, like business organisations, HEIs need to adopt an SR strategy in order to meet the expectations of their stakeholders (students, employers, employees, teachers, and society) (Chen *et al.*, 2015). On the other hand, given their role in social and innovation terms (the so-called "third mission"), HEIs are increasingly called upon to contribute to society: In addition to teaching and research, HEIs have the ability to link their agenda to sustainability matters (Neary and Osborne, 2018).

The concept of university social responsibility (USR) is explored in some literature but with no single definition (Quezada, 2011; Vasilescu *et al.*, 2010; Bokhari, 2017). For Vallaeys (2014), the USR concept is based on the fair and sustainable management of the following impacts generated by an HEI: (1) organisational impacts — that come from the institution itself, its campus and its personnel (labour and environmental impacts); (2) educational impacts — that derive from the academic training given to the students; (3) cognitive impacts — that come from research and (4) social impacts — that result from the relationship with the social environment, networks and partnerships, contracting, and relationship extension with the community/transfer of knowledge to society.

In Latin America, we highlight the work carried out by Professor François Vallaeys to promote the USR, culminating in the publication "Responsabilidad Social Universitaria: Manual de Primeros pasos" (Vallaeys *et al.*, 2009). The importance attributed to this theme led to the approval of the Law of the Peruvian University No. 30220 (2014), which in article 126 obliges universities to comply with their social responsibility through an impact management approach in a transversal way, the same approach promoted in the Green Book about SR and HEIs, published in Portugal (ORSIES, 2018).

Based on the Millennium Development Goals (MDGs, 2002–2015) established in 2000, the SDGs (2015–2030) were formally adopted by all 193 UN member states. Unlike the previous MDGs, SDGs were designed to be universal and capable of being applied to all countries (Neary and Osborne, 2018), placing education at the heart of the strategy to promote SD (Annan-Diab and Molinari, 2017). In fact, the SDG4 — Quality education goal 4.7 intends that, by 2030, all students acquire the knowledge and skills necessary to promote SD, inclusively, among others, through education for SD.

The 2030 agenda and the SDGs will help focus the efforts of governments and academic institutions in obtaining important contributions for development. SD cannot be achieved in isolation to the relationship between HEIs and organisations and society.

Lozano *et al.*, (2013b) propose that for HEIs to become leaders and engines of change in the matter of sustainability, they should ensure that the needs of present and future generations are better understood and constructed so that professional experts on SD can effectively teach and help students to make the transition to "sustainable social standards". To this end, HEIs leaders and staff must be able to catalyse and implement new paradigms and ensure that the SD is the golden thread throughout the higher education system.

In the same line of thought, according to Bokhari (2017), the role of HEIs in the promotion of SD through their commitment to SR requires first the acceptance/belief and conviction of the university, teachers, staff, and students and the deep trust/belief and conviction in the SR issue. When effectively committed to their SR, HEIs are in a privileged position to play a leading role in achieving SD. In fact, by promoting SR practises in their own institutions, HEIs can demonstrate their commitment to the SDGs.

The HEIs' commitment to their social role requires the incorporation of SR in the vision/mission of the institution, ensuring the inclusion of SR in its objectives and strategic plan. It is also essential to create an internal environment to fit the implementation of green and socially responsible activities, programmes, and initiatives. The HEIs should also commit to the development of curricular and extracurricular activities to improve students' educational level and skills in sustainability. It should also support studies/research programmes on SR and economic sustainability as well as publish results and recommendations with a high level of transparency. In other words, elaborate and disseminate RS indicators, which allow for measuring the effort developed in this area, according to the specific goals defined (Bokhari, 2017).

3. Sustainable Development and Accountability in HEIs

The SDGs (2015–2030) were formally adopted by all 193 UN member states. They were designed to be universal and capable of being applied to all countries (Neary and Osborne, 2018), placing education at the heart of the strategy to promote SD (Annan-Diab and Molinari, 2017). In fact, the SDG4 — Quality Education goal 4.7 intends that, by 2030, all students acquire the knowledge and skills necessary to promote SD, inclusively, among others, through education for SD. Within the 2030 Agenda, educational responses are key to the vision of the SDGs. Education is both a goal in itself and a means for attaining all the other SDGs.

Traditionally, the assessment and reporting of organisations' performance, which are the requirements for effective accountability, has been based on the financial accounting model. However, the growing interest in sustainability has led to the evolution of accountability mechanisms and new reporting models to address the non-financial information needs of stakeholders.

Organisations have expressed interest in disseminating information in reports of SR/sustainability to meet the growing demand for transparency and accountability by stakeholders (KPMG, 2008). Likewise, public entities are increasingly governed by more efficient and transparent management in response to the demands/pressures of citizens and other stakeholders, leading to the dissemination of more information on SR/sustainability. Ball and Bebbington (2008) state that public authorities have increased responsibility for the dissemination of information due to the functions inherent in their own SR competencies.

Regarding higher education, some studies seek to evaluate transparency and accountability in HEIs through the analysis of information released on a voluntary basis (Ntim *et al.*, 2017). According to Buchta *et al.* (2018), a responsible HEI should provide reliable information, taking into account the expectations of interested parties, including the students. In fact, according to Quezada (2011), one of the approaches of the USR is related, on the one hand, to the identification of the stakeholders to whom one is accountable to and, on the other hand, in the process of accountability, through the construction of indicators that allow quantifying the impact of the actions carried out under the USR, results that are disseminated with the purpose of providing transparency to the information disclosed to stakeholders.

Dissemination and information on SR/sustainability through reporting is, therefore, a key element in the transparency and accountability of HEIs. The green book on SR and HEIs, published in Portugal by ORSIES (2018) in point 1.7 related to socially responsible communication and marketing, recommends that HEIs adopt SR reporting strategies developed by HEIs, specifically the inclusion of the social responsibility theme in the institutional websites of HEIs and the development of sustainability reports.

On the other hand, Agenda 2030 for SD covers all areas and sectors of any country. It represents an opportunity for the improvement of university management, the relationship with stakeholders and the community, and the articulation and consolidation of education policies with the SDGs. Thus, HEIs will need to be able to assess their impact on the SDGs and review their strategies accordingly, which requires the collection and reporting of new data, while also evolving in the way they report.

4. Role of Education and Reporting to Promote Sustainability Awareness

Providing sustainability awareness requires educational institutes to adapt their vision, policy, and teaching. The increasing involvement of higher education for sustainable development is notable in their four nuclear areas:

- education (providing students with skills, values, and knowledge related to meeting the SDGs);
- research (ensuring that the knowledge generated by the research results is useful and visible to different stakeholders);
- operations (controlling the HEI's own social and environmental impacts);
- community engagement (as key stakeholders who actively participate in the societal dialogue regarding the issues covered by the SDGs).

Considering the first (and main) area — education — the development of students' competences across the sustainability education curriculum is crucial. Student skills can be enhanced by the inclusion of sustainability concepts in their education, such as energy efficiency, risk reduction, green computing, sustainable projects, climate change, and the sustainable consumption of resources (Malik *et al.*, 2019). This will allow for a deep understanding and an awareness among students to effectively address sustainability during their undergraduate projects and later in the world of work and in their professional life.

In order to promote sustainability awareness among students and influence student behaviour, some actions need to be implemented in sustainability literacy. HEIs should offer sustainability courses, demonstrating and supporting students' activities on and off campus to promote sustainable behaviour (Alsaati *et al.*, 2020). HEIs should also involve students and other stakeholders (such as academics, governments, and local municipalities) in their SDG reporting process in order to discuss the relevance of sustainability disclosures. Sustainability reporting is an important communication element that requires effective stakeholder engagement, which implies that the participatory process and stakeholder expectations must be detailed in the report (Ferrero-Ferrero *et al.*, 2018). Therefore, the sustainability report must not only quantify the past but also show awareness of the future.

5. Integrating the SDGs into HEIs' Reporting

According to Lozano *et al.* (2013a), there has been a rapid growth of HEIs that seek to make SD an integral part of the institutional culture and to incorporate sustainability into their curricular plans, research, operations, evaluation, and reporting.

As in any other type of organisation, a sustainability report from a HEI should include economic, social, and environmental information about the management of the institution on its interest groups as well as the corporate governance and management systems implemented. However, HEIs are not required to elaborate mandatory reports on issues related to sustainability (Romolini *et al.*, 2015).

Despite the growing number of companies that are already reporting on sustainability, it is still insignificant compared to the total number of companies operating in the world. Additionally, in the particular case of HEIs, the number of reporting institutions is even smaller (Lozano, 2011; Lozano *et al.*, 2013a). Most of the reports published by HEIs are in Europa (54%) and America (32%), with the rest in Asia and Australia (Lozano *et al.*, 2013a).

In the opinion of Lozano *et al.* (2013a), when preparing a sustainability report in a HEI, it is important to have a holistic perspective, addressing the different interrelationships between indicators, categories, and dimensions, as well as stakeholders throughout the higher education system.

The guidelines/standards developed by the GRI are singled out as the world's foremost internationally recognised and globally accepted sustainability reporting framework (KPMG, 2015). The private sector was the one that most used this form of disclosure, but it is still used on a small scale in the public sector (Adams *et al.*, 2014). To promote its use, a pilot version of the Sector Supplement for Public Agencies (SSPA) was published in 2005 to be applied at different levels of government: regional, central, federal, and local. However, the use of the supplement was minimal and organisations use the general structure of the GRI guidelines more (Tort, 2010; Navarro *et al.*, 2017).

The GRI guidelines have not been developed for HEIs either. However, Lozano (2006) adapted them to include the educational dimension and developed a framework that he called the "Graphical Assessment of Sustainability in Universities" (GASU), providing a set of performance indicators that can be used to prepare a sustainability report by HEIs. This framework was used to analyse 12 universities that published sustainability reports based on the GRI guidelines (Lozano, 2011). In 2011, GASU was adapted to adjust to the G3 version of the GRI, and interconnections between economic, social, environmental, and educational dimensions were added (Lozano and Huisingh, 2011). This tool was used as a reference in the process undertaken to prepare the first draft of the sustainability report of the University of Leeds in the United Kingdom (Lozano *et al.*, 2013a).

In the context of higher education, Kräusche and Pilz (2018) consider that only a part of the GRI indicators can be applied to universities, so a HEI core business cannot be mapped by the GRI guidelines. In this sense, the authors present an integrated report on sustainability developed at a German university.

The integrated report seems to be the organisational report of the future (Katsikas *et al.*, 2017), complementing the sustainability report and being perfectly applicable also to the public sector with some adjustments (Bartocci and Picciaia, 2013; Montecalvo *et al.*, 2018; Rossi, 2018). According to a CIMA report (2016), integrated reporting in public entities promotes a better understanding of the impact of decisions on the value creation process, taking into account a comprehensive range of factors relevant to the process and not just financial considerations in the short term. This way, better decision-making processes, greater transparency, and long-term perspectives are promoted, which is crucial to the sustainability of public services.

In 2013, the International Integrated Reporting Council (IIRC) published "The International <IR> Framework", with guidelines for the elaboration of an integrated report, defining it as a concise document capable of assessing the value creation capacity of organisations, identifying strategic key points and anticipating risks and opportunities, internal or external, in business.

Oprisor *et al.* (2016) consider that the integrated report has been gaining momentum in the public sector, but progress is still rather slow. Some public entities at an international level have been implementing the integrated report successfully, such as the City of London Corporation, Welsh Government, Crown Estate, and other government departments in the United Kingdom, as well as other public entities in South Africa, Russia, New Zealand, Singapore, Italy, etc. (CIMA, 2016).

Although the integrated reporting framework (IIRC, 2013) refers mainly to for-profit companies, it can also be a reference to the higher education sector (Brusca *et al.*, 2018) and can be used with appropriate adaptations (Veltri and Silvestri, 2015).

In this context, in 2016, the British Universities Finance Directors Group has encouraged universities in the UK to implement the integrated report and developed a guide to assist them in this regard, based on the IR framework, adjusting it to the specificities of the higher education sector in the UK. At a later stage, in 2017, the British Universities Finance Directors Group has developed a project in four universities in order to demonstrate how the framework can help them change into a new approach based on "value creation". The practical application of the integrated report in HEIs is therefore at a very early stage, but the academic debate is already starting to be reflected in some studies (Veltri and Silvestri, 2015; Brusca *et al.*, 2018; Hassan *et al.*, 2019).

Four years have passed since the definition of the UN SDGs, under the 2030 Agenda, with the public sector, and HEIs in particular, playing a key role in helping to achieve the SDGs. In this sense, it is important to align an organisation's strategy and the organisational report with the SDGs, making known to stakeholders the current level of commitment to these goals.

The target 12.6 of Agenda 2030 encourages organisations to adopt sustainable practises and to integrate sustainability information into their reporting cycle. Thus, transparent and relevant reports on the SDGs are important to communicate to stakeholders how HEIs are meeting their set goals.

Fleaca *et al.* (2018) conceptualised a model that helps guide HEIs in the process of organisational culture change, aiming the alignment and operationalisation of the HEI strategy with the SDGs. The proposed educational model can be customised and harmonised according to the different circumstances and priorities of the HEIs. The last stage of the process is to report and communicate the progress made by HEIs in favour of the SDGs, referring to the GRI guidelines as the benchmark to adopt.

Integrating the SDGs' theme into the HEI reports represents, therefore, one of the challenges for HEIs. Despite the fact that different frameworks (from the GRI, the International Organization for Standardization, and the United Nations Global Compact (UNGC)) present different ways to approach reporting on sustainability, none of them include specific guidance on SDG disclosures. In order to bridge this gap, in 2015, the UNGC, the GRI, and the World Business Council for Sustainable Development (WBCSD) presented an innovative initiative titled "The SDG Compass: the guide for business action on the SDGs". This tool helps companies to align their strategies, measure and manage their contribution to achieving the SDGs, and puts sustainability at the centre of their business strategy. It also helps companies to identify the GRI standards that can be used to disclose their actions in order to reach the SDGs.

The UNGC Network along with the GRI developed two fundamental documents ("Business Reporting on the SDGs: An Analysis of the Goals and Targets" and "Integrating the Sustainable Development Goals into Corporate Reporting: A Practical Guide") that should be used together as part of the regular reporting cycle of organisations. It is not intended to create a new framework for reporting but provides a structure that seeks to help organisations reveal their contribution to the SDGs that they consider to be a priority and provide relevant information to stakeholders.

However, according to Adams (2017), the SDG Compass does not support disseminators in deciding how to integrate the SDGs into reports, in accordance with UNGC principles or GRI guidelines/ standards. Moreover, the language used in the document is much closer to the language of integrated reporting than to the language of sustainability reporting. In that sense, the author considers that the integrated report is a promising approach for the dissemination of the contribution of organisations to the SDGs. Therefore, she states that organisations should report their contribution to SDG targets along with the six "capitals" provided in the integrated report framework (IIRC, 2013).

Referring specifically to HEIs, Adams (2018) believes that universities have a central role to play in implementing the SDGs, and governments can hold them responsible to contribute that way. The author, thus, considers that the <IR> framework represents an opportunity for organisations, and HEIs, that seek to respond to the SDGs by integrating them into the strategy and the organisational report. HEIs can illustrate how and for whom they create value and develop strategies contributing to the SDGs on the six capitals of IR, as well as identifying the most relevant risks and opportunities.

The recent report by, Adams *et al.* (2020) offers a new approach for organisations to address sustainable development issues aligned to the <IR> framework (IIRC, 2013), the Task Force on Climate-related Financial Disclosure (TCFD), and the GRI. These recommendations are an opportunity to establish a best practise for corporate reporting on the SDGs and enable more effective and standardised reporting and transparency on climate change, social, and other environmental impacts. The recommendations build on a suggested approach to contributing to the SDGs aligned with long-term value creation in Adams' (2017) report. The report set out a five-step process to align an organisation's approach to the SDGs with integrated thinking and long-term value creation for organisations and society as set out in the <IR> framework.

The need for a common set of performance indicators proves to be paramount for stakeholders to compare the contributions of companies to the achievement of the SDGs. The frameworks already developed for SDG reporting are still at a very embryonic stage (Amey and Whooley, 2018) and it is, therefore, necessary to foster their maturing.

In view of the above, major challenges are placed on HEIs in identifying priority SDGs for their activities and stakeholders, incorporating them into their strategy, setting goals for their success, and measuring and reporting on their progress. Integrating the SDG's evaluation in the report implies showing stakeholders their effective performance, resorting to the emerging non-financial reporting models. Whether through sustainability reports or through integrated reports, we understand that what is important is to align these reports with the structure and scope of the SDGs and should, therefore, be a research area to be favoured in the future.

6. Research Design

6.1. *The case in study*

In the scope of higher education, empirical research in this area is not abundant, but the literature is unanimous in considering that sustainability reporting in HEIs is still very embryonic (Lozano, 2011; Sassen and Azizi, 2017; Sepasi *et al.*, 2018; Azizi *et al.*, 2018), including in Portugal (Aleixo *et al.*, 2016; Silva, 2017).

Fonseca *et al.* (2011) state that the studies performed tend to highlight the relevance of indicators of sustainability and report for higher education or discuss pioneer experiences. Many studies focus their analysis on specific case(s) of an institution (Quezada, 2011; Yi *et al.*, 2017; Sepasi *et al.*, 2018) or a region/country (Huerta-Riveros and Gaete-Feres, 2007; Fonseca, *et al.*, 2011; Hinson *et al.*, 2015; Chatelain-Ponroy and Morin-Delerm, 2016; Sassen and Azizi, 2017; Sassen *et al.*, 2018; Azizi *et al.*, 2018).

The dissemination of SR practises developed by HEIs in support of SD can be carried out through their websites, thus ensuring greater proximity to the academic community. In this sense, several studies on SR/sustainability are based on the analysis of the websites of the HEIs (Garde Sánchez *et al.*, 2013; Nejati *et al.*, 2011; Hinson *et al.*, 2015; Aleixo *et al.*, 2016).

In the scope of SDG reporting, empirical research is rare and recent. According to previous research (Schramade, 2017; Bebbington and Unerman, 2018; PwC, 2018; KPMG, 2018; Gunawan *et al.*, 2019; Avrampou *et al.*, 2019; Almontaser and Gerged, 2019; Hummel, 2019; Monteiro *et al.*, 2020; Di Vaio and Varriale, 2020; Acuti *et al.*, 2020; Wang *et al.*, 2020; Tsalis *et al.*, 2020), a few SDGs have been most often mentioned by the companies in their reporting (sustainability reports or integrated reporting). Concerning higher education, we highlight the recent study of Paletta *et al.* (2020) in the University of Bologna. The social responsibility report of the university, which has been published annually since 2012, consists of an extensive publication covering the economic, social, and environmental effects of the entirety of the university fields of action. The university has also published a report on the UN SDGs since 2016. The latest edition of the report was prepared from April 2018 to July 2018. The report presents the key figures of the University of Bologna, followed by 17 sections dedicated to each SDG. The sections define the direct and indirect impact of the university's activities in their four dimensions — training, research, Third Mission, and institution — in order to measure their contribution to the advancement of the 2030 Agenda.

In the Portuguese context, the studies of SD in HEIs are still scarce. We highlight the study by Madeira *et al.* (2011) which developed a set of sustainability indicators for HEIs, which were applied at the Faculty of Engineering of the University of Porto (FEUP). The study by Aleixo *et al.* (2016) sought to assess the practises of SD existing in Portuguese HEIs through an analysis of the information disclosed on their websites. It also analyses the determinant factors of the implementation of SD practises in Portuguese HEIs. The study by Silva (2017), in turn, sought to identify and study the cases of a sustainability report that exist or existed in Portuguese HEIs, contributing to understanding the main benefits that can encourage a greater sustainability report and the main barriers that the HEIs face in the dissemination of such practises.

The report on sustainability is not a common practise in most countries (Alonso-Almeida *et al.*, 2015), nor is it in Portugal. The study by Aleixo *et al.* (2016) concluded that in the case of SD, Portuguese HEIs are at an early stage but incremental, and they already show some awareness on how they communicate their policies and strategies in favour of SD.

In the study by Silva (2017), three HEIs were identified in Portugal, who report or already reported on SR/sustainability through independent reports: the University of Minho (from 2010 to 2015), Faculty of Engineering of the University of Porto (between 2006 and 2012), and Higher Institute of Engineering of Porto (ISEP) (only in 2012).

Ramísio *et al.* (2019) present the implementation of the Sustainability Vision of the University of Minho (between 2009 and 2017) in a holistic and inclusive perspective, demonstrating the engagement and alignment of the academic community and the rectorate. According to the studies by Silva (2017) and Ramísio *et al.* (2019), the University of Minho (UM) presents an advanced and continuous reporting and commitment on sustainability matters.

Considering that, for this study, it was decided to focus the analysis on the UM sustainability report evolution because it presents a more recent, more advanced, and continuous report (Silva, 2017). The UM has been distinguished by the best ever result of a Portuguese institution in the "UI GreenMetric World University Rankings 2017", which evaluates the environmental sustainability indexes of academies around the world. The UM emerges as the first in the country, second in the Iberian Peninsula, 23rd in Europe, and 48th in the world. On this, the first time that it competed, it achieved the best mark for Portugal in eight editions of the ranking and even reached the top 10 worldwide in the category "Education for sustainability".

For the UM, the annual sustainability reports are crucial documents in this long-term vision in identifying the environmental and socio-economic impacts of the institution. Based on these reports, it was the first European university to align with the SDGs of the UN and the first in the country to be included in the International Sustainable Campus Network (ISCN), having joined the UNGC.

The UM is the best institution of higher education in Portugal and the third largest in the Iberian Peninsula to accomplish the UN SDGs, according to the first edition of Times Higher Education "The Impact Rankings". The UM occupies the 83rd position worldwide, thanks to its commitment to sustainability as evidenced by the criteria "partnerships for the implementation of objectives", "quality education", "sustainable cities and communities", "industry, innovation and infrastructures", and "quality health". The result demonstrates the UM's commitment to complying with SDGs, not only through teaching, research, and knowledge transfer but also incorporating them into its internal practises, policies, and procedures, with verifiable evidence of its activities.

6.2. *Methodology*

Similar to related studies, this study used a content analysis methodology to analyse the sustainability reports of the UM published in 2016, referring to the period 2010–2015. Content analysis of the

The Complexities of Sustainability

CSR/sustainability report in higher education has been a widely used method in previous studies related to corporate social/environmental or sustainability reporting (Huerta-Riveros and Gaete-Feres, 2007; Garde Sánchez *et al.*, 2013; Sassen and Azizi, 2017, 2018; Yi *et al.*, 2017; Azizi *et al.*, 2018; Larrán Jorge *et al.*, 2018).

7. Results Analysis and Discussion

The first UM report was published in September 2012 and had by reference the year 2010. Since then, annual reports have been produced, with the exception of the years 2012 and 2013, the information of which has been compiled into a single report because the GRI has changed the guidelines for the G4, and it is necessary to do a new survey and reorganisation of data, aiming to include more indicators (Silva, 2017). The last report was published in December 2016, with reference to the year 2015, and is already in line with the UN SDGs.

According to Ramísio *et al.* (2019), the regular reporting of sustainability indicators, and its internal and external communication, was very important for the implementation of sustainability plans.

Table 1 summarises the analysis of the UM sustainability reports.

The table shows that, since its first report in 2010, until the last one reported in 2015, the university decided to apply the GRI framework. It is the first Portuguese university, the second European, and the sixth worldwide, to make this report according to the GRI guidelines (Silva, 2017).

The report from the UM has followed the evolution of the guidelines: In the first two reports, it used the G3 version; in the 2012–2013 report, and in the following reports, the guidelines of the G4 version had already been followed. The first approach to the UN SDGs was made in the last report.

The UM structured its reports based on the indicators recommended by the GRI in the three common dimensions: environmental, social, and economic. From the 2012–2013 report, it has added the cultural dimension in order to demonstrate the performance of a set of valences with significant impacts on society. It also chose to include

Table 1. Evolution of UM sustainability reports.

| | Report — Reference period(s) | | | | |
	2010	2011	2012–2013	2014	2015
Publication date	2012	2013	2014	2015	2016
Framework used	GRI G3	GRI G3	GRI G4	GRI G4	GRI G4
No. of pages	116	124	164	56	38
Dimensions analysed	Economic Social Environmental	Economic Social Environmental	Economic Social Environmental Cultural	Economic Social Environmental Cultural	Economic Social Environmental Cultural
Level of declaration/ comprehensiveness	C	C	In accordance — Comprehensive	In accordance — Comprehensive	In accordance — Comprehensive
Alignment with SDGs	No	No	No	No	Yes
External verification	No	No	No	No	Yes

Source: Own elaboration.

a subcategory of the social dimension — the student body — in order to reflect the UM's performance in education, which is not considered by the GRI guidelines. This category was even more highlighted in the last report (2015) in a broader and more comprehensive approach. According to Ramísio *et al.* (2019), the accountability of these performance indicators was attributed by the rectorate to existing areas of responsibility that adapted their sectorial reporting framework. Thus, the UM does not follow the structure of other HEIs which choose to join the social and cultural dimensions and add an educational/institutional dimension (Alshuwaikhat and Abubakar, 2008; Lozano, 2011; Alonso-Almeida *et al.*, 2015).[1] This model suited the needs of the UM.

The indicators used increased gradually over time. In the second report, two indicators were added in the economic dimension. From 2012–2013 report, due to the adaptation to the G4 version, the selection of the indicators was made in order to adopt the most demanding option, corresponding to the highest level of comprehensiveness: In Accordance–Comprehensive. In this sense, the UM felt the need to extend the contents already disclosed in previous reports, taking into account new indicators.

According to the results from Silva (2017, p. 23), "before there was little discrimination regarding the reporting of each indicator before we reported half a page of indicators, now we need four pages (. . .). The indicators are now more complete and convey a better understanding of what is intended".

The use of the G4 version, coupled with the fact that the report published in 2014 covers two periods (2012–2013), justifies a significant increase in the size of the report (the first report had 116 pages, and this one has a total of 164 pages).

---

[1] According to the study by Aleixo *et al.* (2016), the UM implemented more than 50% of SD practises considered in the study, and for this result, economic and environmental performance contributed first, followed by social and environmental performance, and lastly the practises in the institutional/educational/political dimension.

Stakeholders increasingly pay more attention to the acts practised by HEIs, analysing if they have sustainable behaviours, they should therefore be involved in the construction of the framework report of social responsibility in HEIs. In order to meet the opinion and interest of the UM stakeholders, the 2012–2013 report does not follow the traditional information structure presented in the GRI guidelines or previous reports. "Through the result of listening to stakeholders and the materiality matrix, it was decided to prioritise the contents to be disseminated, according to the topics that the stakeholders considered most relevant, as well as the importance of each subject for each indicator" (Report 2012–2013, p. 40).

The 2014 and 2015 reports show a drastic reduction in their size (more than half) compared to previous reports. However, the report "has undergone changes regarding the exposition of the content that resulted in more assertive and enthusiastic communication" (Reports of 2014 and 2015, p. 15 and p. 17, respectively). In fact, in addition to presenting data of the period to which they correspond, they present values from previous periods as well as the differentials recorded in the period compared to the preceding period.

In the report published in 2016 (with reference to the 2015 period), the UM began its first approach to the UN SDGs, presenting its contribution to the achievement of the goals. The UM states that it "cannot ignore the implications of integrating the SDGs into the institution and considers these goals critical to the future of humankind and to ensure the constant improvement of the quality of life of human beings. In fact, it is considered that Education, Research and Learning are at the centre of approaches to sustainable development" (p. 14). Thus, in specific appendixes, information is presented that demonstrates the alignment with the 17 SDGs.

The 2015 report clearly references the continuous reporting process, highlighting "the remarkable path in developing strategies that have enabled the institution to increase its levels of sustainability" (p. 5). This pattern is consistent with the evolution of the social/sustainability report verified in the public sector in Portugal (Ribeiro and Monteiro, 2018), suggesting the possibility of mimetic isomorphism for other universities, in terms of increasing reporting disclosure. This report had an external verification for the first time by the GRI. According to Silva (2017, p. 75), the UM "felt the need to have an accreditation that the information contained in the reports is relevant. Collecting data is important but to collect data and request verification of that data to a competent entity, is to make the process more credible".

The previous analysis is based on the sustainability reports published by the UM with reference to the period 2010–2015. According to the results of interviews conducted by Silva (2017), the UM was expected to continue to produce sustainability reports in the coming years. However, strangely, to this date, no further reports have been published. This may, in our opinion, be related to the introduction of the GRI standards in 2016 because it is considered more complex than the previous GRI guidelines or because the university is eventually thinking of evolving into the <IR> framework, similar to other HEIs (for example, those in the UK).

This idea finds some support in the fact that the language used in the latest sustainability report is much closer to the integrated reporting language than to the GRI sustainability reporting language. It is, therefore, pointed out that this type of report of the institution aims to "make public the integrated analysis (underline self-added) of the impacts of the University's activity, in environmental, social, economic and cultural terms, according to the best international practises" (p. 3).

8. Conclusion

Educating for sustainability and raising awareness among students and other stakeholders through actions and their reporting are essential. The literature review leads us to conclude that the level of sustainability reporting in HEIs is still very low. Therefore, political incentives should be developed to improve the social performance of HEIs. For example, the green book (ORSIES, 2018) suggests the creation of incentives for HEIs to develop reporting of their social responsibility actions (e.g. prizes, awards by the trustees).

The 2030 agenda and the SDGs will help to focus the efforts of governments and academic institutions in making important contributions to SD, which cannot be achieved in isolation but rather from the interaction between HEIs, public and private organisations, and society.

The 2030 Agenda gives a new impetus towards aligning harmonisation of sustainability reporting with the SDG monitoring framework. According to Bebbington and Unerman (2018), the SDGs have the potential to inform and advance research and practise on sustainability reporting. They state that "academic investigation is needed to help understand where specific SGD-related accounting initiatives lie on the continuum between pure rhetoric and meaningful action, and to inform the most effective use of the SDGs by a broad range of organizations in developing policies and practises that will contribute toward the achievement of the SDGs" (Bebbington and Unerman, 2018, p. 10).

This study used a content analysis methodology based on the sustainability reports published by the UM referring to the period 2010–2015. The university has always adopted the GRI guidelines, and its sustainability reporting is at a fairly advanced level. In its last published sustainability report, the UM has started linking its reporting with the SDGs for the first time.

This study is the first Portuguese approach to SDG reporting, focusing on an award-winning public Portuguese university. This work can be considered as a starting point for deepening the research of SDG reporting in other entities of the public sector, in addition to HEIs, and their alignment with the SDGs. The focus on the local public sector may be a track to be investigated in the future, continuing the research on the environmental/responsibility reporting already performed at municipal level (Ribeiro *et al.*, 2016; Ribeiro and Monteiro, 2018).

The results will be of interest to policymakers and regulators, who decide to implement and standardise sustainability or integrated reporting at HEIs, as well as to managers and finance directors at universities that wish to follow these new trends. We agree with Herzner and Stucken (2020) that within the university, it might be a good idea to have an entire department/faculty, the professors, or the entire university join the appropriate networks. The findings can serve as a learning process for institutions interested in implementing sustainability reporting practises aligned with the UN goals.

Further development of a SDG reporting framework is a process that requires time and the possibility of refinement as knowledge and data availability improve. It should, therefore, be a priority research area for the future.

Acknowledgements

This study was conducted at the Research Center on Accounting and Taxation (CICF) and was funded by the Portuguese Foundation for Science and Technology (FCT) through national funds (UIDB/04043/2020 and UIDP/04043/2020).

References

Acuti, D., Bellucci, M. and Manetti, G. (2020). Company disclosures concerning the resilience of cities from the sustainable development goals (SDGs) perspective, *Cities*, Vol. 99. DOI:10.1016/j.cities. 2020.102.

Adams, C. (2017). *The Sustainable Development Goals, Integrated Thinking and the Integrated Report.* Published by the International Integrated Reporting Council (IIRC) and ICAS. Available at https://www.integratedreporting.org/wp-content/uploads/2017/09/SDGs-and-the-integratedreport_summary2.pdf

Adams, C. (2018). Debate: Integrated reporting and accounting for suitable development across generations by universities, *Public Money & Management*, Vol. 38, No. 5, pp. 325–327.

Adams, C., Druckman, P. and Picot, R. (2020). *Sustainable Development Goals Disclosure (SDGD) Recommendations.* Published by IFAC, ACCA, ICAS, CA ANZ, IIRC and WBA. Available at http://mail.scaak.org/uploads/files/2020/February/07/Adams_2020_Feedback-on-the-consultation1581066574.pdf

Adams, C., Muir, S. and Hoque, Z. (2014). Measurement of sustainability performance in the public sector, *Sustainability Accounting, Management and Policy Journal*, Vol. 5, No. 1, pp. 46–67.

Adhikariparajul, M., Hassan, A., Fletcher, M. and Elamer, A. A. (2019). Integrated reporting in UK higher education institutions, *Sustainability Accounting, Management and Policy Journal*, Vol. 10, No. 5, pp. 844–876.

Aleixo, A. M., Azeiteiro, U. and Leal, S. (2016). Toward sustainability through higher education: Sustainable development incorporation into Portuguese higher education institutions, *Challenges in Higher Education for Sustainability*, pp. 159–187.

Almontaser, T. and Gerged, A. (2019). Exploring corporate sustainable development goals (SDGs) disclosure in a politically unstable environment: Evidence from the Libyan Oil Industry, *Sustainability, Accounting, Management, and Policy Journal*, [e-journal]. DOI: 10.1108/SAMPJ-04-2019-0136 (In press).

Alonso-Almeida, M. del M., Marimon, F., Casani, F. and Rodriguez-Pomeda, J. (2015). Diffusion of sustainability reporting in universities: Current situation and future perspectives, *Journal of Cleaner Production*, Vol. 106, pp. 144–154.

Alsaati, T., El-Nakla, S. and El-Nakla, D. (2020). Level of sustainability awareness among university students in the Eastern Province of Saudi Arabia, *Sustainability*, Vol. 12, No. 8, p. 3159.

Alshuwaikhat, H. and Abubakar, I. (2008). An integrated approach to achieving campus sustainability: Assessment of the current campus environmental management practises, *Journal of Cleaner Production*, Vol. 16, pp. 1777–1785.

Amey, M. (2018). Corporate reporting on the SDGs: Mapping a sustainable future, *Viewpoint*, December. Available at https://www.sustainability-reports.com/corporate-reporting-on-the-sdgsmapping-a-sustainable-future/

Annan-Diab, F. and Molinari, C. (2017). Interdisciplinarity: Practical approach to advancing education for sustainability and for the sustainable development goals, *The International Journal of Management Education*, Vol. 15, No. 2, pp. 73–83.

Avrampou, A., Skouloudis, A., Iliopoulos, G. and Khan, N. (2019). Advancing the sustainable development goals: Evidence from leading European Banks, *Sustainable Development*, Vol. 27, No. 4, pp. 743–757.

Azizi, L., Bien, C. and Sassen, R. (2018). Recent trends in sustainability reporting by German universities, *Sustainability Management Forum*, [e-journal]. DOI:10.1007/s00550-018-0469-8.

Ball, A. and Bebbington, J. (2008). Editorial: Accounting and reporting for sustainable development in public sector organizations, *Public Money and Management*. Vol. 28, No. 6, December, pp. 323–326.

Bartocci, L. and Picciaia, F. (2013). Towards integrated reporting in the public sector, *Integrated Reporting*, pp. 191–204.

Bebbington, J. and Unerman, J. (2018). Achieving the United Nations sustainable development goals: An enabling role for accounting research, *Accounting, Auditing & Accountability Journal*, Vol. 31, No. 1, pp. 2–24.

Bokhari, A. (2017). Universities' social responsibility (USR) and sustainable development: A conceptual framework, *International Journal of Economics and Management Studies* (SSRG-IJEMS), Vol. 4, No. 12, December, pp. 1–9.

Brusca, I., Labrador, M. and Larran, M. (2018). The challenge of sustainability and integrated reporting at universities: A case study, *Journal of Cleaner Production*, Vol. 188, pp. 347–354.

Buchta, K., Jakubiak, M. and Wilczewski, A. (2018). University social responsibility — Theory vs. practise, *Research Papers of the Wroclaw University of Economics*, Vol. 2018, No. 520, pp. 22–33.

Chartered Institute of Management Accountants (CIMA) (2016). *Integrated Report in the Public Sector*, ISSN Number 978-1-85971-827-8.

Chatelain-Ponroy, S. and Morin-Delerm, S. (2016). Adoption of sustainable development reporting by universities, *Accounting, Auditing & Accountability Journal*, Vol. 29, No. 5, pp. 887–918.

Chen, S., Nasongkhla, J. and Donaldson, J. (2015). University social responsibility (USR): Identifying an ethical foundation within higher education institutions, *Turkish Online Journal of Educational Technology — TOJET*, Vol. 14, No. 4, pp. 165–172.

Di Vaio, A. and Varriale, L. (2020). SDGs and airport sustainable performance: Evidence from Italy on organisational, accounting and reporting practises through financial and non-financial disclosure, *Journal of Cleaner Production*, Vol. 249, No. 10. DOI:10.1016/j.jclepro.2019.11.

Eccles, R. G. and Serafeim, G. (2015). Corporate and integrated reporting: A functional perspective, in S. Mohrman, J. O'Toole and E. Lawler (eds.), *Corporate Stewardship: Organizing for Sustainable Effectiveness*, pp. 156–173, Greenleaf Publishing, Sheffield.

Ferrero-Ferrero, I., Fernández-Izquierdo, M., Muñoz-Torres, M. and Bellés-Colomer, L. (2018). Stakeholder engagement in sustainability reporting in higher education: An analysis of key internal stakeholders' expectations, *International Journal of Sustainability in Higher Education*, Vol. 19, No. 2, pp. 313–336.

Fleaca, E., Fleaca, B. and Maiduc, S. (2018). Aligning strategy with sustainable development goals (SDGs): Process scoping diagram for entrepreneurial higher education institutions (HEIs), *Sustainability*, Vol. 10, p. 1032.

Fonseca, A., Macdonald, A., Dandy, E. and Valenti, P. (2011). The State of sustainability reporting at Canadian Universities, *International Journal of Sustainability in Higher Education*, Vol. 12, No. 1, pp. 22–40.

Garde Sánchez, R., Rodriíguez Boliívar, M., López-Hernández, A. (2013). Online disclosure of university social responsibility: A comparative study of public and private US universities, *Environmental Education Research*, Vol. 19, No. 6, pp. 709–746.

Gunawan, J., Permatasari, P. and Tilt, C. (2019). Sustainable development goal disclosures: Do they support responsible consumption and production? *Journal of Cleaner Production*, Vol. 246, No. 10. DOI: 10.1016/j.jclepro.2019.1.

Hassan, A., Adhikariparajuli, M., Fletcher, M. and Elamer, A. (2019). Integrated reporting in UK higher education institutions, *Sustainability Accounting, Management and Policy Journal*, Vol. 10, No. 5, pp. 844–876.

Herzner, A. and Stucken, K. (2020). Reporting on sustainable development with student inclusion as a teaching method, *The International Journal of Management Education*, Vol. 18, No. 1. DOI:10.1016/j.ijme.2019.10032.

Hinson, R., Gyabea, A. and Ibrahim, M. (2015). Sustainability reporting among Ghanaian Universities, *Communication*, Vol. 41, No. 1, pp. 22–42.

Huerta-Riveros, P. and Gaete-Feres, H. (2007). Responsabilidad social universitaria a traveís de los reportes de sostenibilidad del global reporting initiative: experiencia de una universidad puíblica, *Revista Iberoamericana de Educacioín Superior*, Vol. 8, No. 23. *versión On-line* ISSN 2007-2872.

Hummel, K. (2019). Reporting on the sustainable development goals — Early evidence from Europe, June 2019. Available at: https://ssrn.com/abstract=3411017 (accessed 10 July, 2019).

International Integrated Reporting Council (IIRC) (2013). *The International <IR> Framework.*

Katsikas, E., Rossi, F. and Orelli, R. L. (2017). Setting the Context for Integrated Reporting in the Public Sector in Towards Integrated Reporting (Chapter 1), SpringerBriefs in Accounting, pp. 1–24. DOI:10.1007/978-3-319-47235-5_1

KPMG (2008). KPMG international survey of corporate sustainability reporting 2008. Available at: http://www.kpmg.com/Global/Issues AndInsights/ArticlesAndPublications/Pages/Sustainability-corporate-responsibility-reporting-2008.aspx.

KPMG (2015). KPMG survey of corporate responsibility reporting 2015. Available at: https://home.kpmg/xx/en/home/insights/2015/11/kpmg-international-survey-of-corporate-responsibility-reporting-2015.html.

KPMG (2018). How to report on the SDGs. What good looks like and why it matters, February 2018 Available at: kpmg.com/sdgreporting (accessed 10 July, 2019).

Kräusche, K. and Pilz, S. (2018). Integrated sustainability reporting at HNE Eberswalde — A practise report, *International Journal of Sustainability in Higher Education*, Vol. 19, No. 2, pp. 291–312, [e-journal]. DOI:10.1108/ijshe-07-2016-0145.

Larrán Jorge, M., Javier Andrades, F. and Madueño Jesús, H. (2018). An analysis of university sustainability reports from the GRI database: An examination of influential variables, *Journal of Environmental Planning and Management*, Vol. 62, No. 3, pp. 1–26.

Lozano, R. and Huisingh, D. (2011). Inter-linking issues and dimensions in sustainability reporting, *Journal of Cleaner Production*, Vol. 19, No. 1–2, February, pp. 99–107.

Lozano, R. (2006). A tool for a graphical assessment of sustainability in universities (GASU), *Journal of Cleaner Production*, Vol. 14, No. 9–11, pp. 963–972.

Lozano, R. (2011). The state of sustainability reporting in universities, *International Journal of Sustainability in Higher Education*, Vol. 12, No. 1, pp. 67–78.

Lozano, R., Llobet, J. and Tideswell, G. (2013a). The process of assessing and reporting sustainability at universities: Preparing the report of the university of leeds, *Revista Internacional de Tecnología, Sostenibilidad y Humanismo*, Desembre, Vol. 8, pp. 85–112.

Lozano, R., Lukman, R., Lozano, F., Huisingh, D. and Lambrechts, W. (2013b). Declarations for sustainability in higher education: Becoming better leaders, through addressing the university system, *Journal of Cleaner Production*, Vol. 48, pp. 10–19.

Madeira, A., Caravilla, M. and Oliveira, J. (2011). A methodology for sustainability evaluation and reporting in higher education institutions, *Higher Education Policy*, Vol. 24, pp. 459–479.

Malik, M., Khan, H., Chofreh, A., Goni, F., Klemeš, J. and Alotaibi, Y. (2019). Investigating students' sustainability awareness and the curriculum of technology education in Pakistan, *Sustainability*, Vol. 11, No. 9, p. 2651.

Montecalvo, M., Farneti, F. and De Villiers, C. (2018). The Potential of integrated reporting to enhance sustainability reporting in the public sector, *Public Money & Management*, Vol. 38, No. 5, pp. 365–374.

Monteiro, S., Ribeiro, V. and Lemos, K. (2020). Linking corporate social responsibility reporting with the UN sustainable development goals: Evidence from the Portuguese stock market, in I. Lopes, M. Sanchez-Hernandez, L. Coelho and R. Peixnho (eds.), *Conceptual and Theoretical Approaches to Corporate Social Responsibility, Entrepreneurial Orientation, and Financial Performance*, pp. 134–151. IGI Global publisher. http://doi.org/10.4018/978-1-7998-2128-1.ch007.

Navarro, A, Ruiz, M., Tirado, P. and Ríos, A. (2017). Promoting the sustainability transparency in European local governments. An empirical analysis by administrative cultures, *Sustainability Journal*, Vol. 9, No. 3. DOI:10.20944/preprints201703.0102.v1.

Neary, J. and Osborne, M. (2018). University engagement in achieving sustainable development Goals: A synthesis of case studies from the SUEUAA study, *Australian Journal of Adult Learning*, Vol. 58, No. 3, pp. 336–364.

Nejati, M., Shafaei, A., Salamzadeh, Y. and Daraei, M. (2011). Corporate social responsibility and universities: A study of top 10 world universities' website, *African Journal of Business Management*, Vol. 5, No. 2, January, pp. 440–447.

Ntim, C., Soobaroyen, T. and Broad, M. J. (2017). Governance structures, voluntary disclosures and public accountability, *Accounting, Auditing & Accountability Journal*, Vol. 30, No. 1, pp. 65–118.

Oprisor, T., Tiron-Tudor, A. and Nistor, C. (2016). The integrated reporting system: A new accountability enhancement tool for public sector entities, *Audit Financiar*, Vol. 7, No. 139, July, pp. 747–760.

ORSIES — Observatório da Responsabilidade Social e Instituições de Ensino Superiot (2018). *Livro Verde sobre Responsabilidade Social e Instituições de Ensino Superior.* ISBN 978-972-8976-05-7.

Paletta, A., Fochi, P., Toschi, T. and Ubertini, F. (2020). Adoption of the SDGs as a reporting framework at the Alma Mater Studiorum (University of Bologna) in Italy, in G. Nhamo and V. Mjimba (eds.), *Sustainable Development Goals and Institutions of Higher Education*, Sustainable Development Goals Series, pp. 185–197. https://doi.org/10.1007/978-3-030-26157-3_15.

PricewaterhouseCoopers (PwC) (2018). *From Promise to Reality: Does Business Really Care about the SDGs? And What Needs to Happen to Turn Words into Action.* PwC, London.

Quezada, R. (2011). La responsabilidad social universitaria como desafío para la gestión estrateígica de la Educacioín Superior: el caso de España, *Revista de Educacioín*, Vol. 355, Mayo-Agosto, pp. 109–133.

Ramísio, P. J., Costa Pinto, L. M., Gouveia, N., Costa, H. and Arezes, D. (2019). Sustainability strategy in higher education institutions: Lessons learned from a nine-year case study, *Journal of Cleaner Production*, Vol. 222, pp. 300–309.

Ribeiro, V. and Monteiro, S. (2018). Social and environmental accounting (SEA) research in public sector: The Portuguese case, in D. Crowther, S. Seifi and T. Wond (eds.), *Responsibility and Governance: The Twin Pillars of Sustainability, Series: Approaches to Global Sustainability, Markets, and Governance*, pp. 215–236, Spring Nature Singapure Pte Ltd. DOI:10.1007/978-981-13-1047-8.

Ribeiro, V., Monteiro, S. and Moura, A. (2016). Determinants of sustainability E-reporting in Portuguese municipalities: An institutional and legitimacy theoretical framework. Corporate responsibility and stakeholding, *Developments in Corporate Governance and Responsibility*, Vol. 10, pp. 131–163.

Romolini, A., Fissi, S. and Gori, E. (2015). Quality disclosure in sustainability reporting: Evidence from universities, *Transylvanian Review of Administrative Sciences*, Vol. 11, No. 44, pp. 196–218.

Rossi, F. (2018). Is integrated reporting a new challenge for public sector entities? *African Journal of Business Management*, April, Vol. 12, No. 7, pp. 172–187.

Sassen, R. and Azizi, L. (2017). Voluntary disclosure of sustainability reports by Canadian universities, *Journal of Business Economics*, Vol. 88, No. 1, pp. 97–137.

Sassen, R. and Azizi, L. (2018). Assessing sustainability reports of US universities, *International Journal of Sustainability in Higher Education*, [e-journal]. https://doi.org/10.1108/IJSHE-06-2016-0114.

Sassen, R., Dienes D. and Wedemeier, J. (2018). Characteristics of UK higher education institutions that disclose sustainability reports, *International Journal of Sustainability in Higher Education*, [e-journal]. https://doi.org/10.1108/IJSHE-03-2018-0042.

Schramade, W. (2017). Investing in the UN sustainable development goals: Opportunities for companies and investors, *Journal of Applied Corporate Finance*, Vol. 29, pp. 87–99.

Sepasi, S., Rahdari, A. and Rexhepi, G. (2018). Developing a sustainability reporting assessment tool for higher education institutions: The University of California, *Sustainable Development*, [e-journal]. DOI:10.1002/sd.1736.

Silva, P. (2017). Caracterização do Relato de Sustentabilidade nas Instituições de Ensino Superior Portuguesas, Dissertação para obtenção do grau de Mestre em Contabilidade e Controlo de Gestão pela Faculdade de Economia do Porto.

Taylor, B., Hutchinson, C., Pollack, S. and Tapper, R. (1994). *The Environmental Management Handbook*. Pitman Publishing. ISBN 0-273-60185-7.

Tort, L. (2010). *GRI Reporting in Government Agencies*, [online] Global Reporting Initiative, Amsterdam. Available at: http://www.globalreporting.org/ (accessed 13 August, 2012).

Tsalis, T. A., Malamateniou, K. E., Koulouriotis, D. and Nikolaou, I. E., (2020). New challenges for corporate sustainability reporting: United Nations' 2030 agenda for sustainable development and the sustainable development goals, *Corporate Social Responsibility and Environmental Management*, Vol. 27, No. 4, pp. 1–13.

UN Global Compact Network and GRI (2017). Business reporting on the SDGs: An analysis of the goals and targets. Available at https://www.unglobalcompact.org/library/5361.

UN Global Compact Network and GRI (2018). Integrating the sustainable development goals into corporate reporting: A practical guide. Available at https://www.unglobalcompact.org/library/5628.

Vallaeys, F. (2014). University social responsibility: A new university model against commodification, *Ibero-American Journal of Higher Education*, Vol. 5, No. 12, pp. 105–117.

Vallaeys, F., De la Cruz, C. and Sasia, P. (2009). *Responsabilidad Social Universitaria: manual de primeiros pasos*. Banco Interamericano de Desarrollo, McGraw-Hill; Primera edición.

Vasilescu, R., Barna, C., Epure, M. and Baicu, C. (2010). Developing university social responsibility: A model for the challenges of the new civil society, *Procedia — Social and Behavioral Sciences*, Vol. 2, No. 2, pp. 4177–4182.

Veltri, S. and Silvestri, A. (2015). The free state university integrated reporting: A critical consideration, *Journal of Intellectual Capital*, Vol. 16, No. 2, pp. 443–462.

Vilalta, J. M., Betts, A. and Gomez, V. (2018). Higher education's role in the 2030 agenda: The why and how of GUNi's commitment to the SDGs, in J. Vilalta, A. Betts and V. Gómez (eds.), *Sustainable Development Goals: Actors and Implementation. A Report from the International Conference*, pp. 10–13, GUNi, Barcelona.

Wang, X., Yuen, K., Wong, Y. and Li, K. (2020). How can the maritime industry meet sustainable development goals? An analysis of sustainability reports from the social entrepreneurship perspective, *Transportation Research Part D*, Vol. 78, January 2020, 102173. https://doi.org/10.1016/j.trd.2019.11.002.

Yi, A., Howard, D. and Harun, H. (2017). Sustainability reporting at a New Zealand Public University: A longitudinal analysis, *Sustainability*, Vol. 9, No. 9, pp. 1–11. https://doi.org/10.3390/su9091529.

Chapter 9

The Growth and Regulatory Challenges of Cryptocurrency Transactions in Nigeria

Victor Ediagbonya and Tioluwani Comfort Tioluwani

Abstract

There have been various concerns about the regulation of cryptocurrencies in this era of modern technology. The quest for their regulation has been becoming increasingly topical among various stakeholders because of the possibility of using cryptocurrencies for money laundering. The Central Bank of Nigeria had recently barred banks and financial institutions from dealing in or facilitating transactions in cryptocurrencies, such as bitcoin, warning that banks that fail to act will face severe sanctions. Similarly, the Securities and Exchange Commission has also suspended its plans to regulate cryptocurrency transactions in Nigeria. Both regulators have argued that impending risks are associated with dealing in unregulated digital currencies and not legal tender. This chapter argues that besides the risk of such transactions for an ordinary individual who transacts in cryptocurrencies, it can also be a channel for corrupt individuals to launder stolen monies.

Keywords: Money laundering; cryptocurrency; financial regulation; sustainability; crypto-laundering

1. Introduction

The exchange of goods and services has taken place through different means in human history; some of the methods are frequently tangible, such as the use of coins or paper money (Ayomikun and Omowunmi, 2019). The real foundation of money is still untraceable; however, paper money and coins dating back to the seventh century BC

(Mundell, 2002). The substance of money facilitates transactions and has evolved since the seventh century; now, there are debit cards, internet banking, and cryptocurrency. Undoubtedly, the global financial community is incorporating the latest technological transformation from real currencies to virtual currencies. Polillo (2011) introduced an interesting theory regarding the creation of currencies; the idea suggests that general social processes grant various kinds of organisations the right to generate currencies. Also, he argued for the principle of money as multiple currencies and that through social practises, societies constantly change money in creative ways to better suit their needs. Cryptocurrency, one of these creative ways, is defined as a digital record-keeping system that uses balances to keep track of trading commitments and is accessible to all traders.

Cryptocurrencies as a form of currency allow direct peer-to-peer transactions by eliminating banks or other intermediaries when carrying out these financial transactions (Peters *et al.*, 2015). This peer-to-peer system is based on blockchain, allowing transactions to take place directly between users without the need of an intermediary; it makes the transactions a secret between parties and as such, parties will not be privy to each other's identity (Hameed and Farooq, 2016). This form of secrecy has allowed the black market to grow, as cryptocurrencies have allowed individuals to make illegal financial transactions that are difficult and, in some cases, impossible to track (Heilman *et al.*, 2016). This form of anonymity poses serious threats, as criminals could exploit it for laundering illicit funds, thereby weakening financial systems.

There have been various concerns about the regulation of cryptocurrencies in this era of modern technology. The pseudonymous and decentralised structure makes them especially suitable for criminal activities. The quest for its regulation has become increasingly topical among various stakeholders because of the possibility of using cryptocurrencies for money laundering, also known as crypto-laundering. The Central Bank of Nigeria (CBN) had recently barred banks and financial institutions from dealing in or facilitating transactions in cryptocurrencies, such as bitcoin, warning that banks that fail to act will face severe sanctions. Similarly, the Securities and

Exchange Commission (SEC) has also suspended its plans to regulate cryptocurrency transactions in Nigeria. Both regulators have argued that impending risks are associated with dealing in unregulated digital currencies and not legal tender. This chapter argues that besides the risk of such transactions for an ordinary individual who transacts in cryptocurrencies, it can also be a channel for corrupt individuals to launder stolen monies.

2. Conceptual and Theoretical Overview of Cryptocurrencies and Anti-Money Laundering

Research has shown the link between the concepts of digital currency, virtual currency, and cryptocurrency. Digital currency is a type of virtual currency that is electronically created and stored. They are also assets with zero intrinsic value, whose value is determined by the forces of demand and supply as in other commodity money, such as gold (Salawu and Malaoi, 2018). In 2012, the European Central Bank defined virtual currency as "a type of unregulated, digital money which is issued and usually controlled by its developers, and used and accepted among members of a specific virtual community" (Rose, 2015). Baron *et al.* (2015) described virtual currency as a digital representation of value that people accept as a means of payment. However, it is neither issued by a public authority nor necessarily ascribed to an acceptable currency.

On the other hand, offering an acceptable definition of cryptocurrency is complex and challenging. In 2008, a programmer named Satoshi Nakamoto published a paper titled Bitcoin: A Peer to Peer Electronic Cash System, describing digital currencies, and the year after, the Bitcoin network was founded (Temitope and Folorunso, 2020). The first cryptocurrency was bitcoin, which started trading in January 2009 (Gandal and Halaburda, 2014). After that, other cryptocurrencies have been created using the same innovations that Bitcoin introduced but changing some of the specific parameters of their governing algorithms (Temitope and Folorunso, 2020). One similarity between these currencies is that they are not issued by any central authority and are independent of traditional banks. Bitcoins were launched at the peak of the global economic meltdown of 2007–2009, when various central banks and other regulatory and supervisory bodies, with all their policies, were almost considered incompetent, and the confidence of the investors in the ability of the government to sustain the economy was affected (Raskin and Yermack, 2016). Thus, most researchers suggest that Nakamoto appeared to give an answer to the economic crunch and challenge the authoritative power of the government and banking institutions (He, 2018). Over the past decade, bitcoin and other forms of cryptocurrencies have reformed the financial world by developing a stable form of currency that is not controlled by the government and permits encoded, unidentified transactions (Swartz, 2018). The arrival of cryptocurrency has its root in cryptographic technology with online distributed accounting books that appear to have introduced the finance industry into another phase of development. This phase is a blend of both the central bank functions and accounting functions, as it produces and manages the supply of virtual currencies and produces and manages the record of transactions concurrently (Ahamad *et al.*, 2013). Although cryptography is present in traditional banking services, it plays a different role in both systems.

Therefore, cryptocurrency functions at the entry point of traditional banking services and is also at the core of the system. Cryptocurrency is built around certain cryptographic functions, which can also protect the system from insiders. In addition to this technical definition, cryptocurrency also relies on some specific and formal definitions of global institutions and regulatory agencies. Despite the challenges, it is argued that cryptocurrency has particular benefits compared to the traditional banking system. It added to the global payment industry and the economy in the following ways: privacy, low transaction costs, rapid transfers, immunity to inflation, and scalability due to the refusal to represent traditional financial institutions.

Like the physical currency, cryptocurrency is also prone to several challenges, such as a lack of solid anonymity, scams, terrorism financing, and money laundering. Nakamoto (2008) acknowledged the tragic consequences of handing over the strategic decisions of custodians and recipients of investment income and transaction control to greedy attackers who could steal their payments, disrupt the system, and deceive people based on their technical expertise without considering the legitimacy of their wealth. The loopholes in this coin mining system are enough to reward fraudsters who arbitrarily break the rules, inevitably cause social disobedience, and deceive innocent and inexperienced participants (Nakamoto, 2008).

Reid and Harrigan argue that bitcoin transactions, including cryptocurrency's centralised offerings inclusive of exchanges and pockets, are not entirely anonymous (Reid and Harrigan, 2011). Venkatakrishnan *et al.* (2017) argued that cutting-edge flooding protocols used within the cryptocurrency community no longer sufficiently protect a person's anonymity. Major scams had been perpetrated globally and domestically through rip-offs which have been termed excessive-yield wealth programs. These online Ponzi schemes promised high investment returns with little or no risk on deposits, as victims made Bitcoin deposits into rip-off wallets. Notwithstanding the risks that have been associated with cryptocurrency, the way it grows is fascinating. With this growth, the governments are powerless to the control of the currency. Research has shown that there is no consensus at both the national and international levels regarding cryptocurrency's regulation, especially since it was not the governments that created them (Hughes and Middlebrook, 2015). Bitcoin possesses specific attributes that need to be examined; these attributes make it appealing to customers to adopt it. The next section evaluates four such characteristics which might be taken into consideration when adopting bitcoins. They include anonymity, low service charge, global acceptance, and finally the absence of significant control.

2.1. *Low service charge*

Utilising a cryptocurrency account is considered to be low since the services of experts, such as bankers, who act as intermediaries are not needed to confirm any transactions as seen in the regular banking systems (Salawu and Malaoi, 2018). Although this low service charge has been argued to be unsustainable in the future, cryptocurrencies are considered to be a cheaper option than the traditional banking systems (Salawu and Malaoi, 2018).

2.2. *Anonymity*

Under this feature, the parties do not know the real identity of whom they are transacting with. Most times, this characteristic is considered the main strength of using cryptocurrency. The feature complicates any chance of identifying individuals who engage in illegal transactions and other criminal activities (Zamani and Babatsikos, 2017). On the other hand, individuals who use the single wallet address for various transactions risk having their details exposed to a hacker who can quickly identify the user's alphanumeric password. Also, if the account owner dies suddenly, the wealth automatically goes into extinction, as no one will be able to access the wealth. Though one advantage of using bitcoins is that it can safeguard wealth from hackers, unlike the traditional banking system however, it does not allow the deceased's next of kin to claim the wealth in the virtual world, as this does not form part of the estate of the dead.

2.3. *Absence of central control*

This is an inherent feature of the currency that indicates there is no single supervisor or body specifically in charge of cryptocurrency administration. Parties that use the technology are self-governing. The technology does not enforce any central authority. The network is distributed to all members, and each computer mining bitcoins is a part of the system. Thus, the central authority has no power to dictate rules for owners of bitcoins (Nica *et al.*, 2017).

2.4. *Global recognition*

In contrast to the traditional banking system, cryptocurrency promotes a cashless environment and removes the difficulties posed by cash (Gandal and Halaburda, 2014). This technology is easily accessible to anyone and removes any territorial boundary that might come with any transaction. The ease of transaction that this technology poses, makes it attractive to those who indulge in it. Cryptocurrencies may have the potential to compete against other online payment methods, such as debit/credit cards, Google Pay, Apple Pay, and Paypal, thereby having an enormous effect on both physical currencies and the world payments systems in the long run (Gandal and Halaburda, 2014). However, according to the IMF, the currency does not enjoy full global acceptability as a medium of exchange. Some nations[1] do not accept the use of cryptocurrency as a means of currency transactions and would sanction anyone who engages in the use (Nica *et al.*, 2017).

2.5. *Money laundering*

Money laundering can be defined as channelling illicit funds through outside financial channels to make the funds appear legitimate (MacDowell, 2001). The term originated from activities carried out by organised crime, which used laundry cleaning business to cover up "launder", large amounts of cash earned through blackmail, prostitution, gambling, and piracy.

Money laundering is a global problem as the criminal acts of individuals, illegal businesses, and corporations get their funds from illegal and unethical sources, such as fraud, corruption, trafficking, prostitution, drugs, sales of illegal weapons, and terrorist activities. Thus, money laundering damages the well-being and functioning of the global economy (Buchanan, 2004). The money laundering process is made up of three main steps, which are achieved in one merged transaction or in three different transactions (MacDowell, 2001). The first process is placement; a large amount of illegal funds goes into the financial system used to purchase high-value goods or smuggled out of the country. The idea is to convert cash into other types of assets

---

[1]Nigeria: On 5 February 2021, the CBN issued a circular directive that prohibited all transactions in bitcoins and other virtual currencies. Since 19 June, 2021, Thailand declared dealings in cryptocurrency illegal. Vietnam banned trading in cryptocurrencies in 2014, while Colombia banned transactions in cryptocurrencies since 2016.

as soon as possible to avoid the risk of exposure. The next step in the process is layering, and this step is where the source of the illegal funds are hidden, which is done by creating complex levels of financial transactions to hide audit trails and disguise who the funds really belong to. Some of the preferred methods used are the electronic funds transfer (EFT), conversion into monetary instruments, and investments in legally owned businesses and buying real estate. Finally, the last step is the integration, and under this step, the newly laundered money is integrated into legitimate businesses, thereby making the monies untraceable to illicit activities (Buchanan, 2004).

In the past, money laundering was only done through these established processes using small businesses or even large businesses. However, after the arrival of the Internet, the money laundering process has evolved into a digital state. The money laundering process has gone global, and efforts to tackle money laundering are usually expensive and ineffective. There is a need to curb this, as this could lead to a lack of confidence in the global financial system and affect government bodies worldwide (Schneider, 2008). When funds are transferred to offshore accounts, it will not be easy to track and can be moved across multiple banks to hide the origins of those funds (Picard and Pieretti, 2011).

2.6. *Crypto-laundering*

Cryptocurrencies are good options for money laundering activities for many reasons. First, they can be used to move money pseudonymously or sometimes incognito (Haffke *et al.*, 2019). Second, transactions are carried out through decentralised blockchain transactions. This is because the transactions are not automatically inspected for illicit activities by any supervisory control. Third, the currency can be transferred worldwide without territorial boundaries or checks (Haffke *et al.*, 2019). Generally, there are two ways to use cryptocurrency to launder money: On the one hand, money can come from outside and monies gotten from illicit activities are converted to tokens, preferably in a country with lower or non-existent anti-money laundering (AML) regulations. Similarly, illegally obtained assets, for example, stolen assets, can also be traded for tokens. There is also the possibility of the tokens being acquired illegally.

The three-stage money laundering process discussed above also applies to crypto-laundering, but the workings related to each stage are integrally different. For example, through a process called chain hopping, money laundering is carried out first in the placement stage; funds are transferred from a regular bank to an account with a cryptocurrency exchange service to buy primary coins. Then, in the next stage, the layering stage, the primary coins are exchanged for altcoins to muck up the electronic paper trail, which makes it hard for law enforcement to track the route of the funds (Fruth, 2018). Then, in the integration stage, the money can be converted from altcoins to primary coins and finally to traditional money (Fruth, 2018). Although this description was a bit overly simplified, the description shows a well-devised scheme that avoids many of the warnings AML regulators would look for.

Another means of laundering through cryptocurrency is smurfing, which involves different parties carrying out transactions on behalf of the primary money launderer. The concept behind this is that different people make small transactions at various locations in order to avoid suspicions and being tracked by enforcement agencies. This is not new to money laundering; however, it has become pronounced upon the advent of cryptocurrencies, as it is easy to move the currency across borders without restrictions. This scheme originated with criminals located in Spain, where the criminals were involved in getting and splitting the proceeds from illicit drug activities into 174 bank accounts. Moving to Colombia, the criminals will withdraw the money from accounts using the ATM and cards linked to the accounts. In carrying out these acts, the criminals realised that their transactions could be tracked. The scheme was upgraded to utilising bitcoins and other cryptocurrencies in place of using cash (Fruth, 2018). Thus, the criminals did not have to withdraw the money physically from the accounts where the dirty money was deposited. The criminals used the exchange to convert their illicit proceeds into bitcoins, then change the cryptocurrency into Colombian pesos and deposit it into Colombian bank accounts on the same day (Europol, 2018).

Enforcement authorities eventually discovered the above scheme through the cryptocurrency exchange location (Europol, 2018). Another scheme is the mixing and tumbling method. This is different from the traditional money laundering methods, as new technologies have been utilised to launder cryptocurrencies and make illegal monies look legitimate. One of the most deceitful methods is known as mixing, which is also known as tumbling. The scheme is similar to the concept of mutual funds, whereby different parties collectively gather funds for the general good of the group through investments. However, instead of investing the funds pooled, the money is transferred between exchanges, thus making it very difficult to track the trail of the specific transactions (Ciphertrace, 2019).

An example of the use of the bitcoin cryptocurrency for illegal activities is the successful use and disguise of the Silk Road website. This was the most prominent virtual market for trading drugs. All the transactions on the website could only be carried out through bitcoins, which is done anonymously. This was made possible through the TOR software, which made all users anonymous on the Dark Web (Small, 2015). The Dark Web is a part of the Internet that is not indexed by search engines and can be used for anything, including the purchase of usernames, passwords to hacking services and illegal porn. Based on the anonymity of the website, bitcoin was made the main form of currency (Small, 2015).

The blockchain is a public ledger that enables all users to use all the previous bitcoin transactions, which is presumably advantageous to law enforcement. Bitcoin transactions are interconnected due to the blockchain structure. Thus, every entry is unavoidably the result of the last transaction. This poses a risk to cybercriminals because their transactions are interconnected and can be traced back to illegal sources (Wegberg *et al.*, 2018). The dark web provides services to further anonymise bitcoin to help with money laundering. There are two facets to bitcoin money laundering. First, there are bitcoin mixers or toggle switches, a service designed to separate bitcoin from illegal sources; second, there is a bitcoin exchange, which attempts to convert bitcoin into real currencies anonymously (Wegberg *et al.*, 2018).

The mixing service breaks the funding trail of bitcoin transactions. The customer receives a newly generated bitcoin address to make a deposit. After deducting the mixing fee, the mixing service pays bitcoin from its reservation to the designated address to ensure greater anonymity. The payment is dispersed over time. It also introduces an aspect of the unpredictability of divided amount. A mixer is an anonymiser that confuses the blockchain transaction mixer by linking all transactions to the same bitcoin address and sending these transactions together from different addresses. The mixer sends a complex series of fake transactions, so it is difficult to match coins with any particular transaction. Once a bitcoin portfolio is created, it is almost impossible to trace it back to an illegal source (Wegberg *et al.*, 2018).

Once the bitcoins have been successfully mixed, the exchange services are utilised. With this in mind, the exchange is committed to receiving bitcoins in exchange for any other currency so that users can buy and sell bitcoins online. The changed currency belongs to the user which is ensured through output platforms, such as Luno.[2] Usually, these exit platforms require an effective and active account as an exit strategy. This provides an extra layer of protection for detecting and prosecuting suspicious criminal activities and crimes. Accounts can be purchased on the Dark Web, creating a mechanism for erasing all connections to criminal users (Wegberg *et al.*, 2018). Criminals can use the exchange services provided on the Dark Web or exchange currency through bitcoin ATMs, provided that the amount is low enough not to cause suspicion or trigger authentication requirements (Hyman, 2015). The Silk Road was working as a peculiar bitcoins' bank, wherein each user must have an account for carrying out

---

[2]Luno is a bitcoin-related company with its headquarters in the UK. It facilitates bitcoin storage and transactions, including buying, selling, and paying through bitcoin wallet services. It also operates exchanges between fiat currencies and bitcoin. https://www.luno.com/en/about.

transactions through the website. There may be at least one Silk Road bitcoins address associated with a user. The account on the website is stored on the server that controls the Silk Road. To purchase, users send the mined bitcoins to the Silk Road bitcoin address associated with their account on the website.

After the purchase, the user's currencies are transferred to the escrow system until the transaction is completed, and then, the customer's bitcoins are transferred from the escrow account to the bitcoins address of the Silk Road merchant. Also, a toggle switch was utilised for any buyer who sends all payments through a complex series of almost random fake transactions, almost removing the link the payment has to any bitcoin sent from the website (Sat *et al.*, 2016). This system of criminal activity was later uncovered and terminated, leading to the prosecution of the parties involved in this illicit act.

3. Legal, Regulatory, and Institutional Framework of Cryptocurrencies Regulation and AML in Nigeria

The Nigerian Crypto Assets Market (Crypto Assets Market) is estimated to be worth about USD 350 billion (Mesele, 2021). It is therefore important to have a standard framework for regulating this market set out with clarity. The SEC has provided pointers for the regulation of the Crypto Assets Market; however, there are numerous facets of the Crypto Assets Market that are not similar to the capital market, so the regulation of the capital market will not be applicable to the Crypto Assets Market. The advent of the need for cryptocurrency laws in Nigeria is linked to the notorious Ponzi scheme, Mavrodi Mundial Moneybox (MMM). After MMM momentarily shut down in December 2016, the platform stated that it would adopt bitcoin (Vanguard, 2017). When cryptocurrency attracted Nigerians' attention, the Nigeria Deposit Insurance Commission (NDIC) and the CBN in 2016 took a look into the emergence of bitcoin (Vanguard, 2017). The SEC, the primary regulator of the Nigerian capital market, advised Nigerians against investing in cryptocurrency. It stated that none of the persons, companies, or entities promoting cryptocurrencies had been recognised or authorised by it or by other regulatory agencies in Nigeria to receive deposits from the public or to provide any investment or other financial services in or from Nigeria (SEC, 2017).

It also advised that there is no legislation to protect users or investors if the cryptocurrencies fail or the companies trading in these currencies go bankrupt (CBN, 2017). Also, the CBN issued a national circular to all the banks, warning about virtual currencies and emphasising the point that cryptocurrency is not a recognised legal tender in Nigeria (CBN, 2017). The circular also specified that the banks and other reporting financial institutions, while awaiting substantive legislation or policy by the CBN, must be cautioned by ensuring that they do not use, support, and/or conduct any virtual currency transactions; it also directed those existing customers as virtual currency changers have effective anti-money laundering/counter-financing of terrorism (AML/CFT) control measures to enable them to comply with the identification, review, and monitoring of customer transactions. If the bank or other financial institution is not satisfied with the control imposed by the virtual currency customer/exchange, the relationship must be terminated immediately; furthermore, the CBN has directed that all suspicious transactions of these customers should be reported to the Nigerian Financial Intelligence Unit (NFIU) with immediate effect.

The SEC also released a circular advising the public to take caution with regard to the cryptocurrencies as a means of investing and that there is no legal protection in the event the companies operating them fail and go out of business. In 2018, the CBN issued another press release confirming that cryptocurrencies are not legal tender and that cryptocurrency exchanges are not authorised or regulated by it. The CBN also reiterated its warning that there is a risk of loss when investing in cryptocurrencies. This was a commendable attempt by the regulators of the capital market as cryptocurrency is a volatile currency. There was no effective regulation to protect the users in the event that it fails or the companies go out of business. However, as evidenced by the fundraising for the EndSAR protest in October 2020, with the growth and popularity of cryptocurrency trading, the market has clearly ignored these warnings (Handagama, 2020). The financial year ending in 2020 revealed that Nigerians had transacted about USD 400 million worth of cryptocurrencies (Kene-Okafor, 2021). However, one would argue that this does not reflect the total amount of cryptocurrency transactions that had taken place in that financial year. This is because not all the transactions in cryptocurrencies are documented, so the amount accruing from the total transactions will be more significant than what is stated above.

In general, the use of cryptocurrency as legal tender for the exchange of goods and services in Nigeria has never been fully approved. Due to the dominance of Nigerians investing in cryptocurrency and the recommendations of the Cryptocurrency Regulatory FinTech Roadmap Committee in September 2020, the SEC classified crypto assets as securities that need to be regulated (SEC, 2019). Its overall goal is to ensure that technology and innovation are not encumbered or subdued. The SEC sought to develop standards to promote ethical practises in cryptocurrency trading and promote fair trade and an efficient market (SEC, 2019). The SEC stated that unless the issuer or sponsor proves otherwise in the initial valuation application, all virtual encrypted assets are securities. Thus, requiring the registration of all digital assets token offerings, initial coin offerings (ICOs), security token ICOs, and other blockchain-based offers of digital assets in Nigeria, Nigeria's digital asset products can trade these securities on investment exchanges. In addition, with the possibility of trading these securities on an investment exchange. Also, the SEC has decided to supervise individuals and companies involved in blockchain-related and virtual digital asset services, such as management, investment consulting, and custody or nominee services. Arguably, the SEC's position on cryptocurrencies has created much-needed clarity for the future of cryptocurrencies and the role of fintech companies as cryptocurrency exchanges. However, in February 2021, the CBN changed the direction of cryptocurrencies and issued another circular that its typical ambiguity would not characterise. This time, the CBN will completely prohibit any form of cryptocurrency transactions supported by Nigerian financial institutions. The CBN reiterated that financial institutions are cautioned on the use of cryptocurrencies, prohibiting them from transacting or engaging in cryptocurrency exchanges. Additionally, the CBN directed the financial institutions to identify individuals and companies that conduct cryptocurrency transactions on their systems and ensure that such accounts are closed immediately.

Since the CBN imposed new restrictions, financial institutions immediately began to close accounts that were found to be using cryptocurrencies. Cryptocurrency exchanges, such as Binance, have suspended all Naira deposits. The reaction of Nigerians, especially its negative impact on the fast-growing Nigerian cryptocurrency market and fintech industry, is unfavourable. Additionally, the CBN issued a press release explaining and certifying that its policy statement is correct and that it is not new to prohibit financial institutions from using, storing, trading, and/or processing cryptocurrencies as they had been warned about this previously. The CBN stated that cryptocurrencies are not recognised legal tender in Nigeria and that they hinder supervision, accountability, and regulation, making them vulnerable to criminal activities, such as money laundering, tax evasion, drug trafficking, terrorism, and covering up illegal purchases of weapons and ammunition. The volatility of cryptocurrencies threatens the stability of some countries' financial systems (Sofola *et al.*, 2021).

3.1. *Reactions towards the CBN's restrictions on cryptocurrencies*

There have been several criticisms about the CBN's stance on cryptocurrencies. First, the circular contradicts the SEC's provisions, which provides that all crypto-assets are securities until proven otherwise. Consequently, the later directive by the CBN negates the statement earlier released by the SEC. Also, according to the SEC, they are the only regulatory body that has jurisdiction over cryptocurrency transactions in Nigeria. However, on the other hand, it can be argued that the CBN also has the right to issue directives to financial institutions to fulfil its objective under the CBN Act to advance financial stability in Nigeria. Therefore, there is a degree of regulatory overlap between the CBN and the SEC in Nigeria.

Furthermore, it has been argued that the CBN did not expressly clarify what "cryptocurrency" refers to or constitutes. This shows that the CBN ambiguously banned cryptocurrency transactions, regardless of the type of cryptocurrency traded on the exchange. In other words, the CBN did not distinguish between cryptocurrencies used as legal tender, cryptocurrencies with security functions and features (securities tokens), and cryptocurrencies used to provide users with products and/or services (utility tokens) (Sofola *et al.*, 2021).

Another criticism is that the CBN's circular did not provide any sanctions on the exchange of cryptocurrencies. The CBN only prohibits banks and financial institutions which it regulates from transacting in cryptocurrencies or dealing in cryptocurrency transactions. The CBN's circular does not criminalise the use of and dealing in cryptocurrency. Therefore, engaging in cryptocurrency transactions does not constitute an illegal act because for a person to be arrested, detained or prosecuted, and convicted for a criminal offence, three requirements must be met; there must be a written law where the offence is defined, and the penalty must be prescribed in a written law (S.36 (12), CFRN, 1999). There is no specific regulation in Nigeria that has declared cryptocurrency trading illegal or have attempted to criminalise it, and as such, those who engage in cryptocurrency transactions in Nigeria cannot be arrested in the first place, neither can they be prosecuted nor convicted just because they deal in cryptocurrencies, as this is not an offence known to law, a precedent established by the court in *Aoko v. Fagbemi (1961)*, where it held that a woman could not be convicted for adultery in the southern states of Nigeria because it was not prescribed as an offence in any written law in those states; therefore, it was an offence not known to law.

Nevertheless, the CBN's circular has had some negative impacts on many Nigerians. One noticeable impact of the CBN's policy on closing the accounts of individuals and legal entities that conduct cryptocurrency transactions is that it has other implications: The restriction actually closes the door to the possibility of a cryptocurrency exchange for goods and services in Nigeria, but doing so will unknowingly promote the speculative use and trading of cryptocurrencies, which runs counter to the global trend of cryptocurrency regulation and business practises. For example, in the United States, Tesla recently submitted a USD 1.5 billion bitcoin acquisition application to the U.S. Securities and Exchange Commission and announced that it would accept cryptocurrency as a regular payment in the future (Kovach, 2021). Furthermore, although the restrictions prohibit cryptocurrency transactions in Naira, it has not affected secondary market peer-to-peer trading, where most of the dealing in cryptocurrency in Nigeria occurs. Therefore, the users of cryptocurrencies can still carry out transactions on their own and make payments into their cryptocurrency wallet (Babatunde, 2021).

3.2. *Nigerian AML legal and regulatory framework*

The regulatory framework constitutes laws that adopt the global standards of AML within the country. The first of these happened in 1995, with the enactment of the Money Laundering Decree No. 3 of 1995, which criminalised money laundering with definite offences limited to drugs and drug-related crimes. This was followed by the Money Laundering (Prohibition) Act, 2004, which criminalised laundering of the profits of crime or any unlawful act, incorporated and defined designated non-financial institutions, and delegated regulatory responsibility to the Federal Ministry of Commerce (now the Federal Ministry of Industry, Trade and investment). The adoption of this regulation was effective towards the first attempts at the campaign against financial and economic crimes in Nigeria despite the evidence of substantial loopholes which affected some aspects of the campaign against money laundering (Giaba, 2008). These loopholes were later amended in Money Laundering (Prohibition) Act in 2012.

According to Adeseyoju (2012), no country in West Africa has done more than Nigeria to combat money laundering in the country. The regulatory framework for AML/CFT in Nigeria comprises the regulators and supervisors authorised by the establishing law and other AML/CFT laws to regulate the entry and operation of their respective operators, including the issuance of industry-specific regulations and guidelines. Regulators are responsible for overseeing financial institutions and designated non-financial institutions.

Since introducing the AML/CFT system, Nigeria has established strong institutions to implement government measures and guidelines to reduce money laundering activities against terrorist financing. Some of the institutional frameworks include the Nigerian Financial Intelligence Unit (NFIU), the Economic and Financial Crimes Commission (EFCC), the Independent Corrupt Practices Commission (ICPC), and all other agencies established by law to tackle the 21 predicate offences of money laundering.

3.3. *The nature of money-laundering activities in Nigeria*

Despite all the laudable efforts, there is still evidence of various instances of money laundering in Nigeria (Abiola, 2014). This was brought to light by the UK and US AML agencies. Some academics have stated that prosecutions and some other factors hinder the implementation of AML laws and regulations. It is argued that prosecution is an essential tool in an instrumental conception of law; it is a means to reduce the occurrence of illegal acts or criminal offences (Abiola, 2014). However, in Nigeria, the prosecution in light of money laundering is ineffective, as several factors impede its effectiveness, including delay in prosecution, ineffective judicial system, lack of profound and detailed investigation, lack of funding, ineffective laws, and lack of political will.

Otusanya *et al.*, (2012), in their work, stated that the enactment of AML laws and agencies had not shown professional transparency and ethical conduct. This possibly explains why money laundering is still prevalent in Nigeria. This situation can also be attributed to the advent of technology, according to Sieber (1998):

> "The problems caused by computer crime are bound to intensify in the future. Increasing computerisation, particularly in the administration of deposit money, in the balancing of accounts and stock-keeping, in the field of electronic funds transfer systems, and in the private sector, as well as new computer applications such

as electronic home banking, electronic mail systems, and other interactive videotext systems will lead to increase in the number of offences and losses".

Although this statement was made about two decades ago, it has proven quite accurate. Money laundering has spread across the country with far-reaching impacts. Aluko and Bagheri (2012) asserted that among the financial crimes in Nigeria, money laundering had infiltrated the economic and political spheres, leading to economic digression and political unrest. Although there are AML laws in Nigeria, the implementation of these laws is not effective. The critical question is if these regulations and regulatory institutions are strong enough to carry out the purpose for which they were established. In order to record success with the implementation of these regulations, there is a need for an institutional synergy, political will, and international cooperation (Aluko and Bagheri, 2012). However, in Nigeria, there is no indication of these sects to curb money laundering. As seen in the Guaranty Trust Bank case, the bank failed to take proper precautions and controls against money laundering, screen customers against sanction lists, and revise high-risk accounts' activity. The then Financial Conduct Authority fined Guaranty Trust Bank (UK) Ltd a sum of GBP 525,000 for failings in its AML controls for high-risk customers, as the act was considered severe and led to an unacceptable risk of handling of the proceeds of crimes (Binham, 2013).

4. Challenges of AML Implementation in Nigeria

In a speech, the former Governor of CBN, Sanusi Lamido, described his experience as the apex regulator of Nigerian banks. He states that a particular CEO took over USD 1 billion from her bank (Sanusi, 2012) to purchase properties in different parts of the world; while he and the EFCC were able to secure a conviction and retrieved assets procured by the ill-gotten funds, they encountered many difficulties when they filed a lawsuit against another CEO who stole over NGN 142 billion from the bank under his watch which he used it to purchase shares of his bank, which he transferred overseas to purchase real estate properties. Concerning the second CEO, Sanusi (2012) further stated that they finished the case; however, two weeks before the closing statements were made, the judge was miraculously promoted to the Federal Court of Appeal after three years of trial. The Governor expressed his disappointment with the banking reform and the political environment thus:

> "We were dealing with chief executives that in 2009 had become invincible. They were in the seat of power. They had economic power, and they had bought political protection. They were into political parties, they had financed elections of officers, and they believed that nobody could touch them". (Sanusi, 2012)

It is clear that there is a form of exemption from the law or disregard for the law by directors and politicians who have evaded prosecution or are discharged by some corrupt judges even if they are eventually prosecuted. Therefore, implementing AML laws in Nigeria has numerous challenges, as there is either delay with the prosecution or use of political and/or economic power to avoid prosecution.

5. The Rationale for a Crypto-laundering Ban in Nigeria

The use of cryptocurrencies is the preferred means of exchange for different cyberattacks that target computer systems, some of which include hacking and purchasing illicit weapons or fake identity credentials on the dark web. According to Interpol, this has increased financial crimes, especially money laundering (Interpol, 2021). The use of cryptocurrency for money laundering has been considered cheaper by cybercriminals (Wegberg *et al.*, 2018). Nigeria is one of the countries with the highest use of cryptocurrency, with a high use of the Internet, growth in the youth population, and high use of mobile money markets. However, this increases the threat of laundering money through cryptocurrency, and it should not be ignored, which is why the ban on cryptocurrency is, to a large extent, right (Chilen, 2021).

According to the CBN, the reason for the ban on cryptocurrency is that it has been used to finance various illegal activities, including terrorism and money laundering. The cryptocurrency markets are possibly susceptible to a wide range of criminal activities and financial crimes, including money laundering. Most of these threats appear not only on the blockchain itself but also in the surrounding ecosystem of issuers, VCEs, and wallets that support consumer access to DLT. Enabling these systems will make it difficult for law enforcement and financial institution regulators subject to AML requirements to learn about the new criminal activities. As observed in previous sections, the anonymity of cryptocurrency makes it easy to perpetrate money laundering. Cryptocurrency allows for anonymity by allowing users to transfer wealth without disclosing personal information as in the traditional banking system.

Even though bitcoin exchanges are stored on blockchain records which acts as digital records that serve to recognise a sender and a recipient's digital identities, lawbreakers have the resources to alter their computerised personality from utilising virtual private organisations, intermediary network addresses by basically utilising another person's account, or even making an invented pseudonymous online personality practically making their acts untraceable. The enablement of money laundering by cryptocurrencies is through its convention of anonymity, ease of execution, and flexibility of use. The failure to connect a bitcoin account to a recognisable client following the placement, layering, and incorporation of laundered assets would be difficult for AML implementation (Iyoyojie *et al.*, 2021).

Cryptocurrencies allow their users to exchange or move funds anonymously without the traditional paper trail which could easily be tracked through payment intermediaries. The ability to exchange bitcoins freely for other currencies and transfer through an infinite number of accounts to conceal the origin and trail affects AML laws. Thus, cryptocurrencies, including bitcoins, make it easy for money launderers to move illicit funds quicker, cheaper, and anonymously without any form of suspicion (Iyoyojie *et al.*, 2021). Many other countries have banned the use of cryptocurrency; for example, China banned cryptocurrencies, and so did Venezuela, among others. The ban of cryptocurrencies in Nigeria is, to an extent, justified as it will curtail the development of dangerous trends capable of destroying Nigeria's AML/CFT gains (Chibuzor, 2021).

6. Global Recognition and Sustainability of Cryptocurrency

Cryptocurrency can be resourceful for different individuals, businesses, and corporate organisations worldwide, particularly as it relates to e-commerce. As it presently stands, several unresolved issues are militating against its global acceptance. Cryptocurrency may have the potential to provide cheaper and easier payments, encourage financial inclusion, and enable cross-border transfers. However, doing this is not straightforward, as it needs significant investment and tough policy decisions, one of which includes clarifying the role of the public and private sectors in delivering and regulating cryptocurrencies.

Some countries may consider and are already considering accepting cryptocurrency as a national currency. As some of the currencies are secure and easy to access, the risks and costs outweigh the potential benefits in most cases. The idea of cryptocurrency being accepted as a legal tender globally is crippled by a few weaknesses. Some of these weaknesses may have a series of consequences, while others may basically render the concept of cryptocurrency incapable of global acceptability. We might identify such deficiencies with the cryptocurrency itself or its utilisation for everyday use. Ultimately, they are the motivation behind why cryptographic money is not endorsed for use in the global context by various governments, international financial institutions, and international trades organisations (Joshi, 2021). As discussed in the previous sections, some barriers stand between cryptocurrency and its global adoption.

Moreover, on environmental sustainability, cryptocurrencies such as bitcoin now consume more electricity than the whole of Sweden as their carbon footprint is increasingly becoming a concern (Joshi, 2021). The argument against the global banking industry was that it consumes 100 terawatt-hours annually (Anderson, 2019). However, a study carried out by the University of Cambridge has shown that the bitcoin network utilises over 145 terawatt-hours annually, which would rank in the top 30 electricity consumers if it was a nation (Cambridge, 2021). Electricity is needed due to the crypto mining process, as there is a need for high amounts of computing power.

The rapid growth of cryptocurrencies in the world is leading to an exponential increase in their carbon footprint. The primary cause of the high electricity consumption is the bitcoin consensus algorithm called "proof of work", where the miners need to develop the cryptocurrency while earning coins. This system, if not addressed, could potentially undermine the global implementation of cryptocurrency in the long term. Some algorithms are emerging that could provide more sustainable ways of working, one of which includes "proof of stake". This system is said to consume less energy and computing power, that is, if this system is utilised, it achieves the purpose without further deficiencies (Dove, 2021).

Also, cryptocurrencies will probably not survive in countries with stable growth and exchange rates and trustworthy businesses. Families and businesses would have almost no motivation to price or save in an equal cryptocurrency, such as bitcoin, regardless of whether it was given acceptable legal status. Their value is simply volatile and irrelevant to the real economy. Indeed, even in moderately less steady economies, the utilisation of a globally acceptable reserved currency, for example, the dollar, euro or pound sterling, would probably be more appealing than accepting cryptocurrencies (Adrian, 2021).

An additional expense to the global reception of cryptocurrencies, for example, bitcoin, is macroeconomic security. On the off chance that they valued goods and products in both physical currencies and cryptocurrencies, families and businesses would invest critical time and assets picking which cash to hold rather than taking part in productive exercises. Also, government incomes would be exposed to exchange rate risk if taxes were quoted ahead of time in cryptocurrencies while expenditures generally remained in the local currency or the other way around.

Similarly, monetary policies would lose their effect. National banks cannot set interest rates on foreign currencies. Generally, when a nation takes on foreign currency as its own, it "imports" the reliability of the foreign currency policy and hopes to align its economy and loan costs with the foreign business cycle. Neither of these is conceivable in the case of the acceptability of cryptocurrency. Subsequently, domestic costs could turn out to be highly volatile. Regardless of whether all costs were quoted, for example, in bitcoin, the costs of imported goods and products would, in any case, fluctuate tremendously following the whims of market valuations.

Financial sustainability could also be affected. Without vigorous anti-money laundering legislation and an appropriate enforcement regime, particularly at the international level, criminals could utilise cryptocurrencies to launder ill-gotten wealth for many reasons, as previously discussed. This undoubtedly will endanger the country's financial framework, financial equilibrium, and foreign nations and banks. Furthermore, for the currency to attain the global legal tender status, a payment method must be globally accessible. However, web access and technology expected to move cryptocurrencies stays scant in many nations, including developing and emerging markets, raising the issue of fairness and financial inclusion.

Additionally, the authoritative financial unit should be adequately steady in value to facilitate its utilisation for medium- to long-term financial commitments. Moreover, changes to a country's legal tender status and money-related unit regularly require unpredictable and broad changes to financial laws to avoid making an incoherent general set of laws (Adrian, 2021). The deficiencies inherent in cryptocurrencies usage quite outweigh their advantages, making it difficult for them to gain global acceptability. The lack of acceptance within the international legal order makes it easier for different governments worldwide to ban transactions and dealings in cryptocurrencies. It is doubtful that this is likely to change anytime soon without proper safeguards to address the deficiencies of cryptocurrencies.

7. Recommendations

Cryptocurrency has forced countries to pick either between banning, tolerating, or cooperating with technological innovations (Raskin and

Yermack, 2018). These are different regulatory approaches that will have different effects on the market. China banned cryptocurrency in their country; however, this regulatory approach has proved inefficient. This was an effort by its government to sustain existing regulatory consistency and preserve institutional assets (Cohn and Miao, 2018). The United States, on the other hand, did not ban cryptocurrency but instead maintained a balance between the protection of investors and financing technological innovations, presuming a practical and competent capital market (Cohn and Miao, 2018). Both approaches have their advantages and disadvantages, but there are lessons to pick from the approaches. Crypto-laundering should be a focus of the government of Nigeria. Although cryptocurrency has been banned in Nigeria, it has not stopped Nigerians from trading with it. The reasons for banning cryptocurrencies in Nigeria might seem straightforward; however, it will not completely purge the country of money laundering activities through cryptocurrencies.

It is also clear that applying the Nigerian anti-money laundering legislation is ineffective against secretive organisations, such as the Dark Web. Thus, there is a need for the legislature to regulate exchanges and wallet services. Although there are still no clear plans on regulating cryptocurrencies in Nigeria, it may be helpful for the legislature to deliberate on how to provide policies in regulating cryptocurrencies, especially since the country is currently developing its own. In seeking to regulate it, it is essential that the Nigerian authorities first make sure that the regulation will be proportional to the risks. The risks associated with the currency must be identified and dealt with appropriately.

This chapter recommends that the Nigerian government develop regulations translated into codes through the help and cooperation of relevant regulatory agencies, particularly the CBN and the SEC and other relevant stakeholders. Nigeria is already creating its own cryptocurrency, which might have already adopted regulations through codes to reduce the risk of anonymity in traditional accounts. Therefore, it is proposed that the government encourage cooperation between the above stakeholders to create a regulatory framework that will govern the trades and dealings in cryptocurrencies in Nigeria.

There is also a need for uniform international regulations on cryptocurrencies. Money laundering through the use of cryptocurrencies is not a problem restricted to Nigeria, it is a global issue. Regulatory organisations already exist which have the capability to deal with this task. Therefore, it is recommended that the United Nations Commission on International Trade Law (UNCITRAL) or the Organisation for Economic Co-operation and Development (OECD) develop an ideal law that controls cryptocurrencies on a global scale.

8. Conclusion

Cryptocurrencies are a relatively new technological advancement, but they have quickly taken over the global market. Consequently, cryptocurrencies have been abused in various illegal ways. Criminals have used the currency to launder money through different methods. While the stages of money laundering still apply, the anonymity and the absence of standard global policies governing the currency have created new methods for money laundering. Although the Nigerian government has attempted to address the problem and find lasting solutions, this chapter has shown that the Nigerian AML laws do not regulate cryptocurrencies. The wording is, at best, unclear when applied to crypto-laundering; ultimately, as recommended, more needs to be done at both the national and international levels to curb this problem, as local approaches might not suffice.

References

Abiola, J. (2014). Anti-money laundering in developing economy: A pest analysis of Nigerian situation, *Review of Public Administration and Management Nnadi Azikiwe University*, Vol. 3, No. 6, pp. 63–75.

Adeseyoju, A. (2012). Anti money laundering: FATF moves against WMDs. Financial Africa: New Playground for Crypto Scams and Money Laundering. Available at: https://issafrica.org/iss-today/africa-new-play ground-for-crypto-scams-and-money-laundering.

Adrian, T. (2021). Cryptoassets as national currency? A step too far, international monetary funds. Available at: https://blogs.lmf.org/2021/07/ 26/cryptoassets-as-national-currency-a-step-too-far/.

Ahamad, S. Nair, M. and Varghese, B. (2013). A survey on crypto currencies, a survey on crypto currencies. In *Proc. of Int. Conf. on Advances in Computer Science*, AETACS, pp. 42–48.

Aluko, A. and Bagheri, M. (2012). The impact of money laundering on economic and financial stability and on political development in developing countries, *Journal of Money Laundering Control*, Vol. 15, No. 4, pp. 442–457.

Anderson, W. P. (2019). Cryptocurrency: A viable route to sustainability for financial technology. Available at: https://www.financedigest. com/cryptocurrency-a-viable-route-to-sustainability-for-financial-technology.html.

Aoko, v. F. (1961). *All Nigeria Law Reports*, Vol. 1, p. 400.

Ayomikun, A. S. and Omowunmi, I. E. (2019). Cryptocurrency and its implications on nigeria banking operations, a Paper Presented at the Banking Digital Conference Held on Thursday, 25 July, 2019. At Babcock University, Ilisan, Ogun State. Available at: http://apbe-cibn. org.ng/wp-content/uploads/2020/06/APBE-Papers-2019-Preliminary-FA.pdf.

Babatunde, G. (2021). Bitcoin vendors cash in as P2P trading volume swells By 16% Since CBN Ban. Available at: https://technextng/2021/ 02/11/nigerias-crypto-vendors-cash-in-as-p2p-trading-volume-swells-by-16-since-cbn-order/.

Baron, J., O'Mahony, A., Manheim, D. and Dion-Schwarz, C. (2015). *National Security Implications of Virtual Currency: Examining the Potential of Non-State Actor Deployment*. Rand Publisher California, U.S.A.

Binham, C. (2013). FCA fines Nigeria lender for inadequate money laundering checks. *The Financial Times*, 9 August. Available at: https:// www.ft.com/content/4ba16f82-00fa-11e3-8918-00144feab7de.

Buchanan, B. (2004). Money laundering — A global obstacle, *Research in International Business and Finance*, Vol. 18, No. 1, pp. 115–127.

Cambridge, (2021). Cambridge bitcoin electricity consumption index (CBECI). Available at: https://cbeci.org/.

CBN, (2017) "Circular to banks and other financial institutions on virtual currency operations in Nigeria, Ref No: FPR/DIR/GEN/ CIR/06/010'. Available at: https://www.cbn.gov.ng/out/2017/fprd/ aml%20january%202017%20circular%20to%20fis%20on%20virtual%20 currency.pdf.

CFRN. (1999 as amended). Section 36 (12).

Chibuzor, O. (2021). Weighing the ban on cryptocurrency transactions. Available at: https://www.thisdaylive.com/index.php/2021/02/ 16/weighing-the-ban-on-cryptocurrency-transactions/.

Chilen, R. (2021). Africa: New Playground for crypto scams and money laundering. Available at: https://issafrica.org/iss-today/africa-new-playground-for-crypto-scams-and-money-laundering.

Ciphertrace (2019). Cryptocurrency anti-money laundering report — Q4 2018. Available at: https://ciphertrace.com/cryptocurrency-anti-money-laundering-report-q4-2018/.

Cohn, S. R. and Miao, Y. (2018). The Dragon and the Eagle: Reforming China's securities IPO laws in the U.S. model, Pros and Cons, *Washington University Global Studies Law Review*, Vol. 17, No. 2, pp. 327–363.

Dove, S. (2021). A sustainable future for cryptocurrencies? — Wildfire PR for technology companies. Available at: https://www.wildfirepr.com/blog/a-sustainable-future-for-cryptocurrencies/.

Europol, (2018). Illegal network used cryptocurrencies and credit cards to launder more than eight million Euros from drug trafficking. *Presse Release*, 9 April. Available at: www.europol.europa.eu/newsroom/news/illegal-network-used-cryptocurrencies-and-credit-cards-to-launder-more-eur-8-million-drug-trafficking.

Fruth, J. (2018). 'Crypto-cleansing:' Strategies to fight digital currency money laundering and sanctions evasion. Available at: https://www.reuters.com/article/bc-finreg-aml-cryptocurrency-idUSKCN1FX29I.

Gandal, N. and Halaburda, H. (2014). Competition in the cryptocurrency market. Bank of Canada, Working Paper No. 4, pp. 1–33. Available at: https://www.bankofcanada.ca/wp-content/uploads/2014/08/wp2014-33.pdf.

GIABA (2008). Mutual evaluation report anti-money laundering and combating the financing of terrorism. Available at: https://www.giaba.org/media/f/299_Mutual%20Evaluation%20Report%20of%20Nigeria.pdf.

Haffke, L. Fromberger, M. and Zimmermann, P. (2019). Cryptocurrencies and anti-money laundering: The shortcomings of the fifth AML directive (EU) and how to address them, *Journal of Banking Regulation*, Vol. 21, No. 2, pp. 125–138.

Hameed, S. and Farooq, S. (2016). The art of crypto currencies, *International Journal of Advanced Computer Science and Applications*, Vol. 7, No. 12, pp. 426–435.

Handagama, S. (2020). Protests show bitcoin adoption is accelerating in Nigeria. Available at: https://www.coindesk.com/nigeria-bitcoin adoption.

Ile, D. (2018). Monetary policy in the digital age: Crypto assets may one day reduce demand for central bank money, *A Quarterly Publication of the International Monetary Fund*, Vol. 55, No. 2, pp. 13–16.

Heilman, E. Baldimtsi, F. and Goldberg, S. (2016). Blindly signed contracts: Anonymous on-blockchain and off-blockchain bitcoin transactions, in Clark, J. Meiklejohn, S. Ryan, P. Y. A. Wallach, D. Brenner, M. and Rohloff, K. (eds.), *Financial Cryptography and Data Security*, FC 2016. LNCS, Vol. 9604, pp. 43–60, Springer, Heidelberg. https://doi.org/10.1007/978-3-662-53357-4.

Hughes, S. J. and Middlebrook, S. T. (2015). Advancing a framework for regulating cryptocurrency payments intermediaries, *Yale Journal of Regulation*, Vol. 32, No. 2, pp. 495–507.

Hyman, M. (2015). Bitcoin ATM: A criminal's laundromat for cleaning money, *St. Thomas Law Review*, Vol. 27, No. 2, pp. 287–308.

Interpol (2021). Financial crime threatens people in every aspect of their lives: At home, at work, online and offline. Available at: https://www.interpol.int/en/Crimes/Financial-crime.

Iyoyojie, L. D. Edeh, O. J., Erinne, U. and Umezurike, C. (2021). Cryptocurrency: The search for a legal framework as a world currency, *International Journal of Business & Law Research*, Vol. 9, No. 3, pp. 15–25.

Joshi, N. (2021). What are the main barriers towards a mainstream acceptance of cryptocurrencies? *BBN Times*. Available at: https://www.bbntimes.com/technology/what-are-the-main-barriers-towards-a-mainstream-acceptance-of-cryptocurrencies.

Kene-Okafor, T. (2021). In 2020, Nigerians traded more than $400M worth of crypto on local crypto exchange platforms. Available at: https://techpoint.africa/2021/01/06/nigerians-traded-more-than-400m-worth- crypto-2020/.

Kovach, S. (2021). Tesla buys $1.5 billion in bitcoin, plans to accept it as payment. Available at: https://www.cnbc.com/2021/02/08/tesla-buys-1point5-billion-in-bitcoin.html.

MacDowell, J. (2001). The consequences of money laundering and financial crime, money laundering-economic perspective-state department, *An Electronic Journal of the U.S. Department of State*, Vol. 6, No. 2, pp. 6–8.

Mesele, O. (2021). Framework for the regulation of the Nigerian crypto assets market — Law allianz. Available at: https://www.lawallianz.com/articles/framework-for-the-regulation-of-the-nigerian-crypto-assets-market/.

Mundell, R. (2002). The birth of coinage, Discussion paper #:0102-08 Department of Economics, Columbia University, New York. Available at: https://core.ac.uk/download/pdf/161436657.pdf.

Nakamoto, S. (2008). Bitcoin: A peer-to-peer electronic cash system. Available at: https://bitcoin.org/bitcoin.pdf.

Nica, O. Piotrowska, K. and Schenk-Hoppp, K. R. (2017). Cryptocurrencies: Economic benefits and risks. *University of Manchester, FinTech* working paper No. 2. Available at: https://ssrn.com/abstract=3059856.

Otusanya, O. J., Ajibolade, S. O. and Omolehinwa, O. E. (2012). The role of financial intermediaries in elite money laundering practises: Evidence from Nigeria, *Journal of Money Laundering Control*, Vol. 15, No. 1, pp. 58–84.

Picard, P. M. and Pieretti, P. (2011). Bank secrecy, illicit money and offshore financial centers, *Journal of Public Economics*, Vol. 95, Nos. 7–8, pp. 942–955.

Peters, G. W. Panayi, E. and Chapelle, A. (2015). Trends in cryptocurrencies and blockchain technologies: A monetary theory and regulation perspective, *Journal of Financial Perspectives*, Vol. 3, No. 3, pp. 92–113.

Polillo, S. (2011). Money, moral authority, and the politics of creditworthiness, *American Sociological Review*, Vol. 76, No. 3, pp. 437–464. Washington.

Raskin, M. and Yermack, D. (2018). Digital currencies, decentralised ledgers, and the future of central banking, in P. Conti-Brown and R. Lastra (eds.), *Research Handbook on Central Banking*, pp. 474–486.

Reid, F. and Harrigan, M. (2011). An analysis of anonymity in the bitcoin system, *IEEE Third International Conference on Privacy, Security, Risk and Trust and IEEE Third International Conference on Social Computing*, pp. 1318–1326. DOI:10.1109/PASSAT/SocialCom.2011.79.

Rose, C. (2015). The evolution of digital currencies: Bitcoin, a cryptocurrency causing a monetary revolution, *International Business & Economics Research Journal*, Vol. 14, No. 4, pp. 617–622.

Salawu, M. and Malaoi, T. (2018). Benefits of legislating cryptocurrencies: Perception of Nigerian professional accountants, *Academy of Accounting and Financial Studies Journal*, Vol. 22, No. 6, pp. 1–17.

Sat, D. M., Krylov, G. O., Bezverbnyi, K. E., Kasatkin, A. B. and Kornev, I. A. (2016). Investigation of money laundering methods through cryptocurrency, *Journal of Theoretical and Applied Information Technology*, Vol. 83, No. 2, pp. 244–254.

Sieber, U. (1998). Legal aspects of computer-related crime in the information society, COMCERIME Study, A Report Prepared for the European Commission.

Small, S. (2015). Bitcoin: The napster of currency, *Houston Journal of International Law*, Vol. 37, No. 2, pp. 581–641.

Sanusi, L. S. (2012). The banking reform and its impact on the Nigerian economy, A public lecture delivered at the University of Warwick's Economic Summit, Warwick, 17 February. Available at: https://www.bis.org/review/r120320d.pdf.

Schneider, F. (2008). Money laundering and financial means of organised crime: Some preliminary empirical findings, *Global Business and Economics Review*, Vol. 10, No. 3, pp. 309–330.

SEC (2017). Public notice on investments in cryptocurrencies and other virtual or digital currencies, 12 January. Available at: http://sec.gov.ng/public-notice-on-investments-in-cryptocurrencies-and-other-virtual-or-digital-currencies/.

SEC (2019). Report of the fintech roadmap committee of the Nigerian capital market. Available at: https://sec.gov.ng/report-of-the-fintech-roadmap-committee-of-the-nigerian-capital-market/.

Sofola, K. Eraga, R. and Omowunmi, I. (2021). Cryptocurrencies in Nigeria: An overview of a regulatory framework. Available at: http://kslegal.org/wp-content/uploads/2021/04/Cryptocurrencies-in-Nigeria-.pdf.

Swartz, L. (2018). What was bitcoin, what will it be? The techno-economic imaginaries of a new money technology, *Cultural Studies*, Vol. 32, No. 4, pp. 623–650.

Temitope, J. F. and Folorunso, O. F. (2020). Digital currencies and national development: Prospects and challenges for adoption, *International Journal of Academic Accounting, Finance & Management Research*, Vol. 4, No. 10, pp. 139–145.

Vanguard, (2017). MMM prepares to return, Dumps Naira for bitcoin. *The Vanguard Newspaper*, 9 January. Available at: http://www.vanguardngr.com/2017/01/mmm-prepares-to-return-dumps-naira-for-bitcoin/.

Venkatakrishnan, S. B., Fanti, G. and Viswanath, P. (2017). Dandelion: Redesigning the bitcoin network for anonymity, (Publish Illinios). Available at: http://publish.illinois.edu/science-of-security-lablet/files/2016/07/Dandelion-Redesigning-BitCoin-Networking-for-Anonymity.pdf.

Wegberg, R. V., Oerlemans, J. and Deventer, O. V. (2018). Bitcoin money laundering: Mixed results? An explorative study on money laundering of cybercrime proceeds using bitcoin, *Journal of Financial Crime*, Vol. 25, No. 2, pp. 419–435.

Zamani, E. D. and Babatsikos, I. (2017). The use of bitcoins in light of the financial crisis: The case of Greece, *The 11th Mediterranean Conference on Information Systems (MCIS)*, Genoa, Italy.

Chapter 10

The Impact of Environmental Information Disclosure on Corporate Performance in Building Material Industry

Wang Hong, Bao Xinyuan, and Wang Yidan

Abstract

In the trend of green and low-carbon economy, environmental information disclosure is an effective measure to deal with global climate change and to promote environmental protection. In 2020, China officially put forward the strategic goal of achieving peak carbon dioxide emission by 2030 and achieving carbon neutrality by 2060. In order to form new market competitiveness under these two goals of carbon emission control, companies should actively respond to policies, consciously fulfil their social responsibilities, and sort out and disclose their environmental information, so as to support and achieve decarburisation and environmental protection. We select the unbalanced panel data of A-share listed companies in building materials industry from 2015 to 2019 to empirically analyse the impact of environmental information disclosure on corporate performance in this industry. The results show that: (1) environmental information disclosure and corporate performance are significantly positively correlated at the 1% level; so, improving the quality of environmental information disclosure can effectively boost corporate performance; (2) the effect of the nature of equity on the correlation between environmental information disclosure and corporate performance is very different: the environmental information disclosure of state-owned enterprises has a significant positive effect on corporate performance at the 5% level, while that of non-state-owned enterprises are not significant at all. The purpose of this research is to guide companies in building materials industry to fulfil their environmental responsibilities, actively disclose environmental information, improve the quality of green and low-carbon development, and strive to achieve a positive interaction between sustainable economic and environmental protection. We choose the building materials industry as the object and hope our research can enrich relevant literature in the field of environmental information disclosure, help companies change their traditional concepts, promote the implementation of environmental protection work, enhance their competitive advantages, and make positive contributions to ecological civilisation construction.

Keywords: Environmental information disclosure; corporate social responsibility (CSR); corporate performance; building materials industry; climate change

1. Introduction

The Paris Agreement, which took effect in 2016, put forward the overall goal of holding the temperature increase of the Earth's surface within 2 degrees Celsius and trying to control it within 1.5 degrees Celsius at the end of the 21st century. Carbon neutrality, that is, to balance the total amount of greenhouse gas emissions emitted by man-made activities with the total amount absorbed by nature is an effective measure to achieve this goal on a global scale. In order to achieve this goal, the United Nations Framework Convention on Climate Change requires all parties to report to the United Nations on their 2030 emission reduction targets by the end of 2020 and report national low-emissions strategy for the coming mid-21st century. On 22 September, 2020, at the general debate of the 75th UN General Assembly, general secretary of the People's Republic of China, Xi Jinping, said in his speech that China will increase its contributions to controlling carbon emission, enact and adopt more powerful policies and measures, strive to reach its peak carbon dioxide emissions by 2030, and to reach carbon neutrality by 2060. At the moment, China's environmental problems are still severe: Ecological debt is still large, with the impact of climate and environmental changes on economic and social development becoming more and more obvious. Especially, after the "dual carbon" goal is proposed, how to keep corporate development in tune with low-carbon transformation has become a problem to be solved.

The building materials industry is one of the industries with the largest energy consumption and pollutant emissions in China, so the task of protecting the environment, saving energy, and reducing emission is arduous. However, the environmental information disclosure status of building materials companies is not ideal now. First, some companies pay little attention to environmental information disclosure, and the quality of environmental information disclosed is low. Some companies only disclose simple textual description instead of substantive and quantitative content. Besides, there are huge differences in disclosure between companies. Second, in the existing research on corporate performance of environmental information disclosure, there is a research gap in the building materials industry. Therefore, we take the building materials industry as the object to explore the impact of environmental information disclosure on corporate performance, aiming to find the balance point between business development and low-carbon environmental protection to improve the sustainable development ability as well as profitability of building materials companies.

2. Literature Review

Both domestic and international scholars have studied the relationship between environmental information disclosure and corporate performance from different perspectives. Belkaoui (1976) took 50 listed companies as the research sample and used the event research method to analyse the market response caused by their environmental information disclosure. The result shows that the stock prices of companies with pollution control expense disclosures have short-term positive fluctuations. Lanoie *et al.* (1998) conducted continuous observations on the changing capital market and found companies with environmental information disclosure received better feedback in the capital market. Berman *et al.* (1999) did a statistical analysis on business information and social responsibility information from corporate websites and found that there is no significant relationship between environmental information and corporate performance. Gray *et al.* (2001) found a positive correlation between environmental information disclosure and corporate profitability. Botosan and Plumlee (2002) pointed out in their research that information disclosure improves the liquidity of the stock market, thereby reducing the cost of equity capital through reducing transaction costs or increasing the demand for corporate securities.

Patten and Trompeter (2003), using 112 listed companies in the United States as a research sample, found that the environmental information disclosure of companies reduces the negative impact of government regulations and prevents corporate performance from degrading. Al-Tuwaijri (2004) found that there is a positive correlation between corporate value and the quality of environmental information disclosure after empirical analysis. Clarkson *et al.* (2004) found that companies improving the quality of environmental information disclosure can reduce investors' investment risks as well as their requirements for the value of asset, thereby reducing corporate financing costs and improving financing capabilities.

Wegener (2010) used the CDP report to empirically study the relationship between the stock market and the disclosure of carbon information by Canadian companies, and the result shows that voluntary disclosure of carbon information has a positive impact on the value of the stock market. Saka and Oshika (2014) found that as the content of carbon information disclosure increases, the market value of corporate equity increases as well. Li *et al.* (2015) believes that carbon information disclosure is helpful for corporate value creation. Yan *et al.* (2016) found that earning power can lead to the improvement of corporate carbon information disclosure, but there is a time lag. Ganda (2018), based on the 2010–2015 annual carbon emissions report of South African companies, found that there is a positive correlation between carbon information disclosure and return on assets.

In China, Yin (2006) analysed the impact of earnings on voluntary information disclosure of Chinese listed companies by constructing a voluntary information disclosure indicator system. The results show that the better the earnings performance of companies, the better the voluntary disclosure. Lü and Jiao (2010) took listed companies in the papermaking industry and building materials industry in 2007 as the sample and found through empirical analysis that there is no significant correlation between environmental disclosure and corporate performance. Zhang and Wang (2015) used three-year data of 100 listed companies in heavily polluting industries as the sample and found that there is no significant relationship between voluntary disclosure of environmental information and corporate performance in such industries.

Chang (2015) used the unbalanced panel data of Chinese heavily polluting industries as the sample and found that environmental information disclosure has a significant positive correlation with corporate performance. Li and Shi (2016) found that improving the quality of carbon information disclosure can lead to improvement of corporate performance. Dong *et al.* (2018) found that carbon information disclosure is significantly positively correlated with corporate performance. Pan and Wang (2019) also drew a similar conclusion and found that the nature of the corporate share will lead to differences in the impact of carbon information disclosure on corporate performance: State-owned enterprises (SOEs) are better than non-state-owned enterprises. Apart from the positive relationship between the two, Tian and Song (2019) also found that corporate earnings management reinforced the relationship between the quality of carbon information disclosure and financial performance. Dai and Shi (2019) analysed a three-year data sample of A-share listed companies on the Shanghai Stock Exchange in the heavy polluting industry and found that corporate environmental information disclosure is significantly related to corporate performance.

After sorting out the literature, we found that both domestic and international scholars have stored up abundant research in the field of environmental information disclosure on corporate performance. Compared with other countries, China's research in this field started later and achieved fewer. In addition, the existing researches on environmental information disclosure on corporate performance seldom control industry factors, ignoring the impact of differences among different industries.

Liu and Zheng (2021) believed that we should be aware of the positive impact brought about by environmental information disclosure on promoting enterprises to take emission reduction and environmental protection responsibilities. In addition, we should establish and supervise the mandatory disclosure of corporate-level greenhouse gas emission information at the same time.

The aims of this chapter are as follows:

(1) We focus on the building materials industry which urgently requires regulation of environmental information disclosure. Taking Chinese A-share listed building materials companies in 2015–2019 as a research sample, we explore the impact of environmental information disclosure on corporate economic performance to enrich the research in this field.

(2) Through empirical analysis, we explore the relationship between voluntary disclosure of environmental information and corporate performance, and we provide a reference for building materials companies to proactively respond to climate change, actively take environmental protection responsibilities, and achieve a balance point between corporate development and environmental protection.

3. Theoretical Framework and Hypotheses

According to corporate social responsibility (CSR) theory, companies benefit by disclosing environmental information in many aspects: improving the visibility and transparency of companies fulfilling their environmental responsibilities so that the public can fully understand their achievement in environmental protection and improvement; building an environment-friendly social reputation; enhancing the connection between the company and stakeholders and to gain competitive advantages on the market so that companies can operate, profit, and create value more successfully.

In business management, CSR includes the triple bottom line of economy, society, and environment (Elkington, 1994). According to triple bottom line theory, a business should look beyond the one bottom line of profits to achieve sustainability. Sustainable management is achieved when companies commit to their communities and the environment (Marrewijk, 2003; Norman and MacDonald, 2004; Dixon and Clifford, 2007) as well as their profits in a balanced relationship. Good performance in the financial dimension leads to good future performance in the environmental dimension and vice versa. Thus, there is no dichotomy between environmental performance and financial performance, and the two concepts conflate into one concern: the future management as far as the firm is concerned (Crowther, 2002).

Signalling theory means organisations frequently send out signals that reduce information asymmetry among them and stakeholders and enable them to communicate their organisational image, intentions, behaviour, and performance (Karaman *et al.*, 2020). Signalling theory is related to companies' need to communicate their information to the stakeholders and the market by emitting signals about their commitment to society (Bae *et al.*, 2018). According to signalling theory, environmental informational asymmetry between company and investors will lead to investors' perception of uncertainty about enterprises due to the difficulty and high cost of access to information. However, by disclosing environmental information, companies can reduce the cost for investors to obtain environmental information, transmit positive signals about the company's environmental management and performance, and enhance investors' confidence and favour towards the company so do their positive expectations for the company's future development and investment. Moreover, consumers will have a preference for companies' environment-friendly products and will be willing to pay the environmental premium included. So, the company can increase the turnover of "green products", enhance competitiveness, expand market share, and thus improve corporate performance.

According to stakeholder theory, the behavioural decisions of a company are constrained by both internal and external stakeholders. In addition to seeking profits for shareholders, corporate must consider the impact of stakeholders on their business operation and development and maximise corporate value (Freeman, 1984). Companies actively disclose and improve the quality of environmental information to meet the needs of stakeholders, including government and public, to reduce all kinds of external pressures, to encourage stakeholders to participate in corporate management better, and to contribute to corporate operation and value creation in a positive way. This also helps to enhance the companies' sustainable development capabilities, form long-term competitiveness, and achieve good performance eventually.

For all the above reasons, we propose the following hypothesis.

Hypothesis 1: Environmental information disclosure has a significant positive influence on corporate performance, that is, the higher the information quality, the better the corporate performance.

The difference in the nature of corporate equity leads to differences in management, governance structure, and performance of environmental protection responsibilities. China's SOEs are the backbone of national economic development. On the one hand, SOEs need to make profit as a commercial institution and pursue the goal of maximising and maintaining value. On the other hand, compared with non-SOEs, the decision-making behaviour of SOEs reflects the volition of the government, due to which SOEs should proactively respond to national policies and pay more attention to the medium-term and long-term developments. Facing political pressure and public attention, SOEs will take on more social responsibilities. At present, China is vigorously building an ecological civilisation, developing a green and low-carbon economy. This requires SOEs to play a leading role in upholding and practising the concept of sustainable development and actively disclosing environmental information. Hence, the quality of environmental information disclosure of SOEs is higher than that of non-SOEs, and the effect on corporate performance should be more significant as well. Dai and Shi (2019) examined how the nature of equity impacts the environmental information disclosure and corporate performance.

For all the above reasons, we propose the following hypothesis.

Hypothesis 2: The environmental information disclosure of SOEs has a significant impact on corporate performance, while that of non-SOEs insignificant.

4. Methodology

4.1. *Sampling and method*

The research sample is selected from Straight Flush — a Chinese finance website, including 69 Chinese continuously operating A-share listed building materials companies from 2015 to 2019. After excluding ST and ST* (special treatment) companies and excluding years with missing data, 56 companies (232 annual values in total) remain for further observation. Then, the last 1% data of the two-tailed continuous distribution is processed using the Winsor tailing method by Stata15 and Excel.

Based on annual reports and independent reports issued by companies (including social responsibility reports, environmental reports, sustainability reports, etc.), which can be found on Eastmoney website, Juchao Information website, Shanghai Stock Exchange website, Shenzhen Stock Exchange website, and corporates' official websites, we collected the environmental information of the sample enterprises. Other variables such as financial data, shareholder structure, company sizes, and data from Huibo Investment Research Consulting Network are also used.

4.2. *Modelling*

In this chapter, we use F-test and Hausman test to determine the model of empirical analysis. The result of the F-test is 0.0000 and that of the Hausman robust test is 0.0101. Therefore, we chose the fixed-effects model (FEM) for empirical analysis. The analysis uses the relevant data from 2015 to 2019 of listed companies in the A-share listed building materials industry to construct a fixed-effect panel data model.

First, the following regression model is constructed:

$$ROA_{(i,t)} = \alpha_{(i,t)} + EIDI_{(i,t)} + LnSize_{(i,t)} + Lev_{(i,t)} + Growth_{(i,t)}$$
$$+ LnJsize_{(i,t)} + Top1_{(i,t)} + \varepsilon_{(i,t)}.$$

In this formula, i and t represent the number of A-share listed building materials companies and the year, respectively; ROA is the return of total assets, working as the explained variable; $EIDI$ is the environmental information disclosure index, working as the core explaining variable; other indicators are control variables; and $\varepsilon(i,t)$ is the stochastic disturbance term. These specific indicators and their meanings will be explained in detail in the following three sections.

4.3. *Variables*

4.3.1. *Explained variable: enterprise performance (ROA)*

Enterprise performance refers to the performance of the operator and the operating efficiency of the enterprise during a certain period. Margolis and Walsh (2001) pointed out that more than 70 of the 95 corporate performance research articles use single ratio indicators, such as return on total assets (ROA) and return on net assets (ROE), as corporate performance variables. Zhao (2019) used the Institute for Scientific Information (ISI) database for searching and found that from 2001 to 2010, more than 2,000 out of 3,000 papers, which studied company performance from the perspective of social responsibility, used ROA and ROE as performance metrics. Bi *et al.* (2015) and Lü *et al.* (2018) also use the ROA as an indicator of corporate profitability. ROA can reasonably reflect the profitability of a company and can be hardly affected by the company's non-recurring event. Furthermore, it is also universal, objective, and easily available. Therefore, we use ROA as a proxy variable of corporate performance.

4.3.2. *Explaining variables*

We use EIDI as an independent variable to indicate the quality of corporate environmental information disclosure. We calculate the EIDI after establishing the standard of grading.

First, a quality evaluation index system for environmental information disclosure is established. As shown in Table 1, we mainly refer to the design of disclosure indicators of Bi *et al.* (2012), Shen *et al.* (2014), and Zhu *et al.* (2019) to establish an environmental information disclosure quality evaluation indicator system with a total of 13 indicators. The disclosure methods are divided into qualitative and quantitative disclosures. It scores 0 if the company does not describe the content of the indicator at all; if the company

Table 1. Environmental information disclosure quality evaluation system and scoring standards.

Index	Standard of grading
1. Environmental policy and philosophy	1 for disclosure, 0 otherwise
2. Environmental emergency plan	Same as above
3. Environmental protection training	2 for quantitative disclosure, 1 for qualitative disclosure, and 0 otherwise
4. Environmental protection equipment and technology	Same as above
5. Investment in environmental protection	Same as above
6. Usage of pollution control facilities	Same as above
7. Clean energy development and utilisation	Same as above
8. Annual resource consumption	Same as above
9. Production of environmentally friendly products	Same as above
10. Energy saving and emission reduction	Same as above
11. Pollutant emissions	Same as above
12. Pollutant discharge compliance	Same as above
13. Hazardous waste treatment	Same as above

describes environmental information, it is classified as qualitative disclosure and scores 1; and if the company discloses figures, it is classified as quantitative disclosure and scores 2.

Then, the environmental information disclosure quality score is calculated. Tang *et al.* (2006) pointed out that EIDI is universally used to define the information disclosure level in relevant literature. More specifically, it is used to score these disclosure indicators and to summarise their scores. Cooke (1989), Tang *et al.* (2006), etc. all use the method of direct aggregation. Therefore, we assign scores and add up these 13 indicators to obtain the environmental information disclosure scores of each sample enterprise, $EID_{(i,t)}$, which is the sum of the scores of each indicator disclosed by enterprise i during year t.

Finally, we calculate the EIDI. When measuring environmental information disclosure, Wang *et al.* (2013), Zhang and Wang (2015), and Bi *et al.* (2015) used the total score to divide the maximum possible score of EIDI of sample companies. The purpose of calculating the EIDI is to reduce the volatility of the disclosure score, to reflect the degree of environmental information disclosure of different companies, and to increase the prudence of our research. The maximum possible score of environmental information disclosure of the sample companies is 24. Then, we divide the actual score of the company's environmental information disclosure, $EID_{(i,t)}$, by 24 to obtain, $EIDI_{(i,t)}$, which represents the environmental information of company i in year t.

The calculation formula is

$$EIDI_{(i,t)} = EID_{(i,t)}/24.$$

$EIDI_{(i,t)}$ range from 0 to 1. Environmental information disclosure quality gets higher when its score approaches 1 and lower if its score approaches 0.

4.3.3. *Control variables*

Based on the related literature on environmental information disclosure (e.g. Shen and Feng, 2012; Bi *et al.*, 2015; Zhu *et al.*, 2019), we select the following control variables: company size (LnSize, natural logarithm of total asset at the end of the period), financial leverage (Lev, total liabilities at the end of the period/total assets at the end of the period), corporate growth (Growth, growth in operating income/total operating income in the previous year), size of the board of supervisors (LnJsize, natural logarithm of the number of board members), and share structure (Top1, the shareholding ratio of the largest shareholder).

The variables and their definitions are shown in Table 2.

5. Results

5.1. *Basic statistics*

Table 3 shows that the maximum ROA is 0.226 and the minimum is −0.0801, indicating that the performance of different companies in the building materials industry varies greatly. Some companies have strong profitability, while some do not. The maximum value of the EIDI is 0.750, the minimum value is 0.0417, and the

Table 2.   Variables and definitions.

Variable type	Name	Signal	Calculation
Explained variables	Corporate performance	ROA	Return on total assets
Explaining variables	Environmental information disclosure quality	EIDI	Environmental information disclosure index
Control variables	Corporate size	LnSize	Natural logarithm of total asset at the end of the period
	Financial leverage	Lev	Total liabilities at the end of the period/total assets at the end of the period
	Corporate growth	Growth	Growth in operating income/total operating income in the previous year
	Size of the board of supervisors	LnJsize	Natural logarithm of the number of board members
	Share structure	Top1	Shareholding ratio of the largest shareholder

Table 3.   Basic statistics of variables.

Name	Sample size	Mean	Standard deviation	Minimum	Maximum
ROA	232	0.0583	0.0630	−0.0801	0.226
EIDI	232	0.348	0.183	0.0417	0.750
LnSize	232	8.646	1.237	6.079	12.36
Lev	232	0.454	0.183	0.0658	0.826
Growth	232	0.183	0.294	−0.358	1.367
LnJsize	232	1.260	0.278	0.693	1.946
Top1	232	0.322	0.124	0.111	0.769

Note: ROA represents corporate performance; EIDI represents environmental information disclosure quality; LnSize represents corporate size; Lev represents financial leverage; Growth represents corporate growth; LnJsize represents size of the board of supervisors; and Top1 represents Share structure.

standard deviation is 0.183. This shows that with the increasingly stringent environmental regulations and the increasing pressure of environmental information disclosure requirements, many building materials companies begin to realise the importance of environmental protection and are willing to disclose environmental information related to the company's production and operation to the public. However, the quality of disclosed information varies greatly.

A high leverage ratio means a high debt repayment risk, while a low leverage ratio indicates a poor use of creditor's capital. The maximum leverage ratio, Lev, in the table is 82.6%, the minimum is 6.58%, and the average is 45.4%. The overall leverage ratio of the building materials industry remains at a certain level, but there is a significant difference in financial leverage among companies. The maximum of corporate growth, that is, the growth rate of operating income, is 136.7%, the minimum is −35.8%, and the average is 18.3%. In conclusion, there are huge differences in the growth of different companies in the building materials industry. Some companies are rising rapidly, while some are growing slowly, even showing a downturn or decrease.

5.2. *Regression*

From the regression results in Table 4, it can be seen that the quality of environmental information disclosure and corporate performance are significantly positively correlated at the level of 5%, and every 1%

Table 4.   Overall sample regression.

Variables	ROA	t value
EIDI	0.068**	2.49
LnSize	0.019	1.57
Lev	−0.305***	−6.07
Growth	0.040***	4.03
LnJsize	−0.018	−0.58
Top1	0.234**	2.08
Constant	−0.053	−0.49
Observations	232	
Number of code	56	
R-squared	0.478	
$r2\_a$	0.464	
F	17.18	

Note: $^*p < 0.05$; $^{**}p < 0.01$; $^{***}p < 0.001$. The t value is the robust standard error of cluster heteroscedasticity at the individual level.

increase in the quality of environmental information disclosure leads to a 6.8% increase in corporate performance. The result indicates that hypothesis 1 is statistically supported. This indicates that the quality of information disclosure has a positive effect on corporate performance. In addition, there is no significant correlation between corporate performance and corporate scale, indicating that corporate scale does not determine the quality of corporate performance. There is a significant negative correlation between corporate and financial leverage at 1% level. The lower the financial leverage, the better the corporate performance because a higher financial leverage causes greater corporate debt repayment risk. Corporate performance and corporate growth are positively correlated at 1% level, that is, the higher the growth rate of corporate operating income, the greater the net profit margin of total assets and the better the financial performance.

Ownership structure and corporate performance have a significant positive correlation at 5% level. This means the higher the shareholding ratio of the largest shareholder, the more conducive the improvement of corporate performance because a more concentrated shareholding will benefit the formulation of major decisions and the implementation of corporate strategies. There is no significant relationship between the size of the board of supervisors and corporate performance because the difference in the number of supervisory boards of building materials companies is not obvious, and the effect on corporate performance is not clear.

5.3. *Regression of the grouped nature of equity*

We classify the sample A-share listed building materials companies as state-owned ones and non-state-owned ones by the nature of equity and build regressions of the sample companies in groups. The results are as follows.

The regression results in Table 5 show that the environmental information disclosure of SOEs is significantly related to corporate performance at the level of 5%, while non-SOEs see insignificant results.

Table 5. Regression results of the grouped nature of equity.

Variables	State-owned ROA	t value	Non-state-owned ROA	t value
EIDI	0.055**	2.36	0.051	1.15
LnSize	0.009	0.46	0.026*	1.73
Lev	−0.436***	−5.08	−0.261***	−3.70
Growth	0.053**	2.62	0.035***	2.94
LnJsize	0.051	0.79	−0.027	−0.96
Top1	−0.292**	−2.15	0.320**	2.51
Constant	0.196	1.04	−0.131	−1.07
Observations	85		147	
Number of code	19		37	
R-squared	0.635		0.410	
r2_a	0.607		0.385	
F	19.97		5.581	

Note: $^*p < 0.05$; $^{**}p < 0.01$; $^{***}p < 0.001$.

Compared with non-SOEs, SOEs would be more proactive in responding to national policies and pay more attention to mid-term and long-term developments. Facing policy pressure and public concern, SOEs must take more social responsibilities. At present, China is vigorously building an ecological civilisation, developing a "green" and low-carbon economy. This requires SOEs to play a leading role in upholding and practising the concept of sustainable development and actively disclosing environmental information. Hence, the quality of environmental information disclosure of SOEs is higher than that of non-SOEs, and the effect on corporate performance should be more significant as well.

The result indicates that hypothesis 2 is statistically supported. The results of the new regression are consistent with those of the overall regression in terms of control variables, the regression results of enterprise size, asset-liability ratio, enterprise growth, and the size of the board of supervisors. For SOEs, the ownership structure and corporate performance have a significant negative correlation at the level of 5%. On the other hand, the ownership structure of non-SOEs is significantly positively correlated with corporate performance at the level of 5%, perhaps because of the entrenchment of major shareholders of SOEs.

5.4. *Endogeneity test*

The conclusion of environmental information disclosure affects corporate performance is sceptical: There may be reverse causality, that is, improving the quality of environmental information disclosure can cause an improvement in corporate performance and vice versa. In this regard, we take the current EIDI as the explained variable and use one-period lag value of the corporate performance and control variables for regression after the research model proposed by Zhang and Chen (2017).

As shown in Table 6, "l. Variable Name" represents variables with one-period lag. And the endogeneity test results are relatively consistent with the main test results, so the conclusion does not have endogeneity.

5.5. *Robust test*

The robustness test is carried out by adjusting the model method. Li and Shi (2016) used ROE as a robustness test when studying the relationship between carbon information disclosure and corporate performance. Therefore, we choose the return on equity (ROE) as a corporate performance measurement index and select the top 10

Table 6.   Endogeneity test.

Variables	EIDI	t value
l. ROA	0.784**	2.55
l. LnSize	0.067	1.42
l. Lev	0.042	0.24
l. Growth	0.083**	1.98
l. Jsize	0.035	0.22
l. Top1	−0.360	−0.75
Constant	−0.210	−0.42
Observations	175	
Number of code	51	
R-squared	0.239	
F test	0.00159	
$r2\_a$	0.212	
F	4.238	

Note: "***" means significant at the 1% level, "**" means significant at the 5% level, "*" means significant at the 10% level.

Table 7. Regression of adjusted model.

Variables	ROE	t value
EIDI	0.174***	3.19
LnSize	0.007	0.23
Lev	−0.507***	−4.03
Growth	0.098***	4.04
LnBsize	0.0025	0.49
LnJsize	−0.061	0.76
Top10	0.147	0.65
Constant	0.122	0.36
Observations	232	
Number of code	56	
R-squared	0.361	
$r2\_a$	0.341	
F	8.281	

Note: "***" means significant at the 1% level, "**" means significant at the 5% level, "*" means significant at the 10% level.

largest shareholders. We use the share ratio (Top10) to replace the shareholding ratio of the largest shareholder as a measure of the shareholding structure. And we introduce the board size (LnBsize, the natural logarithm of the board of directors) as a control variable. As a result, a new model is formed as follows:

$$ROE_{(i,t)} = \alpha_{(i,t)} + EIDI_{(i,t)} + LnSize_{(i,t)} + Lev_{(i,t)} + Growth_{(i,t)}$$
$$+ LnBsize_{(i,t)} + LnJsize_{(i,t)} + Top10_{(i,t)} + \varepsilon_{(i,t)}.$$

Using the new model, the original samples are regressed, and the results are as follows:

Table 7 shows that environmental information disclosure and corporate performance are still significantly positively correlated at the level of 1%. The regression results of other control variables are consistent with the overall regression results. Therefore, after adjusting the model, the empirical results are still significant, showing that the empirical results are robust and reliable.

6. Conclusions and Recommendations

This chapter focused on the building materials industry because it is one of the industries with the largest energy consumption and pollutant emissions. Compared with other industries, the building materials industry has more responsibilities in terms of energy conservation, emission reduction, and environmental management. In the age of climate change, it can help companies change their traditional development concepts and disclose environmental information actively. In our empirical study, the results of the models indicate that hypotheses 1 and 2 are statistically supported.

Achieving carbon peak and carbon neutrality is in nature an unprecedented green industrialisation revolution. Under the current background of global warming, environmental information disclosure provides a data basis and decision support for the implementation of carbon emission reduction and environmental protection development and is conducive to the establishment of a national carbon market with "effective supervision, openness and transparency". It can urge enterprises to implement emission reduction and take environmental responsibility. It can help realise the "green recovery" of the world economy in the post-epidemic era as well.

In this chapter, we took the A-share listed companies in Chinese building materials industry from 2015 to 2019 as a sample and used the fixed effect model to analyse and verify the impact of environmental information disclosure on corporate performance empirically. The research conclusions are drawn as follows:

(1) Environmental information disclosure has a positive effect on corporate performance.
(2) The nature of the enterprise has significant differences between the correlation of environmental information disclosure and enterprise performance: the environmental information disclosure of SOEs has a significant positive promotion effect on enterprise performance, while that of non-SOEs is not significant.

In order to cope with environmental pollution and climate change and promote the high-quality transformation of China's economy, it is necessary to consider the economy and the ecological environment together, carry out the concept of green development, vigorously develop a green economy, and improve the quality of environmental information disclosure.

For all the above reasons, we put forward the following suggestions.

First, the government must improve the reward-penalise system to achieve a two-way promotion. That is, on the one hand, through the introduction of mandatory laws and regulations, companies are forced to improve the quality of environmental information disclosure; on the other hand, the government should encourage them to actively disclose environmental information through the implementation of subsidy and strengthened financial support. Second, relevant government departments should promote the establishment of a mutual assistance platform for environmental protection and promote the exchange of ecological protection technologies between SOEs and non-SOEs, so they can work together to improve the quality and performance of environmental information disclosure. Third, enterprises should change their development mindset, understand the mechanism of how the improvement of the quality of environmental information disclosure helps corporate performance, set up independent energy-saving and environmental protection agencies, promote fine environmental protection management, increase the motivation to disclose environmental information, and promote the completion of corporate environmental information disclosure.

References

Al-Tuwaijri, S. A., Christensen, T. E. and Hughes, K. E. (2004). The relations among environmental disclosure, environmental performance, and economic performance: A simultaneous equations approach, *Accounting, Organizations and Society*, Vol. 29, No. 5, pp. 447–471.

Belkaoui, A. (1976). The Impact of the disclosure of the environmental effects of organizational behavior on the market, *Financial Management*, Vol. 5, No. 4, pp. 26–31.

Berman, S., Wicks, A., Suresh, K. and Thomas, M. J. (1999). Does stakeholder orientation matter? The relationship between stakeholder management models and firm financial performance, *The Academy of Management Journal*, Vol. 42, No. 5, pp. 488–506.

Botosan, C. A. and Plumlee, M. A. (2002). A re-examination of disclosure level and the expected cost of equity capital, *Journal of Accounting Research*, Vol. 40, No. 1, pp. 21–40.

Bi, X., Peng J. and Zuo Y. Y. (2012). Environmental information disclosure system, corporate governance and environmental information disclosure, *Accounting research*, Vols. 448–453, No. 7, pp. 39–47, 96.

Bi, X., Gu, L. M. and Zhang, J. J. (2015). Traditional culture, environmental system and enterprise environmental information disclosure, *Accounting Research*, No. 3, pp. 12–19, 94.

Bae, S. M., Masud M. A. K. and Kim J. D. (2018). A cross-country investigation of corporate governance and corporate sustainability disclosure: A signaling theory perspective, *Sustainability*, Vol. 10, No. 8.

Cooke, T. E. (1989). Disclosure in the corporate annual reports of swedish companies, *Accounting & Business Research*, Vol. 19, No. 74, pp. 113–124.

Crowther, D. (2003). A social critique of corporate reporting: A semiotic analysis of corporate financial and environmental reporting, *British Accounting Review*, Vol. 35, No. 4, pp. 401–402.

Clarkson, P. M., Li, Y. and Richardson, G. D. (2004). The market valuation of environmental capital expenditures by pulp and paper companies, *The Accounting Review*, Vol. 79, No. 2, pp. 329–353.

Chang, K. (2015). The impact of environmental information disclosure on performance — An empirical analysis based on the cross-sectional data of china's heavy pollution industry, *Finance and Economics*, No. 1, pp. 71–77.

Dixon, S. and Clifford, A. (2007). Ecopreneurship — A new approach to managing the triple bottom line, *Journal of Organizational Change Management*, Vol. 20, No. 3, pp. 326–345.

Dai, Y. and Shi, M. G. (2019). The effect of enterprise environmental information disclosure on performance — Based on the empirical evidence of listed companies in heavy pollution industry, *Ecological Economy*, Vol. 35, No. 6, pp. 162–169.

Dong, S. L., Zou, A. N. and Liu, B. M. (2018). Research on the relationship between social trust, carbon information disclosure and enterprise performance — Based on China's urban business credit CEI index, *Friends of Accounting*, No. 21, pp. 74–78.

Elkington, J. (1994). Towards the sustainable corporation: Win-win-win business strategies for sustainable development, *California Management Review*, Vol. 36, No. 2, pp. 90–100.

Freeman, R. E. (1984). Strategic management: A stakeholder approach, *Journal of Management Studies*, Vol. 29, No. 2, pp. 131–154.

Gray, R., Javad, M., Power, D. and Sinclair, D. (2001). Social and environmental disclosure and corporate characteristics: A research note and extension, *Journal of Business Finance & Accounting*, Vol. 28, No. 3–4, pp. 327–356.

Ganda, F. (2018). The influence of carbon emissions disclosure on company financial value in an emerging economy, *Environment Development and Sustainability*, Vol. 20, No. 4, pp. 1723–1738.

Karaman, A. S., Kilic, M. and Uyar, A. (2020). Green logistics performance and sustainability reporting practises of the logistics sector: The moderating effect of corporate governance, *Journal of Cleaner Production*, Vol. 258.

Lanoie, P., Laplante, B. and Roy, M. (1998). Can capital markets create incentives for pollution control? *Ecological Economics*, Vol. 26, No. 1, pp. 31–41.

Li, L, Yang, Y. H. and Tang, D. L. (2015). Carbon information disclosure of enterprises and their value creation through market liquidity and cost of equity capital, *Journal of Industrial Engineering and Management*, Vol. 8, No. 1, pp. 137–151.

Li, X. Y. and Shi, Y. Y. (2016). Green development, quality and performance of carbon information disclosure, *Economic Management*, Vol. 38, No. 7, pp. 119–132.

Lü, J. and Jiao, S. Y. (2011). An empirical study on the relationship between environmental disclosure, environmental performance and performance, *Journal of Shanxi University of Finance and Economics*, Vol. 33, No. 1, pp. 109–116.

Lü, M. H., Xu, G. H., Shen, Y. and Qian, M. (2018). Heterogeneous debt governance, contractual incompleteness and environmental information disclosure, *Accounting Research*, No. 5, pp. 67–74.

Liu, H. Y. and Zheng, S. (2021). Experience and policy suggestions on greenhouse gas emission information disclosure, *Climate Change Research Exhibition*, pp. 1–11.

Margolis, J. D. and Walsh, J. P. (2001). *People and Profits? The Search for a link between a Company's Social and Financial Performance*, Taylor and Francis.

Marrewijk, M. V. (2003). Concepts and definitions of CSR and corporate sustainability: Between agency and communion, *Journal of Business Ethics*, Vol. 44, pp. 95–105.

Norman, W. and MacDonald, C. (2004). Getting to the bottom of "triple bottom line, *Business Ethics Quarterly*, Vol. 14, pp. 243–262.

Patten, D. M. and Trompeter, G. (2003). Corporate responses to political costs: An examination of the relation between environmental disclosure and earnings management, *Journal of Accounting and Public Policy*, Vol. 22, No. 1, pp. 83–94.

Pan, S. Q. and Wang, F. (2019). Can the level of carbon information disclosure improve the financial performance of enterprises — Empirical experience based on shanghai stock exchange a shares, *Journal of Anhui Normal University*, Vol. 47, No. 6, pp. 133–141.

Shen, H. T. and Feng, J. (2012). Public opinion supervision, government supervision and enterprise environmental information disclosure, *Accounting Research*, No. 2, pp. 72–78, 97.

Shen, H. T., Huang, Z. and Guo, F. R. (2014). Confession or defense-A study on the relationship between enterprise environmental performance and environmental information disclosure, *Nankai Management Review*, Vol. 17, No. 2, pp. 56–63, 73.

Saka, C. and Oshika, T. (2014). Disclosure effects, carbon emissions and corporate value, *Sustainability Accounting Management & Policy Journal*, Vol. 5, No. 1, pp. 22–45(24).

Tang, Y. L., Chen, Z. L., Liu, X. and Li, W. H. (2006). Empirical study on environmental information disclosure and influencing factors of listed companies in China, *Management World*, No. 1, pp. 158–159.

Tian, Y. and Song, Y. J. (2019). Carbon information disclosure, earnings quality and financial performance of heavily polluting enterprises, *Accounting Communication*, No. 3, pp. 87–91.

Wegener, M. (2010). *The Carbon Disclosure Project, an Evolution in International Environmental Corporate Governance: Motivations and Determinants of Market Response to Voluntary Disclosures*. Brock University.

Wang, X., Xu, X. D. and Wang, C. (2013). Public pressure, social reputation, internal governance and corporate environmental information disclosure — Evidence from Chinese manufacturing listed companies, *Nankai Management Review*, Vol. 16, No. 2, pp. 82–91.

Yan, Q., Shaukat, A. and Tharyan, R. (2016). Environmental and social disclosures: Link with corporate financial performance, *The British Accounting Review*, Vol. 48, No. 1.

Yin, F. (2006). Research on the relationship between voluntary information disclosure and earnings performance of listed companies, *Financial and Accounting Newsletter (Academic Edition)*, No. 3, pp. 3–5, 12.

Zhang, C. C. and Chen, H. C. (2017). Product market competition, property right nature and internal control quality, *Accounting Research*, No. 5, pp. 75–82, 97.

Zhang, Y. J. and Wang, B. (2015). Research on the relationship between voluntary environmental information disclosure and financial performance in heavy pollution industry, *Accounting Communication*, No. 24, pp. 72–75.

Zhao, C. L. (2019). Research on the impact of corporate social responsibility on performance, *Northeast University of Finance and Economics*, Vol. 01, No. 1, pp. 83–84.

Zhu, W., Sun, Y. X. and Tang, Q. (2019). Substantive disclosure or selective disclosure: The impact of corporate environmental performance on the quality of environmental information disclosure, *Accounting Research*, No. 3, pp. 10–17.

Chapter 11

Board Directors' Home Regions and Social Disclosure: Evidence from French Firms Listed in SBF 120

Nadia Ben Farhat Toumi and Rim Khemiri

Abstract

This chapter examines the impact of directors' home regions on employee human rights policy (EHRP) disclosure in the French context. We classify foreign directors into four home regions, namely, Anglo-American, European, Asian, and Middle Eastern regions. Logistic regression analyses are conducted, referring to a sample of 73 French firms that were listed on the Euronext Paris Stock Exchange and members of the SBF 120 index over the period from 2008 to 2018. EHRP disclosure data are collected from the Bloomberg database and indicate whether the firm has disclosed EHRP information in its annual report or CSR statement. Results provide evidence that board home region diversity is positively and significantly associated with EHRP disclosure. Results also show that the presence of Anglo-American and Asian directors is positively associated with EHRP disclosure. Surprisingly, European directors are less concerned about EHRP disclosure. Furthermore, we provide evidence that there is no relationship between the presence of directors from the Middle East and EHRP disclosure. The chapter highlights the need to reconsider the composition of French boards by promoting the presence of directors from different home regions. Specifically, the authors support the recommendations of the AFEP-MEDEF (2020) regarding the need to intensify international recruitment when selecting new board members.

Keywords: Employee human rights policy disclosure; CSR, directors' home regions; board diversity, Anglo-American; European; Asian; Middle Eastern directors

1. Introduction

France is often thought of as a strike-prone country, especially its private sector. Institutes reveal that France remains among the leading countries in terms of social movements. There were 118 days of strikes per year per 1,000 employees between 2008 and 2017.[1] Among the more recent social protests highlighting growing inequalities among employees is the *"gilets jaunes"* (Yellow Jackets or Vests) movement. This social movement has prompted companies to reconsider their corporate social responsibility (CSR) strategies by strengthening their commitments to their employees. Specifically, companies demonstrate greater concern for the rights of their employees by investing in social practises that protect employees' interests. In the past decade, companies have increasingly applied CSR to ensure their employees' satisfaction. This is manifested notably through CSR reporting which is viewed as a privileged tool for dialogue with employees and trade unions alike (Campbell, 2007).

We advance on the premise that CSR reporting is likely to improve transparency as to the social impacts of company activities. Social disclosure relates to both the quantity and the quality of information that is reported. Points covered include professional equality, awareness raising and training about non-discrimination, recruitment of disabled people, and employee rights. This study focuses on "employee human rights policy" in the form of initiatives implemented to ensure the protection of all workers' rights. This information indicates whether a company has disclosed such initiatives in its annual report or CSR statement. Employee human rights policy (EHRP) is a component of the social index and so part of the ESG index. It provides useful information about the prevention of all forms of discrimination, the exercise of trade unionism, the improvement of labour conditions, and the prohibition of child labour.

Earlier studies have argued that CSR policies are usually developed and approved by the board of directors (Katmon *et al.*, 2019; Muttakin *et al.*, 2018). Consistent with the academic literature, directors' profiles, including factors such as their background, gender,

---

[1]https://www.boeckler.de/pdf/p_wsi_pb_31_2019.pdf.

or nationality, might influence the CSR decision-making process. After the recent economic crisis and the changes in international markets, it has been widely recommended that companies recruit foreign directors with international skills and experience for their boards of directors (Dardour *et al.*, 2018). The literature on board composition has usually stated that foreign directors have a positive influence on CSR practises (Harjoto *et al.*, 2018; Kang *et al.*, 2019). Coming from different institutions, regions, and cultures, they convey their own values, norms, and behaviours which determine their attitudes (Chang *et al.*, 2017; Cheung *et al.*, 2010; Harjoto *et al.*, 2015; Zhang *et al.*, 2013). According to Masulis *et al.* (2012), foreign directors' expertise in their home countries and their ties to local business, social, and political circles can all be valuable for host companies.

In line with the above, this study addresses the following question: *Does a board with home region diversity have an impact on employee human rights policy disclosure?* More specifically, we examine the effect of the presence of directors from Anglo-American, European, Asian, and Middle Eastern regions on EHRP disclosure by French companies. By home regions, we refer to the country from which the directors of the board of directors originates. This information is provided in the annual report of the companies: it is referred to as nationality or citizenship. We have categorised the regions according to the purpose of our research. The first classification concerns the differences between the European and Anglo-American governance models (La Porta *et al.*, 2008; Sison, 2009). The second category is based on the United Nations classifications: the Asian and Middle Eastern countries.

We study a sample of French companies listed on the stock exchange during the period 2008–2018. France can boast of some highly developed legal reforms in the CSR field (Statement on extra-financial performance, 2017; Grenelle Law, 2007, 2010; NRE, 2001) and high CSR rankings (eighth in the European ranking in 2018). In achieving a greater commitment to CSR at the European and international levels, France also established a specialised form of diplomacy on CSR attached to the Ministry for Europe and Foreign Affairs. Moreover, French companies are recognised as a benchmark in terms of working conditions, social protection, and human rights within the company or the community. Hence, French employees are considered legal citizens. This notion of employee citizenship has been incorporated into legislation to strengthen workers' rights in companies (Rey, 1980). Our sample period (2008–2018) covers these regulations.

Drawing on the resource-based view (RBV) of the firm as well as on intergroup contact theory and institutional theory, this study provides empirical evidence of the impact of directors' home regions on this specific aspect of CSR. Indeed, results indicate that the presence of Anglo-American directors is positively associated with EHRP disclosure. This finding is consistent with institutional theory, which argues that managers are likely to imitate their business counterparts, complying with the regulators and following the institutional understandings of the host firm (Jackson and Apostolakou, 2010; Humphreys and Brown 2008). Surprisingly, European directors are less concerned about EHRP disclosure. Given the implicit importance of the social dimension in Europe, it appears that Europeans do not feel the need to disclose information relating to employees' rights. In addition, directors from Asian countries are positively and significantly associated with the social dimension. On the other hand, directors from Middle Eastern countries have not affected this dimension. Overall, the results suggest that disclosure of EHRP depends on home regions.

Studying this issue results in several significant contributions. First, this is one of a small number of studies that focus on directors' home regions. Each region is characterised by an institutional system with specific cultural values (Jamali *et al.*, 2020; Matten and Moon, 2008). Therefore, because CSR practises vary across regions and countries, directors act and interpret CSR information differently. In addition, foreign directors' background with respect to social and environmental commitments can promote and protect the interests of employees in the company. Second, previous studies have generally focused on the impact of the diversity of nationalities on CSR. This study contributes to the CSR literature by going beyond this relationship and specifically documenting the impact of

Anglo-American, European, Asian, and Middle Eastern directors on employees' human rights policy disclosure. Thus, it is important to consider that this impact differs with each directors' home region. Third, our study contributes to the literature on corporate boards and governance by identifying a new characteristic of directors that affects CSR disclosure. We supplement earlier studies of board characteristics by highlighting the importance of a director's home region in relation to CSR. Our analysis provides evidence that the expertise of directors from Anglo-American and Asian countries benefits French firms releasing CSR information. Finally, this is the first study to associate this new attribute of directors (their home region) with CSR disclosure.

The remainder of this chapter is structured as follows. The second section reviews the relevant literature and the theoretical foundation in order to develop our hypotheses. The third section describes the sample, data, and models. The fourth section reports and discusses the main empirical findings. Finally, the fifth section concludes.

2. Literature Review and Development of Hypotheses

We start our literature review by shedding light on EHRP. We then investigate home region diversity and CSR by relying on resource-based theory, intergroup contact theory, and institutional theory.

2.1. *Employee human rights policy*

A company's employees are regarded as key to long-term sustainable operations and as primary stakeholders (Freeman, 1984). Firms that purport to behave in a highly ethical manner towards their workforce are likely to be perceived as more socially responsible (Cohen *et al.*, 2012). The concept of responsibility towards the workforce is rather a process of satisfying institutionalised norms relating to the interests of employees through collective negotiation. These negotiations are carried forward through trade union organisations. Trade union activity on an international scale (Wailes *et al.*, 2011) has promoted the standardisation of labour practises in companies and has emerged as an important practise for CSR (Lee *et al.*, 2013;

Shen and Zhu, 2011). Trade unions in Europe can employ a variety of mechanisms to influence CSR policy within companies. For example, French trade unions have strong links with the principal political parties. Such processes are likely to be more effective in protecting workers' human rights. Therefore, CSR activities are the result of the adoption of laws from agreements negotiated and signed by corporate governance and trade union organisations (Barreau and Arnal, 2010; Sobczak and Havard, 2015).

Previous studies have found that workers are very demanding in terms of human rights (Chauhan and Chauhan, 2008). Underestimating the importance of these rights can generate dissatisfaction and strikes (Rosati *et al.*, 2018), negatively impacting productivity and harming firms' reputations (Parsa *et al.*, 2018). By adopting EHRP, a company has the opportunity to improve workers' motivation, resulting in a greater likelihood that employees will meet the company's targets. Regulation levels and implementation mechanisms that protect employees' rights are considerably stronger and more widely developed in Western countries than in developing countries (Crane and Matten 2010; McPhail and Ferguson, 2016). Differences between countries concerning EHRP disclosure are not uncommon. Thus, the perception of this social aspect will be different among directors given the cultural and institutional differences across regions. Gallhofer, Haslam, and Van Der Walt *et al.* (2011) highlight the importance of mechanisms of corporate governance, such as the role played by the board of directors in the promotion and the protection of employees' human rights. These rights are an indispensable element of CSR according to the international legal framework (Human Rights Council, 2011). Therefore, the board, as the ultimate decision-making group, significantly influences CSR activities (Dawkins and Lewis, 2003; Waddock and Graves, 1997). In the case of board characteristics, empirical studies observed that the presence of foreign directors can affect CSR disclosure (Dardour *et al.*, 2018; Katmon *et al.*, 2019), CSR performance (Béji *et al.*, 2020), or a philanthropic practise (Kang *et al.*, 2019). Thus, the presence of directors from different home regions can also affect the disclosure of CSR and subsequently the EHRP disclosure.

2.2. *Home region diversity and CSR*

The diversity of demographic characteristics of the board, such as directors' nationalities, has positive effects on CSR disclosure (Katmon *et al.*, 2019). Specifically, foreign directors may provide new perspectives, enhance board effectiveness, and provide a higher potential for taking advantage of opportunities (Béji *et al.*, 2020; Estelyi and Nisar, 2016; Hahn and Lasfer, 2016).

Previous literature on the relationship between board diversity and CSR generally relies on resource-based theory (RBV) (Barney 1991; Branco and Rodrigues 2006). From an RBV perspective, the board provides a competitive advantage and contains resources that are valuable, rare, inimitable, and difficult to substitute (Galbreath, 2016; Katmon *et al.*, 2019; Yu and Choi, 2016). Moreover, RBV theory supports the idea that the heterogeneity of resources and competencies are valuable company resources (Rao and Tilt, 2016). This is necessary to improve the effectiveness of the board of directors and corporate policy-making processes, including corporate CSR information (Galbreath, 2005; Hahn and Lasfer, 2016; Hoopes *et al.*, 2003). Board nationality diversity, and by extension home region diversity, could constitute a valuable source of international information and experience required to promote CSR. Foreign directors are supposed to improve the CSR disclosure of a company by virtue of their previous experience with CSR in international markets (Estelyi and Nisar, 2016; Harjoto *et al.*, 2018). Their recruitment could provide access to new international opportunities and generate economic and political ties that might contribute to more socially responsible activities. According to Béji *et al.* (2020), the presence of foreign directors has a positive impact on environmental performance and community involvement. Their presence on the board increases its monitoring role and improves strategic decisions related to public and social activities as well as their reporting (Kang *et al.*, 2019; Muttakin *et al.*, 2015). Moreover, board directors are also considered to be working groups that supervise management's activities with respect to CSR. In line with intergroup contact theory, diversity could improve group performance, as members of a diverse team provide a greater source of knowledge, perspectives, ideas, and conflict-resolution skills, which improves group performance capacity. In fact, cross-cultural studies have shown that diverse groups composed of people from different cultural backgrounds or even home regions are more likely to have a cooperative orientation and to diminish individualistic behaviour than a homogeneous team does. This may affect the group decision-making process. A few empirical studies show that boards with origin diversity are likely to improve CSR (Harjoto *et al.*, 2018; Katmon *et al.*, 2019; Rao and Tilt, 2016). Furthermore, in this study, diversity refers to affiliation to home regions. Nevertheless, the presence of foreign directors may not be positive for the board. In fact, Katmon *et al.* (2017) argue that the presence of different nationalities on the board generates intercultural communication issues and is likely to have a negative influence on CSR (Branco and Rodrigues, 2008).

Both RBV and intergroup contact theory support the view that a diverse board affects CSR disclosure. We argue that Anglo-American, European, Asian, and Middle Eastern directors could bring in different perspectives that contribute to robust decision-making and the development of a social practise. More specifically, this is EHRP disclosure. Therefore, we look to test the following hypothesis:

Hypothesis 1: A board with home region diversity is positively associated with employee human rights policy disclosure.

2.3. *Institutional theory and CSR*

2.3.1. *Anglo-American versus European directors and CSR*

Foreign directors have diverse values and cultural contexts according to their origin or regions, which implies different institutional settings on the board. These institutional and cultural differences may or may not generate greater involvement in CSR disclosure and practises (Jamali *et al.*, 2020; La Porta *et al.*, 1998, 2008; Matten and Moon, 2008). A cluster of clues suggests that institutional differences, such as norms and cultural context (Ball and Craig, 2010), a nation's history (La Porta *et al.*, 1998; Sison, 2009), the business system (Jackson and Apostolakou, 2010; Jamali *et al.*, 2020), and corporate governance mechanisms (Harjoto *et al.*, 2018; Kang *et al.*, 2019) influence CSR practises and disclosure.

Consistent with Sison (2009) and Matten and Moon (2008), we argue that there are differences in the interpretation of the CSR concept from Anglo-American and European perspectives. The European approach can be described as stakeholder-oriented, less results-driven, and thus inclined towards a civic republican or communitarian type. Anglo-American culture is inclined towards what is described as individualistic, shareholder-oriented, and subsequently more results-driven. Most earlier studies argue that directors from Anglo-American countries are less engaged in CSR activities (Harjoto *et al.*, 2018; Kang *et al.*, 2019) and are more protective of shareholders' interests. However, these authors found also that directors from European countries improve CSR and represent both shareholders and stakeholders. Overall, these studies indicate that the presence of European directors is positively related to CSR. The preceding discussion suggests that Anglo-American directors are negatively associated with CSR. Therefore, they would be less likely to release social information such as EHRP disclosure. As a result, we have the following:

Hypothesis 2: *The presence of directors from Anglo-American countries is negatively associated with employee human rights policy disclosure.*

Hypothesis 3: *There is a positive relationship between the presence of European directors and employee human rights policy disclosure.*

2.3.2. *Asian directors and CSR*

Previous literature revealed that CSR is entrenched in Western or Anglo-American norms and regulations (Peters *et al.*, 2011; Sison, 2000). Nevertheless, CSR is a universal concept, whose understanding and practises differ according to economic, social, and cultural environments (Munro, 2013; Chapple and Moon, 2005). Prior literature in emerging countries revealed that culture and institutional contexts influence CSR practises (Maurice and Sorge, 2000; Nguyen *et al.*, 2018; Preuss and Barkemeyer, 2011). Previous studies argue that the implementation and nature of CSR in emerging markets differs considerably from that of their counterparts in mature economies (Shaomin *et al.*, 2010; Munro, 2013; Katmon *et al.*, 2019). Emerging countries are characterised by weak institutional structures, weak application of norms and regulations, and corruption (Chapple and Moon, 2005; Nguyen *et al.*, 2018). Thus, CSR adoption in emerging markets is perceived as challenging, given the conflicting social, environmental, and governance issues involved (Chapple and Moon, 2005). Through international markets, emerging countries are more exposed to ideas and culture from Western countries and Europe. This provides different perspectives about global issues, such as climate change and labour rights. This may be a factor in driving CSR-related changes in social attitudes. As a result, citizens from emerging countries are likely to be more concerned about social and environmental issues (Chapple and Moon, 2005).

Recently, studies in emerging economies have argued that environmental and ethical concerns have significantly increased in emerging markets, especially in Asia (Khan *et al.*, 2013; Kang *et al.*, 2019). One of the motivations for this rising attention is the growing interconnection between Asian and Western economies as well as the specific CSR norms and behaviours that are due to institutional and cultural differences (Wang and Coffey, 1992; Post *et al.*, 2011; Chang *et al.*, 2017; Kang *et al.*, 2019). Therefore, citizens of Asian countries will be more likely to be engaged in socially responsible activities. For this research, Asian directors were classified by geographical region (Chapple and Moon, 2005; Baughn *et al.*, 2007; Munro, 2013).

Consequently, in line with the previous studies mentioned above, we draw the fourth hypothesis as follows:

Hypothesis 4: There is a positive relationship between the presence of Asian directors and employee human rights policy disclosure.

2.3.3. *Middle Eastern directors and CSR*

According to Jamali and Sidani (2011), CSR in the Middle East has been growing in importance in recent years. Middle Eastern companies, which are more characterised by philanthropy and charity, have shifted their focus to social and environmental issues that affect development and economic challenges (Daaja and Szabados, 2018). Moreover, philanthropy is the most common feature of the corporate social framework in the Middle East.

Prior studies in the Middle Eastern market revealed that the principal objective of adopting CSR activities is to increase a company's reputation, including better relations with stakeholders and the community (Yawar, 2009). The Middle East depends on its natural resources but some countries remain affected by political and macroeconomic instability. Consequently, there is a significant difference among Middle Eastern nations in applying and practising CSR (Amran *et al.*, 2013; Robertson, 2009; Jamali and Karam, 2018). Thus, citizens of Middle Eastern countries will be more likely to be more responsive to CSR commitments according to their culture and institutional contexts. For this study, Middle Eastern directors were defined by the geographical area that includes the territory of the UAE, Israel, Lebanon, Saudi Arabia, Egypt, Iraq, Qatar, Jordan, and Iran (Tranfield *et al.*, 2003; Koleva, 2018).

Due to the lack of sufficient studies about the association between the presence of directors from Middle Eastern countries and CSR involvement in the French context and in line with institutional theory, we develop the following hypothesis:

Hypothesis 5: There is a relationship between the presence of directors from the Middle East and employee human rights policy disclosure.

3. Methodology

3.1. *Sample and data sources*

The initial sample consists of all French listed firms belonging to the SBF 120 index during the period from 2008 to 2018. The SBF

Table 1.   Sample selection process.

Initial sample (119 listed SBF 120 companies)	**119**
• Firms no longer in the index	11
• Firms belonging to the financial sector	7
• Firms whose annual report does not mention any information on the nationality of its directors	13
• Firms with missing data	15
Total sample	**73**

120 index is one of the benchmark indices in the Euronext Paris market. It represents more than 75% of the market capitalisation of the Paris stock market and includes the largest French firms in terms of market capitalisation and liquidity. All the data were collected from the Bloomberg database, and the nationality of each director was identified from annual reports. For directors with several nationalities, our selection was based on the first nationality. Missing data were completed using various reference documents from listed companies. In all, 119 listed SBF 120 companies are rated by Bloomberg, mainly from 2008 onwards. Due to the unavailability of some data, the final sample is made up of 73 companies observed over the years 2008 to 2018, yielding 803 observations (Table 1).

The industry distribution of companies, based on the international Industry Classification Benchmark (ICB)[2] classification, is reported in Table 2. In order to avoid the workforce being too small by sector, companies were grouped under five headings: technology, media, industry, services, and other sectors. As shown in Table 2, the industry distribution is marked by a strong overrepresentation of firms in the manufacturing sector (61.64% of the sample), while media companies are poorly represented (6.85% of the sample).

---

[2]The classification was created by FTSE Group and Dow Jones Index. It came into force on January 2, 2006, for all companies listed in Amsterdam, Brussels, Lisbon, and Paris. This new sector coding breaks companies down into 10 industries, 18 super-sectors, 39 sectors, and 104 sub-sectors.

Table 2. Sample distribution by industry.

Industry	Number of observations	Number of firms	Percentage of firms
Technology	88	8	**10.96**
Media	55	5	**6.85**
Manufacturing	495	45	**61.64**
Services	88	8	**10.96**
Other sectors	77	7	**9.59**
Total	**803**	**73**	**100.00**

3.2. *Measures*

We classify home regions of directors based on five categories. First, we use the studies by La Porta *et al.* (1998, 2008) and by Matten and Moon (2008) to classify countries according to corporate governance models. Thus, as we have a European and Anglo-American approach, we classify directors from European countries in the "European Region" category and directors from Anglo-American countries in the "Anglo-American Region" category. Next, we classify the directors from Asian and Middle Eastern countries into two different regions based on the United Nations' regional classifications.[3] Finally, for directors from regions that are very poorly represented in our sample, we classify them in the "Other Regions" category.

To measure the diversity of directors' home regions, we use Blau's heterogeneity index (1977). This is one of the most commonly used indicators of variation in categorical data. It is calculated using the following formula:

$$1 - \sum_{i=1}^{N} Pi^2,$$

where P is the share of individuals in a category and N is the number of categories.

---

[3]https://www.un.org/en/sections/where-we-work/index.html.

As set out in this formula, for a variable with five possible categories (e.g. home regions), if only one category is to be found on the board (same home regions), then the Blau index is equal to zero. This index reaches a maximum value of 0.2 when directors are perfectly balanced between these five categories (20% European, 20% Anglo-American, 20% Middle Eastern, 20% Asian, and 20% other regions). Table 3 defines the variables that were selected, their meaning, and their measures.

Based on previous studies, we include several features of the boards and the companies that are found to be related to CSR activities. Size is an often used variable for monitoring firm size. The larger the firm, the more pressure it encounters in terms of satisfying stakeholders' expectations in social CSR activities (Gallo and Christensen, 2011; Katmon *et al.*, 2019; Levy *et al.*, 2010; Waddock and Graves, 1997). We also monitor firm age (AGE) because the company's visibility and pressure from the public become more important as the firm grows, driving it to engage in more social CSR activities (Harjoto *et al.*, 2018; Kang *et al.*, 2019). We include debt ratio (RD) and ROA since financial resources and conditions can affect business investment in CSR (Barnea and Rubin, 2010; Hillman *et al.*, 2001). We also consider board characteristics, such as board size (BS), because larger boards are more likely to operate effectively on issues related to CSR activities (Chang *et al.*, 2017; Jizi, 2017; Rahman and Bukair, 2013). Finally, we monitor board independence (PIN) (Jo and Harjoto, 2011; Katmon *et al.*, 2019) expecting that companies with greater board independence will enhance involvement in more CSR activities. Table 3 defines the variables selected, their meaning, and their measures.

3.3. *Empirical model*

Several logistic regressions were performed on the panel data to study the impact of directors' home region on EHRP disclosure (EHRP_D). The logistic regressions are justified by the fact that our dependent variable is a binary variable. A total of six estimates of our model were performed. Model 1 of directors' home region diversity

Table 3. Variables, definitions, and sources.

Variable	Measure	Definition	Source	Authors
Dependent variable				
Employee Human Rights Policy	**EHRP_D**	The disclosure of a policy to ensure protection of the rights of all of its workers 1 if the company has disclosed this initiative, 0 if not	*Bloomberg*	
Independent variables				
Blau-Home regions	*Blau-HR*	Blau Index of home regions diversity on the board	*Annual report of listed companies*	Dardour et al. (2018), Harjoto et al. (2018), Katmon et al. (2019); Porta et al. (1998);
% European directors	**PrE**	The percentage of European directors on the board		
% Anglo-American directors	**PrANGAM**	The percentage of Anglo-American directors		Matten and Moon (2008)
% Middle East directors	**PrME**	The percentage of directors from the Middle East on the board		*United Nations' regional classifications*
% Asian directors	**PrAS**	Percentage of directors from Asia on the board		*United Nations' regional classifications*
% Other regions	**PrOR**	The percentage of other home regions on the board		Author's classifications

(*Continued*)

Table 3. *(Continued)*

Variable	Measure	Definition	Source	Authors
Control variables				
	SIZE	The logarithm of the total workforce	*DataStream*	Waddock and Graves (1997)
	AGE	The age of the firm calculated from the date of creation of the company until 2018	*Company's website*	Khan *et al.* (2013)
	RD	The ratio of total debt to total assets	*Datastream*	Kang *et al.* (2019), Harjoto (2018)
	PIN	Percentage of independent directors	*Datastream*	Jo and Harjoto, (2011)
	ROA	Return on Assets	*Datastream*	Campbell (2007)
	BS	The number of directors on the Board	*Datastream*	Jizi (2017), Chang *et al.* (2019)
Business Sectors	T	Technology		
	ME	Media		
	IND	Industry		
	SE	Services		
	ASEC	Other sectors		

is presented as follows:

$$(EHRP\_D)_{it} = \beta_0 + \beta_1(Blau\text{-}Home\ regions)_{it} + \beta_2(SIZE)_{it}$$
$$+ \beta_3(AGE)_{it} + \beta_4(RD)_{it} + \beta_5(PIN)_{it}$$
$$+ \beta_6(ROA)_{it} + \beta_7(BS)_{it}\beta_8(T)_{it} + \beta_9(ME)_{it}$$
$$+ \beta_{10}(IND)_{it} + \beta_{11}(SE)_{it} + \beta_{12}(OSEC)_{it} + \varepsilon_{it}.$$

4. Results and Discussion

4.1. *Descriptive statistics*

Table 4 presents descriptive statistics for all variables that are used in this study. We note that 78.46% of the companies in the sample chose to disclose EHRP, compared to 21.54% that did not. We further show that the average percentage of European directors (0.868) is higher than the percentage scores for directors of other regions. This result can be explained by a higher proportion of European directors on boards of companies listed on the SBF 120. We further observe that the diversity index of the Blau-Home regions variable is, on average, equal to 0.207. Regarding the characteristics of the companies, the performance indicators reveal that the average rate of return on equity is 4.50%. The average debt ratio of the companies is 29.10%, and it may be zero for some companies. The average age of the companies is 83.65 years, and it varies between 2 and 387 years. The percentage of independent directors is, on average, 52.64%, which indicates that the companies respect the governance codes. In fact, the proportion of independent directors should be half of the board members in companies with dispersed capital and no controlling shareholders (AFEP-MEDEF, 2020).

Table 5 provides the correlation matrix for all variables. The correlation analysis does not highlight any major problems. The only issue of concern is the percentage of European directors (prE) and the percentage of Anglo-American directors (prANGAM) that are significantly and negatively correlated ($-0.917^* > 0.8$). To ensure that this does not unduly affect the results, the logistic analysis was performed without these two variables in the same model.

Table 4.   Descriptive statistics.

Continuous variables	N	Mean	Q1	Q2	Q3	Std. Dev	Minimum	Maximum
Independent variables								
Blau-HR	803	0.207	0.000	0.193	0.320	0.165	0.000	0.640
E	803	12.039	10	12	15	3.348	2	21
prE	803	0.868	0.800	0.894	1.000	0.121	0.400	1.000
ANGAM	803	1.313	0	1	2	1.205	0	5
prANGAM	803	0.101	0.000	0.076	0.153	0.101	0.000	0.444
ME	803	0.034	0	0	0	0.196	0	2
prME	803	0.002	0.000	0.000	0.000	0.014	0.000	0.200
AS	803	0.169	0	0	0	0.464	0	3
prAS	803	0.012	0.000	0.000	0.000	0.035	0.000	0.250
OR	803	0.202	0	0	0	0.446	0	2
prOR	803	0.015	0.000	0.000	0.000	0.033	0.000	0.166
Control variables								
SIZE	803	10.258	9.318	10.553	11.579	1.666	5.929	13.073
AGE	803	83.656	35.000	59.000	116.000	72.436	2.000	387.000
ROA	803	4.509	2.336	4.370	6.557	5.634	−49.595	48.319
RD	803	0.291	0.161	0.254	0.393	0.242	0.000	2.537
PIN	803	52.642	40.000	50.000	66.000	18.434	0.000	100.000
BS	803	13.760	11.000	14.000	16.000	3.024	5.000	22.000

Binary variables	Frequencies
Dependent variable EHRP_D	78.46
Control variables	
T	10.96
ME	6.85
IND	61.64
SE	10.96
ASEC	9.59

Notes: All variable definitions are presented in Table 3. Table 5 shows ***, **, and * as significant at the 0.01, 0.05, and 0.10 levels, respectively. The **E, ANGAM, ME, AS**, and **OR** regions represent the number of European directors, Anglo-American directors, Middle East directors, Asian directors, and other regions, directors, on the board, respectively.

Table 5. Correlation matrix.

Variable	EHRP_D	Blau-HR	prE	prANGAM	prME	prAS	prOR	SIZE	AGE
EHRP_D	1.000								
Blau-HR	−0.033	1.000							
prE	0.046	−0.979***	1.000						
prANGAM	−0.059*	0.880***	−0.917***	1.000					
prME	0.045	0.176***	−0.149***	0.022	1.000				
prAS	−0.000	0.305***	−0.282***	0.022	−0.043	1.000			
prOR	−0.008	0.476***	−0.473***	0.259***	0.082**	−0.098***	1.000		
SIZE	0.391***	−0.001	0.042	−0.065*	0.084**	0.078**	−0.077**	1.000	
AGE	0.154***	−0.000	0.016	−0.005	0.059*	−0.039	−0.028	0.335***	1.000
ROA	−0.083**	0.006	−0.007	0.051	0.059*	−0.187***	0.046	−0.049	0.028
RD	−0.141***	−0.082**	0.075**	−0.070**	0.112***	−0.076***	−0.026	−0.171***	0.082**
PIN	0.038	0.298***	−0.276***	0.208***	0.043	0.191***	0.146***	0.012	−0.114***
BS	0.222***	−0.196***	0.248***	−0.270***	0.050	−0.049	−0.051	0.231***	0.158***
T	0.036	−0.031	0.029	−0.024	0.015	−0.067*	0.035	−0.005	−0.112***
ME	−0.121***	−0.064*	0.071**	−0.036	0.017	−0.051	−0.103***	−0.235***	−0.045
IND	0.022	0.069**	−0.070**	0.044	−0.177***	0.114***	0.077**	0.054	0.100**
SE	0.048	0.001	0.007	−0.022	0.194***	−0.042	0.001	0.093***	0.184***
ASEC	−0.024	0.0292	−0.031	0.052	0.062	−0.016	−0.054	−0.029	−0.172***

(*Continued*)

Table 5. (*Continued*).

Variable	ROA	RD	PIN	BS	T	ME	IND	SE	ASE
EHRP_D									
Blau-HR									
prE									
prANGAM									
prME									
prAS									
prOR									
SIZE									
AGE									
ROA	1.000								
RD	0.195***	1.000							
PIN	−0.158***	−0.079**	1.000						
BS	−0.062*	0.078**	−0.151***	1.000					
T	−0.086**	0.006	0.122***	−0.107***	1.000				
ME	0.256***	0.202***	−0.035	0.006	−0.088**	1.000			
IND	−0.001	−0.139***	−0.020	−0.066*	−0.412***	−0.343***	1.000		
SE	−0.114***	0.044	−0.123***	0.172***	−0.114***	−0.095***	−0.444***	1.000	
ASEC	−0.006	−0.022	0.089**	0.011	−0.106**	−0.088**	−0.412***	−0.114***	1.000

Notes: All variable definitions are presented in Table 3. ***, **, and * significant at the 0.01, 0.05, and 0.10 levels, respectively.

4.2. *Logistic regression results*

In cases where the variable to be explained is binary, it is recommended that logistic regression be used. The results are presented in Table 6. A total of six models were tested. The results of our models will be interpreted on the basis of both the regression coefficient (β) and its statistical significance (p).

4.2.1. *The effect of home region diversity on employee human rights policy disclosure*

The logistic analysis presented in Table 6 shows that the basic model (Model 1) is globally significant. The positive and significant coefficient of the Blau_Home region index ($\beta1 = 2.381$; $p = 0.056$) indicates a significant and positive influence of home region diversity on EHRP disclosure (EHRP_D) of listed companies. This result is consistent with our first hypothesis and with earlier empirical studies (Chang *et al.*, 2017; Dardour *et al.*, 2018; Harjoto *et al.*, 2018; Hoang and Abeysekera, 2016; Jo and Harjoto, 2011). The first interpretation is that home region diversity is a valuable asset to the firm and that is rare, tough to imitate, and not easy to replace. It contributes to attaining competitive advantage through the consideration of CSR, especially EHRP disclosure. CSR is therefore an important element of corporate strategy leading to competitive advantages, innovation, and opportunities. The second interpretation is compatible with intergroup theory which suggests that counterfactual experiences enhance group decision-making and performance. This explanation is consistent with Harjoto *et al.* (2018), who argue that foreign directors from diverse cultures (Anglo-American, Europe, Asian, Middle Eastern) behave more cooperatively than culturally homogeneous groups. A board that is heterogeneous in terms of skills and international experience enhances the board's functions and strengthens relationships with stakeholders. This enables the improvement of CSR disclosure (Katmon *et al.*, 2019). Our results support partially the institutional theory, which suggests that a national institutional framework can

Table 6. Logistic regression results.

Variable	Model 1 β	Model 2 β	Model 3 β	Model 4 β	Model 5 β	Model 6 β
Blau-HR	2.3811*					
prE		-3.8369**				
prANGAM			3.5996*			
prME				12.2389		
prAS					14.0536*	
prOR						2.9429
SIZE	1.4312***	1.4352***	1.4649***	1.4426***	1.5681***	1.4629***
AGE	0.0208*	0.0205*	0.0208*	0.0222*	0.0252**	0.0219*
ROA	-0.0503*	-0.0521*	-0.0504*	-0.0538*	-0.0533*	-0.0512*
RD	-1.4242	-1.4227	-1.3283	-1.6500	-1.4462	-1.4931
PIN	0.0631***	0.0626***	0.0661***	0.0675***	0.0623***	0.0664***
BS	0.1529*	0.1694*	0.1629*	0.1504	0.0839	0.1441
T	-21.2648	-21.1056	-21.3048	-19.9778	-26.8309	-21.2804
ME	-21.8328	-21.6568	-21.9408	-20.5397	-27.9362	-21.7466
IND	-22.1109	-21.9952	-22.1565	-20.6639	-27.9018	-21.9782
SE	-22.8439	-22.7051	-22.9311	-21.6708	-28.8196	-22.9062
ASEC	-21.6001	-21.5049	-21.6976	-20.1595	-26.9601	-21.3973
Constant	4.6617	8.1496	4.2157	3.4251	9.6646	4.5772
N	803	803	803	803	803	803
Wald Chi 2	41.22***	41.22***	41.58***	37.50***	39.26***	37.98***
R^2 of Nagelkerke	0.1787	0.1785	0.1785	0.1793	0.1797	0.1791

Note: All variable definitions are presented in Table 3. ***, **, and * significant at the 0.01, 0.05, and 0.10 levels, respectively.

transmit CSR influences through its political and education systems as well as its cultural systems. This theory focuses on the impact of global forces of legitimisation which are manifested in forms of coercive isomorphism and mimetic processes in national influences on CSR (DiMaggio and Powell, 1983). International regulatory pressures (Global Reporting Initiative (GRI), UN Global Compact, NGOs, etc.) are growing with globalisation and global competition and require firms to address human rights and labour issues. Hence, mimetic isomorphism may be a factor which provides a partial explanation, as foreign directors may have board membership in other international firms. The involvement of foreign directors in international markets can raise awareness among the board's other members about different CSR disclosure at the local level and thus make decisions that are more in line with stakeholder expectations (Fuente *et al.*, 2017). They have access to a wider range of social networks, broad and international experience and capabilities, and are more exposed to cross-cultural issues (Béji *et al.*, 2020). To sum up, our results are largely in line with the recommendations of good governance codes to diversify the international experience of directors (AFEP-MEDEF, 2020).

4.2.2. *The effect of Anglo-American directors on employee human rights policy disclosure*

Table 6 shows that the presence of Anglo-American directors (prANGAM) is positively and significantly related to the social commitment of companies through the EHRP disclosure (EHRP_D) (β = 3,599; p = 0.070), which rejects our second hypothesis. This is in contradiction with the results of Sison (2009) and Kang *et al.* (2019) that highlight the negative association between Anglo-American directors and CSR in the Asian and American contexts. Consistent with institutional theory, when directors become involved in cross-border activities mainly in EU countries, they adapt and adopt CSR practises according to the institutional requirements of these host countries (Garcia-Sanchez *et al.*, 2016). They change their behaviour in order to improve their reputation and gain the acceptance of the host companies. Another possible explanation is the constraining nature of the CSR regime in Anglo-American countries (Crifo and Rebérioux, 2015). Indeed, according to these authors, Anglo-Americans consider CSR as a voluntary commitment, while Europeans view it as mandatory. They tend to be more ethical, which is more likely to be disclosed in voluntarily CSR information (Humphreys and Brown, 2008; Jackson and Apostolakou, 2010). Moreover, our findings are also consistent with the results of Crifo and Rébérioux (2016) and Bénabou and Tirole (2010), who argue that companies can be proactive for certain CSR measures. This conclusion reinforces the explanation of our results and possibly affirms the proactivity of Anglo-American directors with regard to social information.

The results can be also explained by the importance of CSR disclosure for shareholders. Indeed, CSR does not harm shareholder value (Margolis *et al.*, 2009). Firms disclose CSR information to achieve financial and extra-financial results (Crifo and Rébérioux, 2015). By releasing CSR information, firms can achieve more attractive stock market returns, notably by improving their reputation in the market and maximising their value (Sahut *et al.*, 2018; Ziegler *et al.*, 2007).

These findings are consistent with RBV theory, suggesting that boards with foreign directors enjoy greater competitive advantages. The diversified knowledge and current or past social commitments of Anglo-American directors are a valuable asset to the firm (Béji *et al.*, 2020; Katmon *et al.*, 2019). By their involvement in international markets, their social networks, and their wide international experience, Anglo-American directors are more exposed to cross-cultural issues. This suggests that foreign directors are better at raising awareness among other members about different CSR disclosures and thus make decisions that are more in line with stakeholder expectations (Béji *et al.*, 2020; Fuente *et al.*, 2017; Garcia-Sanchez *et al.*, 2016). The findings confirm the view of McNamara *et al.* (2017) that the perception of EHRP by Anglo-American countries is associated more with effective commitment and cultural perception.

4.2.3. *The effect of European directors on employee human rights policy disclosure*

Regarding European directors, results show a negative and significant association between these directors and EHRP disclosure ($\beta = -3{,}836$; $p = 0.025$). Therefore, our Hypothesis 3 is not supported. Unlike Harjoto *et al.* (2018) and Habisch *et al.* (2010), who argue that the presence of European directors in US companies or Asian firms is associated with more CSR disclosure, we found that directors from European countries communicate less on EHRP in the French context.

One explanation could be that European directors act according to a specific context. Many studies argue that European companies disclose more information when they are publicly traded on a US market (Bancel and Mittoo, 2001; Matten and Moon, 2008). In fact, according to Gamerschlag *et al.* (2011), the institutional context is an important factor for the commitment to CSR. Thus, European directors enhance social information or not depending on the institutional context. A possible interpretation of this result may relate to the fact that European directors are more likely to be concerned with environmental or philanthropic information than social information. These findings are in line with those of Crifo and Rébérioux (2016) and Bénabou and Tirole (2010), who underline the importance of certain CSR dimensions in regard to others, as could be the case for European directors who favour the disclosure of the environmental dimension over the social dimension.

Based on the above-mentioned findings, civil law countries (European approach) have stronger unions, as well as stricter consumer protection laws, to protect a broader range of stakeholders. In fact, stakeholders are likely to benefit from more protection in civil law countries than in common law countries. This means there is a tacit pressure on directors in civil law countries to behave in a socially responsible manner. It is a common practise that goes beyond compliance with regulatory requirements (Bénabou and Tirole, 2010; Liang and Renneboog, 2017). Accordingly, European directors are less likely to release social information depending on stakeholders' demands. For instance, employees play an important role in a firm as a stakeholder group, and so, there is no requirement to communicate more information about employees' rights. Another interpretation is that because European directors are faced with the same regulations and processes in CSR, they share similar views and are more likely to have common perspectives and opinions. This degree of cohesiveness and uniformity can lead to a lack of objectivity. As a result, due to their lack of diversity of opinion, European members may fail to challenge the decisions of the board of directors, weakening the board and so reducing the quality of CSR. This is in line with RBV theory which supports the idea that a homogeneous board is likely to produce failed and inefficient governance (Sarra, 2012; Zhang, 2012). Moreover, our findings could provide evidence that the European model converges towards a shareholder-oriented system. This is in line with La Porta *et al.* (2008, 1998), who argue that countries have to turn towards a more efficient common law system based on transparency and independent relationships. In fact, the institutional setting has changed, and some of these changes have introduced Anglo-American practises. Consequently, European directors are probably less convinced by CSR disclosure and are more focused on shareholder interests, thus converging towards the Anglo-American approach (Jeffers, 2005).

4.2.4. *The effect of Asian directors on employee human rights policy disclosure*

With regard to the fourth Hypothesis 4, the regression results suggest a significant and positive relationship ($\beta = 14{,}053$; $p = 0.099$) between the presence of directors from Asia and corporate social commitment. This finding is in line with our expectations (Hypothesis 4 validated) and with the works, of Khan *et al.*, (2013) and Harjoto *et al.*, (2018). These authors highlight the development of CSR in Asian countries. For example, in Japan and China, firms emphasise the value of CSR in improving investor confidence and the reputation of firms (Chapple and Moon, 2005). Importation of the CSR concept into these countries has been based on the European model, advocating the interests of stakeholders. Thus, directors from Asian countries have been widely influenced by Western-style management practises. Asian government regulations in terms of CSR focus in particular on employment issues, where employers are required by law to report on the health, safety, and labour issues of their workers (Vogel, 2005). Thus, we have shown that directors from Asian countries tend to be more concerned with social issues, notably EHRPs. On this level, Oh *et al.* (2011) indicate that sociocultural environment and national institutions affect the CSR activities. In this sense, Western management practises and internationalisation are strongly influencing current CSR trends in Asia.

Another possible explanation is that in Asia, French investments are steadily increasing, which allows the effective and rapid replication of CSR management skills across key Asian markets.

However, it is important to retain a certain degree of caution with regard to this analysis of the results. In fact, there is a cultural disparity between the different Asian countries, which may differently impact the appropriation of social engagement from one country to another. In China, for example, the focus is on working conditions, health, and human rights (MacBean, 2003). While, in India, CSR practises are illustrated by philanthropic actions and community projects (Chapple and Moon, 2005).

4.2.5. *The effect of Middle Eastern directors on employee human rights policy disclosure*

For this category of directors, no significant impact could be noted ($p = 0.346$). Thus, Hypothesis 5, according to which there is a relationship between the presence of directors from the Middle East and EHRP disclosure, is not verified. This result can be explained by the low percentage of such directors on French boards of directors. In these countries, where religion and culture predominate, the principle of donations called "*zakat*" is more firmly rooted in large companies (Brammer *et al.*, 2007b; Munro, 2013). In this sense, it is possible to argue that directors from Middle Eastern countries tend to donate to local and regional causes rather than defend labour and human rights. This would constitute a CSR dimension that is more favoured than others, which could, by extension, justify our findings.

Therefore, it can be argued from the results obtained that the aversion of Middle Eastern directors to social issues may be because of the lack of CSR-related regulations in the Middle East as well as the lack of experience about the social dimension of CSR.

Although the Middle Eastern market is affected by global trends, it has retained its traditional characteristics and has restricted the degree to which these global and Western values can be adopted (Jamali and Mirshak, 2007).

According to institutional theory, formal and informal factors such as rules, culture, political spheres, and religion should be able to impact CSR dimensions (Jamali, 2010; Jamali and Neville, 2011; Al-Abdin *et al.*, 2017). These studies explain that by the fact that philanthropy is grounded in cultural, family, and religious traditions. On this level, directors from the Middle East are more likely to be concerned with philanthropic activities (Jamali and Sidani, 2012) than employee human rights.

4.2.6. *Interpretation of control variables*

Our interpretation of the control variables will be based on the results of Model 1, shown in Table 6. The size of the firm has a positive and significant impact ($\beta2 = 1{,}431$; $p = 0.000$) on the EHRP disclosure. This is consistent with previous studies (Dardour *et al.*, 2018; Shaukat *et al.*, 2016; Waddock and Graves, 1997). The larger the firm, the more information it discloses about CSR practises. Because of their exposure to public opinion, large firms have an interest in paying greater attention to stakeholders, and they have greater resources to satisfy societal expectations (Wu, 2006). Similarly, the independence of directors ($\beta5 = 0.063$; $p = 0.001$) has a significant and a positive influence on EHRP disclosure within companies listed on the SBF 120. Our results corroborate those of Dardour *et al.* (2018), Harjoto *et al.* (2018), and Jo and Harjoto (2011). The presence of independent directors promotes the consideration of the interests of different stakeholders (Post *et al.*, 2011). As for the impact of the firm's age, it is also positive and significant ($\beta 3 = 0.020$; $p = 0.085$). This result probably shows that older, established firms are more socially committed than younger firms. This result is consistent with those of Khan *et al.* (2013). Regarding the size of the board (BS), the impact is also positive and significant ($\beta 7 = 0.152$; $p < 0.1$), which explains that a larger board can better focus on stakeholder demands for information related to CSR (Guerrero-Villegas *et al.*, 2018). Finally, we found that the firm's debt ratio and the sector of activity do not have a significant influence. This could be attributable to the low variance of these variables.

5. Conclusion

The purpose of this study is to examine whether directors' home regions impact EHRP disclosure by French companies. In order to do so, our social measure data were sourced from the Bloomberg database for listed firms on the SBF 120, covering a period between 2008 and 2018. This study provides empirical evidence about the effect of the directors' home regions on EHRP disclosure.

Our results indicated that a board with home region diversity is positively related to EHRP disclosure. This finding provides new evidence that home region/nationality diversity promotes social dimension. Our results support RBV theory of the firm which recognises opportunity for a heterogeneous board of directors to improve board function. We find also that the presence of Anglo-American directors is positively associated with EHRP disclosure. This finding is consistent with institutional theory, which argues that managers are likely to imitate their business counterparts, complying with the regulators and following the institutional understandings of the host firm (Humphreys and Brown, 2008; Jackson and Apostolakou, 2010). Surprisingly, European directors are less concerned about EHRP disclosure. Given the implicit importance of the social dimension in Europe, it appears that Europeans do not feel the need to disclose information related to ensuring employees' rights. Consistent with the view that boards which are more diverse are more effective, we find that directors from Asian countries have a positive and significant influence on human rights policy for workers. However, Middle Eastern directors have no association with the social dimension, which implies that those directors do not have enough expertise about the social issues of the company.

These findings have different implications. First, recent demands by the governance codes for the internationalisation of boards of directors can lead to more socially responsible companies. Second, the study highlights the need to take into account a more significant quota of foreign board members. This recruitment could be a response to the needs of increasingly international investors in French companies. Specifically, our study supports the recommendations of the AFEP-MEDEF (2020) regarding the need to increase international skills and expertise when selecting new board members. While governments are encouraging policies to recommend that companies appoint foreign directors to their boards, it is timely and important to understand the consequences of the foreign directors' presence and their interrelation with openness to international markets. French firms can use the international background and expertise of directors from different home regions to enhance CSR disclosure and specifically employee human rights disclosure. Third, our research helps companies, managers, shareholders, and stakeholders to reconsider the composition of their board by promoting the presence of directors from different home regions.

To complete our analysis, it would be useful to study all dimensions of CSR. Future research will involve focusing on the proactiveness of foreign directors with respect to each aspect of CSR. It would also be useful to widen the sample for analysing home region diversity in a different context than France. We acknowledge that our results must be interpreted with caution in light of several issues. First, directors' regions of origin may not necessarily reflect their culture, norms, and values. Second, directors may have multiple nationalities but only list one in the annual governance report, which may not be their home region. Finally, countries within the same geographical region may be culturally different, therefore leading to different levels of CSR practises.

References

Al-Abdin, A., Roy, T. and Nicholson, J. D. (2017). Researching corporate social responsibility in the middle east: The current state and future directions, *Corporate Social Responsibility and Environmental Management*, Vol. 25, No. 1, pp. 47–65. http://doi.wiley.com/10.1002/csr.1439.

AFEP-MEDEF (2020). Corporate governance code of listed corporations. Available at: https://afep.com/wp-content/uploads/2018/06/Afep-Medef-Code-revision-June-2018-ENG.pdf.

Amran, A., Ping, S. L. and S. Devi, S. (2013). The influence of governance structure and strategic corporate social responsibility toward sustainability reporting quality, *Business Strategy and the Environment*, Vol. 23, No. 4, pp. 217–235.

Ball, A. and Craig, R. (2010). Using neo-institutionalism to advance social and environmental accounting, *Critical Perspectives on Accounting*, Vol. 21, No. 4, pp. 283–293. DOI:10.1016/j.cpa.2009.11.006.

Bancel, F. and Mittoo, U. R. (2001). European managerial perceptions of the net benefits of foreign stock listings, *European Financial Management*, Vol. 7, No. 2, pp. 213–236. DOI:10.1111/1468-036X.00153.

Barnea, A. and Rubin, A. (2010). Corporate social responsibility as a conflict between shareholders, *Journal of Business Ethics*, Vol. 97, pp. 71–86. https://doi.org/10.1007/s10551-010-0496-z.

Barney, J. (1991). Firm resources and sustained competitive advantage, *Journal of Management*, Vol. 17, No. 1, pp. 99–120. https://doi.org/10.1016/S0742-3322(00)17018-4.

Barreau, J. and Arnal, J. (2010). Responsabilité sociale de l'entreprise, comité d'entreprise européen et négociation collective transnationale. L'exemple du groupe ACCOR, *Négociations*, Vol. 4, No. 2, pp. 21–35.

Baughn, C. and Bodie, N. and McIntosh, J. C. (2007). Corporate social and environmental responsibility in Asian countries and other geographical regions, in *Corporate Social Responsibility and Environmental Management*, John Wiley & Sons, Vol. 14, No. 4, September, pp. 189–205.

Béji, R., Yousfi, O., Loukil, N. and Omri, A. (2020). Board diversity and corporate social responsibility: Empirical evidence from France, *Journal of Business Ethics*. https://doi.org/10.1007/s10551-020-04522-4

Beínabou, R. and Tirole, J. (2010). Individual and corporate social responsibility, *Economica*, Vol. 77, No. 305, pp. 1–19.

Blau, P. M. (1977). *Inequality and heterogeneity: A primitive theory of social structure*, Vol. 7. Free Press, New York.

Branco, M. C. and Rodrigues, L. L. (2006). Corporate social responsibility and resource-based perspectives, *Journal of Business Ethics*, Vol. 69, pp. 111–132. https://doi.org/10.1007/s10551-006-9071-z.

Brammer, S., Williams, G. and Zinkin, J. (2007b). Religion and attitudes to corporate social responsibility in a large cross-country sample, *Journal of Business Ethics*, Vol. 71, pp. 229–243.

Campbell, J. L. (2007). Why would corporations behave in socially responsible ways? An institutional theory of corporate social responsibility, *Academy of Management Review*, Vol. 32, No. 32, pp. 946–967. https://doi.org/10.2307/20159343.

Chang, Y. K., Oh, W. Y., Park, J. H. and Jang, M. G. (2017). Exploring the relationship between board characteristics and CSR: Empirical evidence from Korea, *Journal of Business Ethics*, Vol. 140, pp. 225–242. https://doi.org/10.1007/s10551-015-2651-z.

Chapple, W. and Moon, J. (2005). Corporate social responsibility (CSR) in Asia: A seven-country study of CSR web site reporting, *Business and Society*, Vol. 44, No. 4, pp. 415–441. https://doi.org/10.1177/0007650305281658

Chauhan, S. P. and Chauhan, D. (2008). Human obsolescence. A wake–up call to avert a crisis, *Global Business Review*, Vol. 9, No. 1, pp. 85–100. https://doi.org/10.1108/EBHRM-04-2020-0043.

Cheung, Y. L., Tan, W., Ahn, H. J. and Zhang, Z. (2010). Does corporate social responsibility matter in Asian emerging markets? *Journal of Business Ethics*, Vol. 92, pp. 401–413. http://dx.doi.org/10.1007/s10551-009-0164-3

Cohen, E., Taylor, S. and Muller-Camen, M. (2012). HRM's role in corporate social and environmental sustainability, *SHRM Foundation's Effective Practice Guidelines Series*.

Crane, A. and Matten, D. (2010). Business ethics: Managing corporate citizenship and sustainability in the age of globalization, Oxford University Press.

Crifo, P. and Rebérioux, A. (2015). Gouvernance et responsabilité sociétale des entreprises: nouvelle frontière de la finance durable? *Revue d'Economie Financière*, Vol. 117, pp. 205–223.

Crifo, P. and Rebérioux, A. (2016). Corporate governance and corporate social responsibility: A typology of OECD countries, *Journal of Governance and Regulation*, Vol. 5, No. 2, pp. 14–27. DOI:10.22495/jgr_v5_i2_p2.

Daaja, Y. and Al-Szabados, G. N. (2018). The middle east perspective of corporate social responsibility, *International Journal of Engineering and Management Sciences*, Vol. 3, No. 4, pp. 282–291. https://doi.org/10.21791/IJEMS.2018.4.24.

Dardour, A., Ben Farhat Toumi, N. and Boussaâda, R. (2018). Composition du conseil d'administration et divulgation d'informations RSE, *Finance Contrôle Stratégie*, Vol. 4. https://doi.org/10.4000/fcs.2674.

Dawkins, J. and Lewis, S. (2003). CSR in stakeholder expectations and their implications for company strategy, *Journal of Business Ethics*, Vol. 44, No. 2–3, pp. 185–193. https://doi.org/10.1023/A:1023399732720.

DiMaggio, Paul J. and Walter W. Powell. (1983). The iron cage revisited: Institutional isomorphism and collective rationality in organizational fields, *American Sociological Review*, Vol. 48, No. 2, [American Sociological Association, Sage Publications, Inc.], pp. 147–160. https://doi.org/10.2307/2095101.

Estelyi, K. S. and Nisar, T. M. (2016). Diverse boards: Why do firms get foreign nationals on their boards? *Journal of Corporate Finance*, Vol. 39, No. C, pp. 174–192. DOI:10.1016/j.jcorpfin.2016.02.006.

Freeman, E. (1984). *Strategic Management: A Stakeholder Approach.* Cambridge University Press.

Fuente, J. A., Garciía-Sanchez, I. M. and Lozano, M. B. (2017). The role of the board of directors in the adoption of GRI guidelines for the disclosure of CSR information, *Journal of Cleaner Production*, Vol. 141, pp. 737–750. https://doi.org/10.1016/j.jclepro.2016.09.155.

Gallhofer, S., Haslam, J. and Van Der Walt, S. (2011). Accountability and Transparency in Relation to Human Rights: A Critical Perspective reflecting upon accounting, corporate responsibility and ways forward in the context of globalization, *Critical Perspectives on Accounting*, Vol. 22, No. 8, pp. 765–780. https://doi.org/10.1016/j.cpa.2011.07.002.

Galbreath, J. (2005). Which resources matter the most to firm success? An exploratory study of resource-based theory, *Tech-novation*, Vol. 25, No. 9, pp. 979–987. https://doi.org/10.1016/j.technovation.2004.02.008.

Galbreath, J. (2016). When do board and management resources complement each other? A study of effects on corporate social responsibility, *Journal of Business Ethics*, Vol. 136, No. 2, pp. 281–292. https://www.jstor.org/stable/24736131.

Gallo, P. J. and Christensen, L. J. (2011). Firm size matters: An empirical investigation of organizational size and ownership on sustainability-related behaviors, *Business and Society*, Vol. 50, No. 2, pp. 315–349. https://doi.org/10.1177/0007650311398784.

Gamerschlag, R., Möller, K. and Verbeeten, F. (2011). Determinants of voluntary CSR disclosure: Empirical evidence from Germany, *Review of Managerial Science*, Vol. 5, No. 2–3, pp. 233–262. DOI:10.1007/s11846-010-0052-3.

Garcia-Sanchez, I. M., Cuadrado-Ballesteros, B. and Frias-Aceituno, J. V. (2016). Impact of the institutional macro context on the voluntary disclosure of CSR information, *Long Range Planning*, Vol. 49, No. 1, pp. 15–35. DOI:10.1016/j.lrp.2015.02.004.

Grenelle Law (2007/2010). Law on national commitment for the environment. Available at: https://www.legifrance.gouv.fr/jorf/id/JORF TEXT000022470434/.

Guerrero-Villegas, J., Pérez-Calero, L., Hurtado-González, J. M. and Giráldez-Puig, P. (2018). Board attributes and corporate social responsibility disclosure: A meta-analysis, *Sustainability*, Vol. 10, No. 12, pp. 1–22.

Habisch, A., Patelli, L., Pedrini, M. and Schwartz, C. (2010). Different talks with different folks: A comparative survey of stakeholder dialogs in Germany, Italy, and the US, *Journal of Business Ethics*, Vol. 100, No. 3, pp. 381–404. https://doi.org/10.1007/s10551-010-0686-8.

Hahn, P. D. and Lasfer, M. (2016). Impact of foreign directors on board meeting frequency, *International Review of Financial Analysis*, Vol. 46, pp. 295–308. DOI:10.1007/s10551-013-1801-4.

Harjoto, M. A., Laksmana, I. and Lee, R. (2015). Board diversity and corporate social responsibility, *Journal of Business Ethics*, Vol. 132, No. 4, pp. 641–660. https://doi.org/10.1007/s10551-014-2343-0.

Harjoto, M. A., Laksmana, I. and Yang, Y. W. (2018). Board nationality and educational Background diversity and corporate social performance, *Corporate Governance: The International Journal of Business in Society*. https://doi.org/10.1108/CG-04-2018-0138.

Hillman, A. J., Keim, G. D. and Luce, R. A. (2001). Board composition and stakeholder performance: Do stakeholder directors make a difference? *Business and Society*, Vol. 40, pp. 295–314. DOI:10.1177/000765030104000304

Hoang, T. C. and Abeysekera, I. S. (2016). Board diversity and corporate social disclosure: Evidence from Vietnam, *Journal of Business Ethic*, Vol. 151, No. 3, pp. 1–20. https://doi.org/10.1007/s10551-016-3260-1.

Hoopes, D. G., Madsen, T. L. and Walker, G. (2003). Guest editors' introduction to the special issue: Why is there a resource-based view? toward a theory of competitive heterogeneity, *Strategic Management Journal*, Vol. 24, No. 10, pp. 889–992.

Human Rights Council (2011). Available at: https://www2.ohchr.org/english/press/hrc/kit/garesolution.pdf.

Humphreys, M. and Brown, A. D. (2008). An analysis of corporate social responsibility at credit line: A narrative approach, *Journal of Business Ethics*, Vol. 80, No. 3, pp. 403–418. http://dx.doi.org/10.1007/s10551-007-9426-0.

Jackson, G. and Apostolakou, A. (2010). Corporate social responsibility in western Europe: An institutional mirror or substitute? *Journal of Business Ethics*, Vol. 94, No. 3, pp. 371–394. https://doi.org/10.1007/s10551-009-0269-8.

Jamali, D. and Neville, B. (2011). Convergence versus divergence of CSR in developing countries: An embedded multi-layered institutional lens, *Journal of Business Ethics*, Vol. 102, pp. 599–621. https://doi.org/10. 1007/s10551-011-0830-0.

Jamali, D. and Sidani, Y. (2011). Is CSR counterproductive in developing countries: The unheard voices of change, *Journal of Change Management*, Vol. 11, No. 11, pp. 69–71. http://dx.doi.org/10.1080/14697017. 2011.548940.

Jamali, D. and Sidani Y. (eds.) (2012). *CSR in the Middle East: Fresh Perspectives*. American University of Beirut, Springer.

Jamali, D. and Karam M. K. (2018). Corporate social responsibility in developing countries as an emerging field of study: CSR in developing countries, *International Journal of Management Reviews*, Vol. 20, No. 11.

Jamali, D. and Mirshak, R. (2007). Corporate social responsibility (CSR): Theory and practise in a developing country context, *Journal of Business Ethics*, Vol. 7, No. 2, pp. 243–262.

Jamali, D., Jain, T., Samara, G. and Zoghbi, E. (2020). How institutions affect CSR practises in the middle East and North Africa: A critical review, *Journal of Word Business*, Vol. 55, No. 5, pp. 1090–9516. https://doi.org/10.1016/j.jwb.2020.101127.

Jeffers, E. (2005). Corporate governance: Toward converging models? *Global Finance Journal*, Vol. 16, No. 2, pp. 221–232.

Jizi, M. (2017). The influence of board composition on sustainable development disclosure, *Business Strategy and the Environment*, Vol. 26, No. 5, pp. 640–655. https://doi.org/10.1002/bse.1943.

Jo, H. and Harjoto, M. A. (2011). Corporate governance and firm value: The impact of corporate social responsibility, *Journal of Business Ethics*, Vol. 103, pp. 351–383. https://doi.org/10.1007/s10551-011-0869-y.

Kang, Y. S, Huh, E. and Lim, M. H. (2019). Effects of foreign directors' nationalities and director types on corporate philanthropic behavior: Evidence from Korean firms. *Sustainability*, Vol. 11, No. 11, pp. 1–18. https://doi.org/10.3390/su11113132.

Katmon, N., Zuriyati, Z., Norlia, M., Norwani, M. and Farooque, O. A. (2017). Comprehensive board diversity and quality of corporate social responsibility disclosure: Evidence from an emerging market, *Journal of Business Ethics*, pp. 1–35.

Katmon, N., Zuriyati, Z., Norlia, M. M., Omar, and Al Farooque, N. (2019). Comprehensive board diversity and quality of corporate social responsibility disclosure: Evidence from an emerging market, *Journal of Business Ethics*, Vol. 157, pp. 447–481. https://doi.org/10.1007/ s10551-017-3672-6.

Khan, A., Muttakin, M. B. and Siddiqui, J. (2013). Corporate governance and corporate social responsibility disclosures: Evidence from an emerging economy, *Journal of Business Ethics*, Vol. 114, No. 2, pp. 207–223. https://dx.doi.org/10.2139/ssrn.2050630.

Koleva, P. (2018). A systematic review on corporate social responsibility literature in the middle east: Conceptual gaps and challenges, in S. Idowu, C. Sitnikov, D. Simion, and C. Bocean (eds.), *Current Issues in Corporate Social Responsibility. CSR, Sustainability, Ethics & Governance*, Springer, Cham. https://doi.org/10.1007/978-3-319-704 49-4_15.

La Porta, R. L., Lopez-de-Silanes, F., Shleifer, A. and Vishny, R. W. (1998). Law and finance. *Journal of Political Economy*, Vol. 106, No. 6, pp. 1113–1155. https://doi.org/10.1086/250042.

La Porta, R., Lopez-de-Silanes, F. and Shleifer, A. (2008). The economic consequences of legal origins, *Journal of Economic Literature*, Vol. 46, No. 2, pp. 285–332. DOI:10.1257/jel.46.2.285

Lee, E. M., Park, S. Y. and Lee, H. J. (2013). Employee perception of CSR activities: Its antecedents and consequences. *Journal of Business Research*, Vol. 66, No. 10, pp. 1716–1724. https://doi.org/10.1016/j.jbusres.2012.11.008.

Levy, D. L., Szejnwald Brown, H. and De Jong, M. (2010). The contested politics of corporate governance: The case of the global reporting initiative, *Business and Society*, Vol. 49, No. 1, pp. 88–115. https://doi.org/10.1177/0007650309345420.

Liang, H. and Renneboog, L. (2017). On the foundations of corporate social responsibility, *Journal of Finance*, Vol. 72, No. 2, pp. 853–910. https://doi.org/10.1111/jofi.12487.

Macbean, N. (2003). *Corporate Social Responsibility in China: Is It Any of Your Business?* China-Britain Trade Review.

Margolis, J. D., Elfenbein, H. and Walsh, J. (2009). Does it pay to be good... and does it matter? A meta-analysis and redirection of research on corporate social and financial performance, *Corporate Law: Law et Finance eJournal*.

Masulis, R., Wang, C. and Xie, F. (2012). Globalizing the boardroom — The effects of foreign directors on corporate governance and firm performance, *Journal of Accounting & Economics*, Vol. 53, No. 3, pp. 527–554. DOI:10.1016/j.jacceco.2011.12.003.

Matten, D. and Moon J. (2008). Implicit and explicit CSR: A conceptual framework for a comparative understanding of corporate social responsibility, *The Academy of Management Review*, Vol. 33, No. 2, pp. 404–424. https://doi.org/10.5465/amr.2008.31193458.

Maurice, M. and Sorge, A. (eds.) (2000). *Embedding organisations: Societal Analysis of Actors, Organisations and Socio-economic Context.* John Benjamins, Amsterdam, The Netherlands.

McNamara, T. K., Carapinha, R., Catsouphes, M. P., Valcour, M. and Lobel, S. (2017). Corporate social responsibility and employee outcomes: The role of country context, *Business Ethics: A European Review*, Vol. 26, No. 4, pp. 413–427. https://doi.org/10.1111/beer.12163.

McPhail, K. and Ferguson, J. (2016). The past, the present and the future of accounting for human rights, *Accounting, Auditing and Accountability Journal*, Vol. 29, No. 4, pp. 526–541. https://doi.org/10.1108/AAAJ-03-2016-2441.

Munro V. (2013). Stakeholder preferences for particular corporate social responsibility (CSR) activities and social initiatives (SIs): CSR initiatives to assist corporate strategy in emerging and frontier markets, *Journal of Corporate Citizenship*.

Muttakin, M. B., Khan, A. and Subramaniam, N. (2015). Firm characteristics, board diversity and corporate social responsibility: Evidence from Bangladesh, *Pacific Accounting Review*, Vol. 27, No. 3, pp. 53–372. https://doi.org/10.1108/PAR-01-2013-0007.

Muttakin, M. B., Khan, A. and Mihret, D. G. (2018). The effect of board capital and CEO power on corporate social responsibility disclosures, *Journal of Business Ethics*, Vol. 150, No. 1, pp. 41–56. DOI:10.1007/s10551-016-3105-y.

New Regulations Economic Law (2001). Available at: https://www.legifrance.gouv.fr/citoyen/jorf_nor.ow?numjo=ECOX0000021L.

Nguyen, M., Bensemann, J. and Kelly, S. (2018). Corporate social responsibility (CSR) in Vietnam: A Conceptual Framework, *International Journal of Corporate Social Responsibility*, Vol. 3, No. 9. https://doi.org/10.1186/s40991-018-0032-5.

Oh, W. Y., Chang, Y. K. and Martynov, A. (2011). The effect of ownership structure on corporate social responsibility: Empirical evidence from Korea, *Journal of Business Ethics*, Vol. 104, pp. 283–297.

Parsa, S., Roper, I., Muller-Camen, M. and Szigetvari, E. (2018). Have labour practises and human rights disclosures enhanced corporate accountability? The case of the GRI framework, *Accounting Forum*, Vol. 42, No. 1, pp. 47–64. https://doi.org/10.1016/j.accfor.2018.01.001.

Peters, S., Miller, M. and Kusyk, S. (2011). How relevant is corporate governance and corporate social responsibility in emerging markets? *Corporate Governance*, Vol. 11, No. 4, pp. 429–445. https://doi.org/10.1108/14720701111159262.

Post, C., Rahman, N. and Rubow, E. (2011). Green governance: Boards of directors' composition and environmental corporate social responsibility, *Business and Society*, Vol. 50, No. 1, pp. 189–223. https://doi.org/10.1177/0007650310394642.

Preuss, L. and Barkemeyer, R. (2011). CSR priorities of emerging economy firms: Is Russia a different shape of BRIC? *Corporate Governance*, Vol. 11, No. 4, pp. 371–385. https://doi.org/10.1108/14720701111159226.

Rahman, A. A. and Bukair, A. A. (2013). The influence of the Shariah supervision board on corporate social responsibility disclosure by Islamic banks of gulf co-operation council countries, *Asian Journal of Business and Accounting*, Vol. 6, No. 2, pp. 65–104.

Rao, K. and Tilt, C. (2016). Board composition and corporate social responsibility: The role of diversity, gender, strategy and decision making, *Journal of Business Ethics*, Vol. 138, No. 2, pp. 327–347. https://doi.org/10.1007/s10551-015-2613-5.

Rey, F. (1980). Corporate social performance and reporting in France, In L. E. Preston (ed.), *Research in Corporate Social Performance and Policy*, Vol. 2, pp. 291–325, JAI, Greenwich, CT.

Robertson, D. C. (2009). Corporate social responsibility and different stages of economic development: Singapore, Turkey, and Ethiopia, *Journal of Business Ethics*, Vol. 88, pp. 617–633. https://doi.org/10.1007/s10551-009-0311.

Rosati, F., Costa, R., Calabrese, A. and Pedersen, E. R. G. (2018). Employee attitudes towards corporate social responsibility: A study on gender, age and educational level differences, *Corporate Social Responsibility and Environmental Management*, Vol. 25, No. 6, pp. 1306–1319. https://doi.org/10.1002/csr.1640.

Sahut, J. M., Mili, M. and Teulon, F. (2018). Gouvernance, RSE et performance financière: vers une compreíhension globale de leurs relations? *Management et Avenir*, Vol. 101, No. 3, pp. 39–59. https://doi.org/10.3917/mav.101.0039.

Sarra, J. (2012). Class act: Considering race and gender in the corporate boardroom, *St. John's Law Review*, Vol. 79, No. 4, pp. 1121–1160.

Sison, A. J. G. (2000). Integrated risk management and global business ethics, *Business Ethics. A European Review*, Vol. 9, No. 4, October, pp. 288–295.

Sison, A. G. (2009). From CSP to corporate citizenship: Anglo-American and continental European Perspective, *Journal of Business Ethics*, Vol. 89, No. 3, pp. 235–246. DOI:10.1007/s10551-010-0395-3.

Shaomin, L., Fetscherin, M., Alon, I. and Ye, K. (2010). Corporate social responsibility in emerging markets: The Importance of the Governance Environment, *Management International Review*. DOI:10.2307/41426815.

Shaukat, A., Qiu, Y. and Trojanowski, G. (2016). Board attributes, corporate social responsibility strategy, and corporate environmental and social performance, *Journal of Business Ethics*, Vol. 135, No. 3, pp. 569–585.

Shen, J. and Jiuhua-Zhu, C. (2011). Effects of socially responsible human resource management on employee organisational commitment, *The International Journal of Human Resource Management*, Vol. 22, No. 15, pp. 3020–3035. DOI:10.1080/09585192.2011.599951.

Sobczak, A. and Havard, C. (2015). Stakeholders' influence on French unions' CSR strategies, *Journal of Business Ethics*, Vol. 129, No. 2, pp. 311–324. https://doi.org/10.1007/s10551-014-2159-y.

Statement on Extra-financial Performance (2017). Law of the ordinance and decrees of July and August (2017) (French regulation). Available at: https://www.legifrance.gouv.fr/jorf/id/JORFTEXT000035401863.

Tranfield, D., Denyer, D. and Smart, P. (2003). Towards a methodology for developing evidence-informed management knowledge means of systematic review, *British Journal of Management*, Vol. 14, No. 3, pp. 207–222.

Vogel, (2005). Is there a market for virtue: The business case for corporate social responsibility, *California Management Review*, Vol. 47, No. 4, pp. 19–45.

Waddock, S. A. and Graves, S. B. (1997). The corporate social performance-financial performance Link. *Strategy and Management*, Vol. 18, No. 4, pp. 303–319. https://doi.org/10.1002/.

Wailes, N., Bamber, G. and Lansbury, R. (2011). International and comparative employment relations: An introduction, in G. Bamber, R. Lansbury and N. Wailes (eds.), *International Comparative Employment Relations*, pp. 1–35.

Wang, J. and Coffey, S. (1992). Board composition and corporate philanthropy, *Journal of Business Ethics*, Vol. 11, p. 771.

Wu, M. (2006). Corporate social performance, corporate financial performance and Firm size: A meta-analysis, *Journal of American Academy of Business*, Vol. 8, No. 1, pp. 163–171.

Yawar, H. M. (2009). *CSR Pakistan Evolution*. Rise and Impact of Socio-economic Development Capital Business (Pvt) Ltd. Gulberg III, Lahore, Pakistan.

Yu, Y. and Choi, Y. (2016). Stakeholder pressure and CSR adoption: The mediating role of organizational culture for Chinese companies, *Social Science Journal*, Vol. 53, No. 2, pp. 226–235. https://doi.org/10.1016/j.soscij.2014.07.006.

Zhang, L. (2012). Board demographic Diversity, independence, and corporate social performance, *Corporate Governance: The International Journal of Business in Society*, Vol. 12, No. 5, pp. 686–700. https://doi.org/10.1108/14720701211275604.

Zhang, J. Q., Zhu, H. and Ding, H. B. (2013). Board composition and corporate social responsibility: An empirical investigation in the Post Sarbanes-Oxley Era, *Journal of Business Ethics*, Vol. 114, No. 3, pp. 381–392. https://doi.org/10.1007/s10551-012-1352-0.

Ziegler, A., Schroeder, M. and Rennings, K. (2007). The effect of environmental and social performance on the stock performance of European corporations, *Environmental and Resource Economics*, Vol. 37, No. 4, pp. 661–680. https://doi.org/10.1007/s10640-007-9082-y.

Index

Printed in the United States
by Baker & Taylor Publisher Services